KAZUKI TAKAHASHI

I'm smoking in this picture, but smoking less is better for your health, Yoshida-san! I quit five years ago!

SHIN YOSHIDA

I keep saying I'm going to quit smoking and get my diving license, but it's been years and I still haven't done either one. I'll do my best, Takahashi Sensei! (´^^;)

NAOHITO MIYOSHI

Whenever I get stuck, I read Takahashi Sensei's original manga. It gets the juices flowing and gets me moving! You're awesome, Takahashi Sensei! I love that ordinary Jonouchi-kun!

Volume 5
SHONEN JUMP Manga Edition

Original Concept by **KAZUKI TAKAHASHI**
Production Support: STUDIO DICE
Story by **SHIN YOSHIDA**
Art by **NAOHITO MIYOSHI**

Translation & English Adaptation TAYLOR ENGEL AND IAN REID, HC LANGUAGE SOLUTIONS
Touch-up Art & Lettering JOHN HUNT
Designer STACIE YAMAKI
Editor MIKE MONTESA

Published by VIZ Media, LLC
P.O. Box 77010
San Francisco, CA 94107

10 9 8 7 6 5 4 3 2 1
First printing, July 2014

www.viz.com

www.shonenjump.com

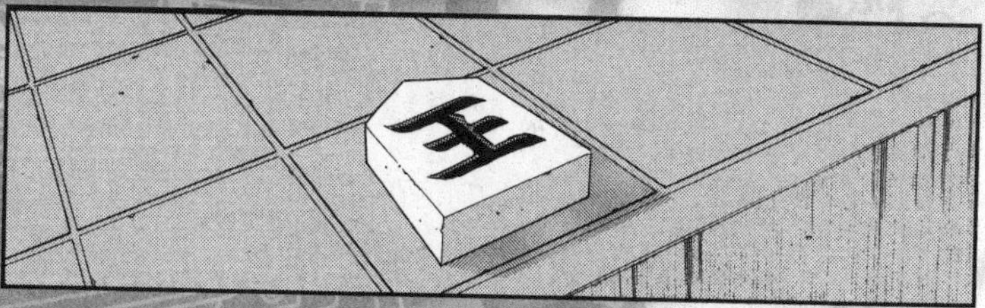
王

Yu-Gi-Oh! ZEXAL

VOLUME 5:
Line World!!

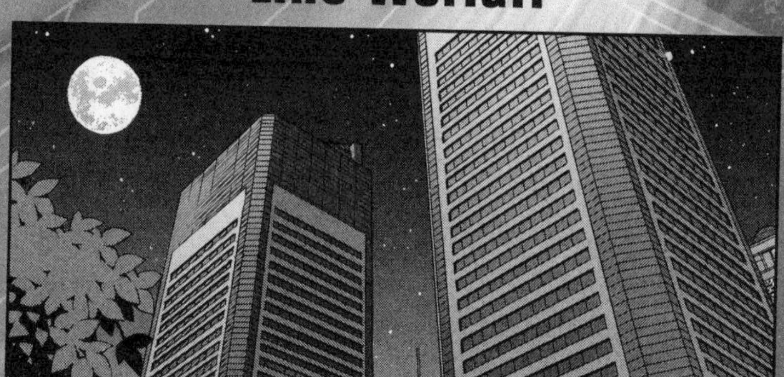

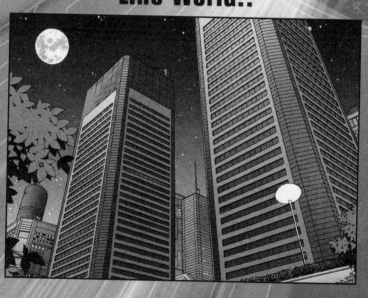

Original Concept by **KAZUKI TAKAHASHI**
Production Support: **STUDIO DICE**
Story by **SHIN YOSHIDA**
Art by **NAOHITO MIYOSHI**

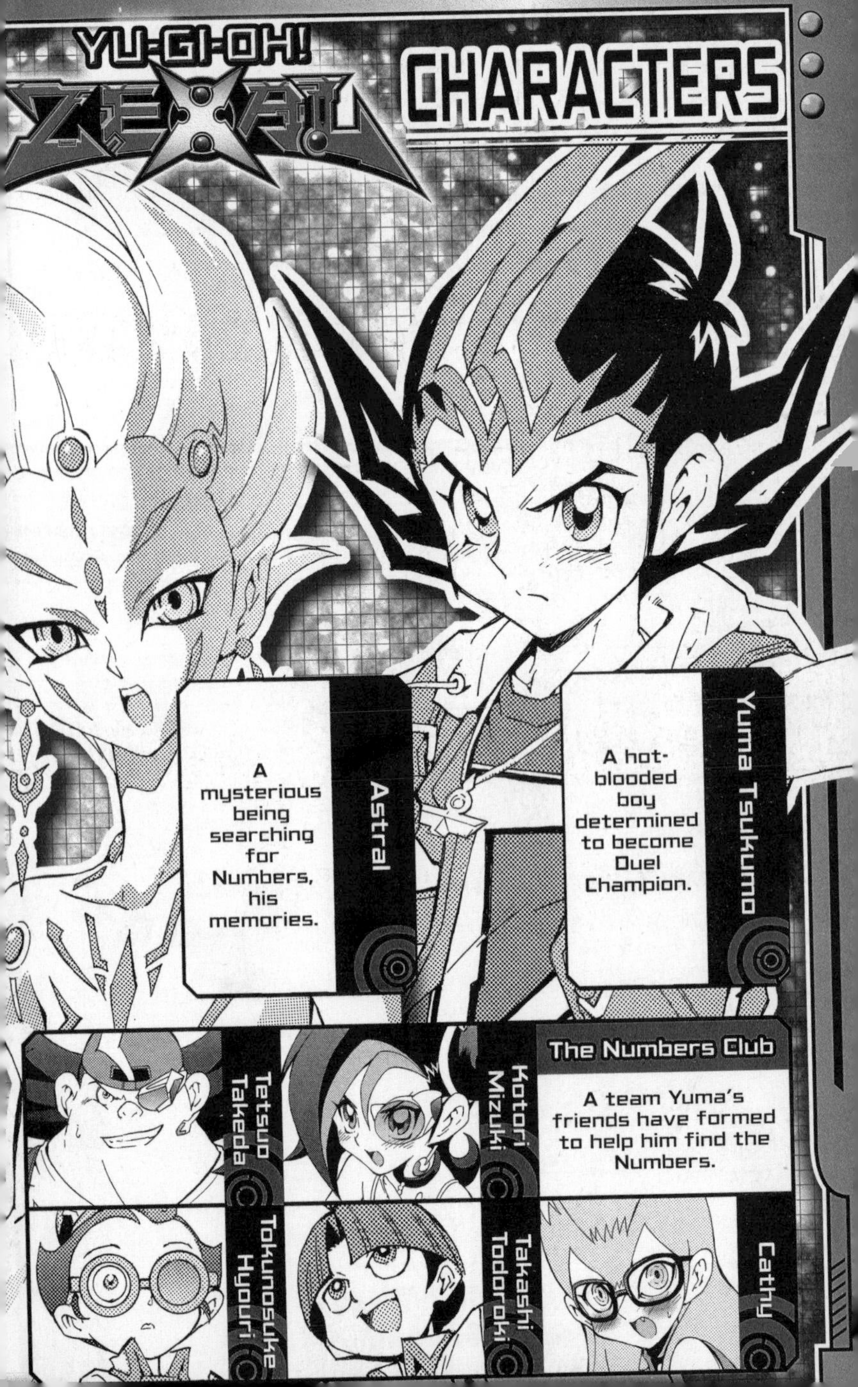
YU-GI-OH! ZEXAL
CHARACTERS
Yuma Tsukumo
A hot-blooded boy determined to become Duel Champion.
Astral
A mysterious being searching for Numbers, his memories.
The Numbers Club
A team Yuma's friends have formed to help him find the Numbers.
Kotori Mizuki
Tetsuo Takeda
Cathy
Takashi Todoroki
Tokunosuke Hyouri

Kyoji Yagumo

Kyoji hunts the Numbers cards for Dr. Faker.

Ryoga Kamishiro

Goes by the nickname "Shark." His fate is tied to Yagumo's.

Kaito

A Numbers Hunter who is searching for Numbers to save his little brother.

Mr. Heartland   Dr. Faker

These two villains are collecting Numbers to destroy the Astral world.

Luna

She is trying to destroy the Numbers cards along with Ryoga.

Haruto

He possesses the power to destroy the Astral world.

Yuma tackles every challenge that comes his way, and he doesn't give up. Although his skills are suspect, he's crazy about dueling!

One day, Yuma's rival Tetsuo has his deck stolen by Shark, the school's biggest delinquent and duelist, and Yuma ends up dueling Shark. During the duel, the charm Yuma's parents gave him opens a mysterious door, and a strange being called Astral appears!!

Astral is a genius duelist, but only Yuma can see him. Astral's lost memories have become special cards called "Numbers."

But standing in their way are Dr. Faker, who's trying to use the power of the Numbers cards to destroy the Astral world, and Kaito, who's hunting the Numbers to help his little brother! Yuma and company beat the enemy's assassins in duels one after another. Meanwhile, Ryoga and Luna start working to wipe out the Numbers.

Then Yagumo, who has teamed up with Dr. Faker and taken command of the Numbers Retrieval Strategy, declares war on Ryoga, Kaito and Yuma! The curtain rises on the Numbers War!!

Previously...

YU-GI-OH! ZEXAL

VOLUME 5
Line World!!

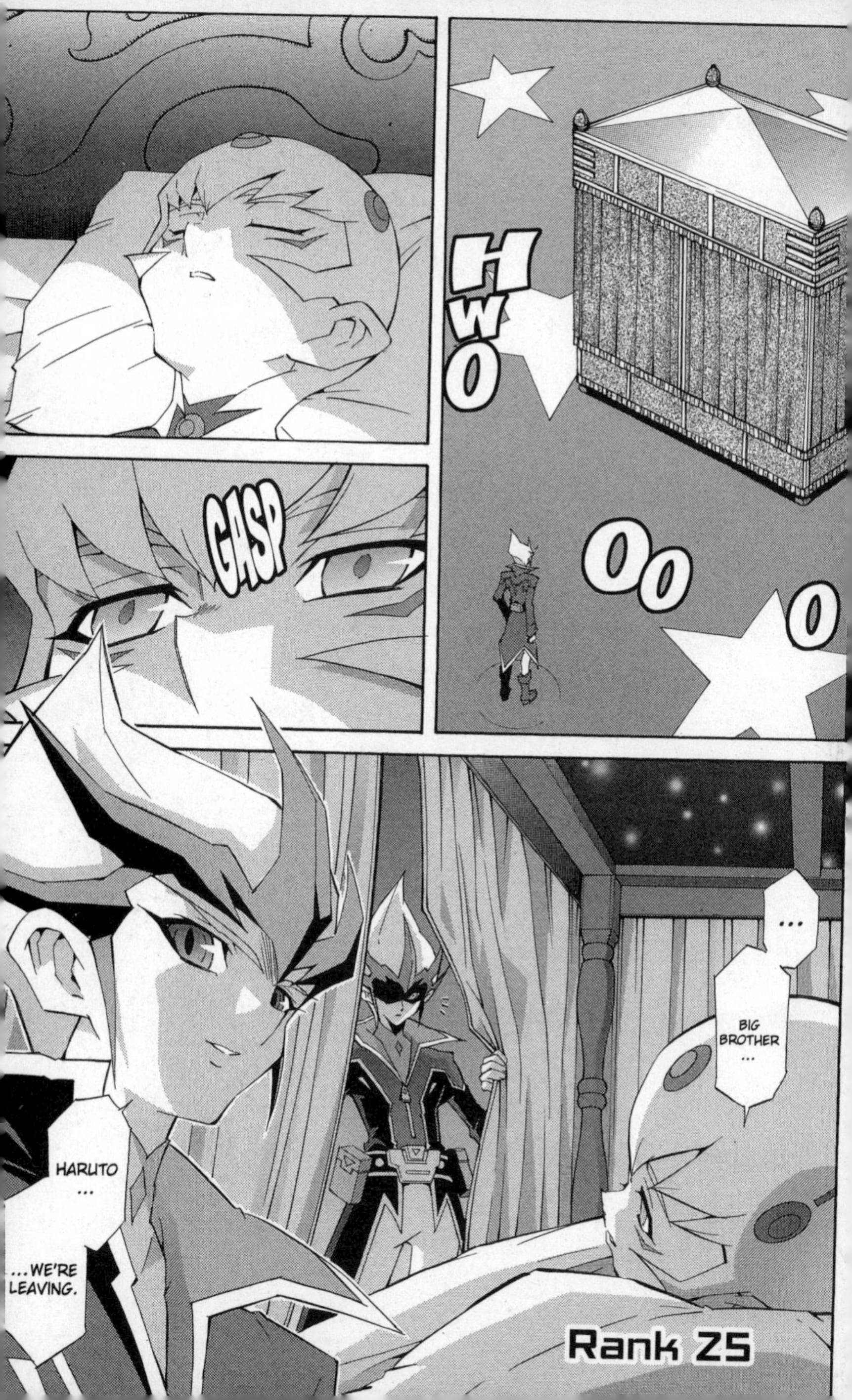

HWOOOO
GASP
...
BIG BROTHER ...
HARUTO ...
...WE'RE LEAVING.
Rank 25

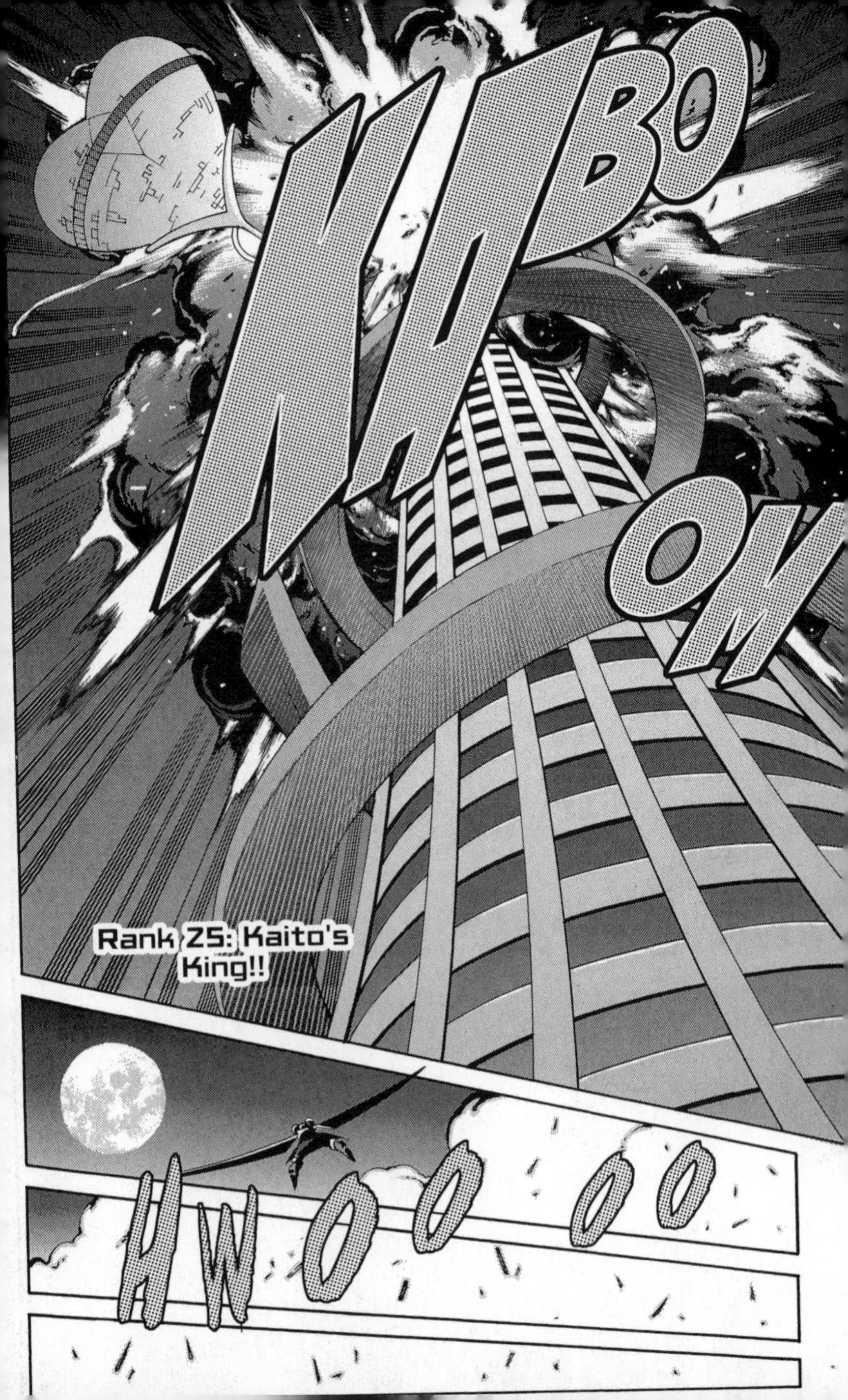

KABOOM
Rank 25: Kaito's King!!
HWOOOOO

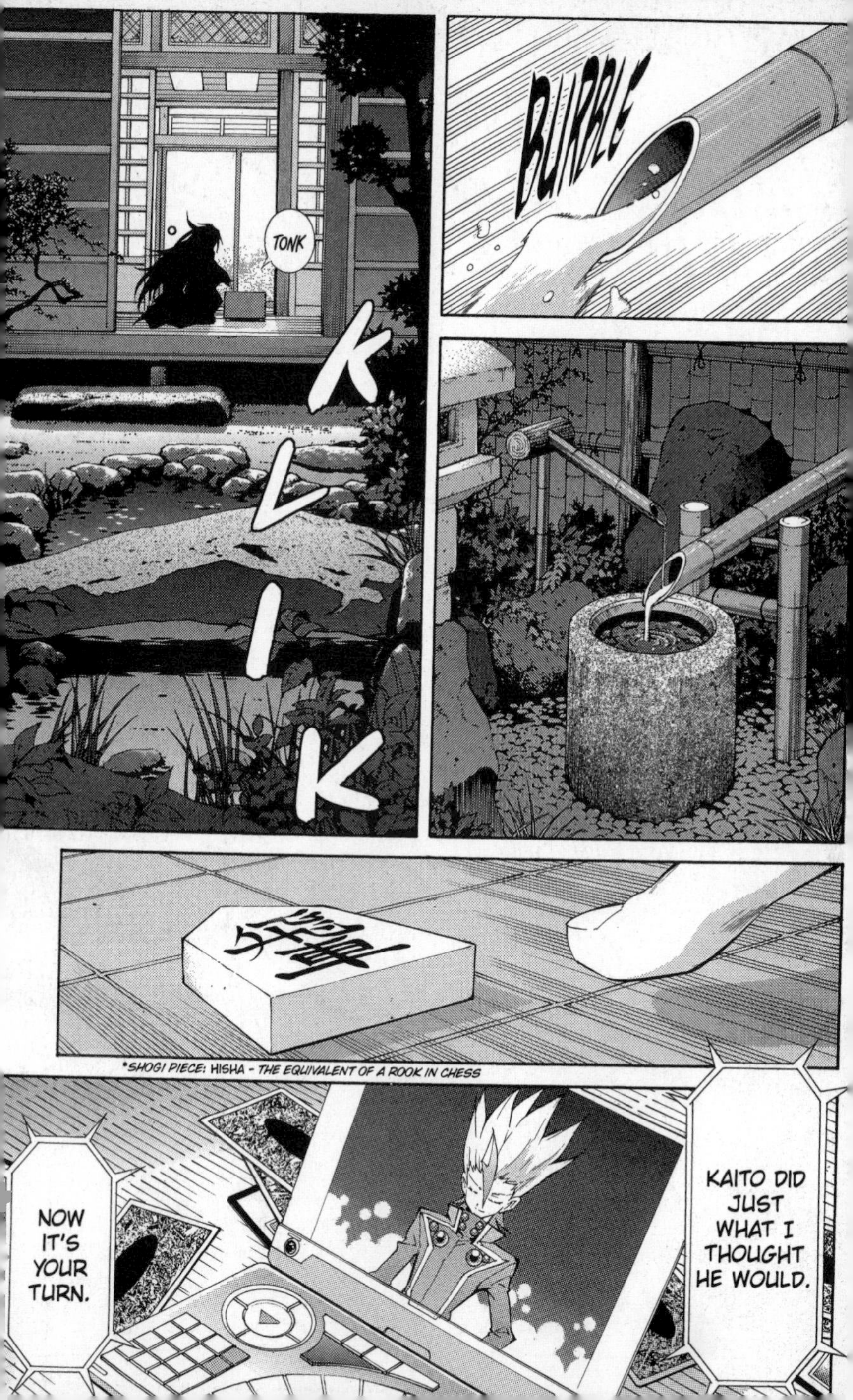
BUBBLE
TONK
KLIK
KAITO DID JUST WHAT I THOUGHT HE WOULD.
NOW IT'S YOUR TURN.
*SHOGI PIECE: HISHA - THE EQUIVALENT OF A ROOK IN CHESS

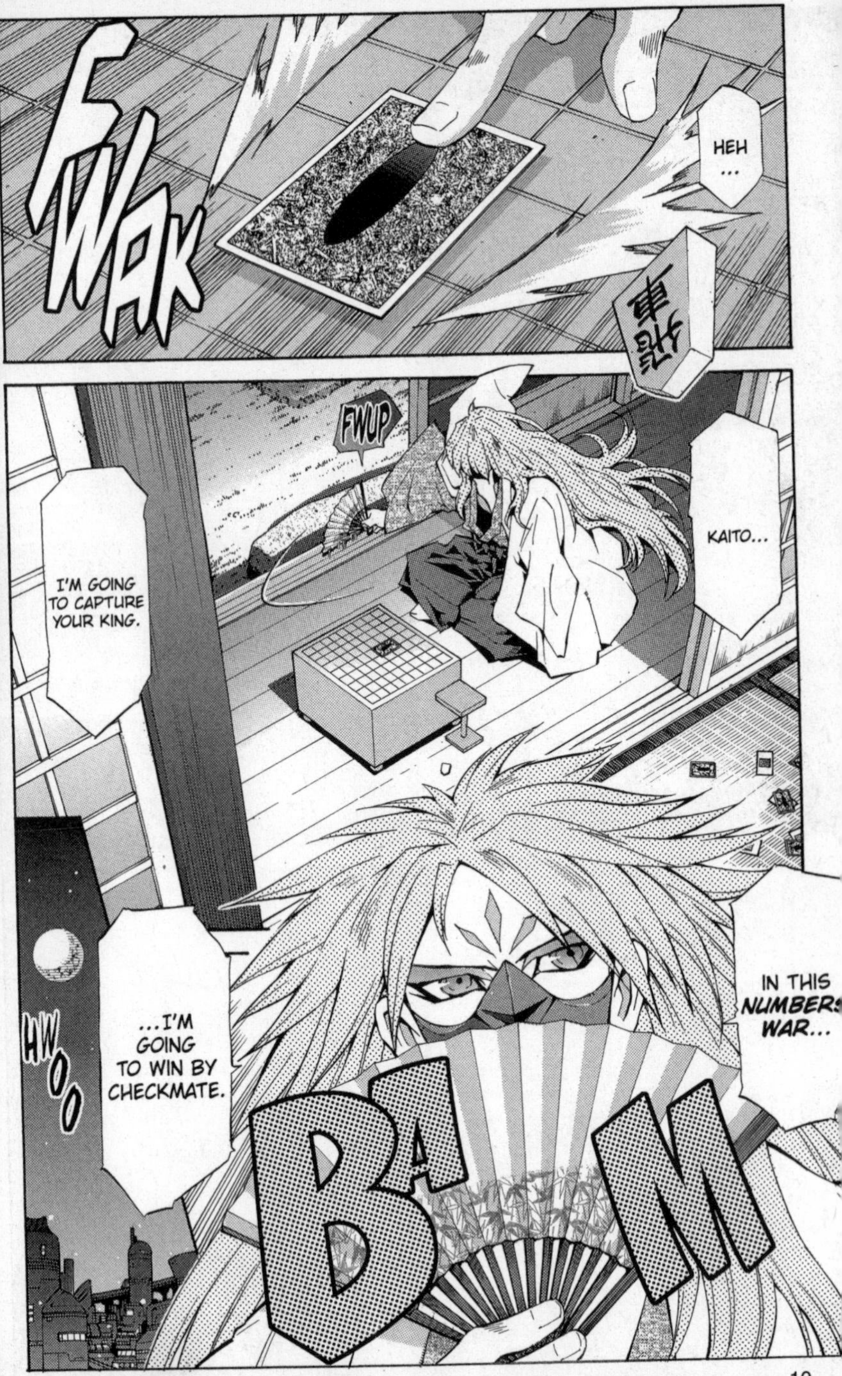
FWAK
HEH ...
KAITO...
FWUP
I'M GOING TO CAPTURE YOUR KING.
IN THIS NUMBERS WAR...
...I'M GOING TO WIN BY CHECKMATE.
BAM
HWOOO

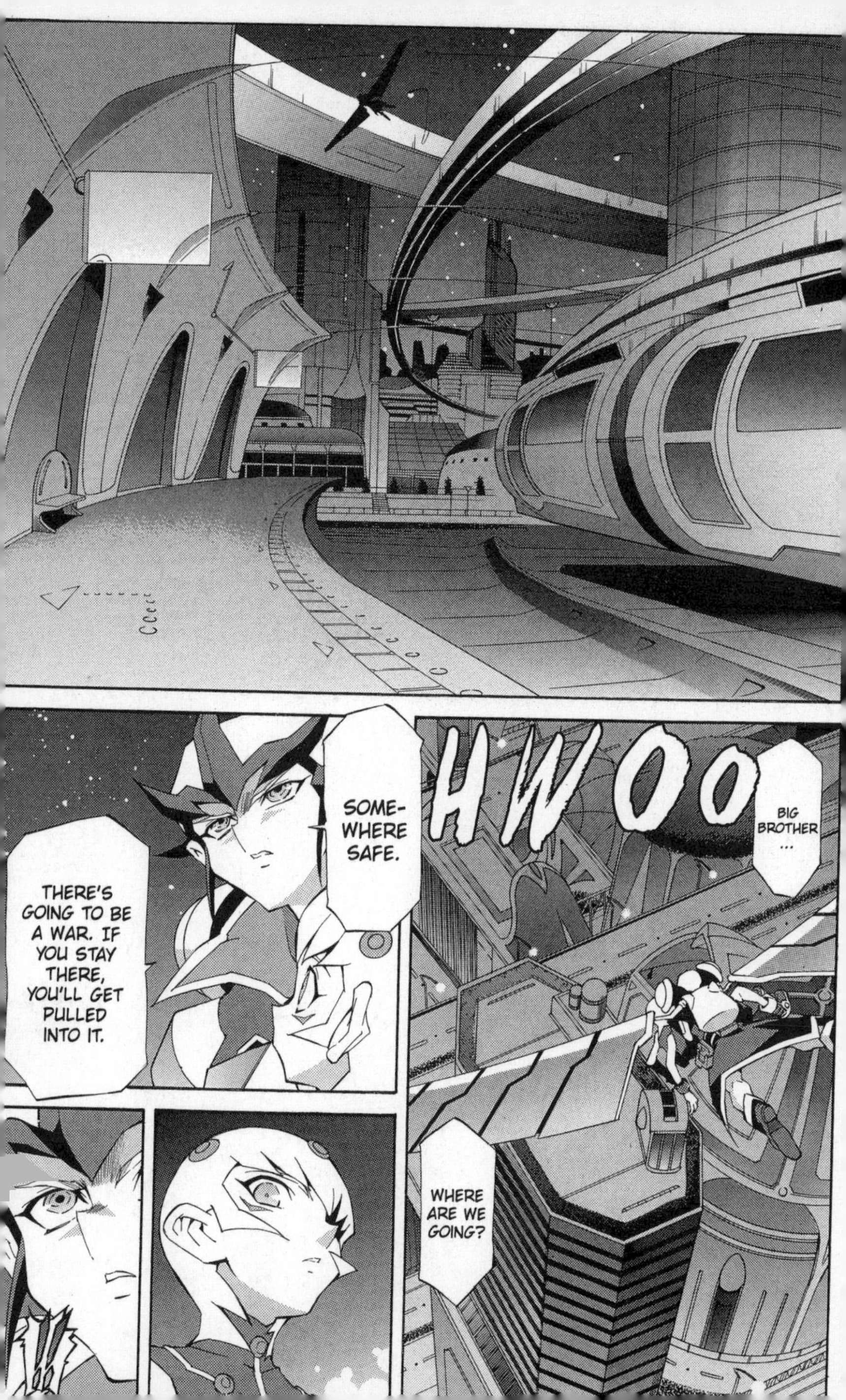
HWOO
BIG BROTHER...
WHERE ARE WE GOING?
SOME-WHERE SAFE.
THERE'S GOING TO BE A WAR. IF YOU STAY THERE, YOU'LL GET PULLED INTO IT.

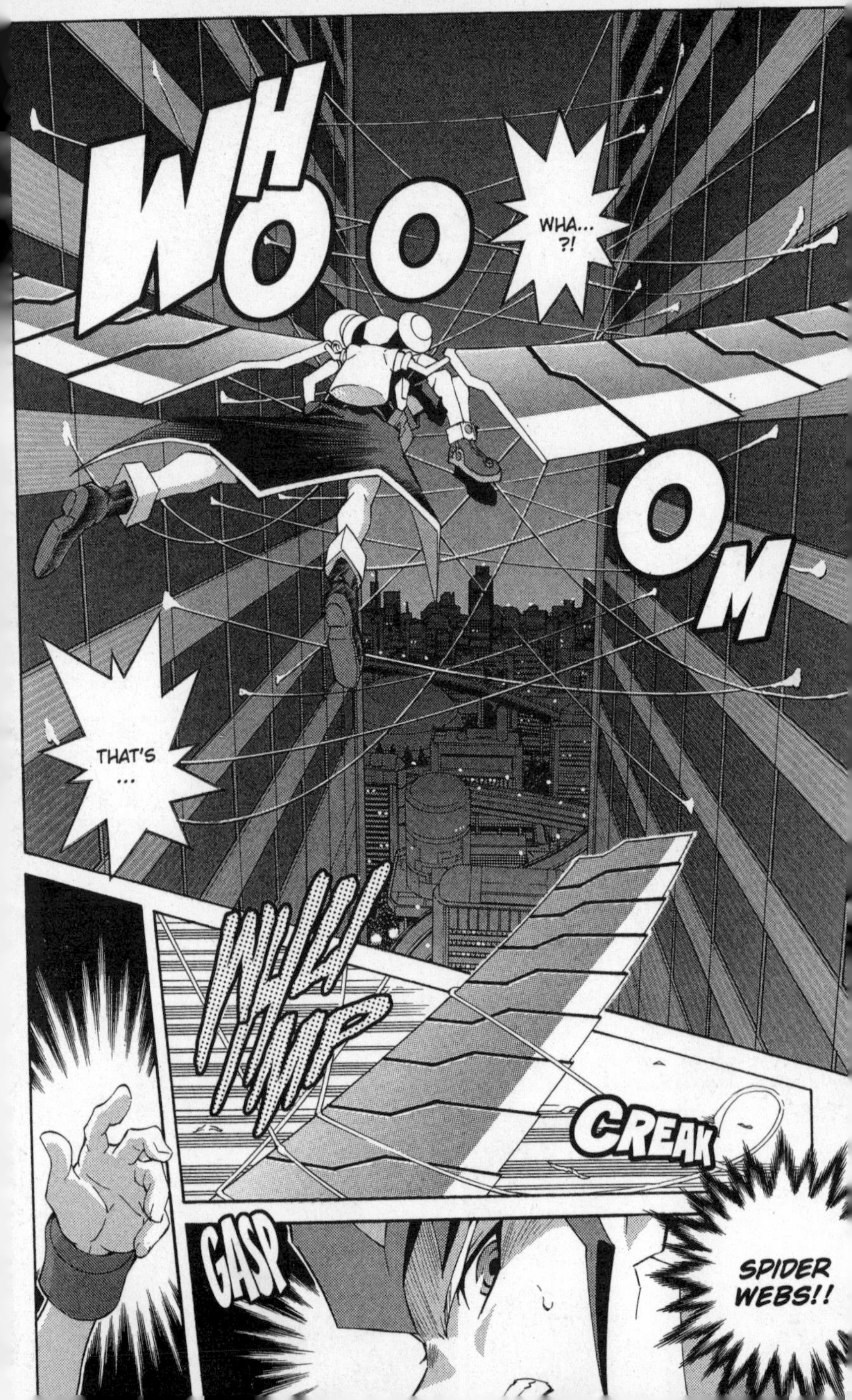
WHA...?!
WHOOOOM
THAT'S...
CREAK
WHIP
SPIDER WEBS!!
GASP

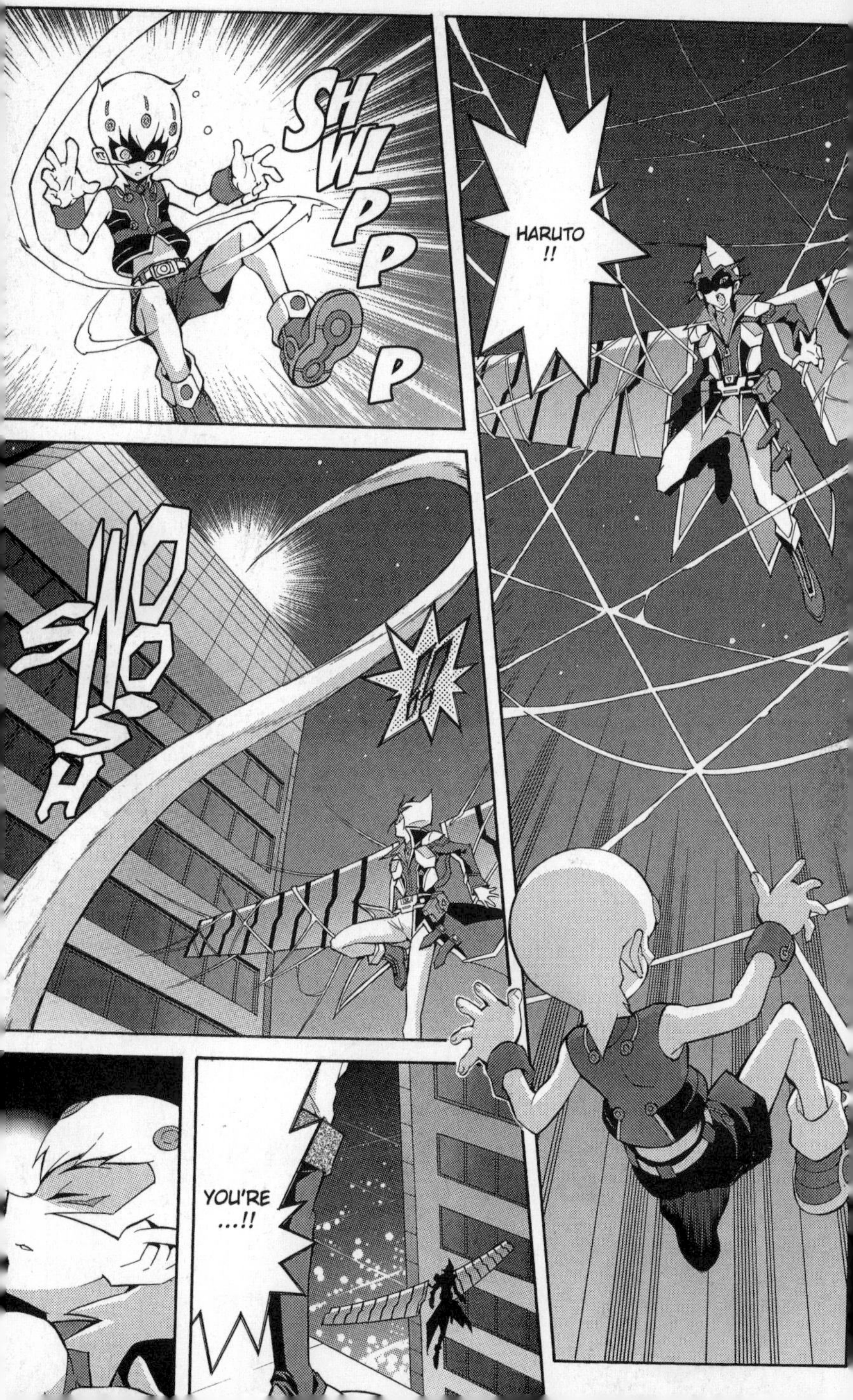
HARUTO !!
SHWIPPP
SWOOSH
!!
YOU'RE ...!!

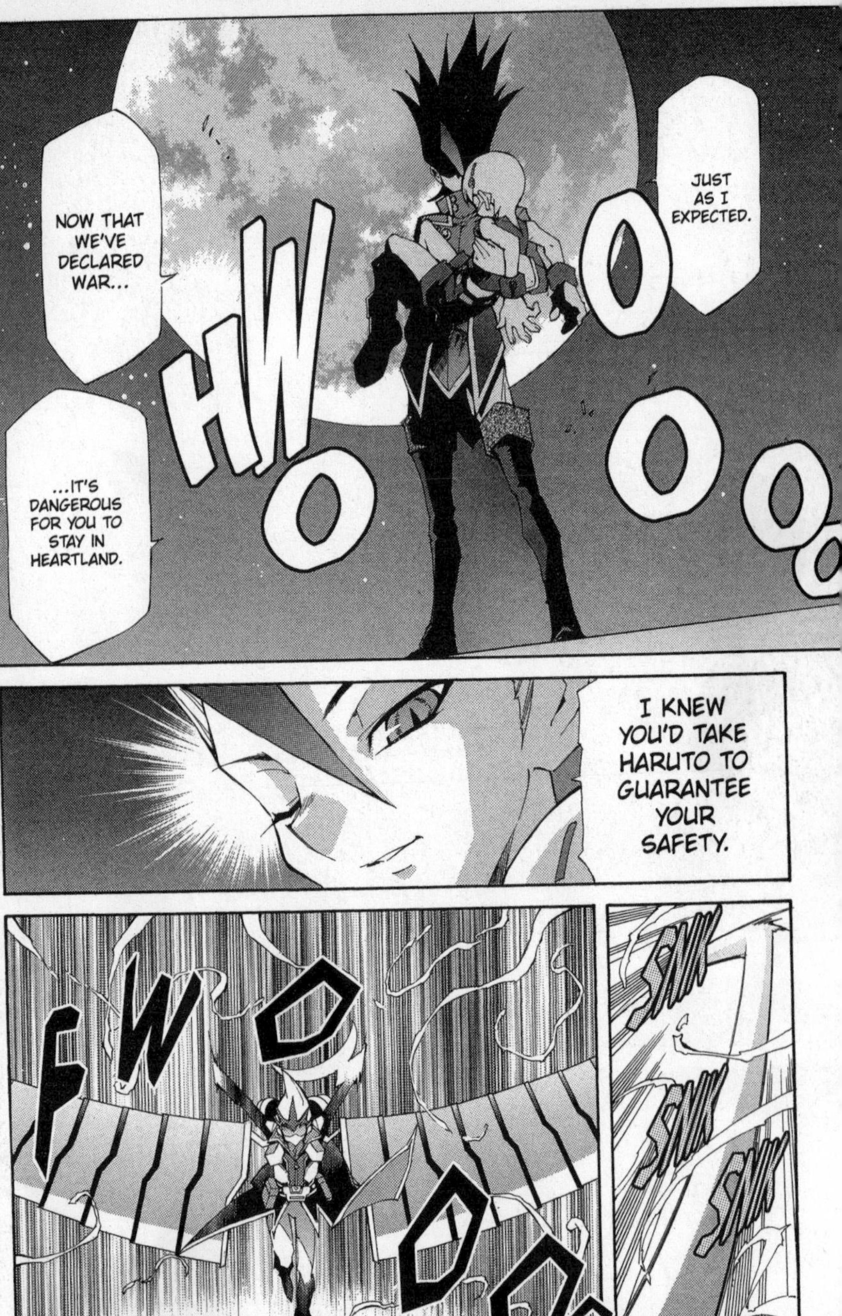
JUST AS I EXPECTED.
HWOOOOOO
NOW THAT WE'VE DECLARED WAR...
...IT'S DANGEROUS FOR YOU TO STAY IN HEARTLAND.
I KNEW YOU'D TAKE HARUTO TO GUARANTEE YOUR SAFETY.
FWOOOOO

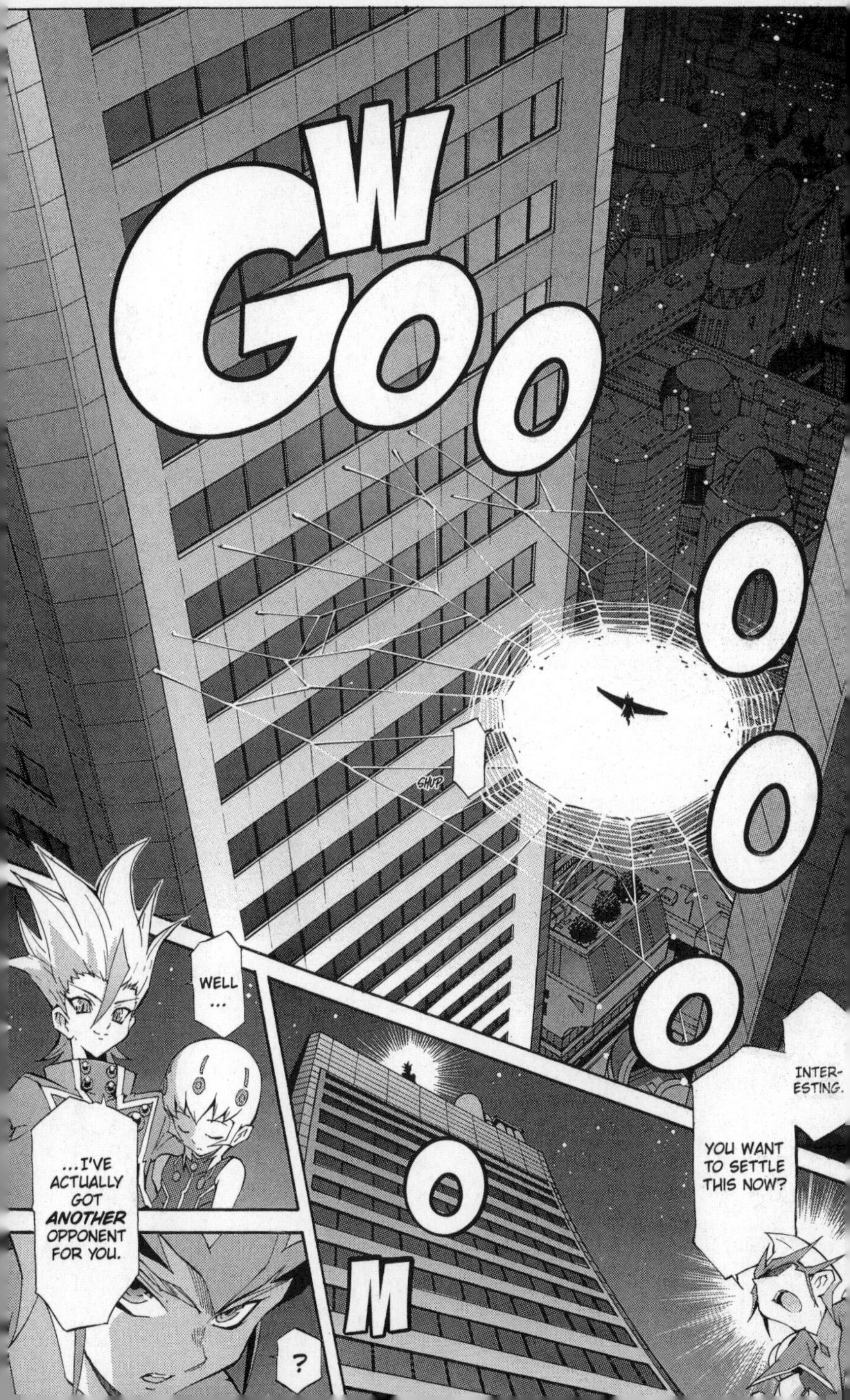
GWOOOOOOOM
SHUP
INTER-ESTING.
YOU WANT TO SETTLE THIS NOW?
WELL ...
...I'VE ACTUALLY GOT ANOTHER OPPONENT FOR YOU.
?

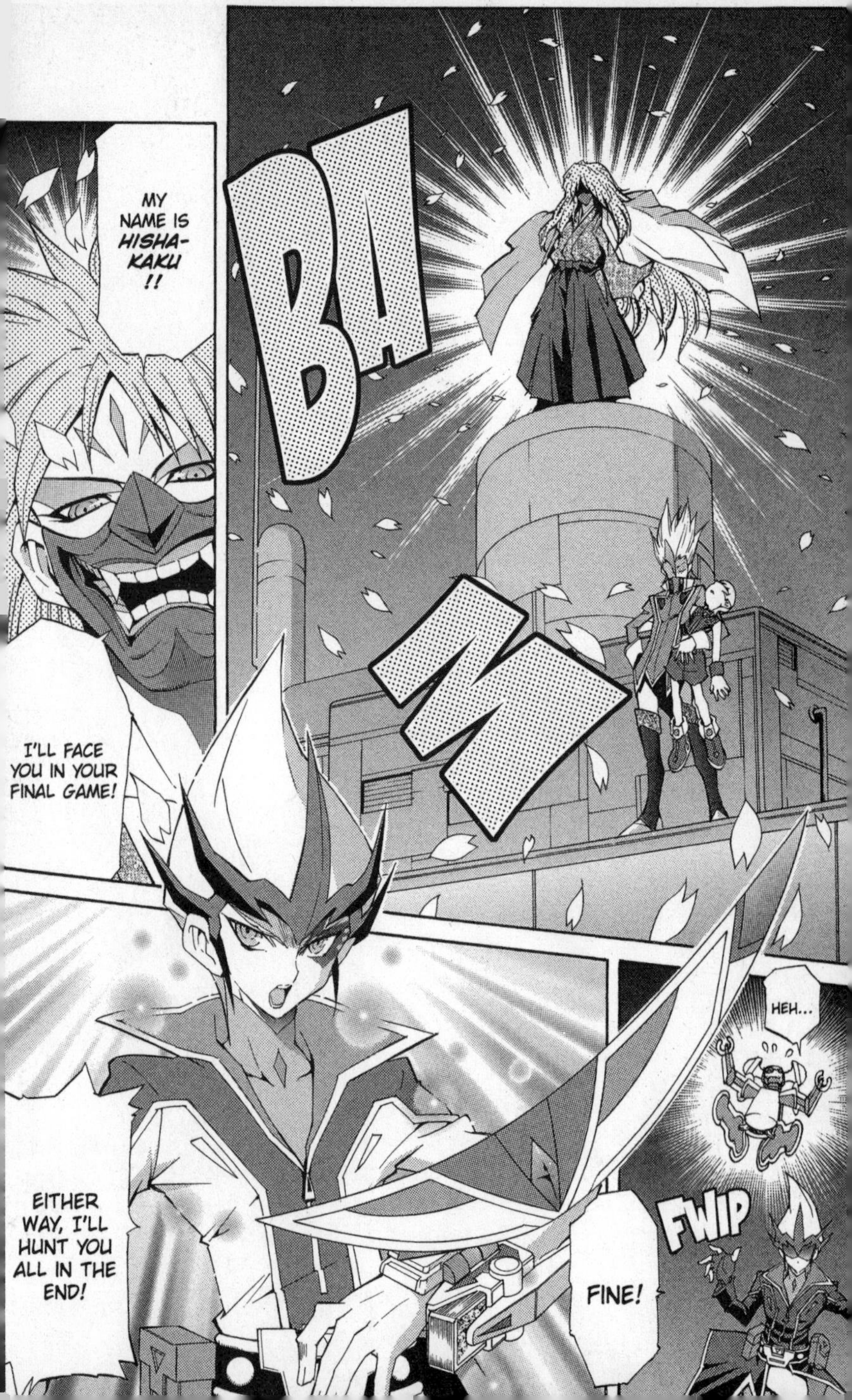
BA
M
MY NAME IS HISHA-KAKU!!
I'LL FACE YOU IN YOUR FINAL GAME!
HEH...
FWIP
FINE!
EITHER WAY, I'LL HUNT YOU ALL IN THE END!

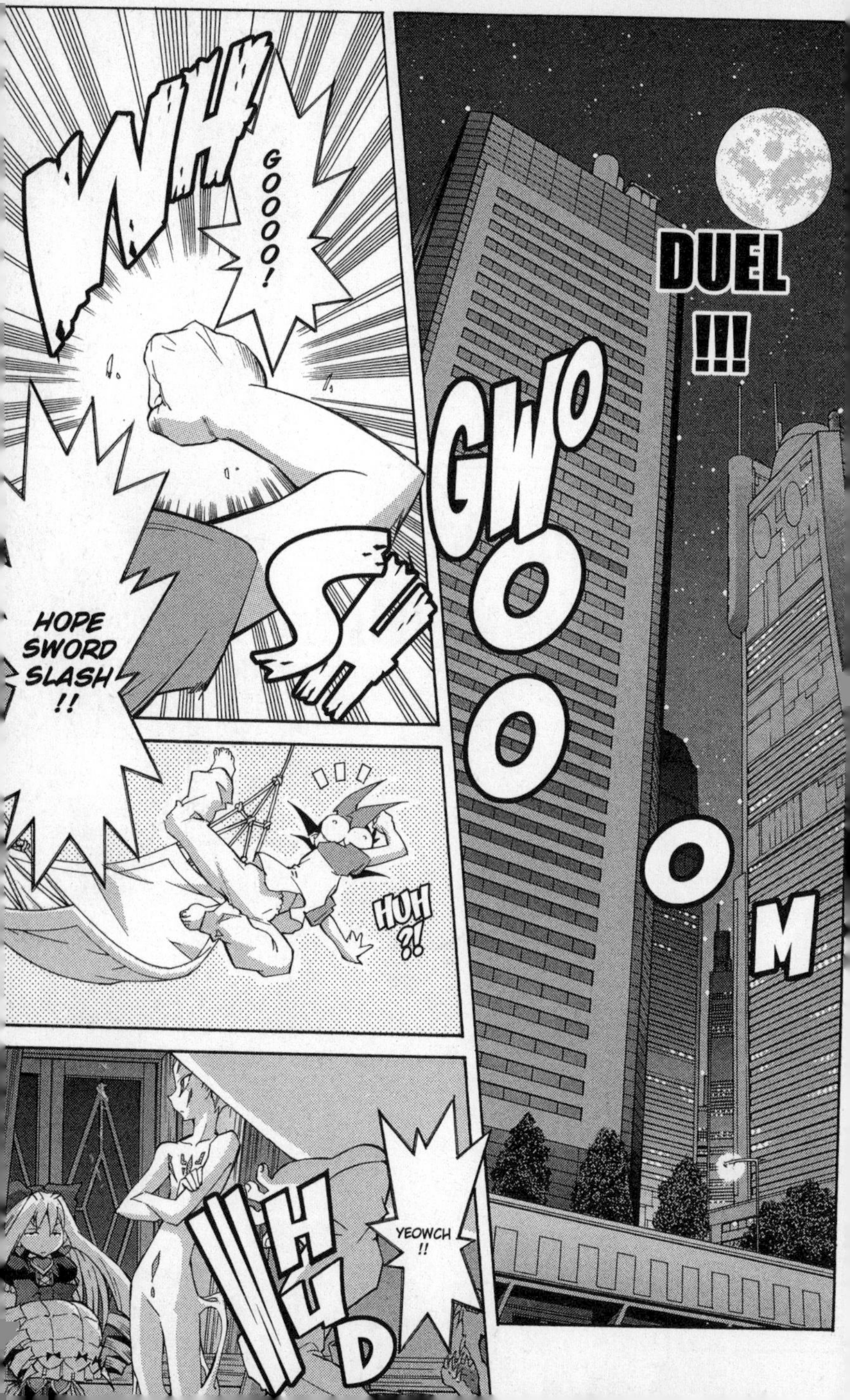

DUEL !!!
GWOOOOOM
WH
GOOOOO!
SH
HOPE SWORD SLASH !!
HUH ?!
YEOWCH !!
HUD

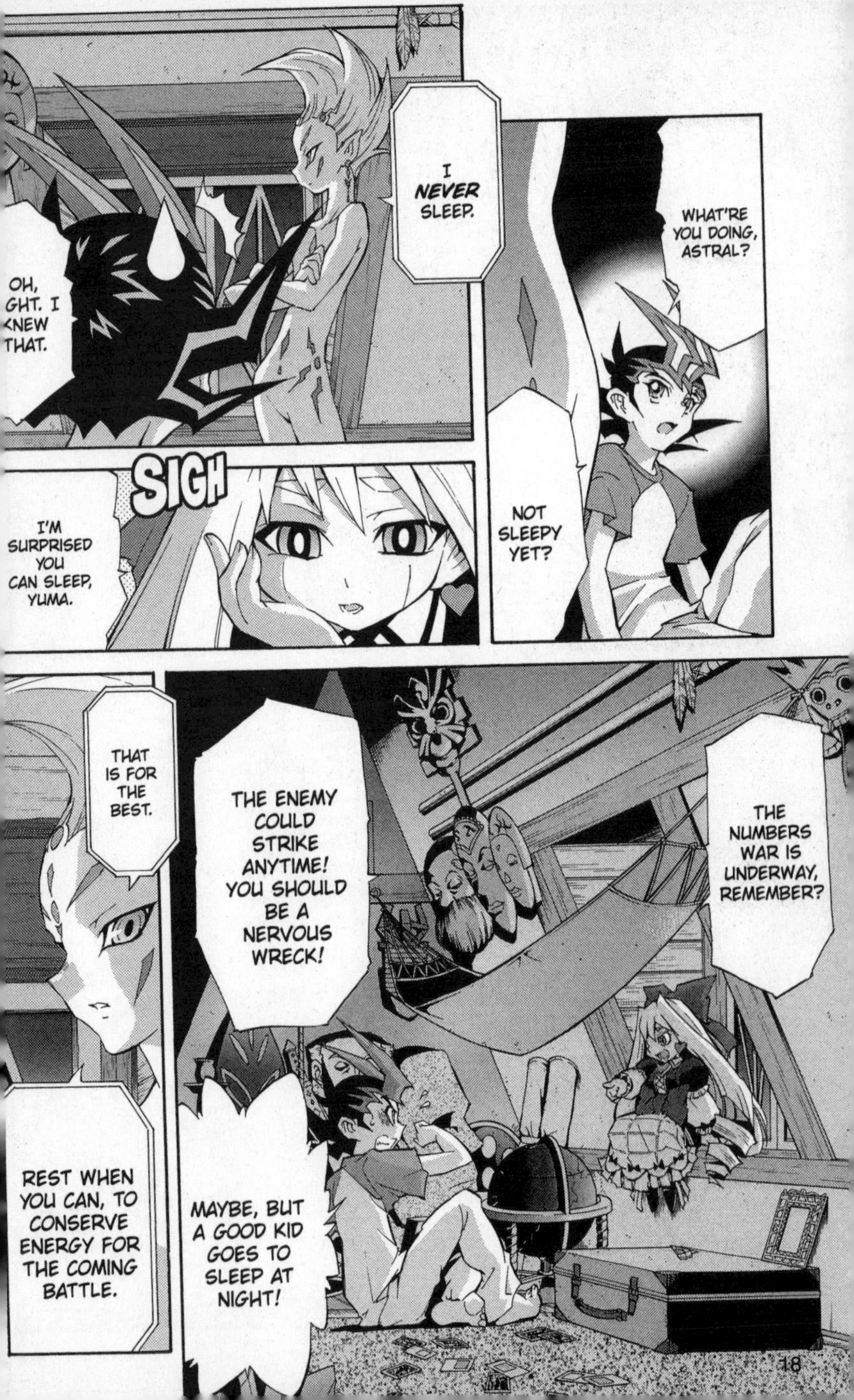

WHAT'RE YOU DOING, ASTRAL?
NOT SLEEPY YET?
I NEVER SLEEP.
OH, GHT. I KNEW THAT.
SIGH
I'M SURPRISED YOU CAN SLEEP, YUMA.
THE NUMBERS WAR IS UNDERWAY, REMEMBER?
THE ENEMY COULD STRIKE ANYTIME! YOU SHOULD BE A NERVOUS WRECK!
MAYBE, BUT A GOOD KID GOES TO SLEEP AT NIGHT!
THAT IS FOR THE BEST.
REST WHEN YOU CAN, TO CONSERVE ENERGY FOR THE COMING BATTLE.

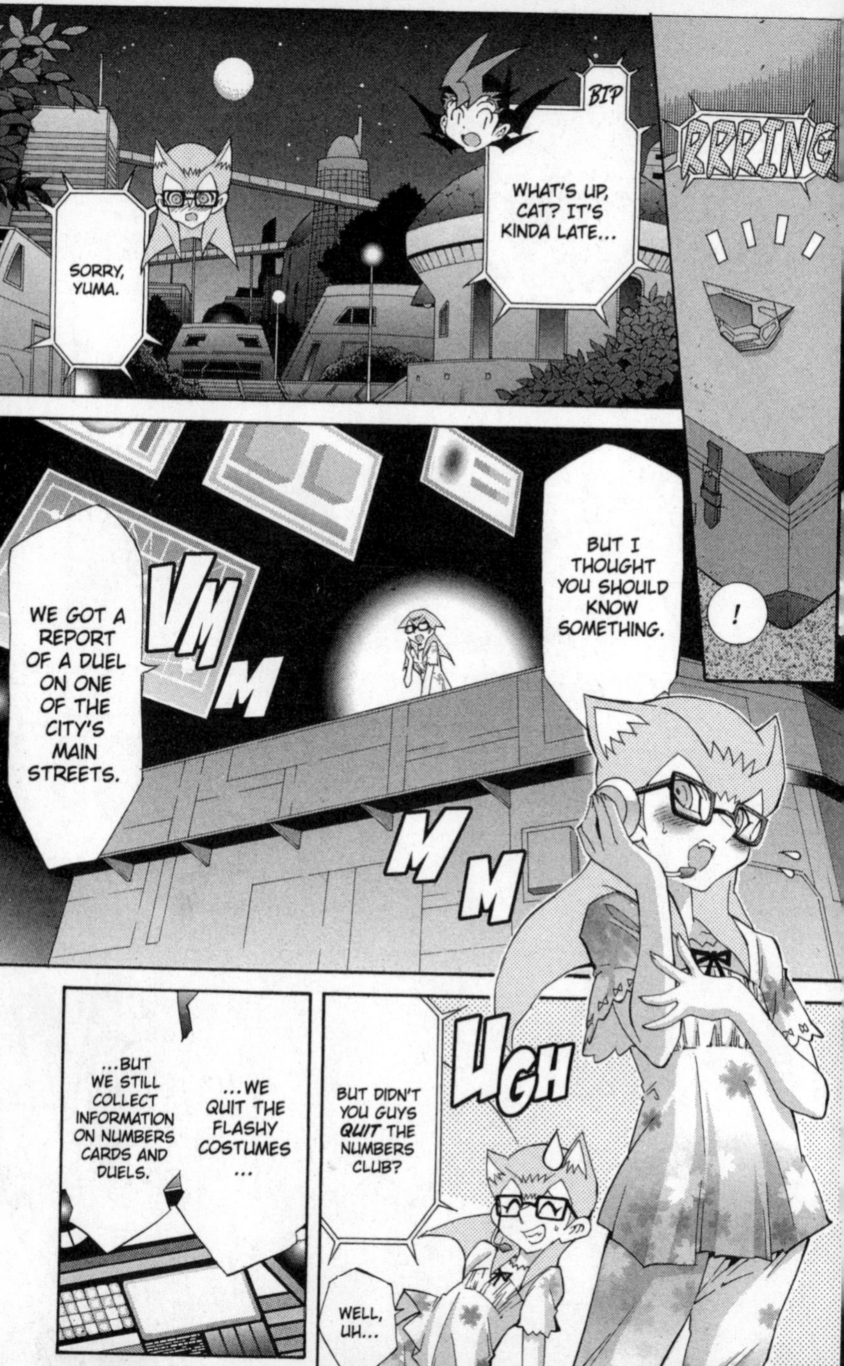
RRRING
!!!!
!
BIP
WHAT'S UP, CAT? IT'S KINDA LATE...
SORRY, YUMA.
BUT I THOUGHT YOU SHOULD KNOW SOMETHING.
VMM
M
WE GOT A REPORT OF A DUEL ON ONE OF THE CITY'S MAIN STREETS.
MM
M
UGH
BUT DIDN'T YOU GUYS *QUIT* THE NUMBERS CLUB?
WELL, UH...
...WE QUIT THE FLASHY COSTUMES...
...BUT WE STILL COLLECT INFORMATION ON NUMBERS CARDS AND DUELS.

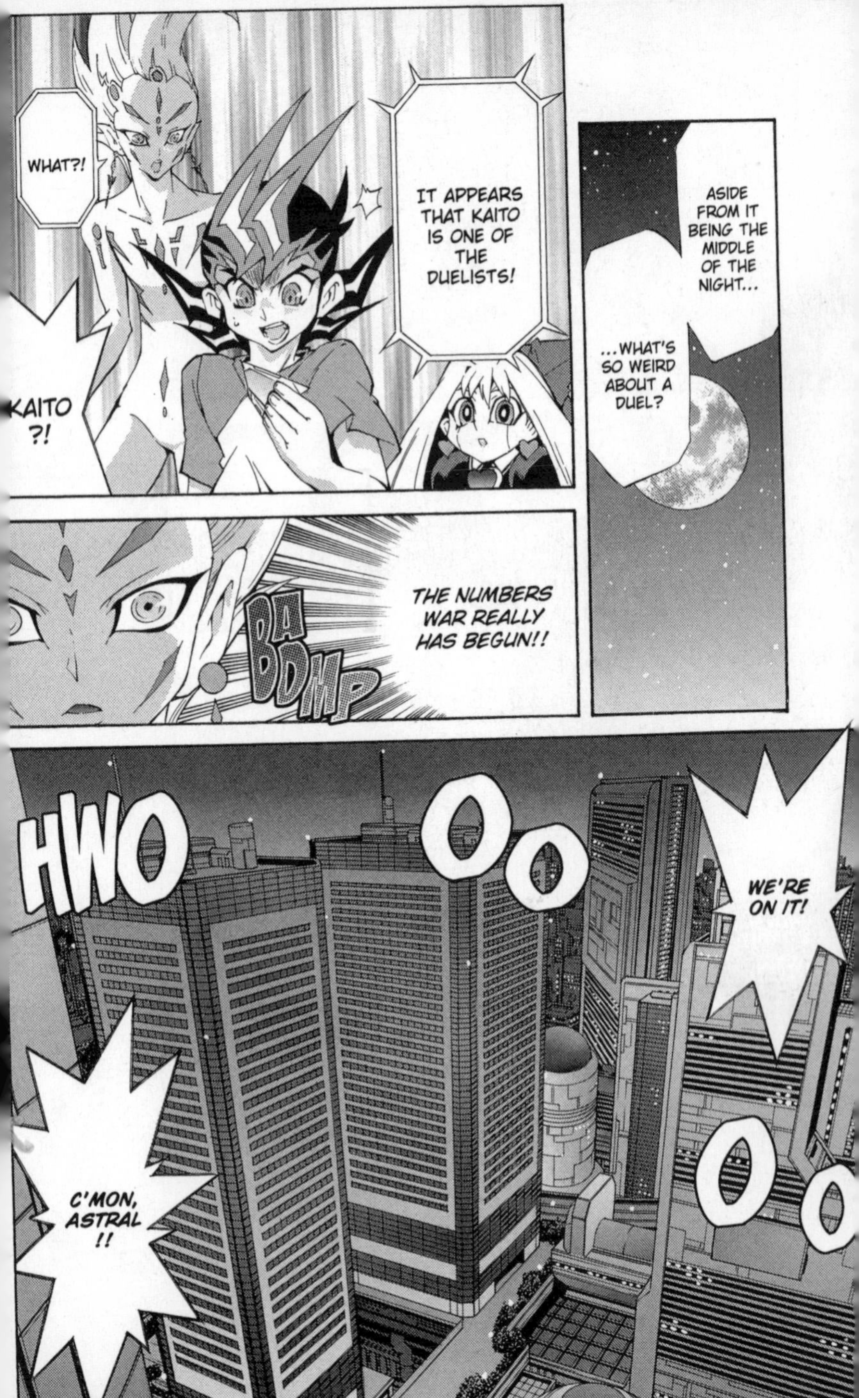
ASIDE FROM IT BEING THE MIDDLE OF THE NIGHT...
...WHAT'S SO WEIRD ABOUT A DUEL?
IT APPEARS THAT KAITO IS ONE OF THE DUELISTS!
WHAT?!
KAITO ?!
THE NUMBERS WAR REALLY HAS BEGUN!!
BA DMP
WE'RE ON IT!
HWOOOOO
C'MON, ASTRAL !!

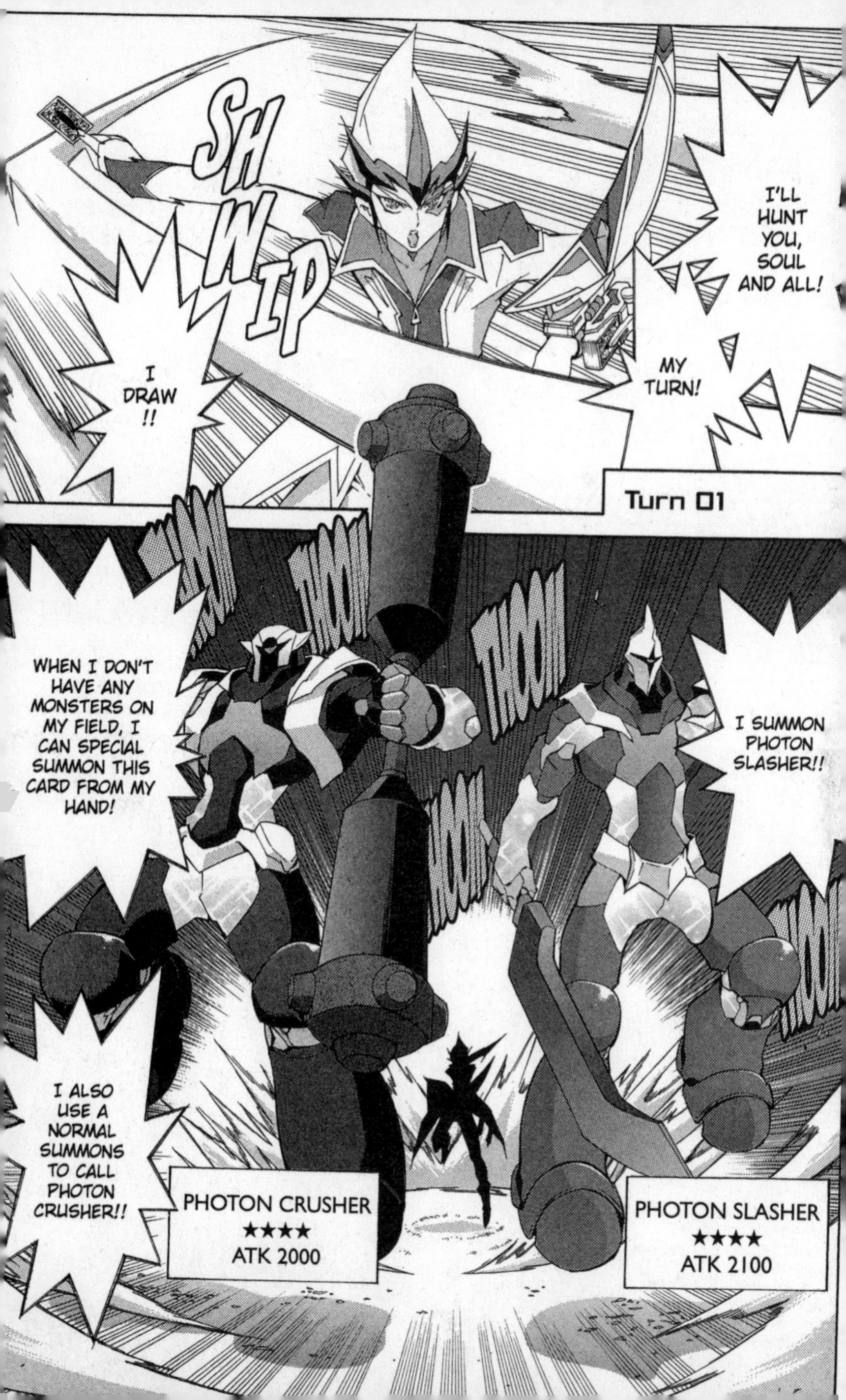
I'LL HUNT YOU, SOUL AND ALL!
MY TURN!
SHWIP
I DRAW!!
Turn 01
THOOM
THOOM
I SUMMON PHOTON SLASHER!!
WHEN I DON'T HAVE ANY MONSTERS ON MY FIELD, I CAN SPECIAL SUMMON THIS CARD FROM MY HAND!
PHOTON SLASHER ★★★★ ATK 2100
I ALSO USE A NORMAL SUMMONS TO CALL PHOTON CRUSHER!!
PHOTON CRUSHER ★★★★ ATK 2000

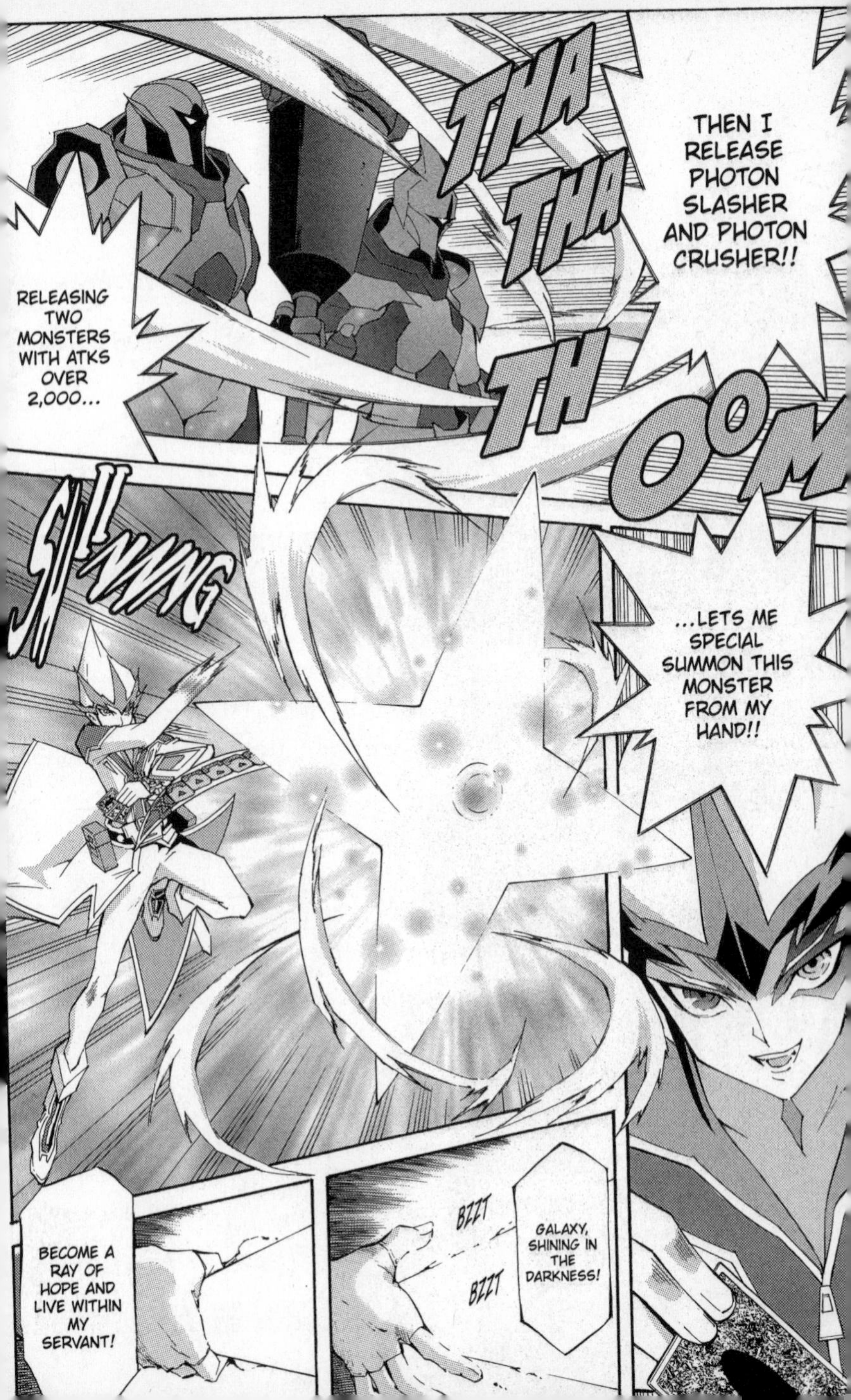
THEN I RELEASE PHOTON SLASHER AND PHOTON CRUSHER!!
THA
THA
THOOM
RELEASING TWO MONSTERS WITH ATKS OVER 2,000...
...LETS ME SPECIAL SUMMON THIS MONSTER FROM MY HAND!!
GALAXY, SHINING IN THE DARKNESS!
BZZT
BZZT
BECOME A RAY OF HOPE AND LIVE WITHIN MY SERVANT!

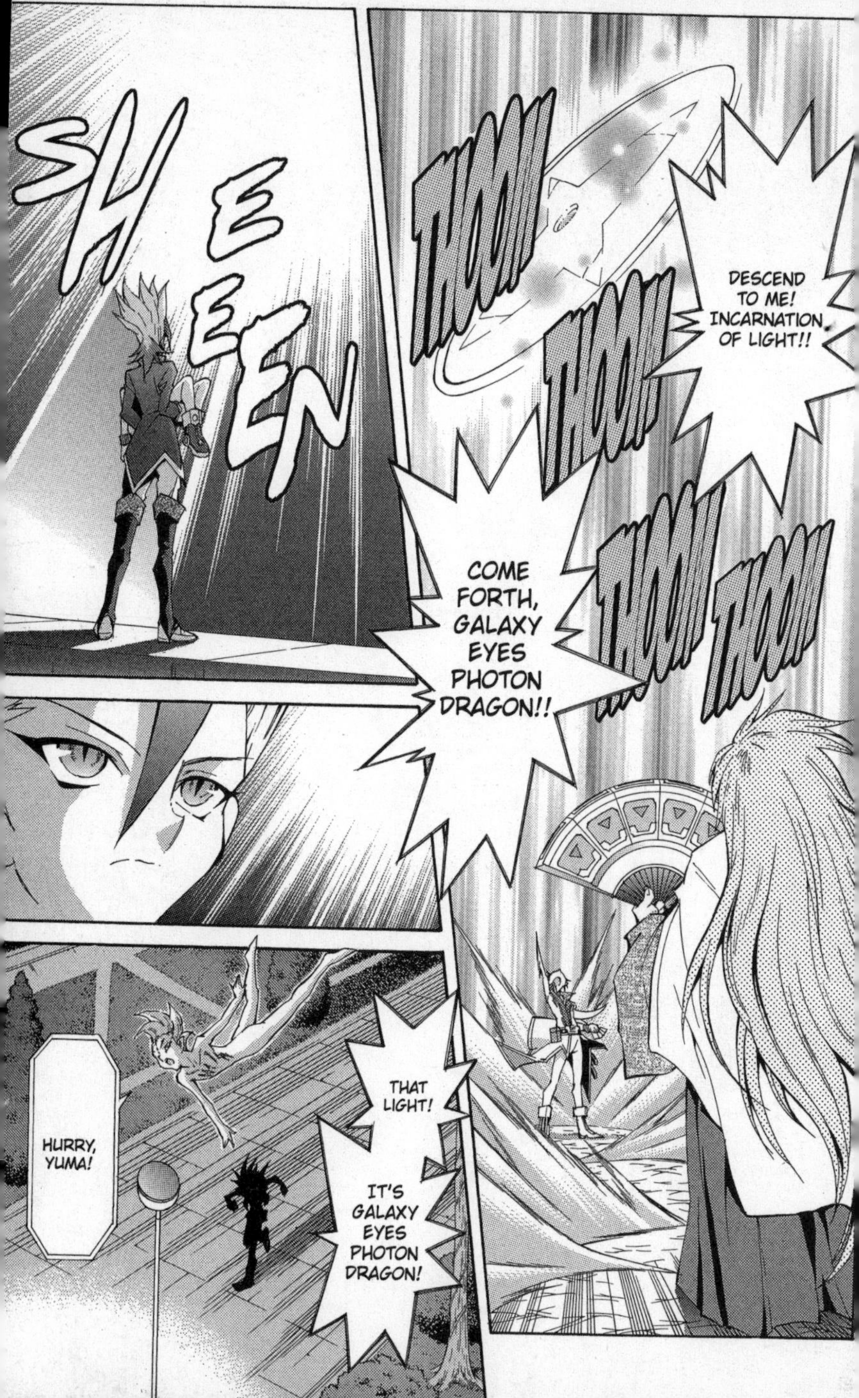

DESCEND TO ME! INCARNATION OF LIGHT!!
THOOM
THOOM
THOOM
COME FORTH, GALAXY EYES PHOTON DRAGON!!
THOOM
THOOM
SHEEEN
THAT LIGHT!
IT'S GALAXY EYES PHOTON DRAGON!
HURRY, YUMA!

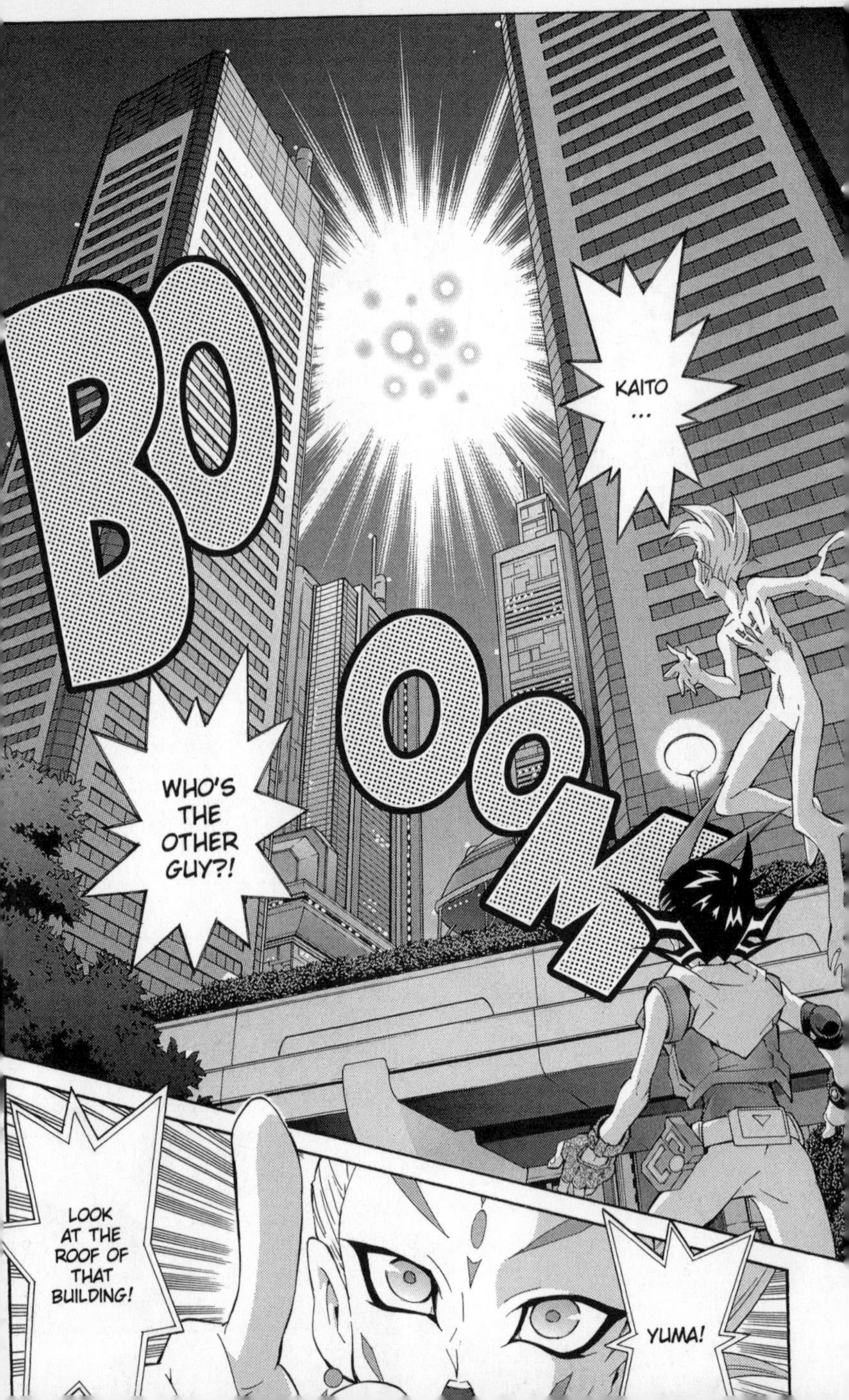
KAITO ...
BOOOM
WHO'S THE OTHER GUY?!
YUMA!
LOOK AT THE ROOF OF THAT BUILDING!

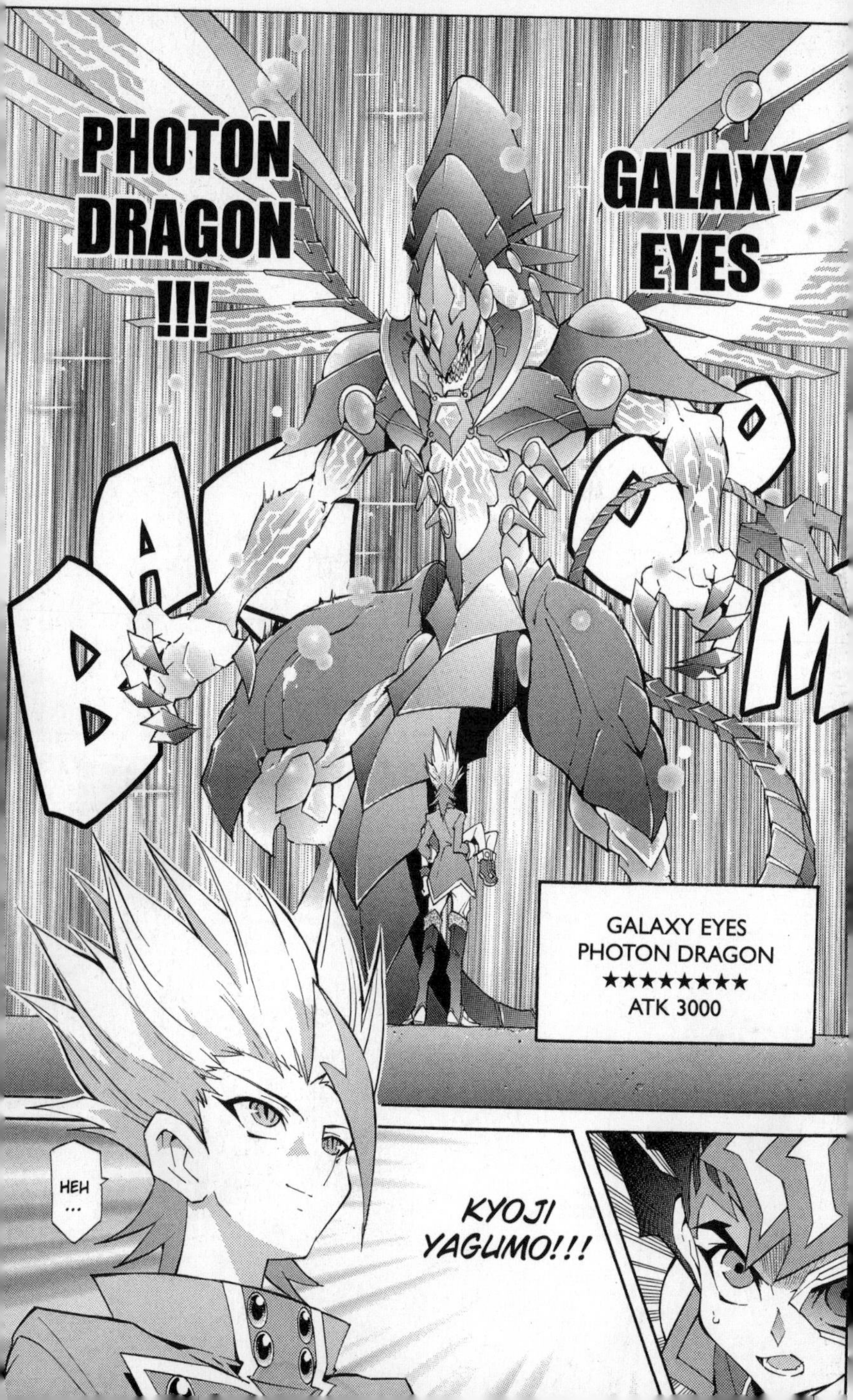
GALAXY EYES
PHOTON DRAGON !!!
GALAXY EYES
PHOTON DRAGON
★★★★★★★★
ATK 3000
KYOJI YAGUMO!!!
HEH ...

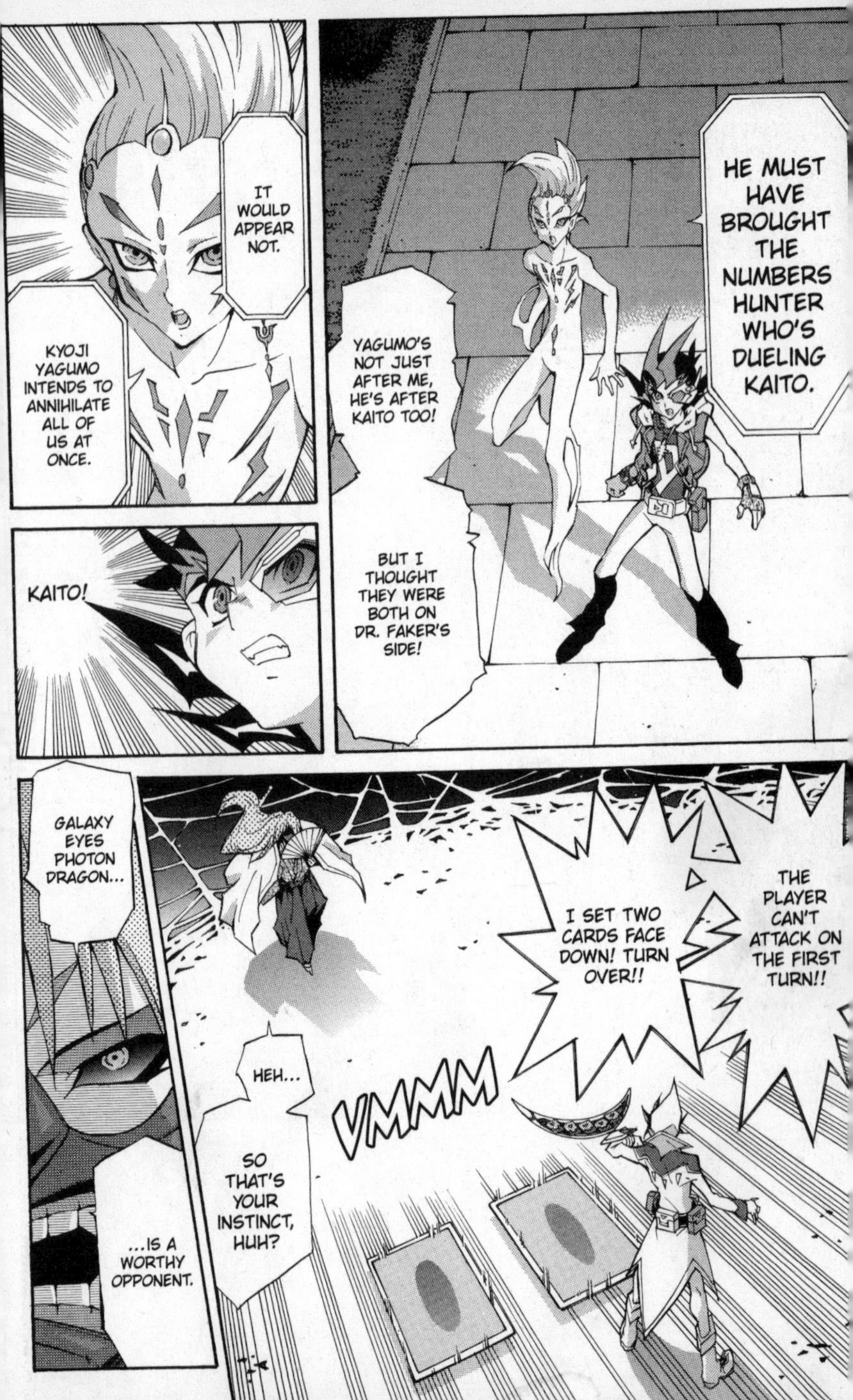
HE MUST HAVE BROUGHT THE NUMBERS HUNTER WHO'S DUELING KAITO.
YAGUMO'S NOT JUST AFTER ME, HE'S AFTER KAITO TOO!
BUT I THOUGHT THEY WERE BOTH ON DR. FAKER'S SIDE!
IT WOULD APPEAR NOT.
KYOJI YAGUMO INTENDS TO ANNIHILATE ALL OF US AT ONCE.
KAITO!
THE PLAYER CAN'T ATTACK ON THE FIRST TURN!!
I SET TWO CARDS FACE DOWN! TURN OVER!!
VMMM
HEH...
SO THAT'S YOUR INSTINCT, HUH?
GALAXY EYES PHOTON DRAGON...
...IS A WORTHY OPPONENT.

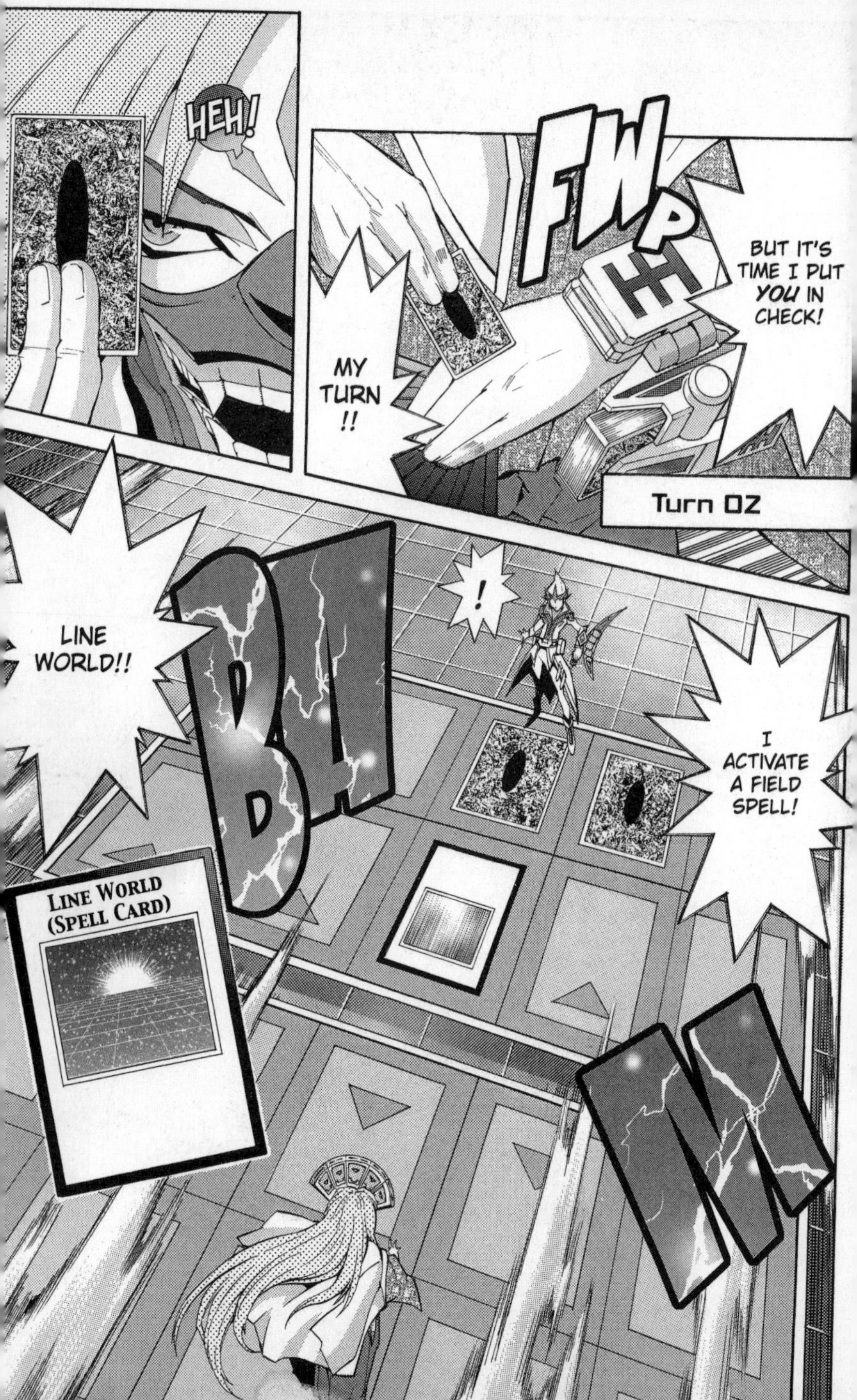

FWP
BUT IT'S TIME I PUT YOU IN CHECK!
MY TURN !!
Turn 02
HEH!
!
I ACTIVATE A FIELD SPELL!
BAM
LINE WORLD!!
LINE WORLD (SPELL CARD)

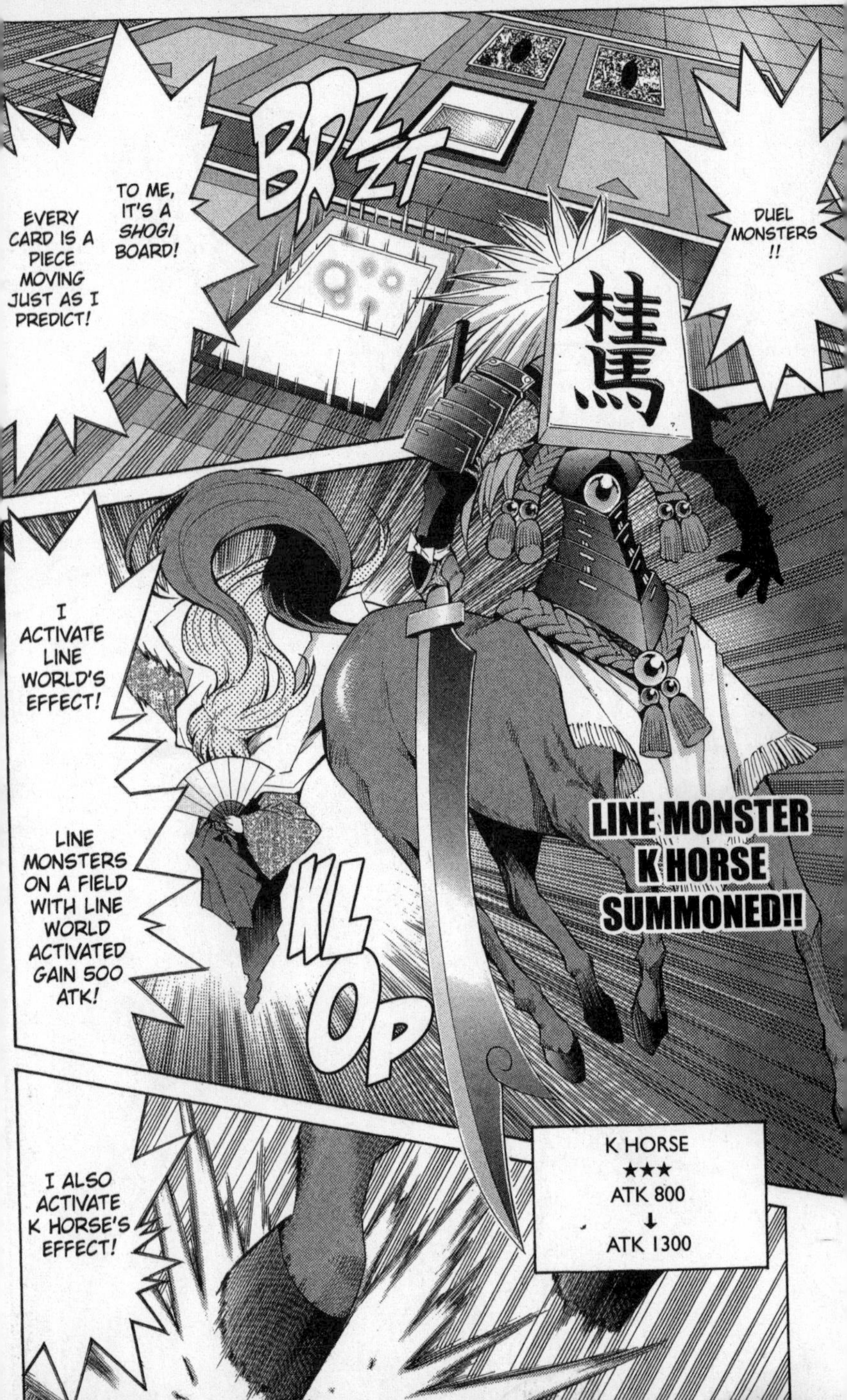
DUEL MONSTERS !!
BRZZT
TO ME, IT'S A SHOGI BOARD!
EVERY CARD IS A PIECE MOVING JUST AS I PREDICT!
桂馬
LINE MONSTER K HORSE SUMMONED!!
KLOP
I ACTIVATE LINE WORLD'S EFFECT!
LINE MONSTERS ON A FIELD WITH LINE WORLD ACTIVATED GAIN 500 ATK!
K HORSE ★★★ ATK 800 ↓ ATK 1300
I ALSO ACTIVATE K HORSE'S EFFECT!

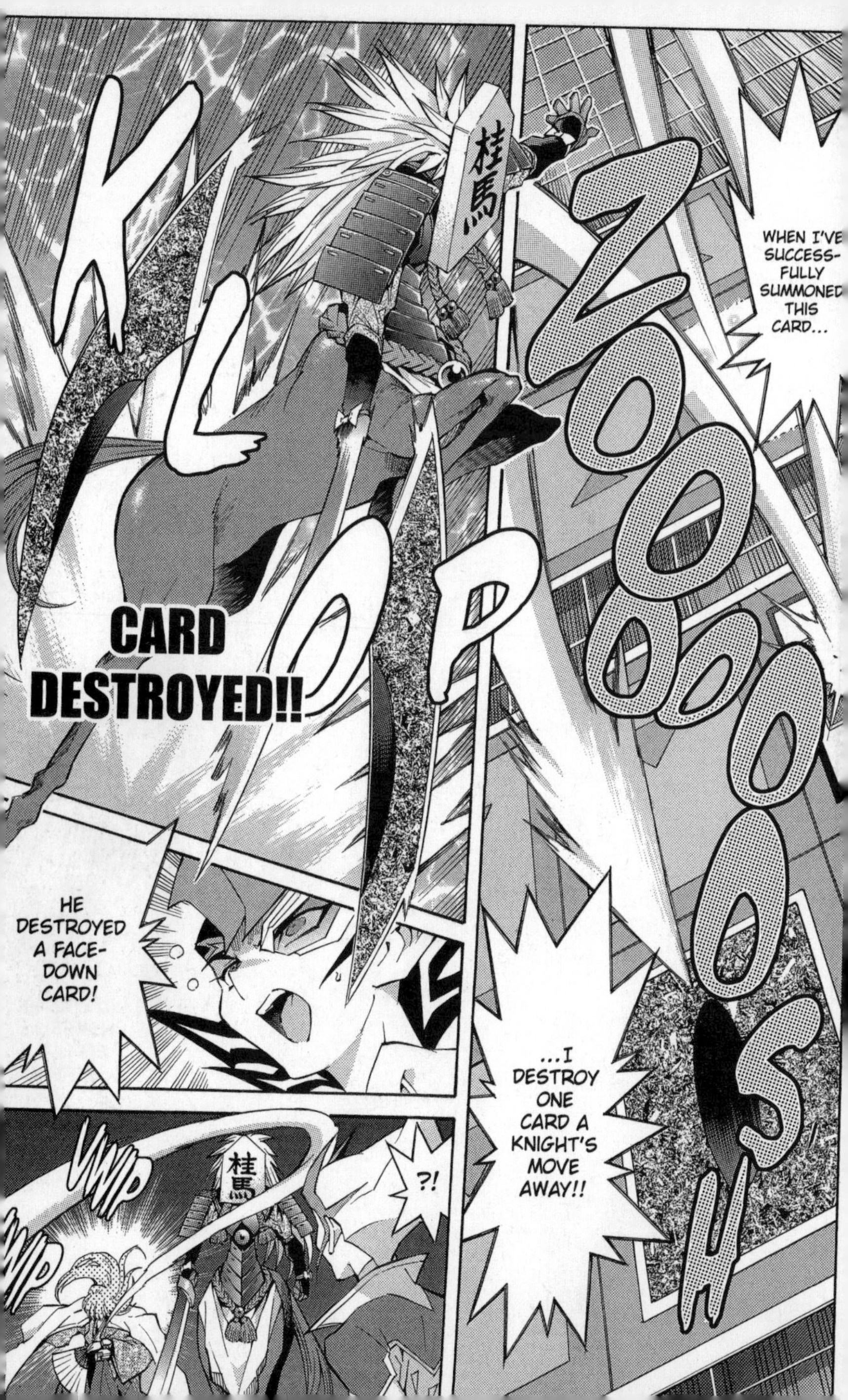

WHEN I'VE SUCCESS-FULLY SUMMONED THIS CARD...
桂馬
ZOOOOOOSH
...I DESTROY ONE CARD A KNIGHT'S MOVE AWAY!!
KLOP
CARD DESTROYED!!
HE DESTROYED A FACE-DOWN CARD!
?!
桂馬

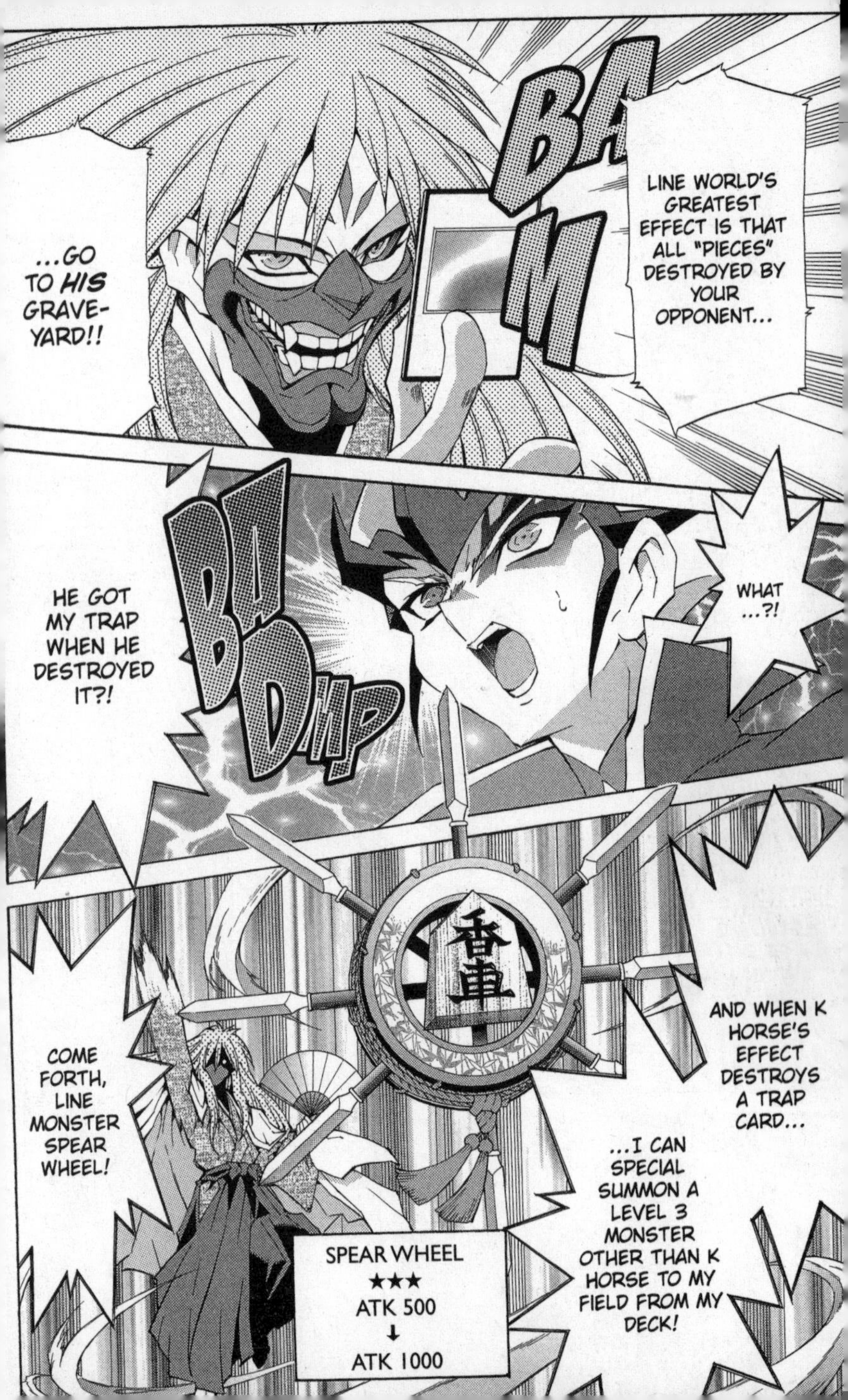
LINE WORLD'S GREATEST EFFECT IS THAT ALL "PIECES" DESTROYED BY YOUR OPPONENT...
BAM
...GO TO HIS GRAVEYARD!!
WHAT ...?!
BA DMP
HE GOT MY TRAP WHEN HE DESTROYED IT?!
香車
AND WHEN K HORSE'S EFFECT DESTROYS A TRAP CARD...
...I CAN SPECIAL SUMMON A LEVEL 3 MONSTER OTHER THAN K HORSE TO MY FIELD FROM MY DECK!
COME FORTH, LINE MONSTER SPEAR WHEEL!
SPEAR WHEEL ★★★ ATK 500 ↓ ATK 1000

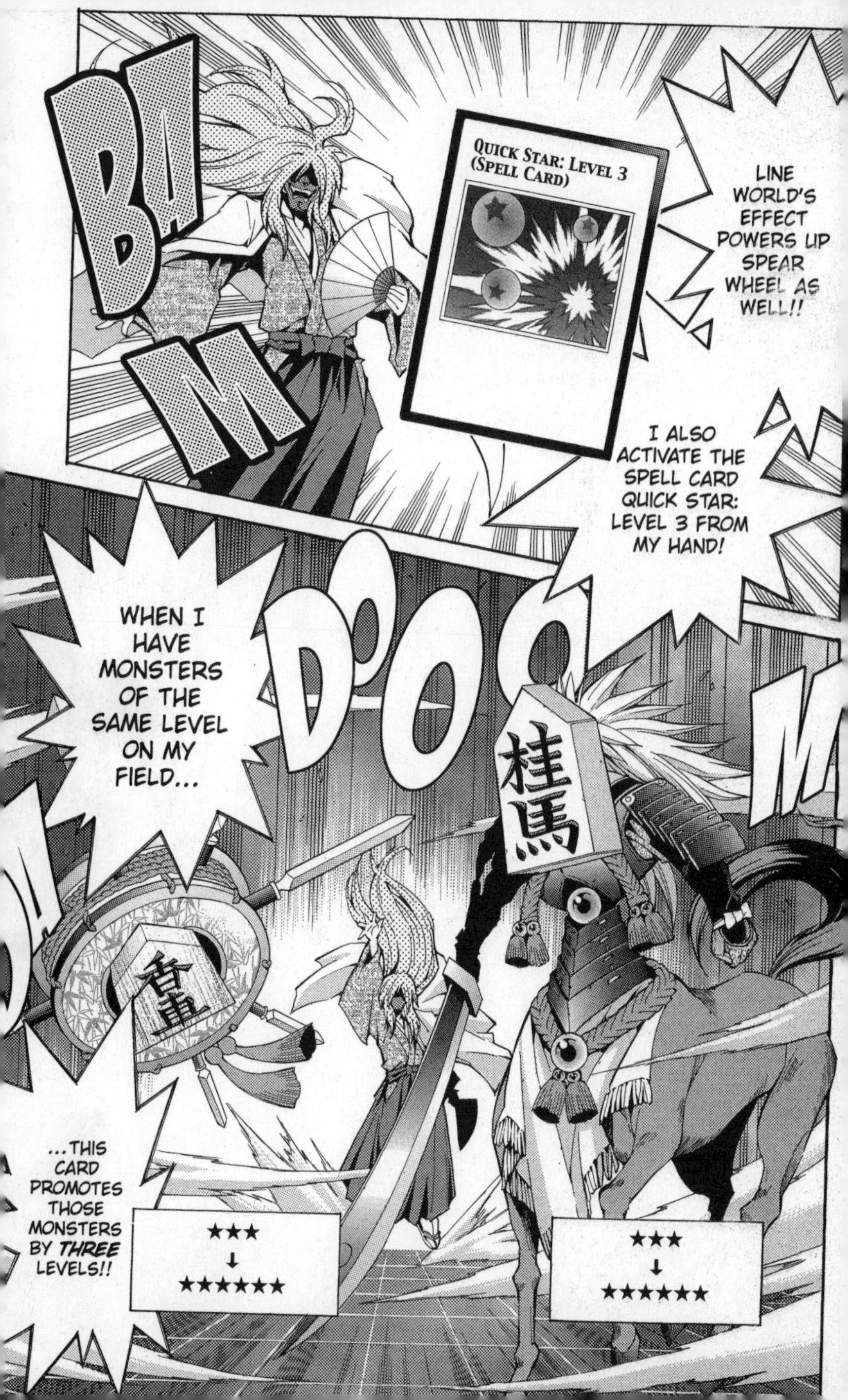
LINE WORLD'S EFFECT POWERS UP SPEAR WHEEL AS WELL!!
QUICK STAR: LEVEL 3 (SPELL CARD)
I ALSO ACTIVATE THE SPELL CARD QUICK STAR: LEVEL 3 FROM MY HAND!
BAM
DOOOM
WHEN I HAVE MONSTERS OF THE SAME LEVEL ON MY FIELD...
...THIS CARD PROMOTES THOSE MONSTERS BY *THREE* LEVELS!!
★★★ ↓ ★★★★★★
★★★ ↓ ★★★★★★

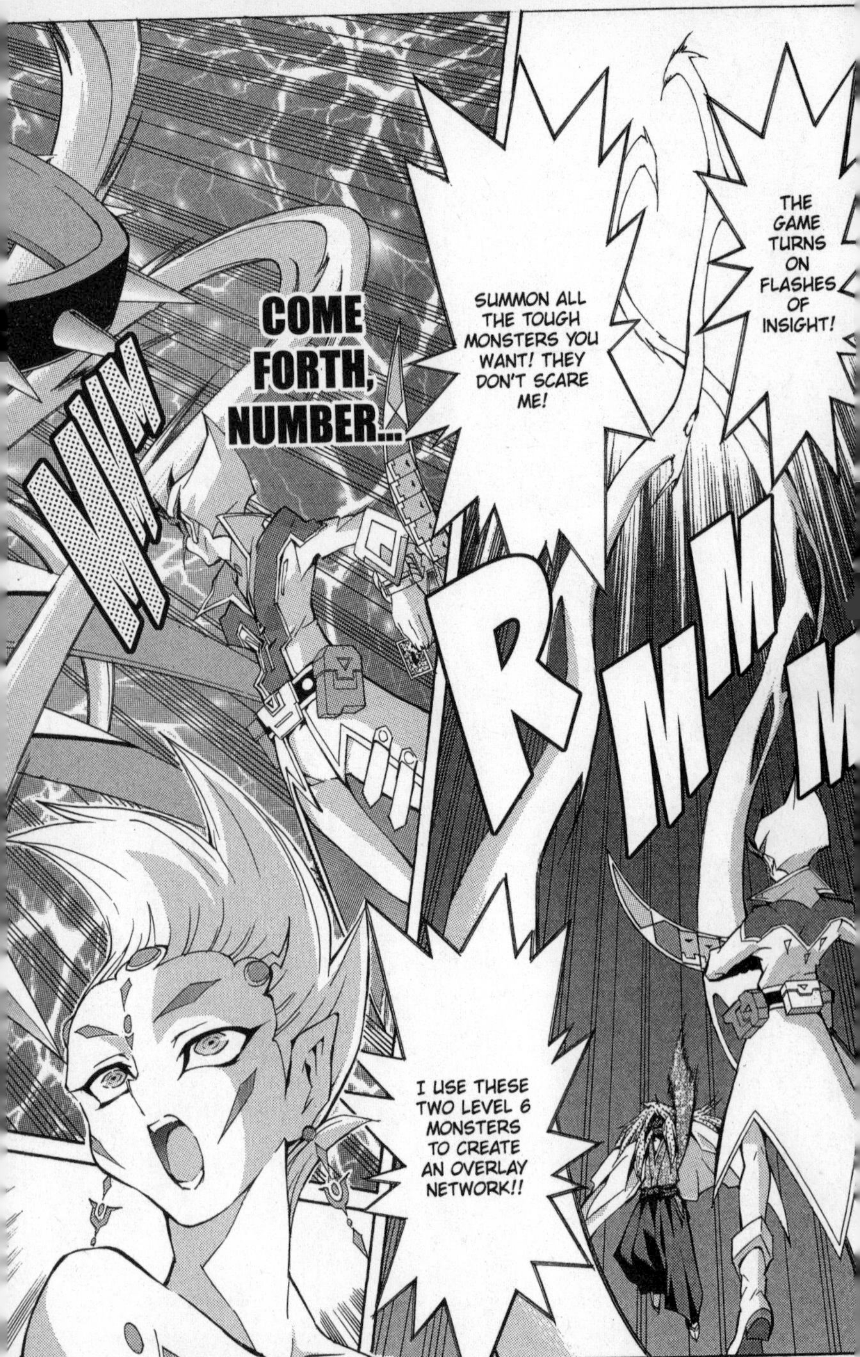
THE GAME TURNS ON FLASHES OF INSIGHT!
SUMMON ALL THE TOUGH MONSTERS YOU WANT! THEY DON'T SCARE ME!
I USE THESE TWO LEVEL 6 MONSTERS TO CREATE AN OVERLAY NETWORK!!
COME FORTH, NUMBER...

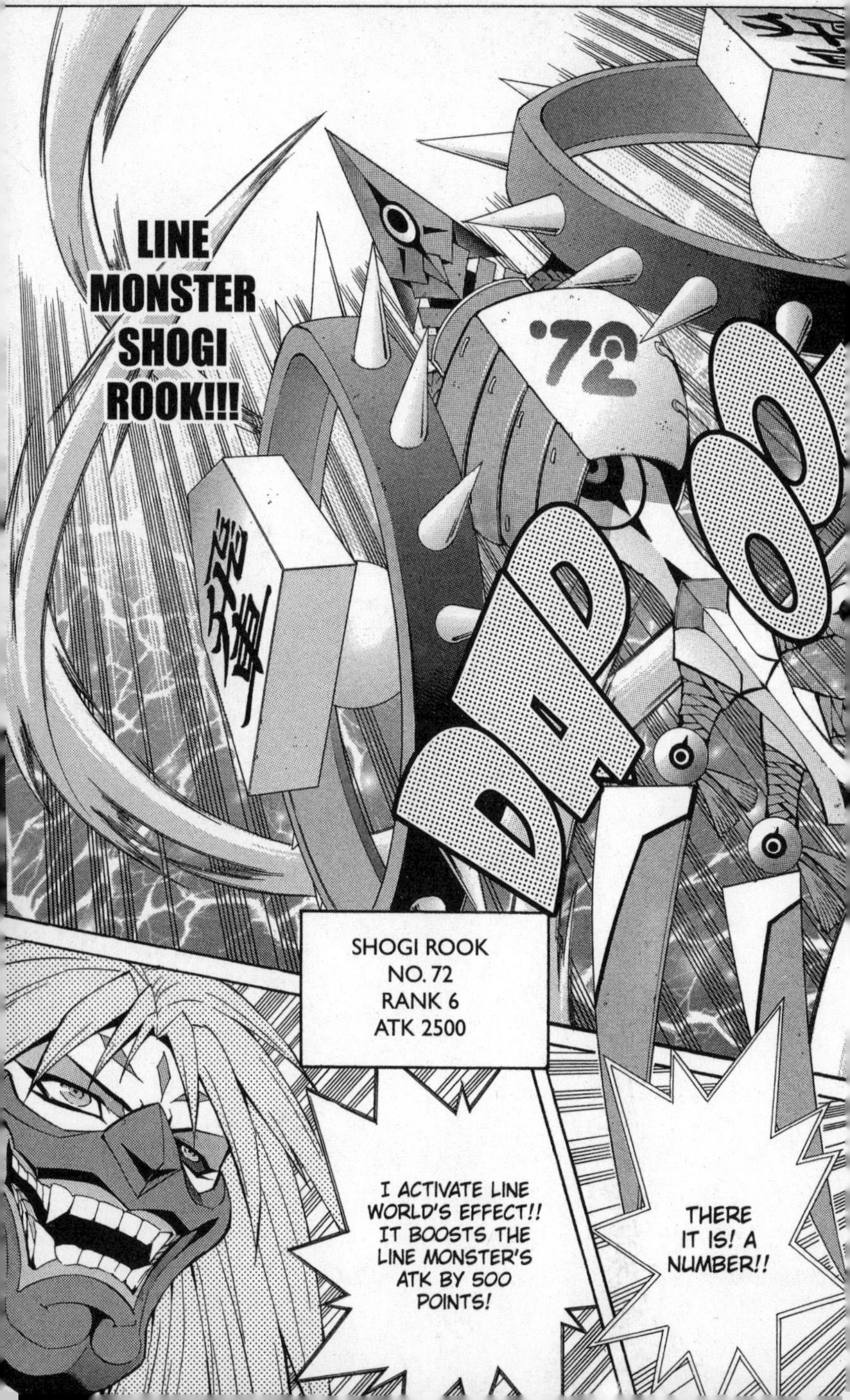
LINE MONSTER SHOGI ROOK!!!
72
SHOGI ROOK NO. 72 RANK 6 ATK 2500
THERE IT IS! A NUMBER!!
I ACTIVATE LINE WORLD'S EFFECT!! IT BOOSTS THE LINE MONSTER'S ATK BY 500 POINTS!

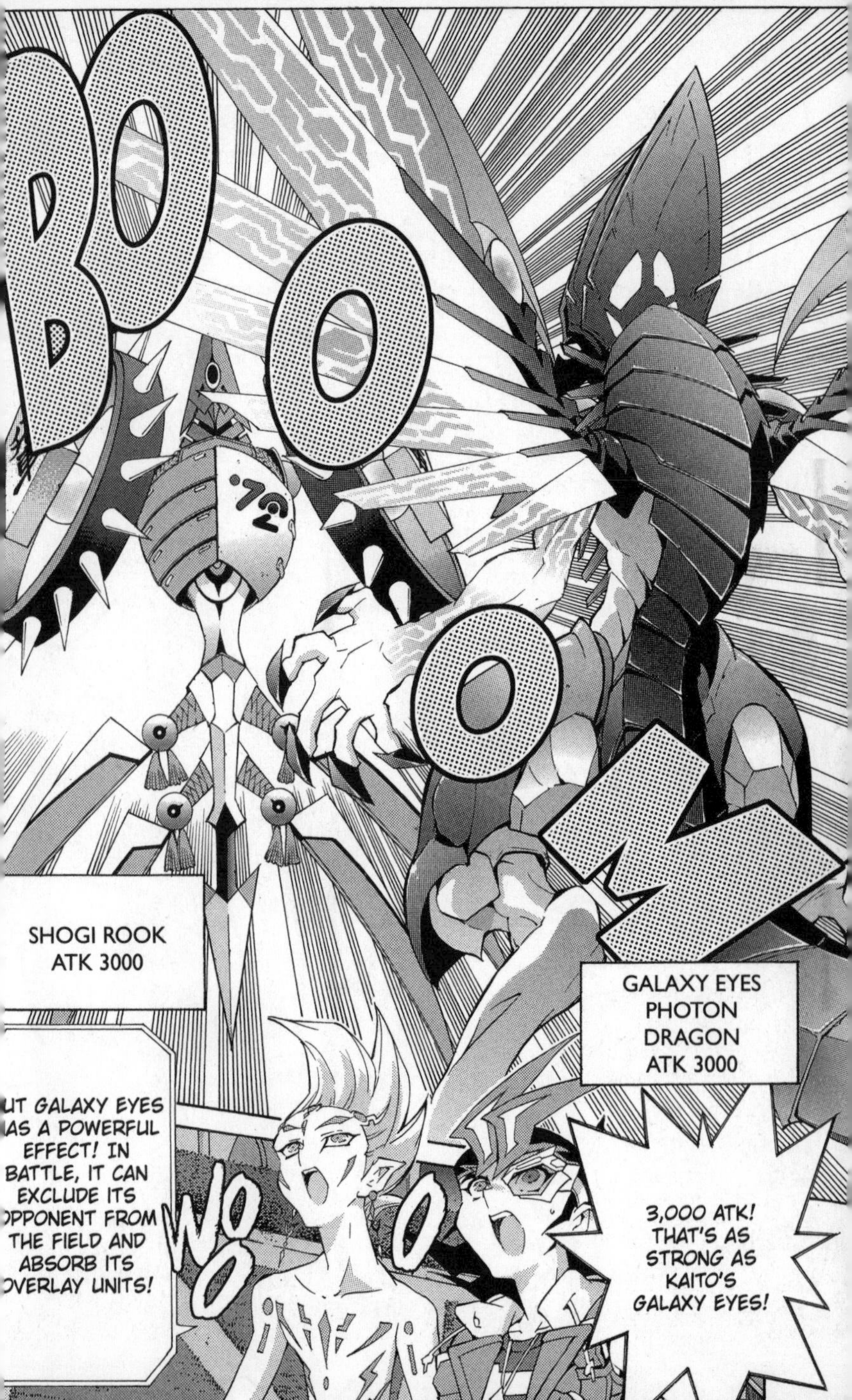
BOOOM
GALAXY EYES PHOTON DRAGON ATK 3000
SHOGI ROOK ATK 3000
3,000 ATK! THAT'S AS STRONG AS KAITO'S GALAXY EYES!
WOOO
UT GALAXY EYES AS A POWERFUL EFFECT! IN BATTLE, IT CAN EXCLUDE ITS PPONENT FROM THE FIELD AND ABSORB ITS OVERLAY UNITS!

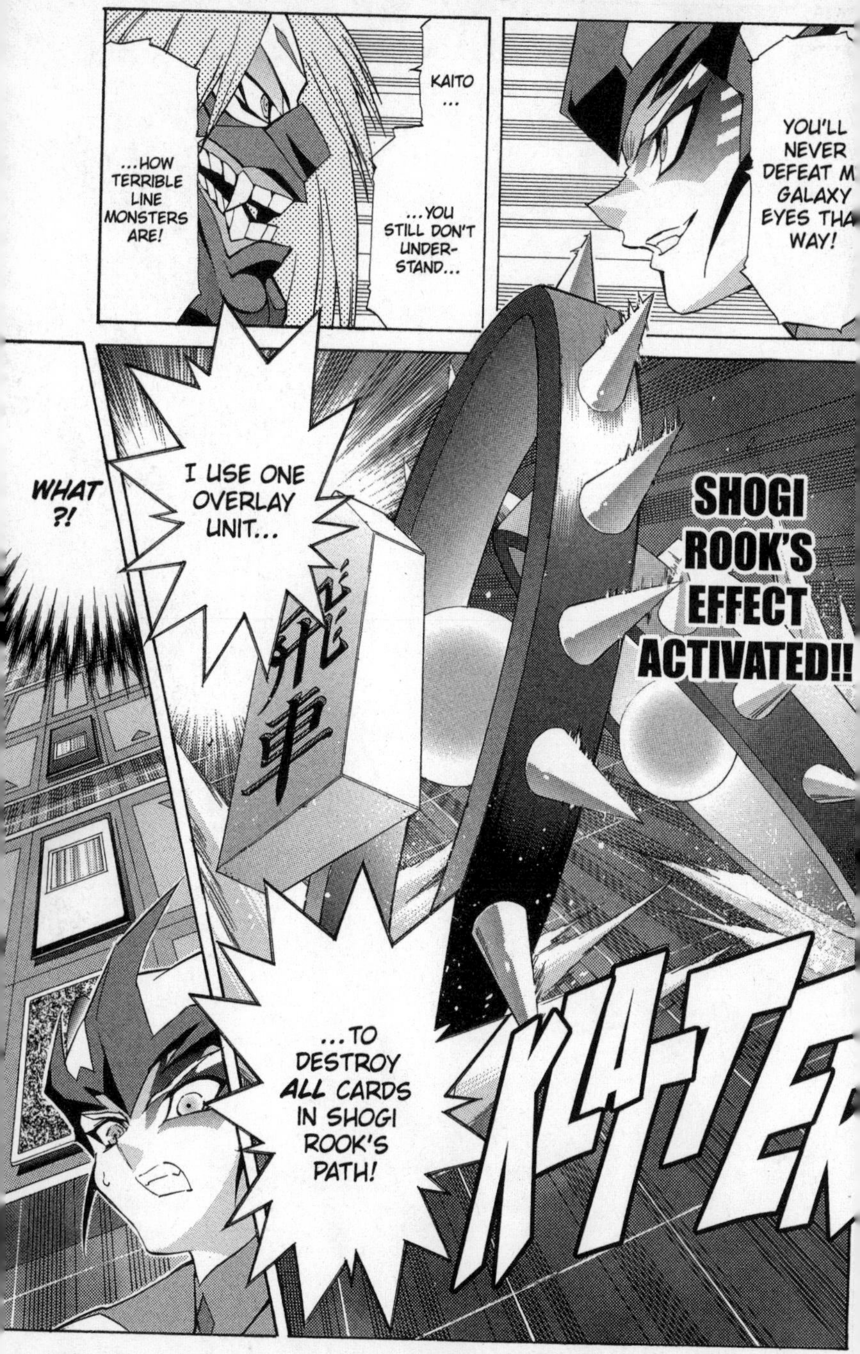

YOU'LL NEVER DEFEAT M GALAXY EYES THA WAY!
KAITO...
...YOU STILL DON'T UNDER-STAND...
...HOW TERRIBLE LINE MONSTERS ARE!
SHOGI ROOK'S EFFECT ACTIVATED!!
I USE ONE OVERLAY UNIT...
飛車
WHAT?!
...TO DESTROY ALL CARDS IN SHOGI ROOK'S PATH!
KLA-TER

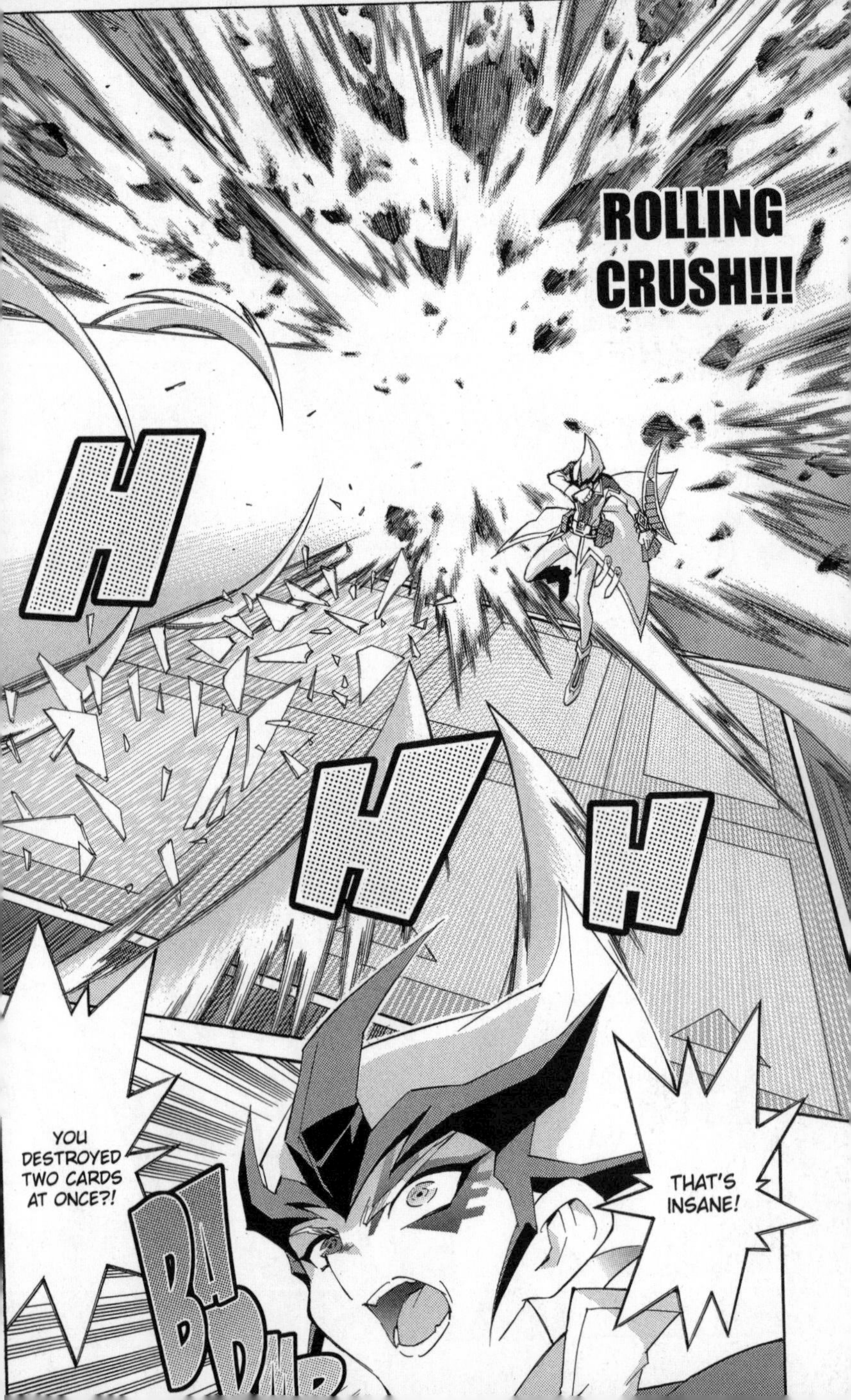
ROLLING CRUSH!!!
H
H
H
THAT'S INSANE!
YOU DESTROYED TWO CARDS AT ONCE?!

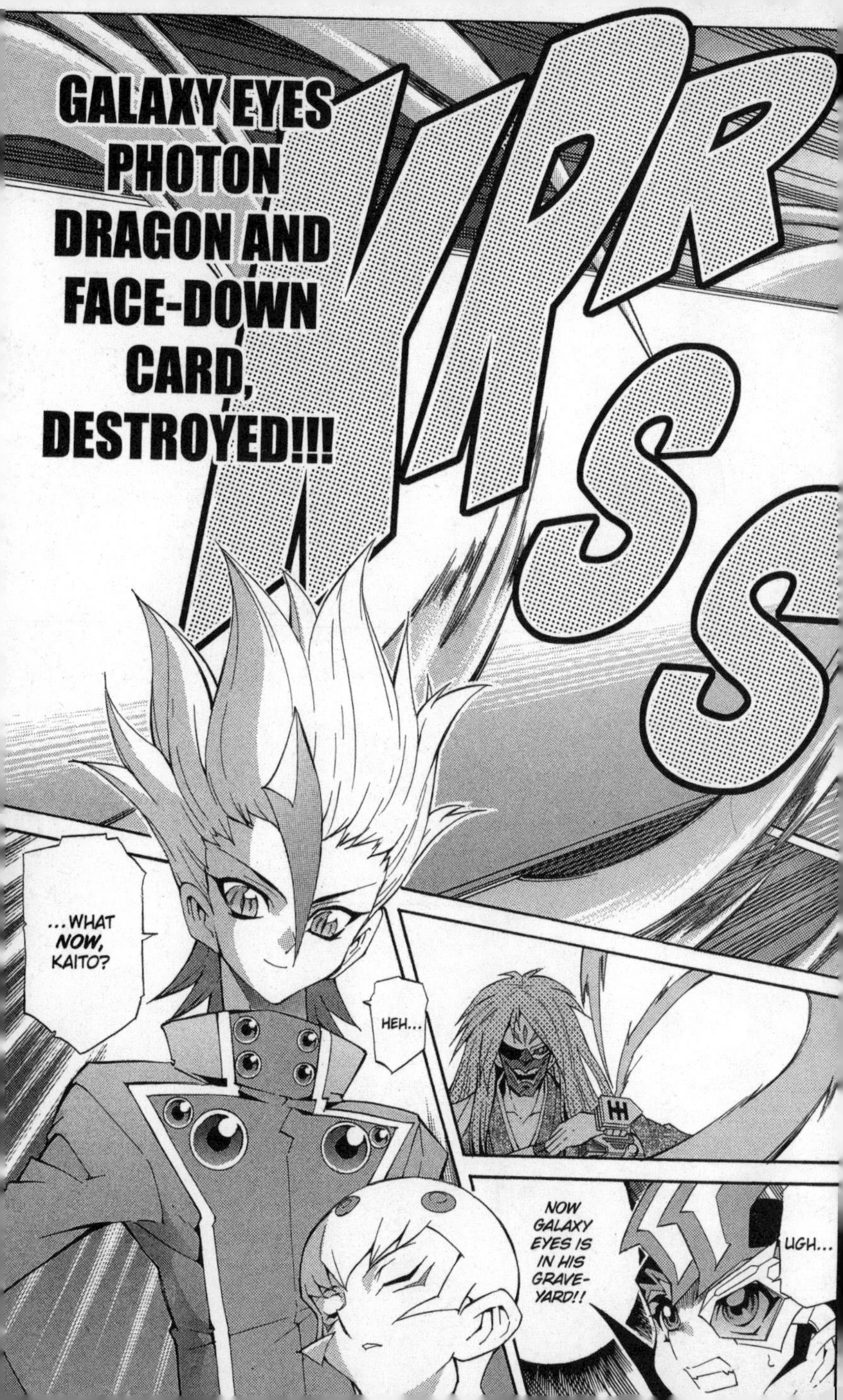
GALAXY EYES PHOTON DRAGON AND FACE-DOWN CARD, DESTROYED!!!
HEH...
UGH...
NOW GALAXY EYES IS IN HIS GRAVE-YARD!!
...WHAT NOW, KAITO?

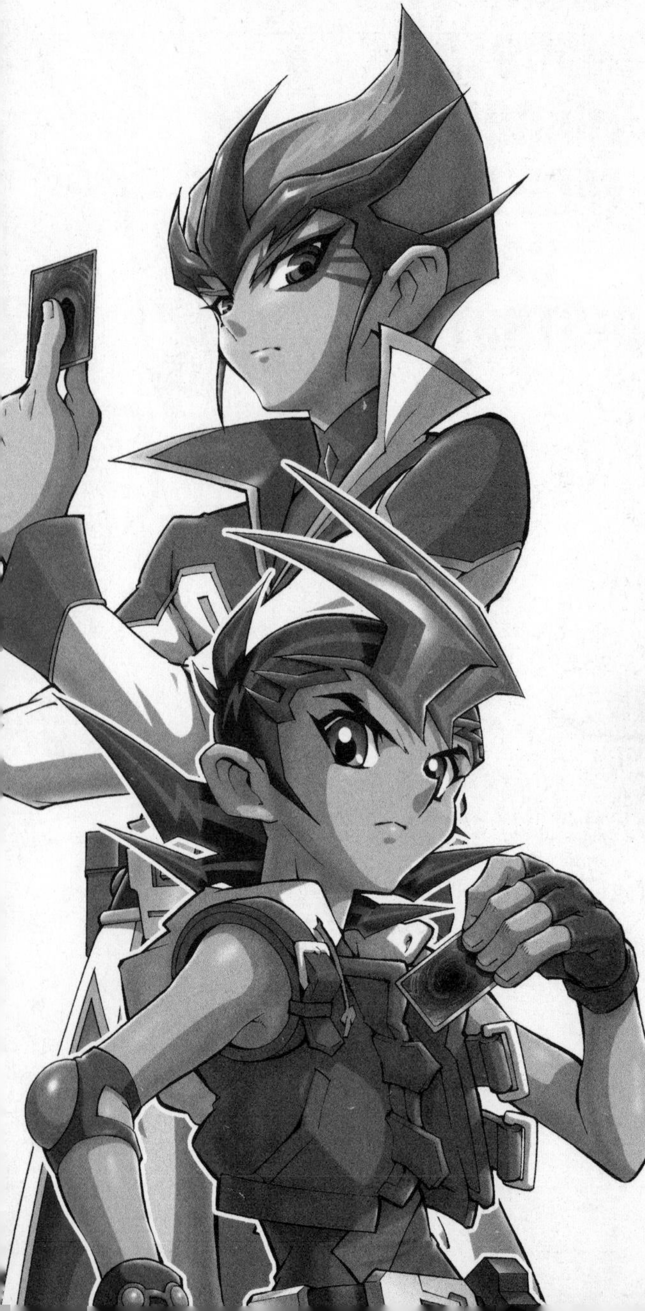

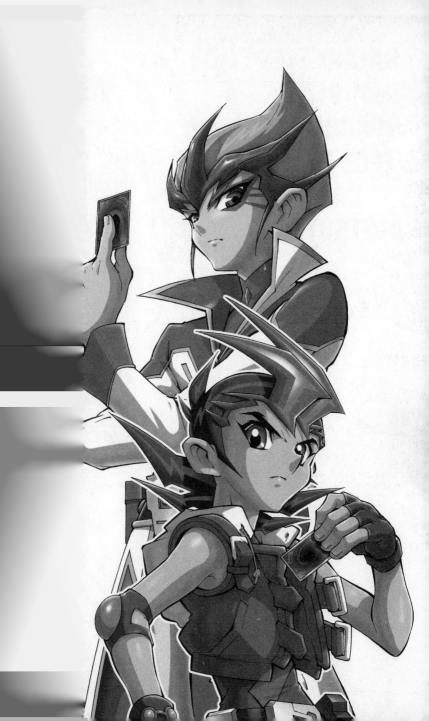

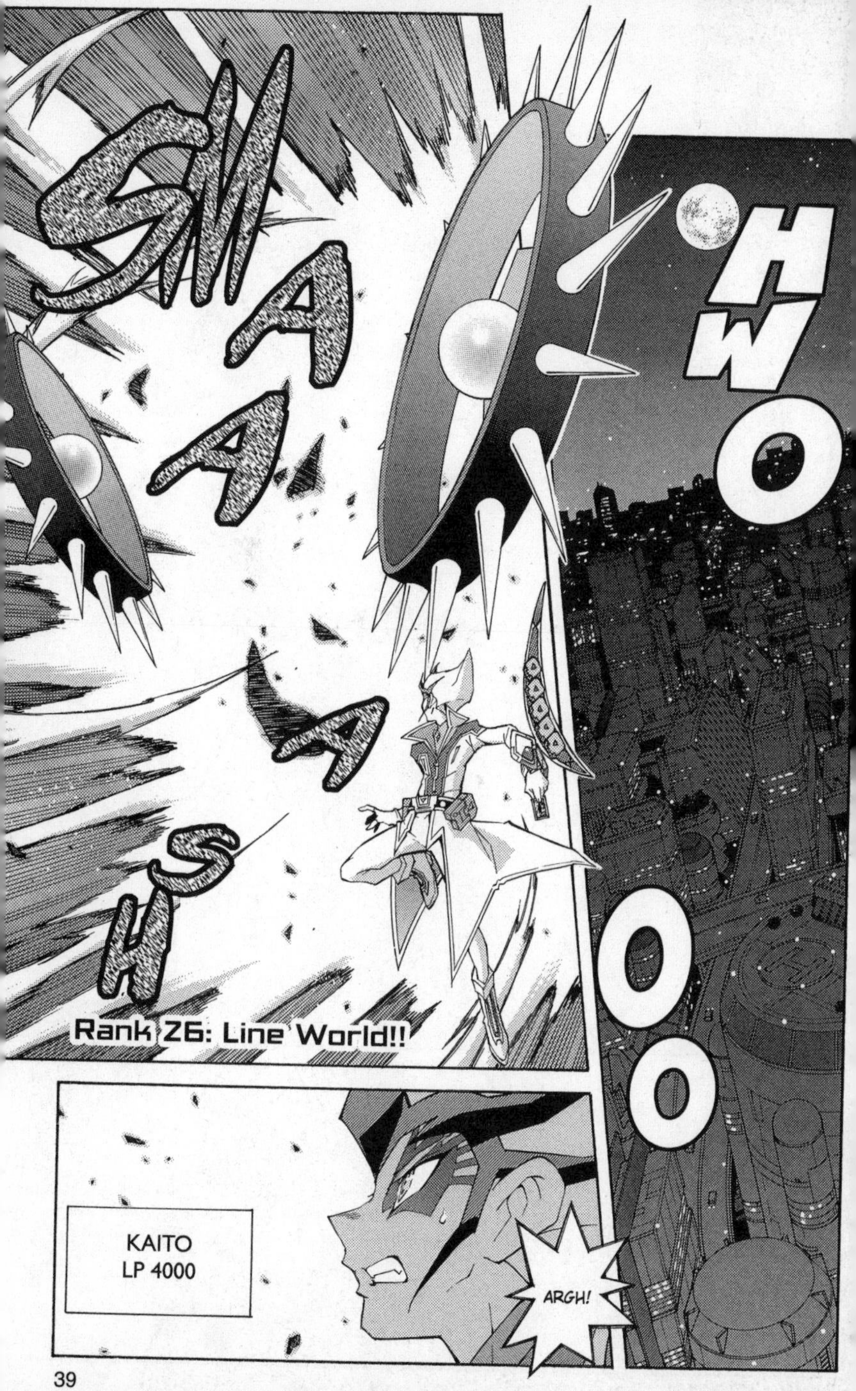
HWOOO
SMAAASH
Rank 26: Line World!!
ARGH!
KAITO
LP 4000

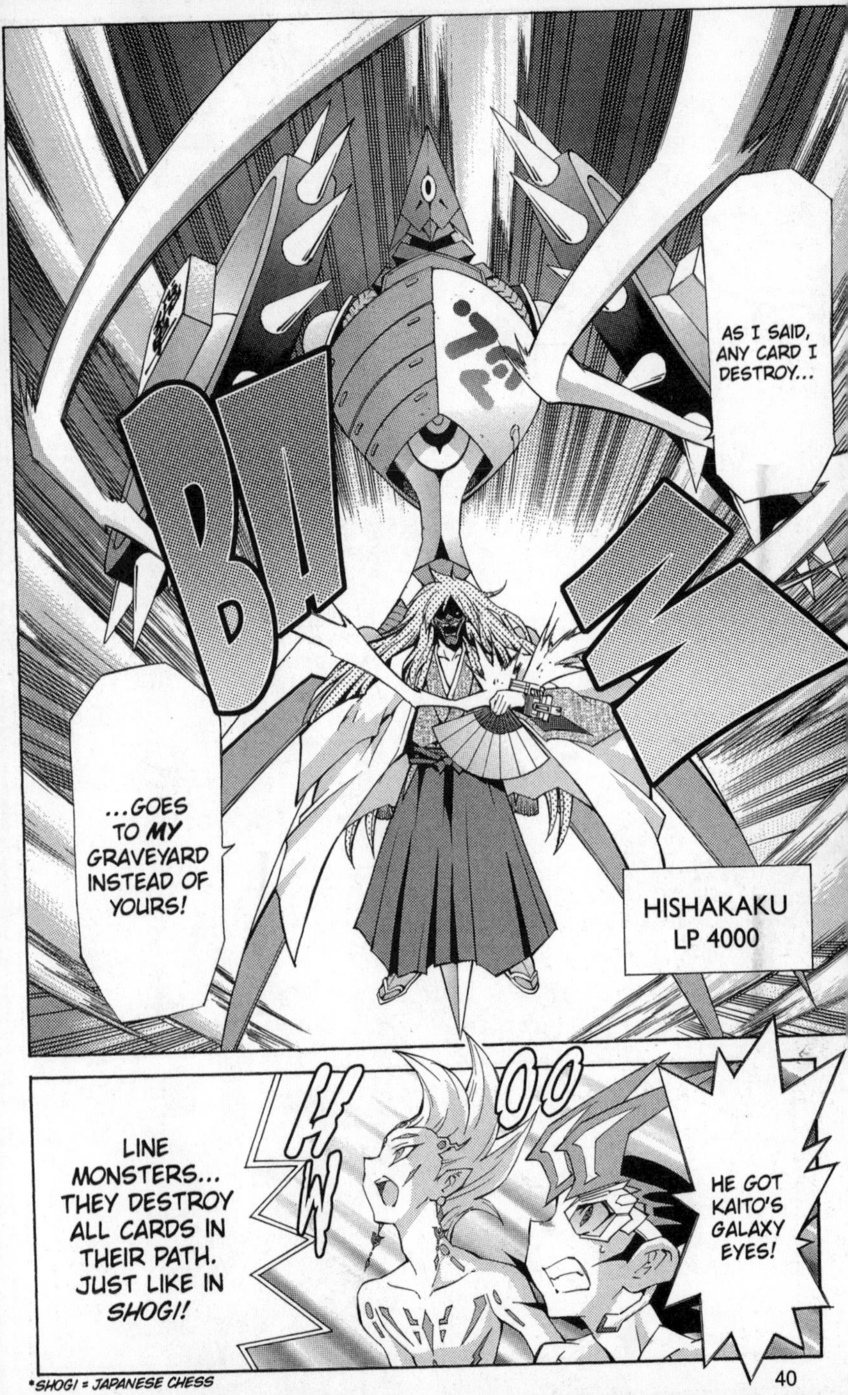
AS I SAID, ANY CARD I DESTROY...
...GOES TO *MY* GRAVEYARD INSTEAD OF YOURS!
HISHAKAKU LP 4000
HE GOT KAITO'S GALAXY EYES!
LINE MONSTERS... THEY DESTROY ALL CARDS IN THEIR PATH. JUST LIKE IN *SHOGI*!

*SHOGI = JAPANESE CHESS

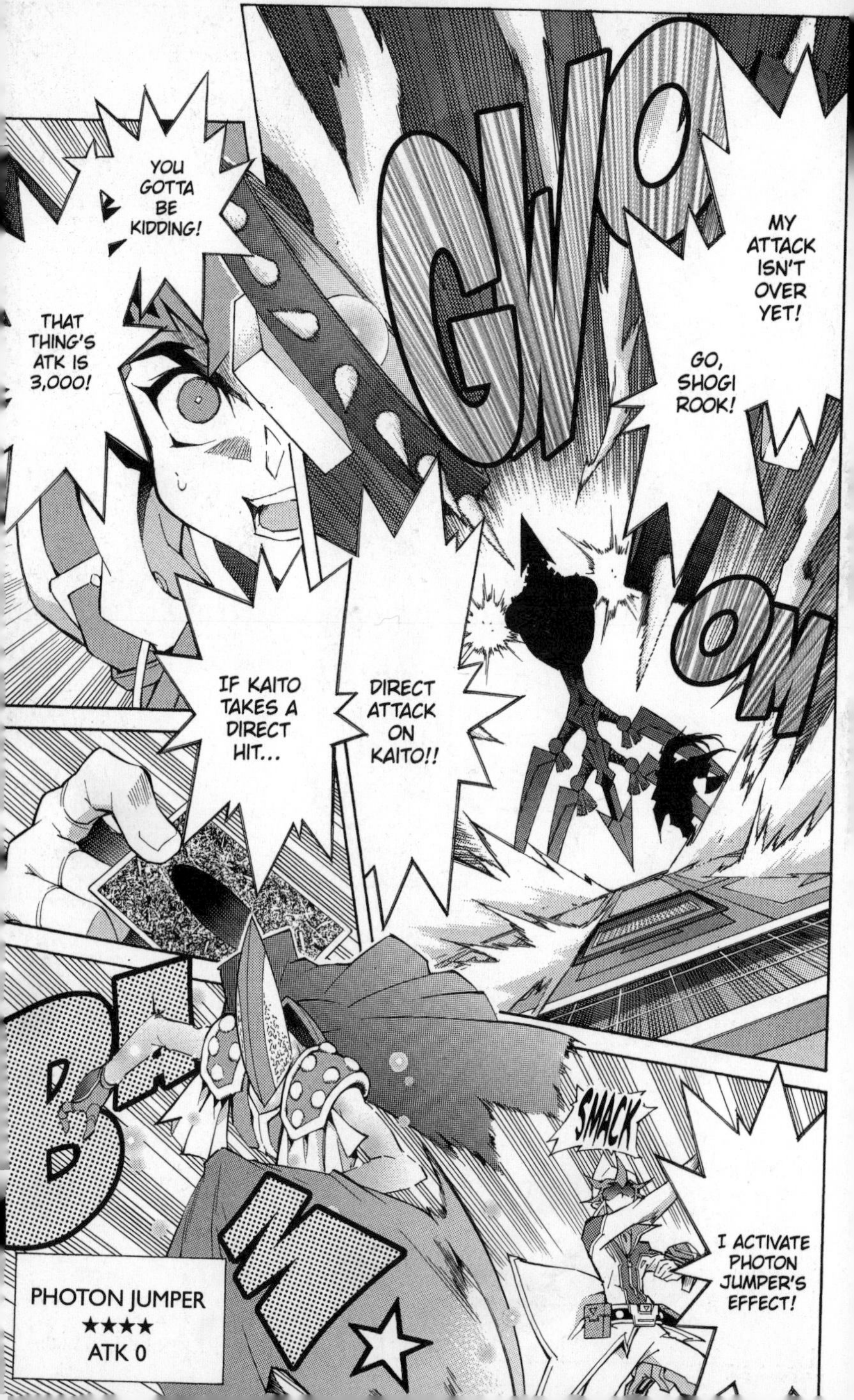
MY ATTACK ISN'T OVER YET!
GO, SHOGI ROOK!
YOU GOTTA BE KIDDING!
THAT THING'S ATK IS 3,000!
DIRECT ATTACK ON KAITO!!
IF KAITO TAKES A DIRECT HIT...
SMACK
I ACTIVATE PHOTON JUMPER'S EFFECT!
PHOTON JUMPER
★★★★
ATK 0

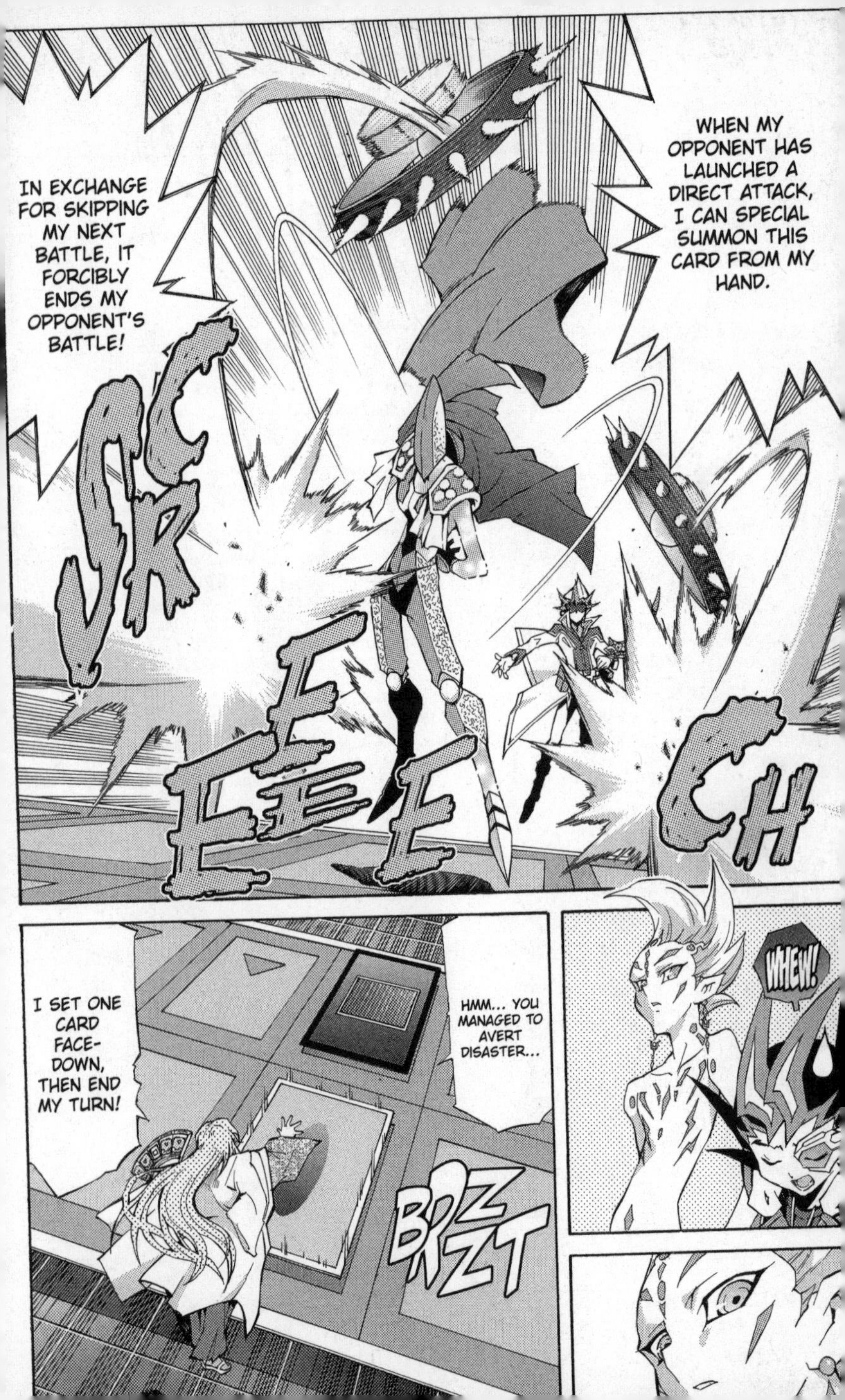
WHEN MY OPPONENT HAS LAUNCHED A DIRECT ATTACK, I CAN SPECIAL SUMMON THIS CARD FROM MY HAND.
IN EXCHANGE FOR SKIPPING MY NEXT BATTLE, IT FORCIBLY ENDS MY OPPONENT'S BATTLE!
SCREEEECH
WHEW!
HMM... YOU MANAGED TO AVERT DISASTER...
I SET ONE CARD FACE-DOWN, THEN END MY TURN!
BRZZT

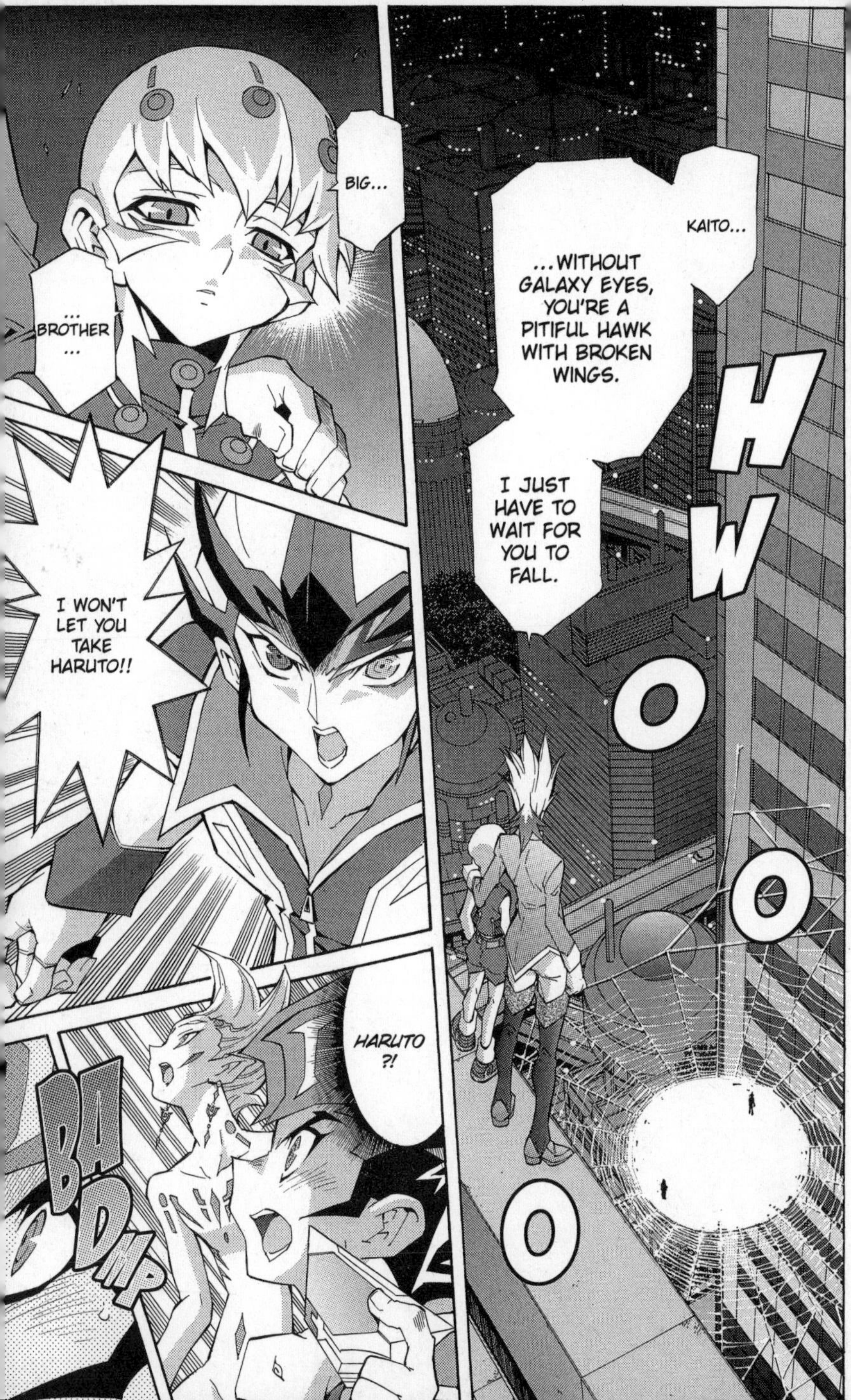
KAITO...
...WITHOUT GALAXY EYES, YOU'RE A PITIFUL HAWK WITH BROKEN WINGS.
I JUST HAVE TO WAIT FOR YOU TO FALL.
HWOOOO
BIG...
...BROTHER...
I WON'T LET YOU TAKE HARUTO!!
HARUTO?!
BADMP

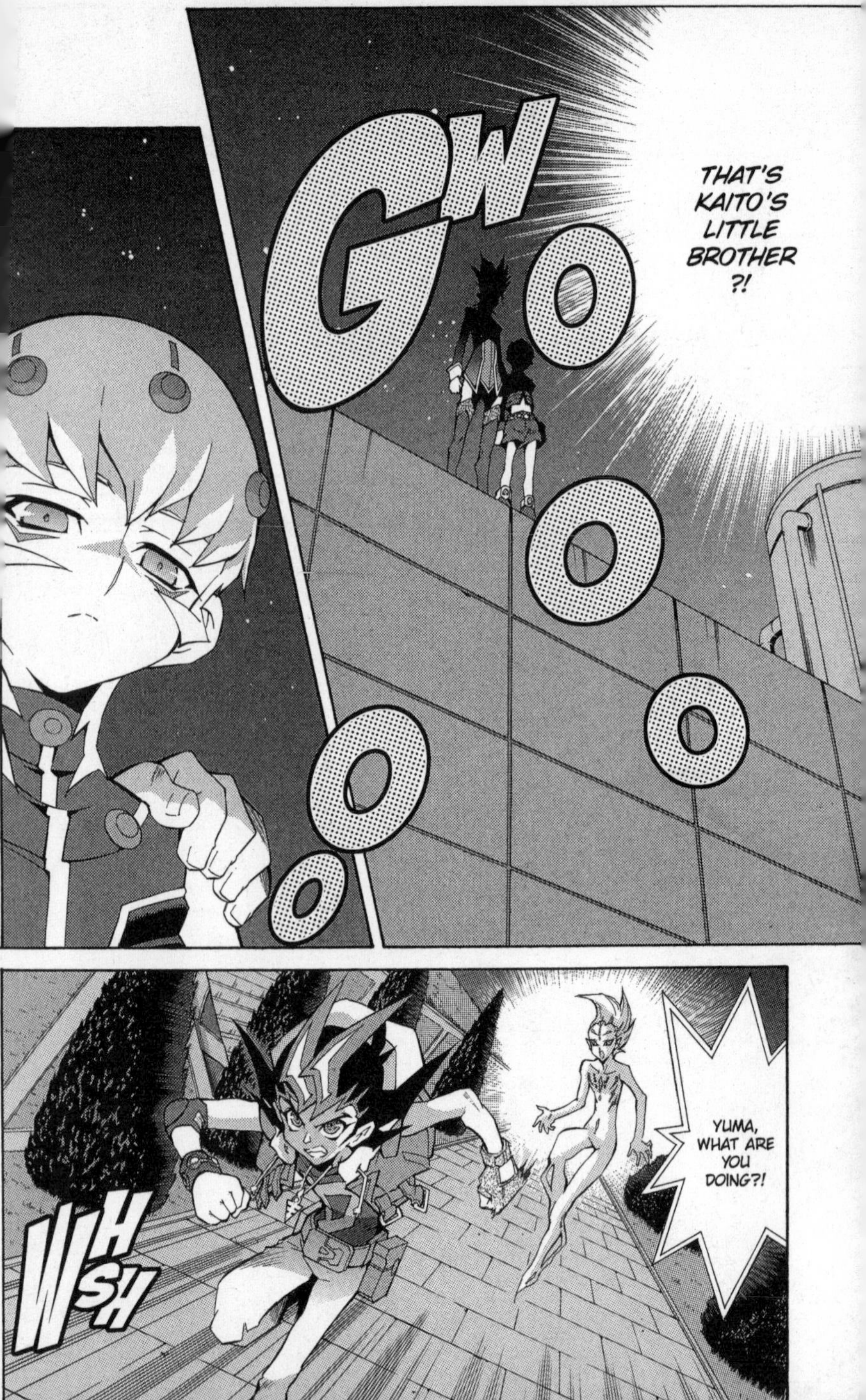
THAT'S KAITO'S LITTLE BROTHER?!
GWOOOOO
YUMA, WHAT ARE YOU DOING?!
WHSH

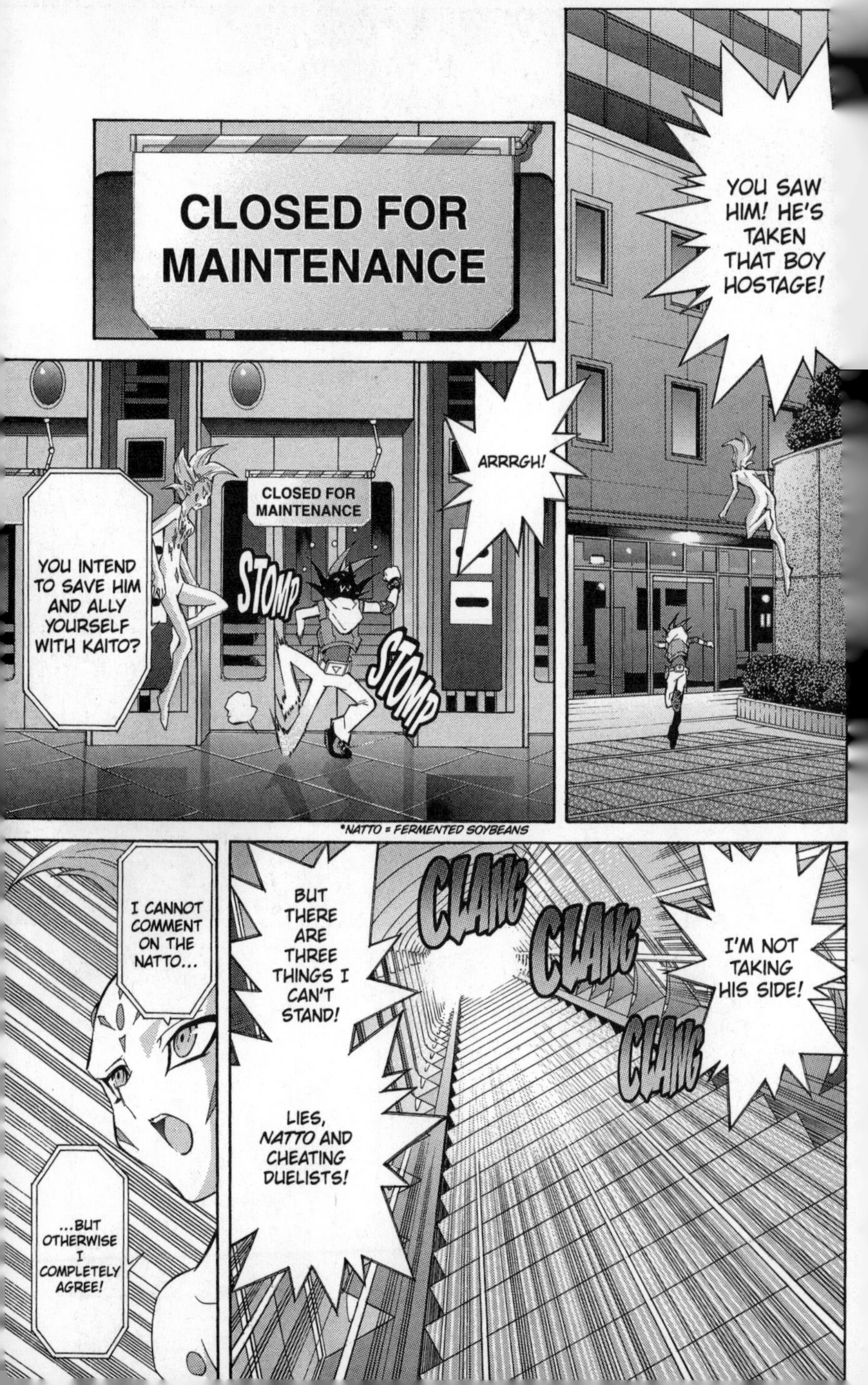
YOU SAW HIM! HE'S TAKEN THAT BOY HOSTAGE!
CLOSED FOR MAINTENANCE
ARRRGH!
CLOSED FOR MAINTENANCE
STOMP
STOMP
YOU INTEND TO SAVE HIM AND ALLY YOURSELF WITH KAITO?
I'M NOT TAKING HIS SIDE!
CLANG
CLANG
CLANG
BUT THERE ARE THREE THINGS I CAN'T STAND!
LIES, *NATTO* AND CHEATING DUELISTS!
I CANNOT COMMENT ON THE NATTO...
...BUT OTHERWISE I COMPLETELY AGREE!

*NATTO = FERMENTED SOYBEANS

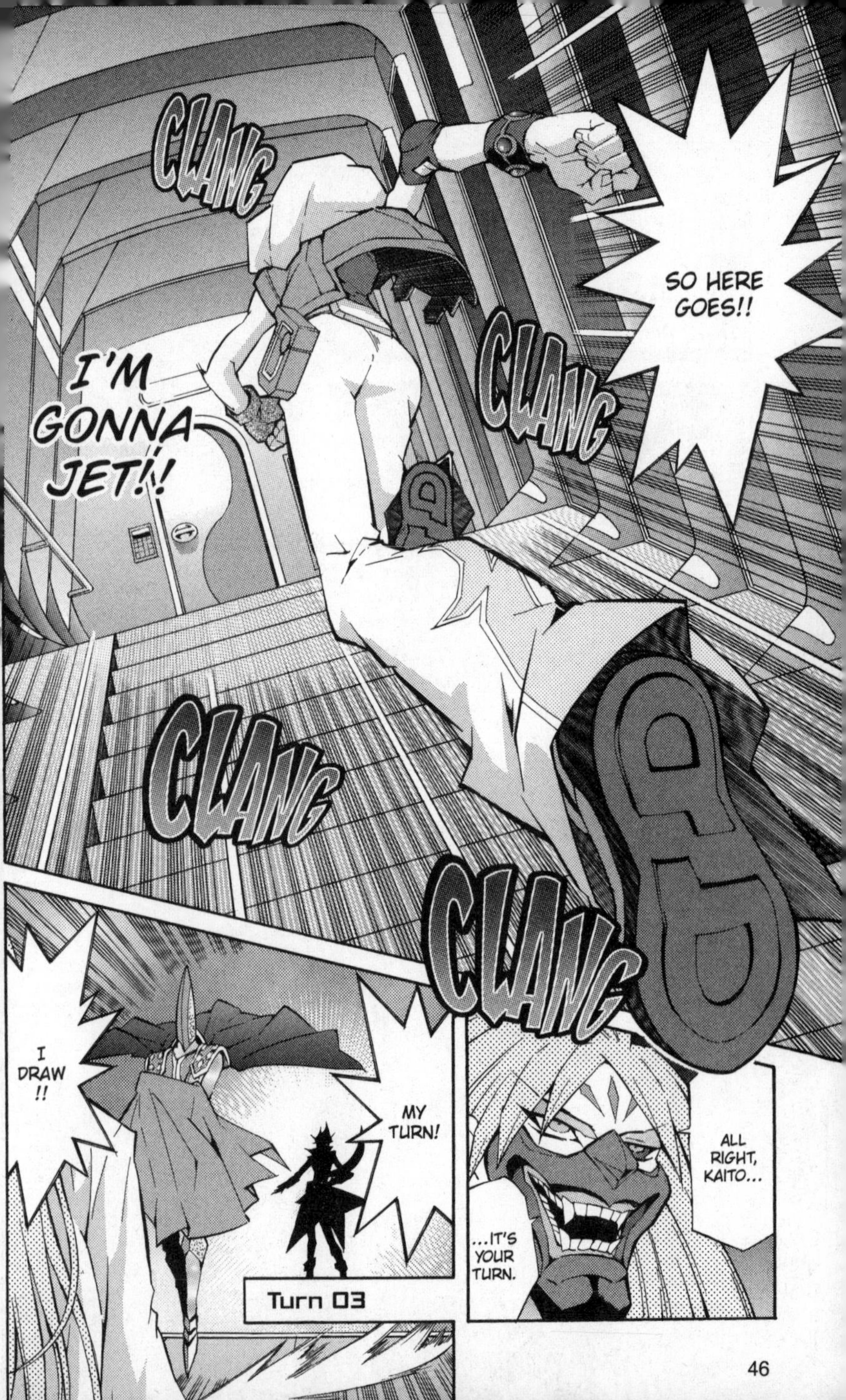
CLANG
SO HERE GOES!!
CLANG
I'M GONNA JET!!
CLANG
CLANG
ALL RIGHT, KAITO...
...IT'S YOUR TURN.
MY TURN!
I DRAW!!
Turn 03

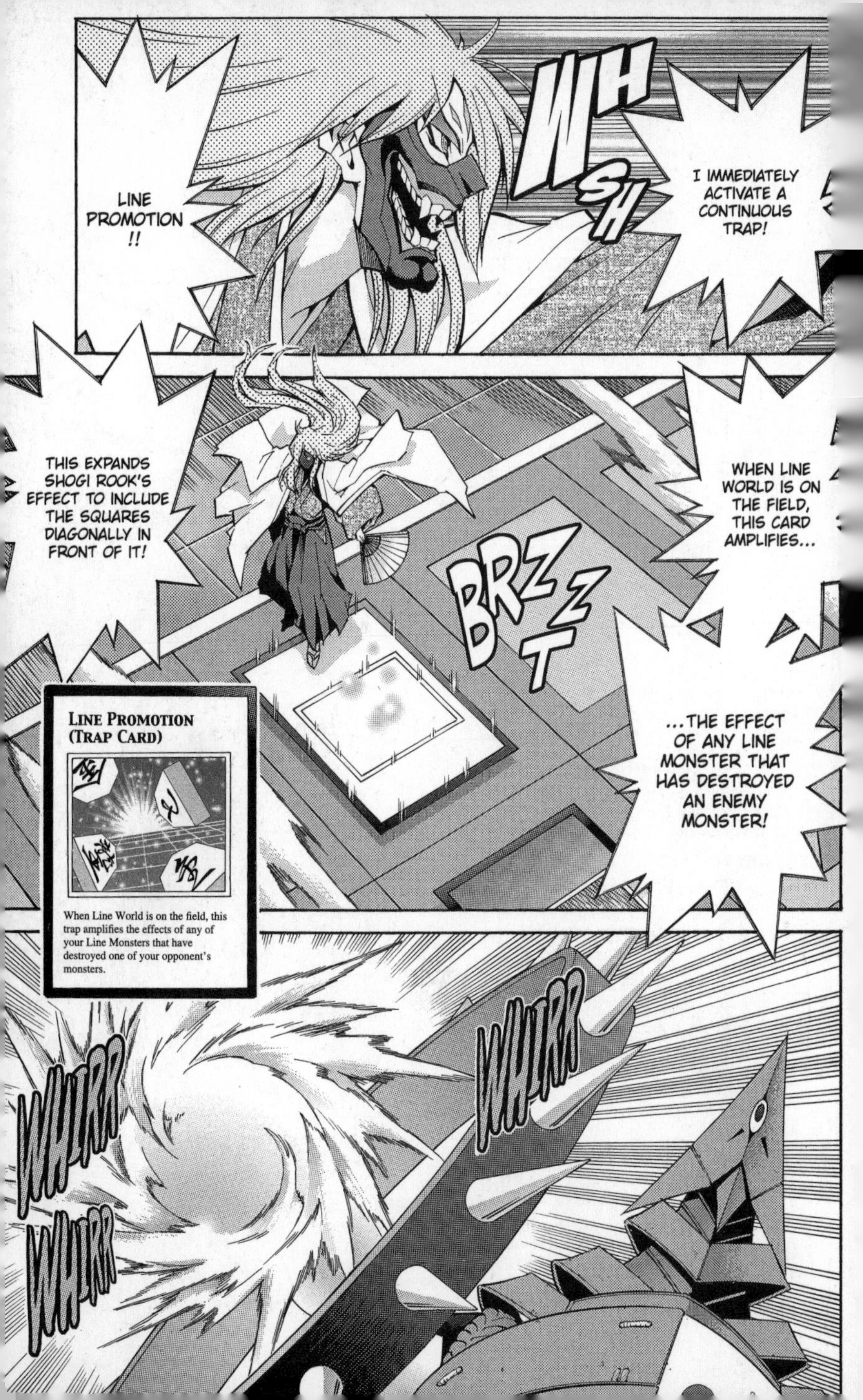
I IMMEDIATELY ACTIVATE A CONTINUOUS TRAP!
WHSH
LINE PROMOTION !!
WHEN LINE WORLD IS ON THE FIELD, THIS CARD AMPLIFIES...
...THE EFFECT OF ANY LINE MONSTER THAT HAS DESTROYED AN ENEMY MONSTER!
BRZZZT
THIS EXPANDS SHOGI ROOK'S EFFECT TO INCLUDE THE SQUARES DIAGONALLY IN FRONT OF IT!
LINE PROMOTION (TRAP CARD)
When Line World is on the field, this trap amplifies the effects of any of your Line Monsters that have destroyed one of your opponent's monsters.
WHIRR
WHIRR
WHIRR

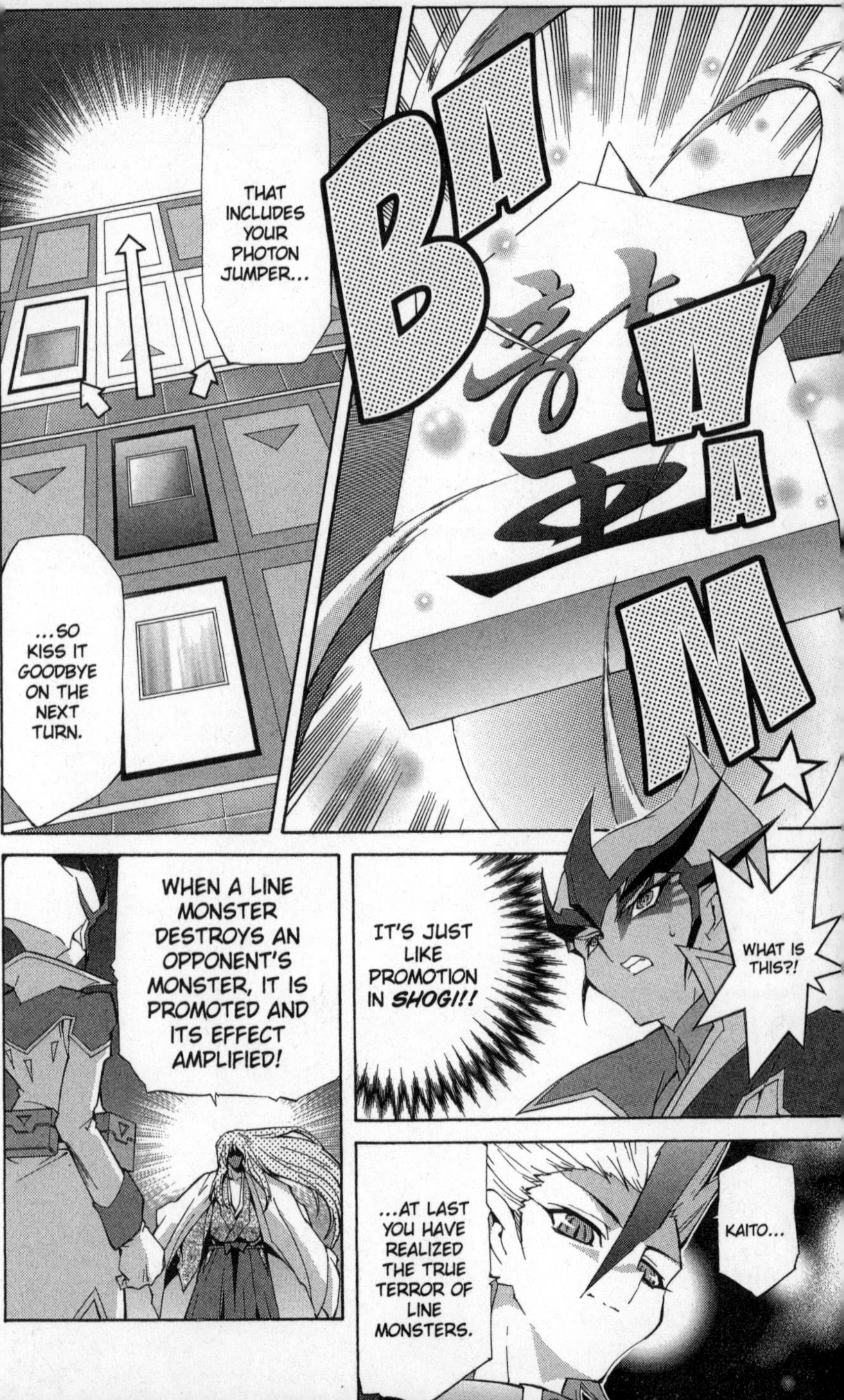
BAAAM☆
THAT INCLUDES YOUR PHOTON JUMPER...
...SO KISS IT GOODBYE ON THE NEXT TURN.
WHAT IS THIS?!
IT'S JUST LIKE PROMOTION IN *SHOGI*!!
KAITO...
...AT LAST YOU HAVE REALIZED THE TRUE TERROR OF LINE MONSTERS.
WHEN A LINE MONSTER DESTROYS AN OPPONENT'S MONSTER, IT IS PROMOTED AND ITS EFFECT AMPLIFIED!

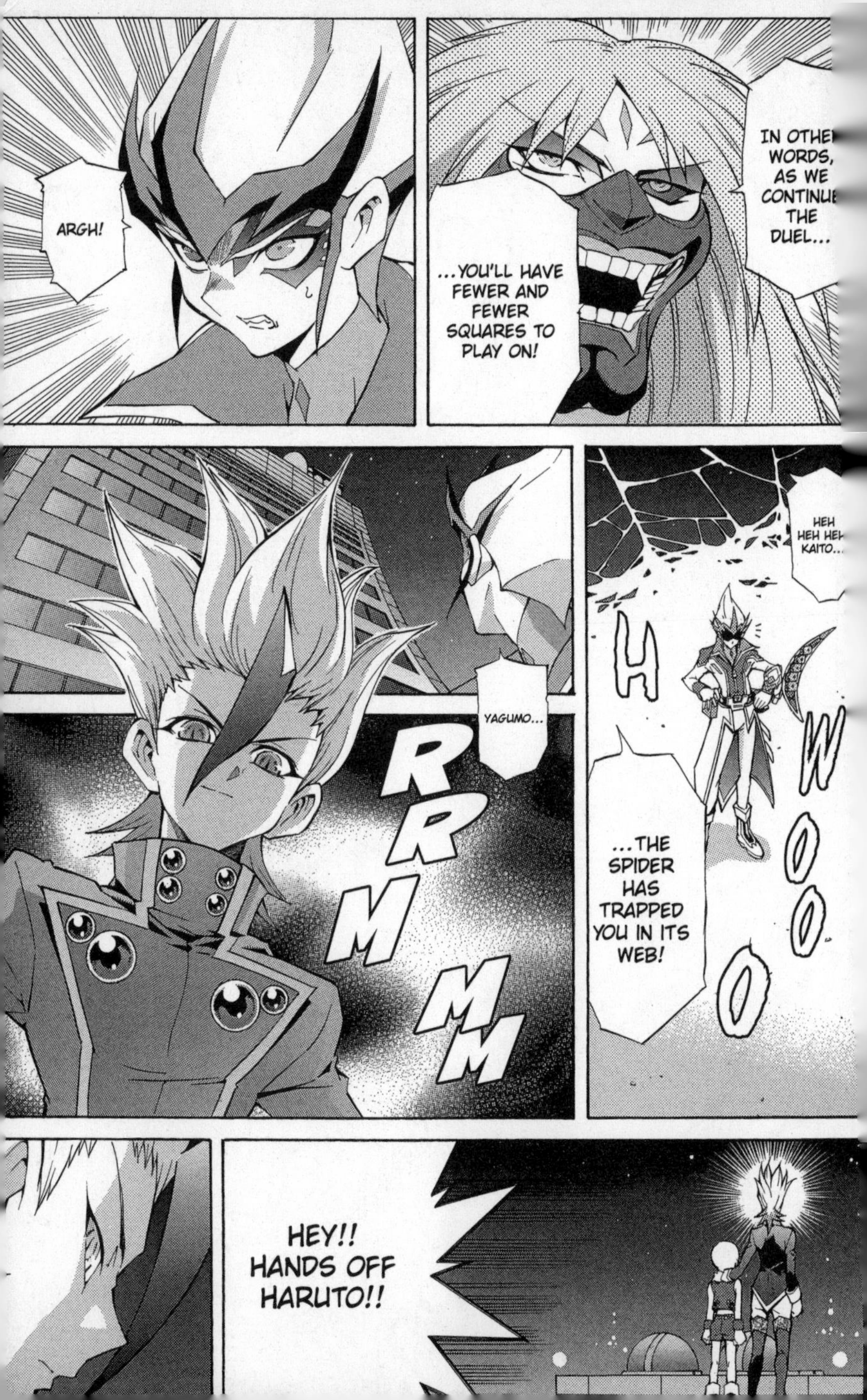
IN OTHER WORDS, AS WE CONTINUE THE DUEL...
...YOU'LL HAVE FEWER AND FEWER SQUARES TO PLAY ON!
ARGH!
HEH HEH HEH KAITO...
...THE SPIDER HAS TRAPPED YOU IN ITS WEB!
HWOOOO
YAGUMO...
RRMMM
HEY!! HANDS OFF HARUTO!!

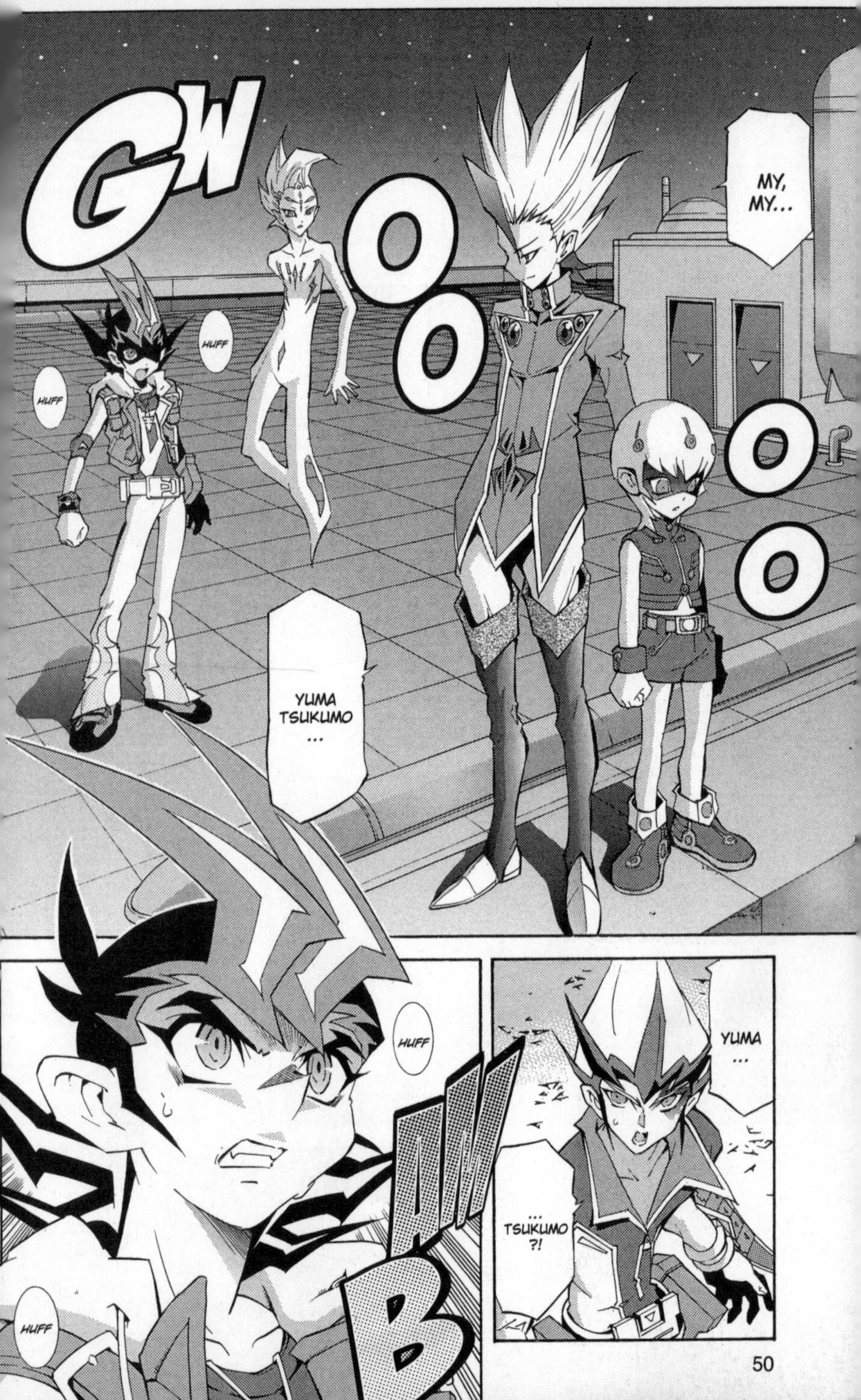
MY, MY...
GWOOOO
HUFF
HUFF
YUMA TSUKUMO ...
YUMA ...
... TSUKUMO ?!
HUFF
BAM
HUFF

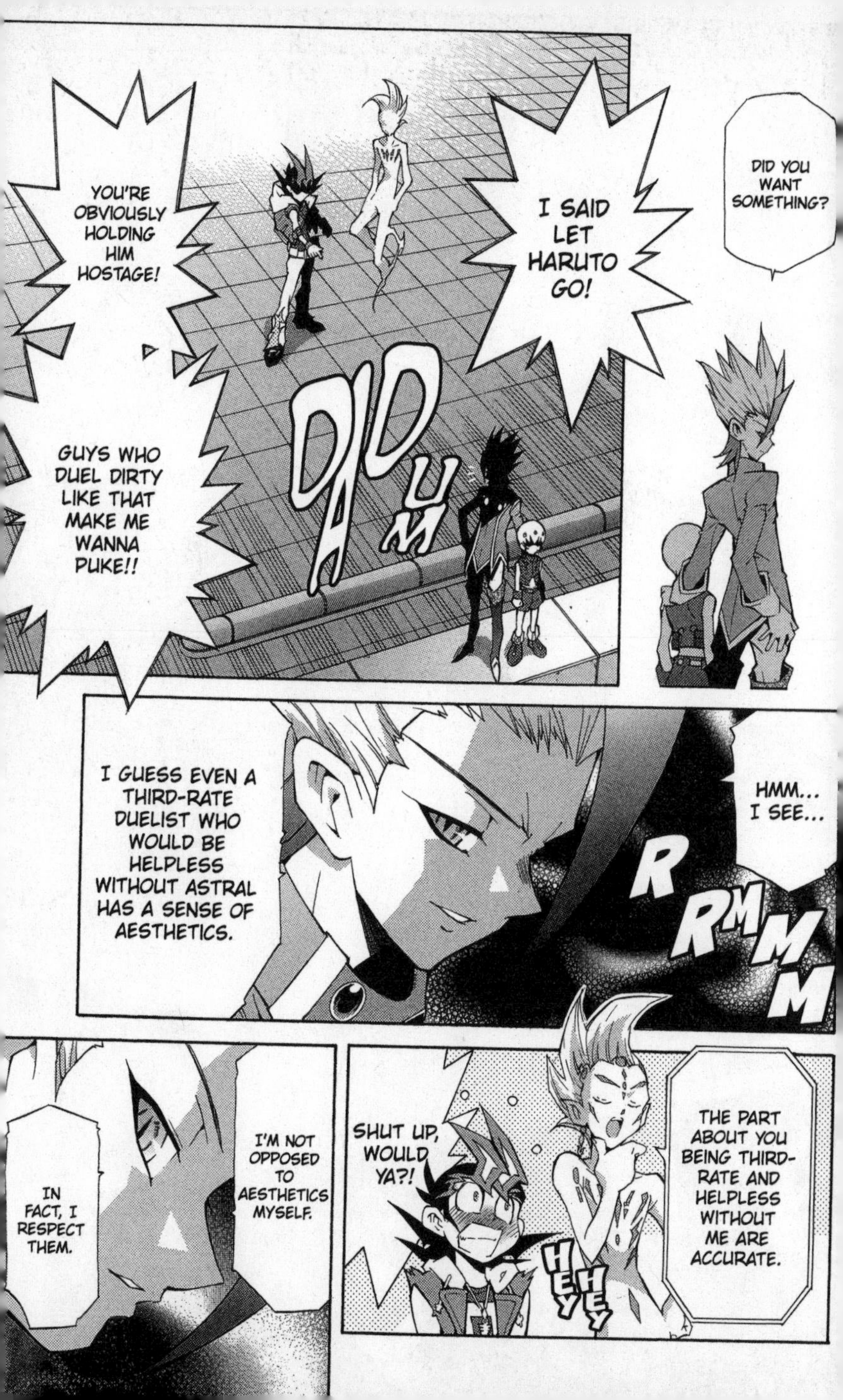

DID YOU WANT SOMETHING?
I SAID LET HARUTO GO!
YOU'RE OBVIOUSLY HOLDING HIM HOSTAGE!
GUYS WHO DUEL DIRTY LIKE THAT MAKE ME WANNA PUKE!!
HMM... I SEE...
I GUESS EVEN A THIRD-RATE DUELIST WHO WOULD BE HELPLESS WITHOUT ASTRAL HAS A SENSE OF AESTHETICS.
RRMMMM
THE PART ABOUT YOU BEING THIRD-RATE AND HELPLESS WITHOUT ME ARE ACCURATE.
SHUT UP, WOULD YA?!
HEY HEY
I'M NOT OPPOSED TO AESTHETICS MYSELF.
IN FACT, I RESPECT THEM.

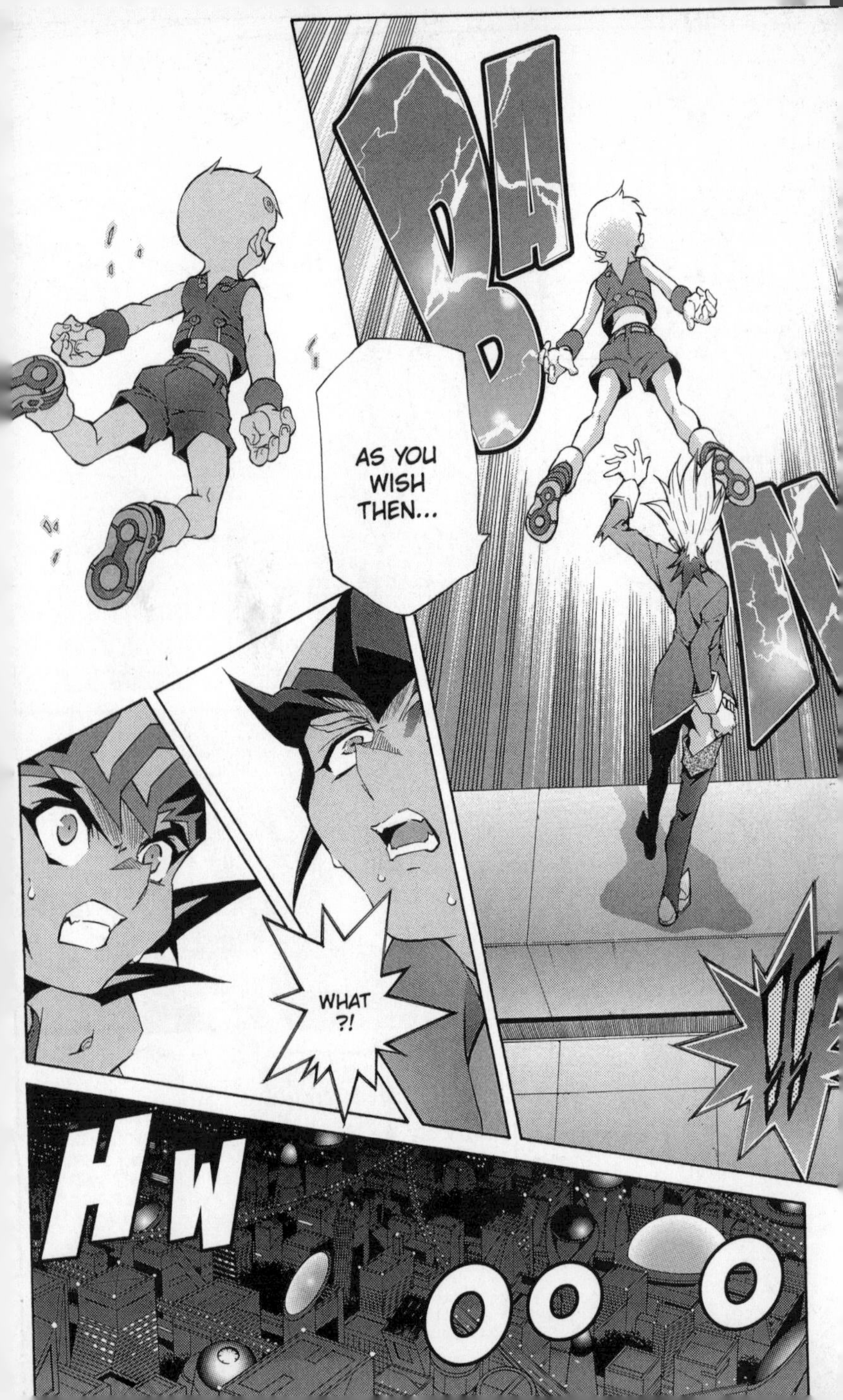
AS YOU WISH THEN...
!!
WHAT ?!
HWOOO

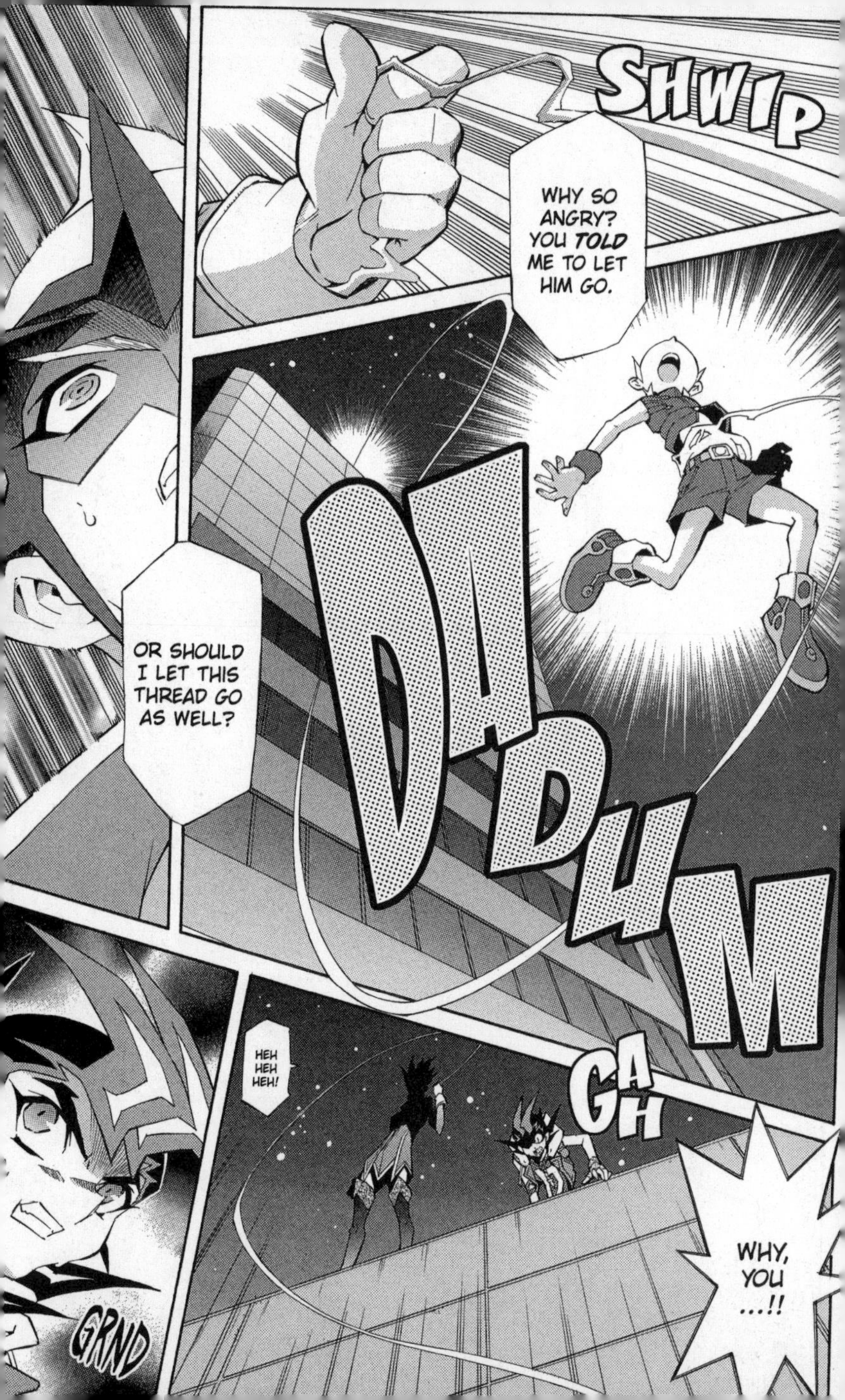
SHWIP
WHY SO ANGRY? YOU TOLD ME TO LET HIM GO.
DADUM
OR SHOULD I LET THIS THREAD GO AS WELL?
GAH
WHY, YOU ...!!
HEH HEH HEH!
GRND

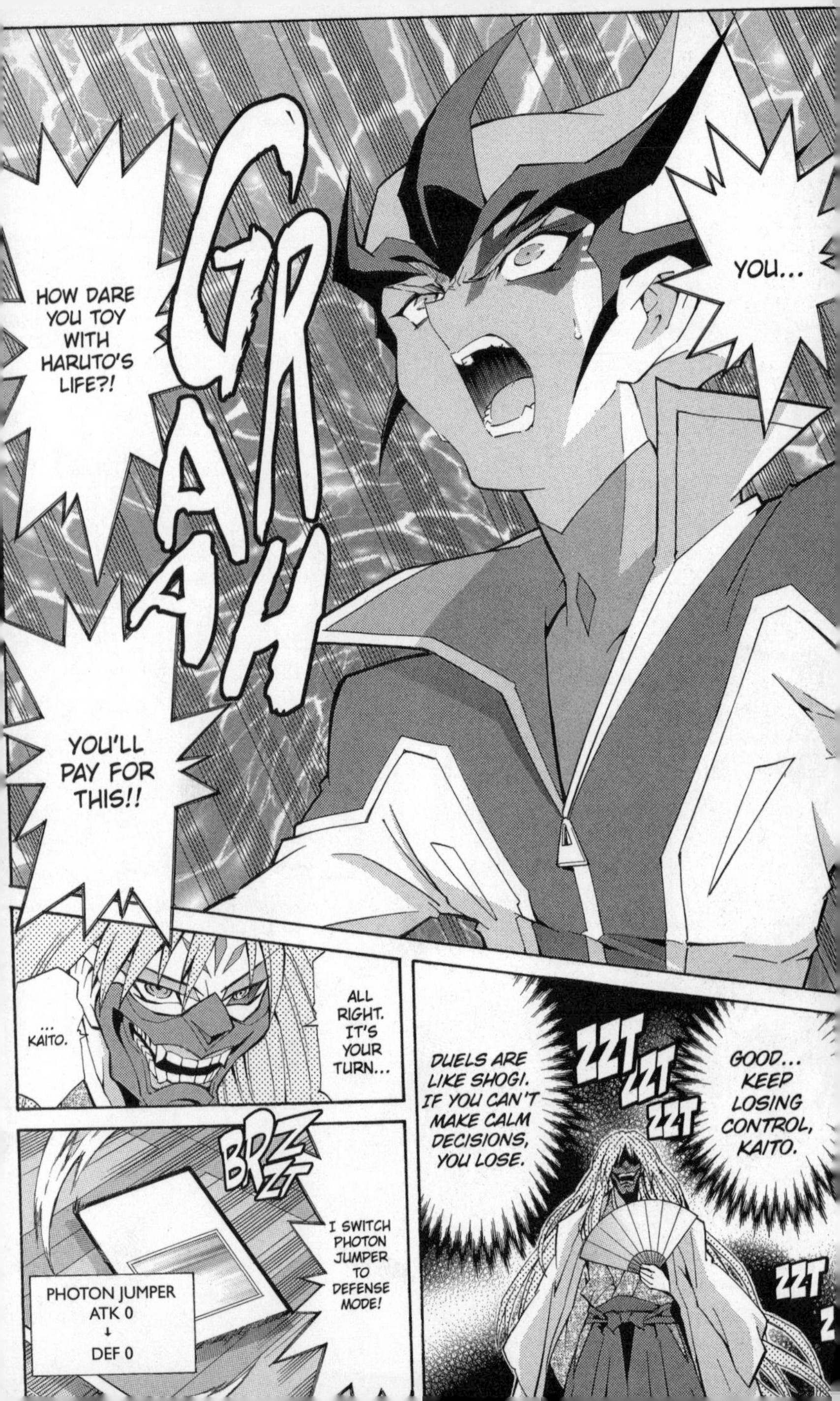
YOU...
GRAAAH
HOW DARE YOU TOY WITH HARUTO'S LIFE?!
YOU'LL PAY FOR THIS!!
GOOD... KEEP LOSING CONTROL, KAITO.
ZZT ZZT ZZT
DUELS ARE LIKE SHOGI. IF YOU CAN'T MAKE CALM DECISIONS, YOU LOSE.
ZZT
ALL RIGHT. IT'S YOUR TURN...
... KAITO.
BRZZT
I SWITCH PHOTON JUMPER TO DEFENSE MODE!
PHOTON JUMPER ATK 0 ↓ DEF 0

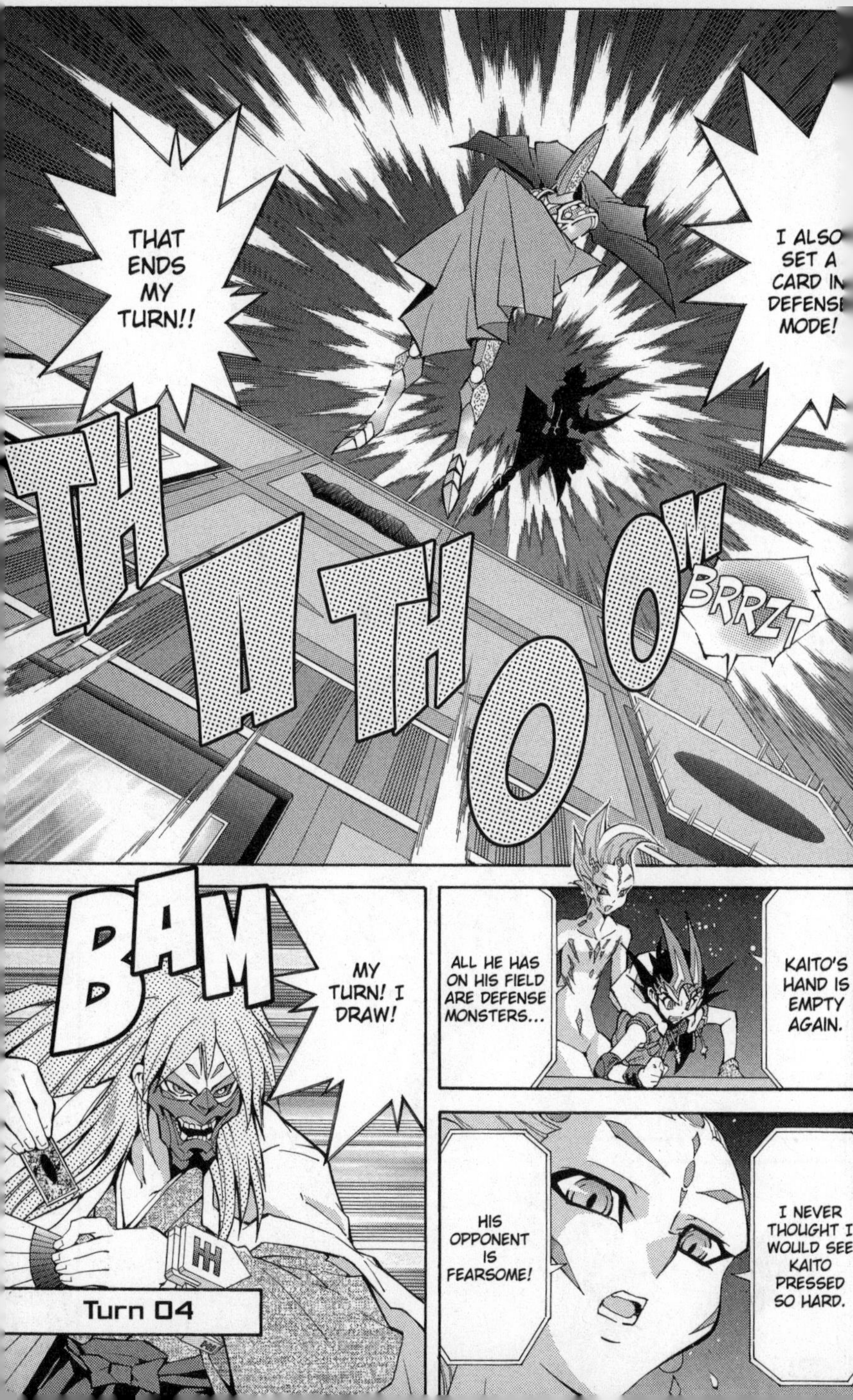
I ALSO SET A CARD IN DEFENSE MODE!
THAT ENDS MY TURN!!
THATHOOM
BRRZT
KAITO'S HAND IS EMPTY AGAIN.
ALL HE HAS ON HIS FIELD ARE DEFENSE MONSTERS...
I NEVER THOUGHT I WOULD SEE KAITO PRESSED SO HARD.
HIS OPPONENT IS FEARSOME!
BAM
MY TURN! I DRAW!
Turn 04

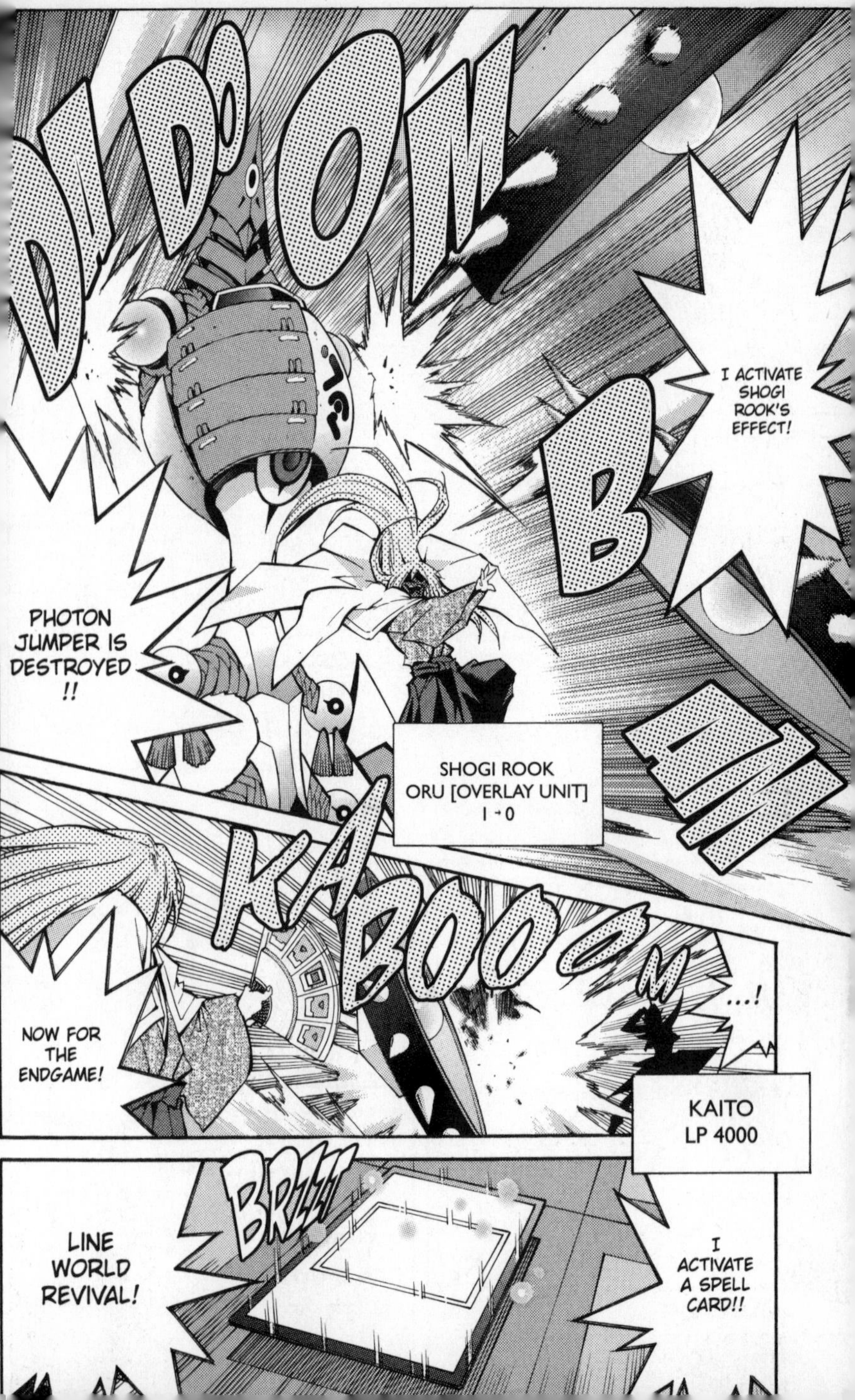
I ACTIVATE SHOGI ROOK'S EFFECT!
SHOGI ROOK
ORU [OVERLAY UNIT]
1→0
PHOTON JUMPER IS DESTROYED !!
...!
KABOOOM
NOW FOR THE ENDGAME!
KAITO
LP 4000
I ACTIVATE A SPELL CARD!!
LINE WORLD REVIVAL!

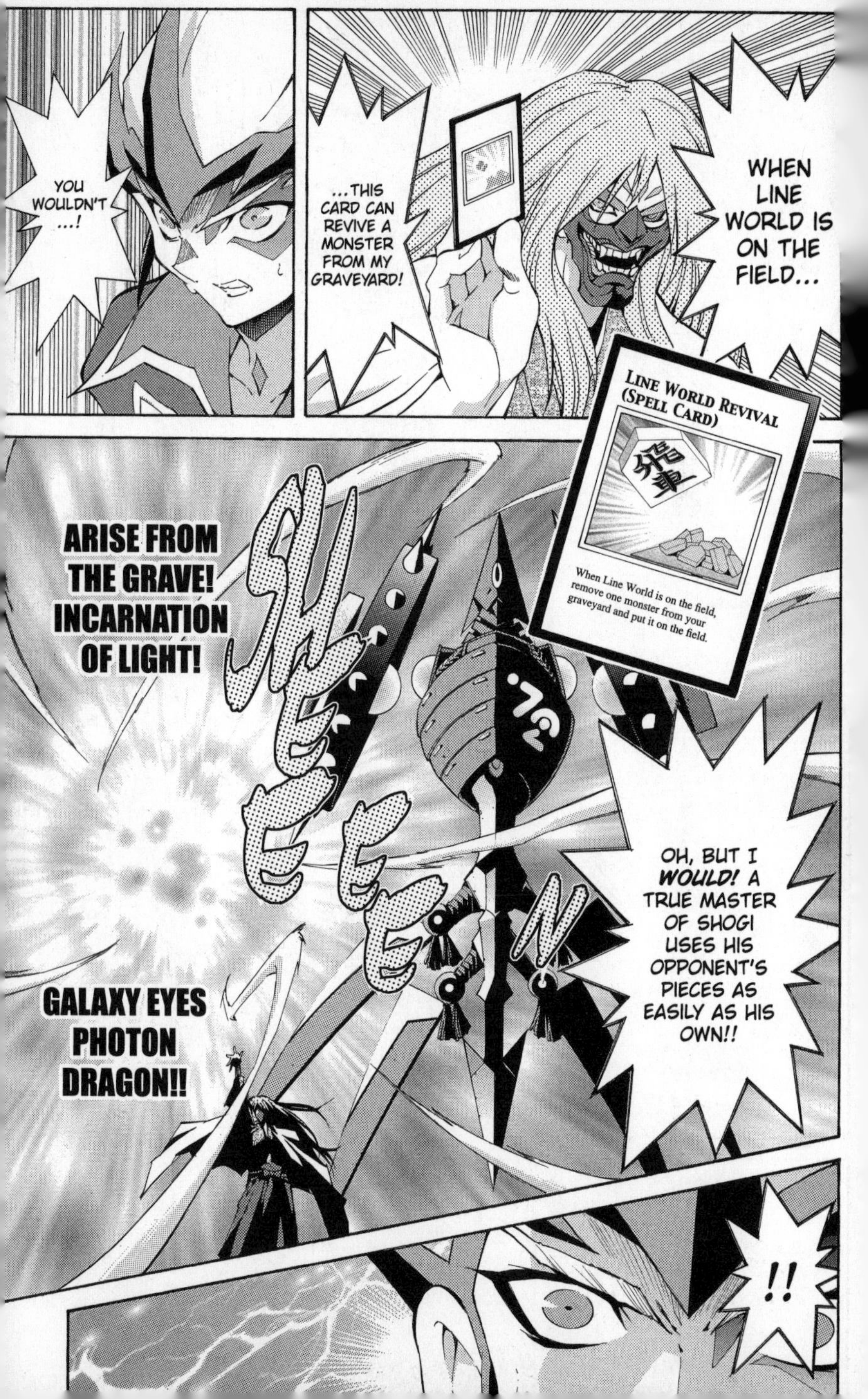
WHEN LINE WORLD IS ON THE FIELD...
...THIS CARD CAN REVIVE A MONSTER FROM MY GRAVEYARD!
LINE WORLD REVIVAL (SPELL CARD)
When Line World is on the field, remove one monster from your graveyard and put it on the field.
YOU WOULDN'T ...!
OH, BUT I *WOULD!* A TRUE MASTER OF SHOGI USES HIS OPPONENT'S PIECES AS EASILY AS HIS OWN!!
ARISE FROM THE GRAVE! INCARNATION OF LIGHT!
SHEEEEN!
GALAXY EYES PHOTON DRAGON!!
!!

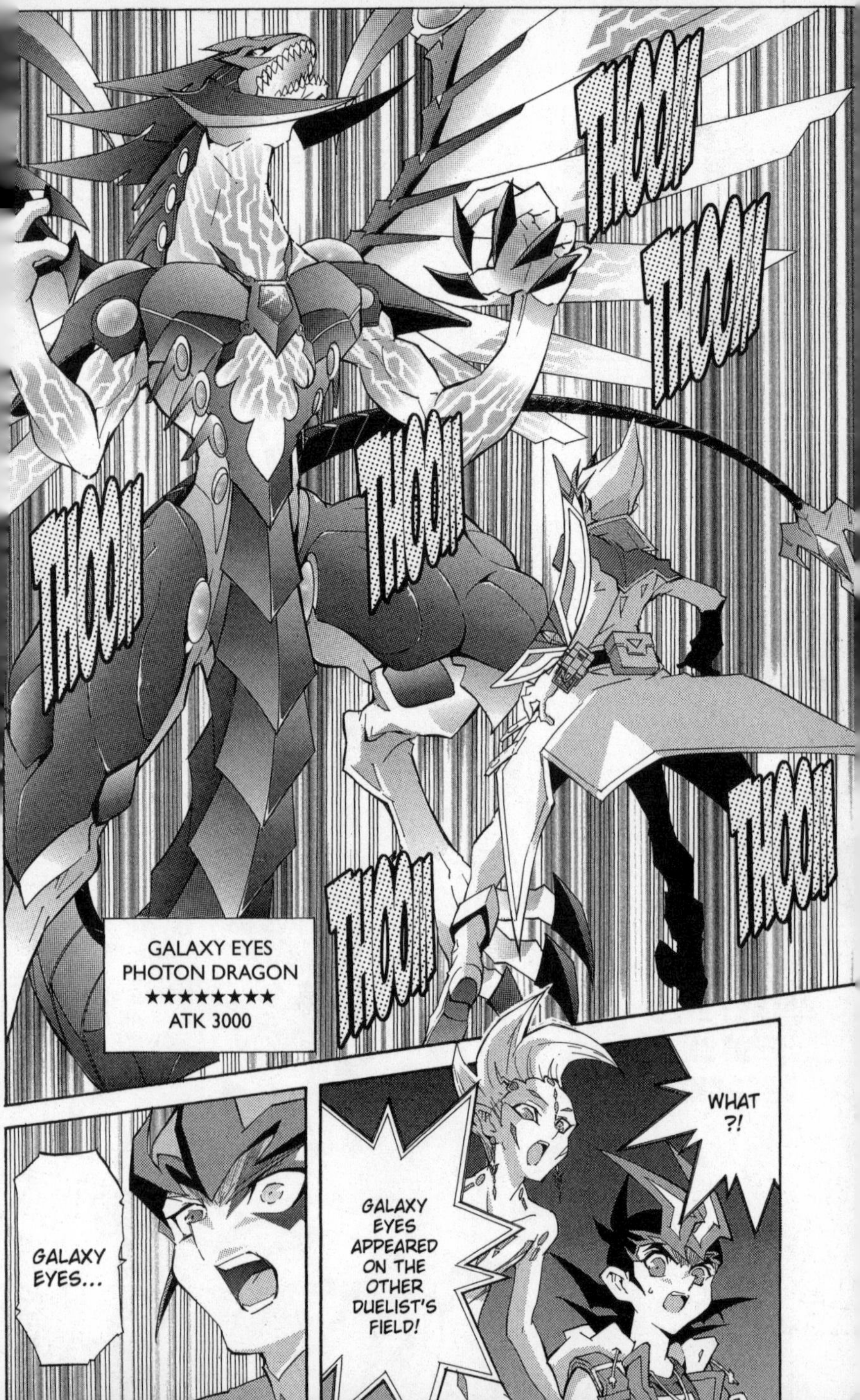
THOOM
THOOM
THOOM
THOOM
THOOM
THOOM
GALAXY EYES PHOTON DRAGON ★★★★★★★★ ATK 3000
WHAT ?!
GALAXY EYES APPEARED ON THE OTHER DUELIST'S FIELD!
GALAXY EYES...

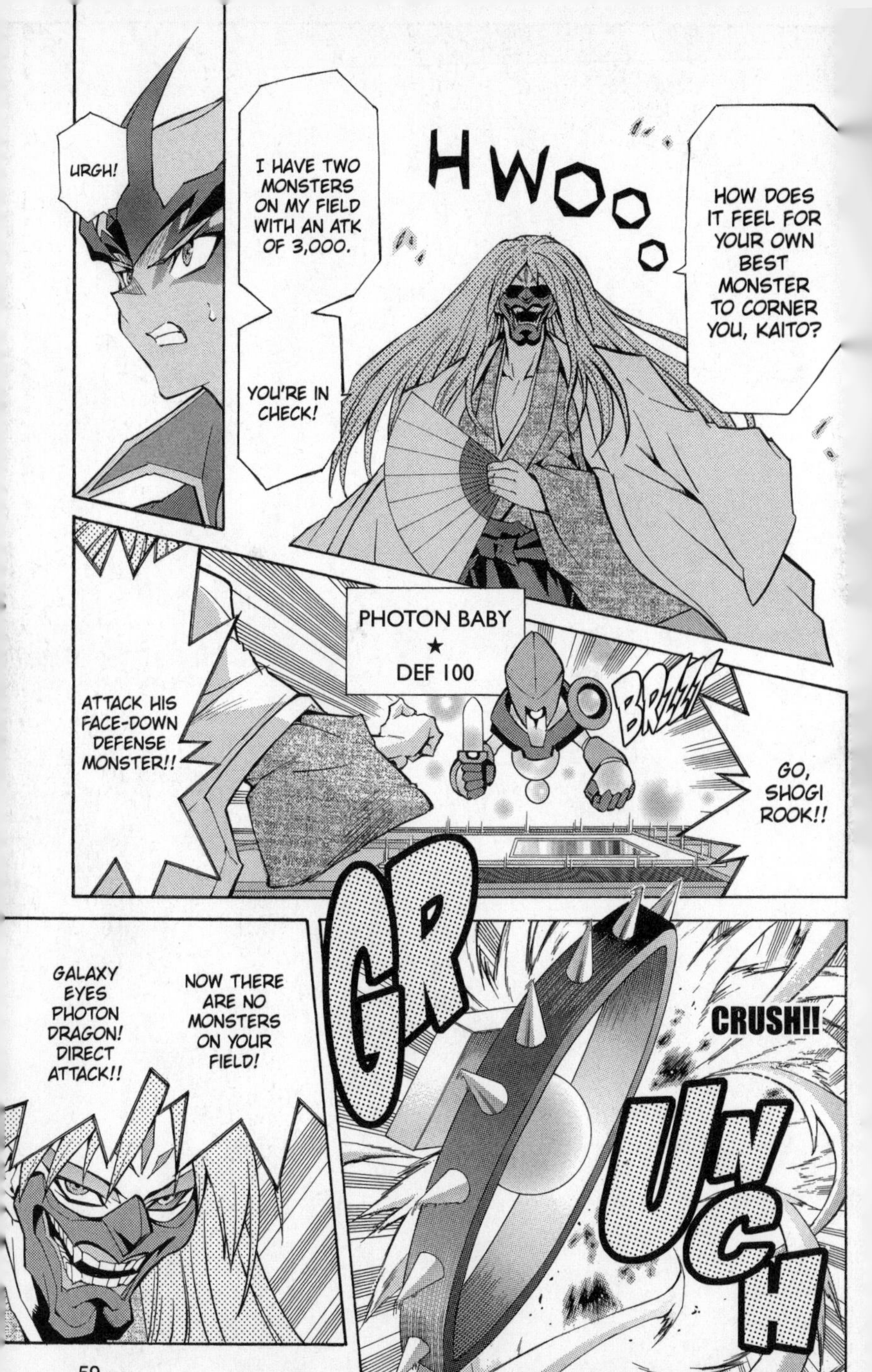
HOW DOES IT FEEL FOR YOUR OWN BEST MONSTER TO CORNER YOU, KAITO?
HWOOO
I HAVE TWO MONSTERS ON MY FIELD WITH AN ATK OF 3,000.
YOU'RE IN CHECK!
URGH!
PHOTON BABY ★ DEF 100
BRZZT
GO, SHOGI ROOK!!
ATTACK HIS FACE-DOWN DEFENSE MONSTER!!
CRUNCH
CRUSH!!
NOW THERE ARE NO MONSTERS ON YOUR FIELD!
GALAXY EYES PHOTON DRAGON! DIRECT ATTACK!!

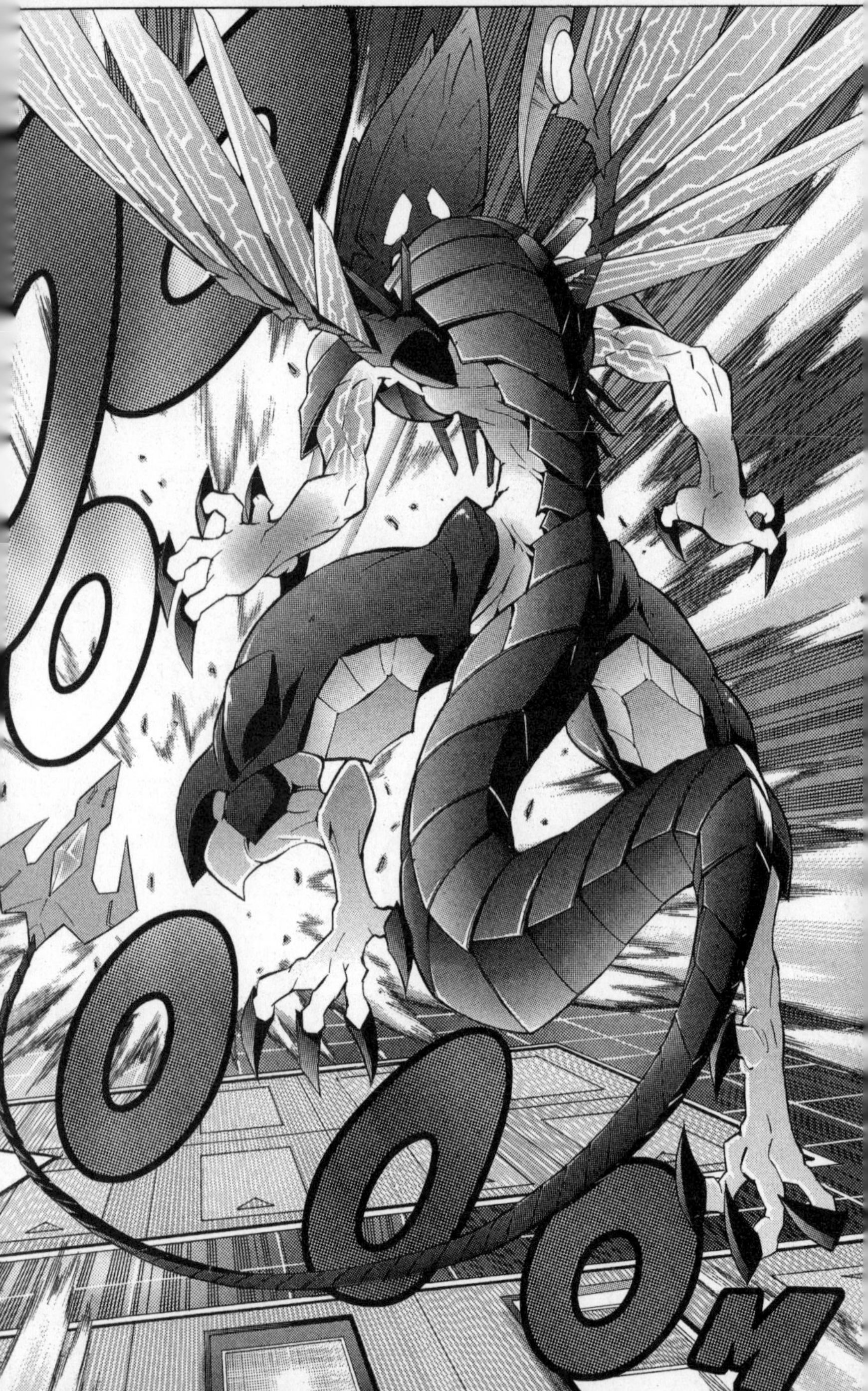
BOOOOOM

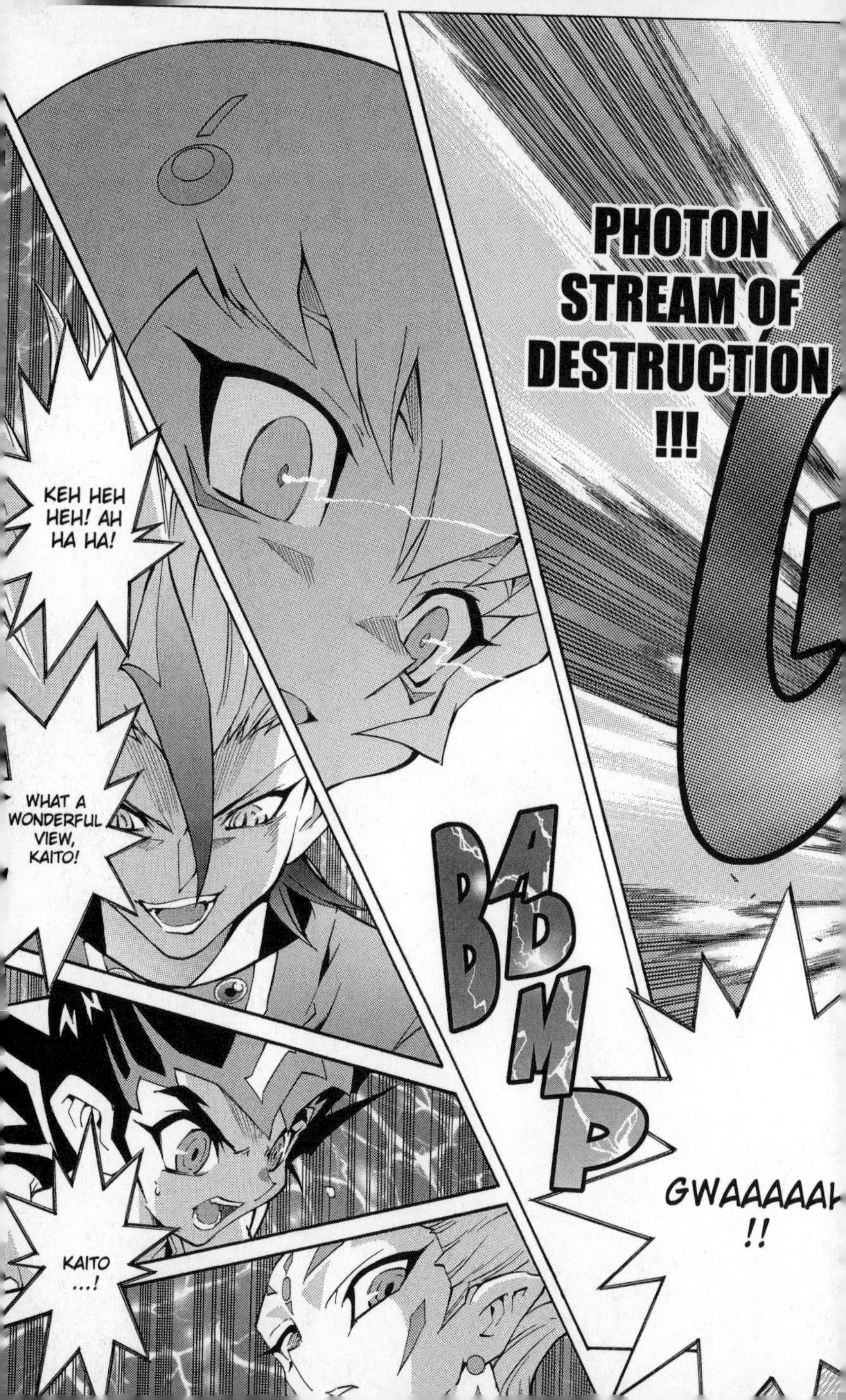
PHOTON STREAM OF DESTRUCTION !!!
BADMP
KEH HEH HEH! AH HA HA!
WHAT A WONDERFUL VIEW, KAITO!
GWAAAAAH !!
KAITO ...!

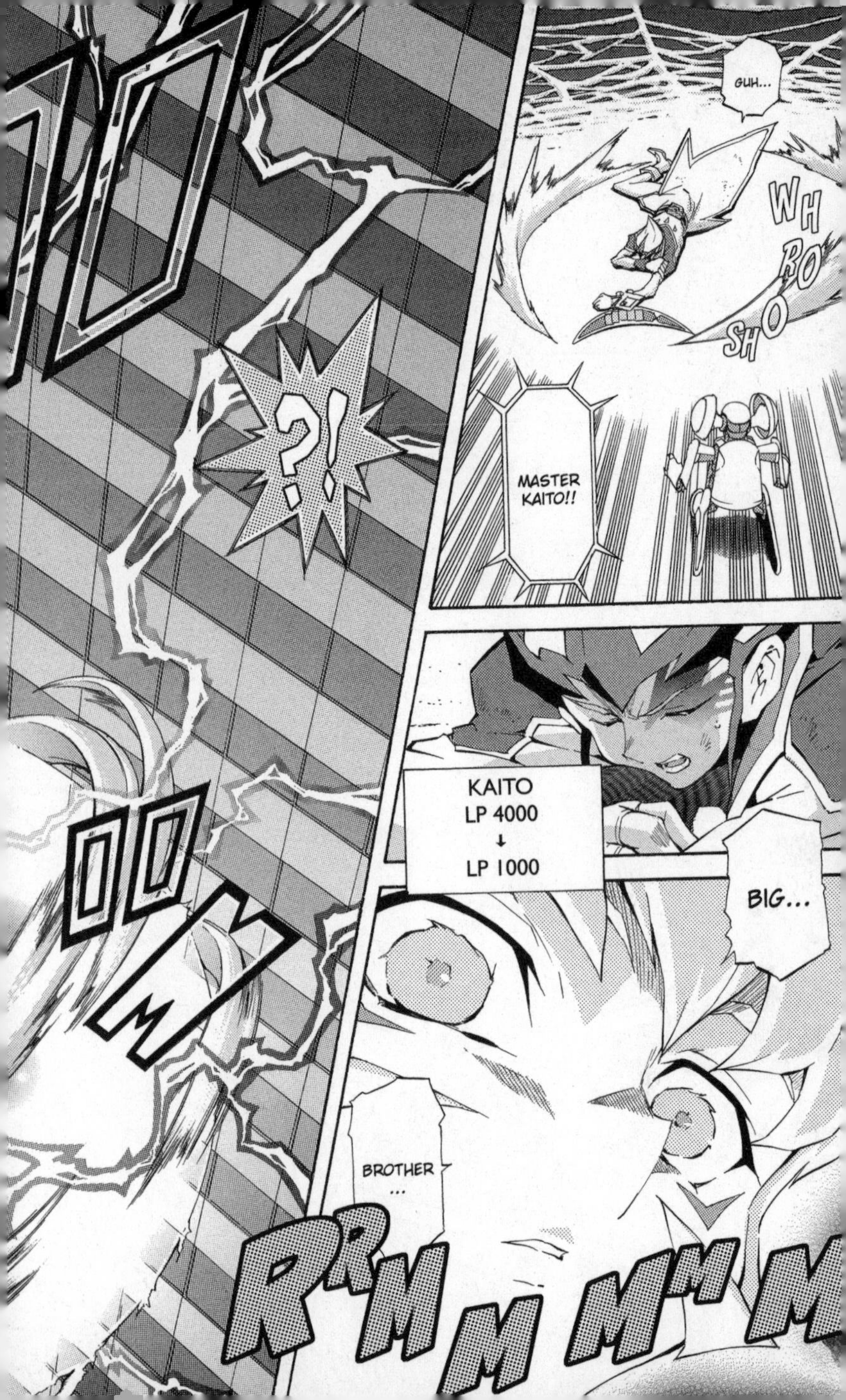
GUH...
WHROOSH
MASTER KAITO!!
KAITO
LP 4000
↓
LP 1000
BIG...
BROTHER
...
RRMMMMMM
?!
DOOM

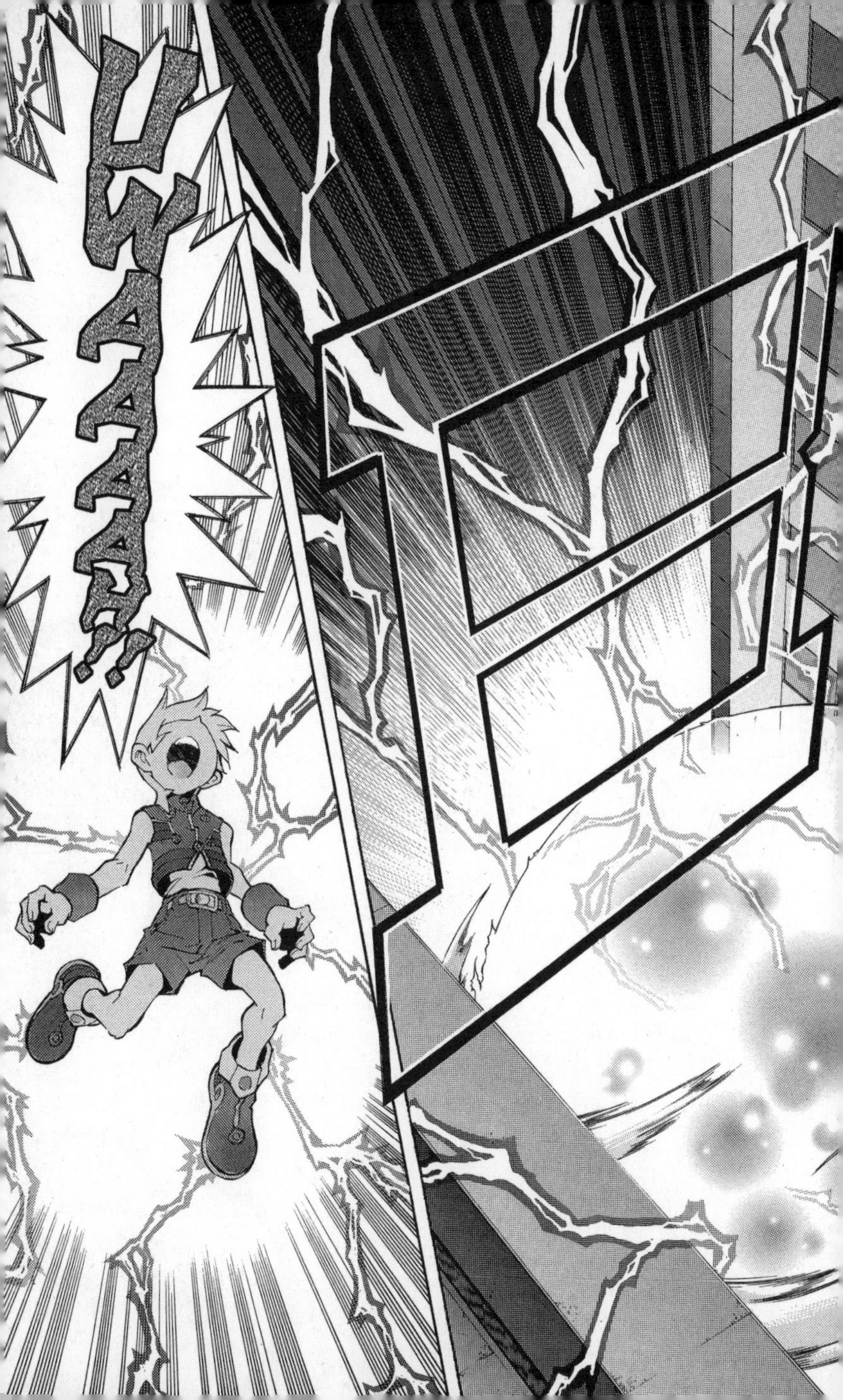
UWAAAAGH!!

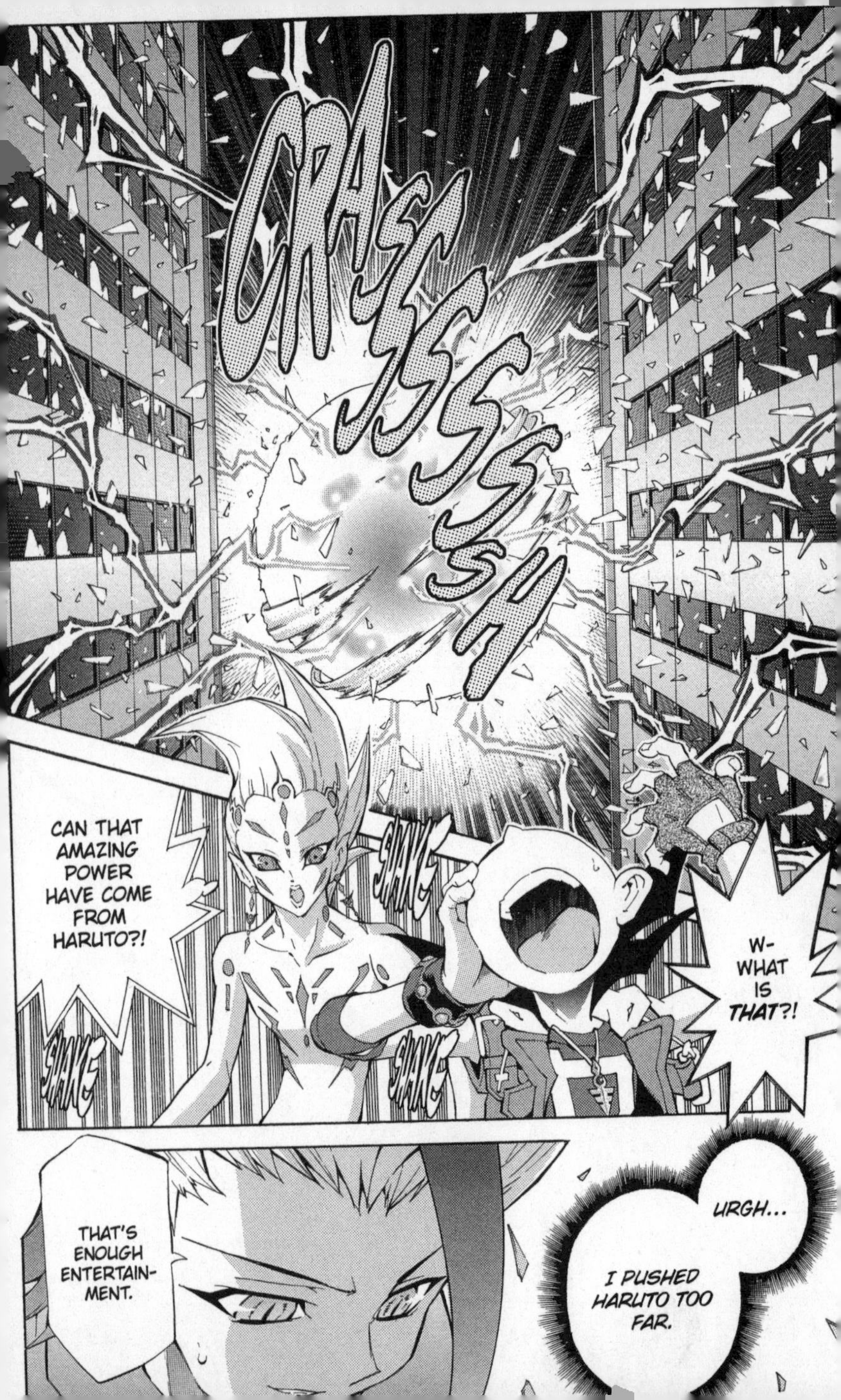
CRASSSSSH
W-WHAT IS THAT?!
SHAKE
SHAKE
CAN THAT AMAZING POWER HAVE COME FROM HARUTO?!
SHAKE
SHAKE
URGH...
I PUSHED HARUTO TOO FAR.
THAT'S ENOUGH ENTERTAIN-MENT.

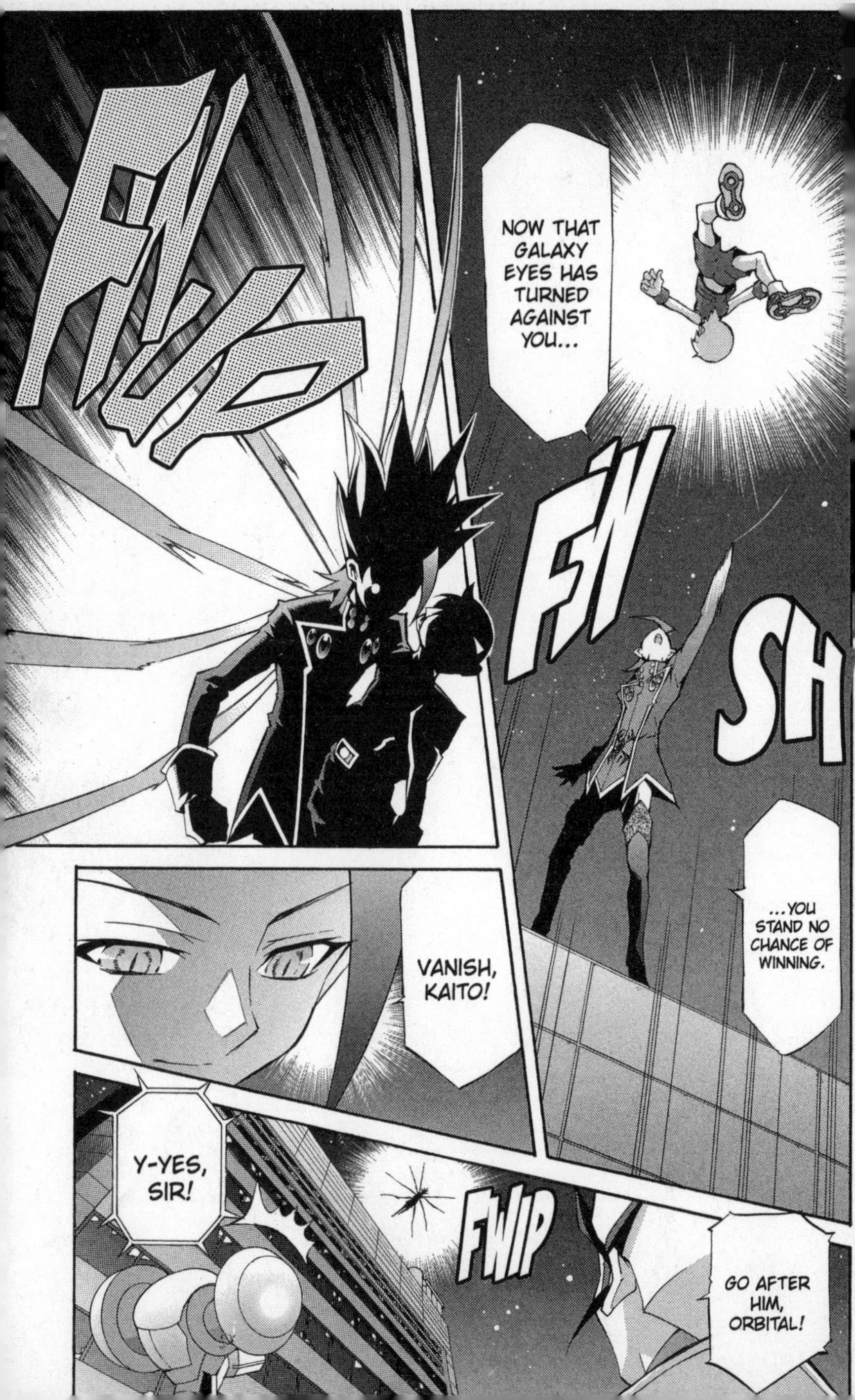
NOW THAT GALAXY EYES HAS TURNED AGAINST YOU...
FSH
SH
...YOU STAND NO CHANCE OF WINNING.
VANISH, KAITO!
GO AFTER HIM, ORBITAL!
FWIP
Y-YES, SIR!

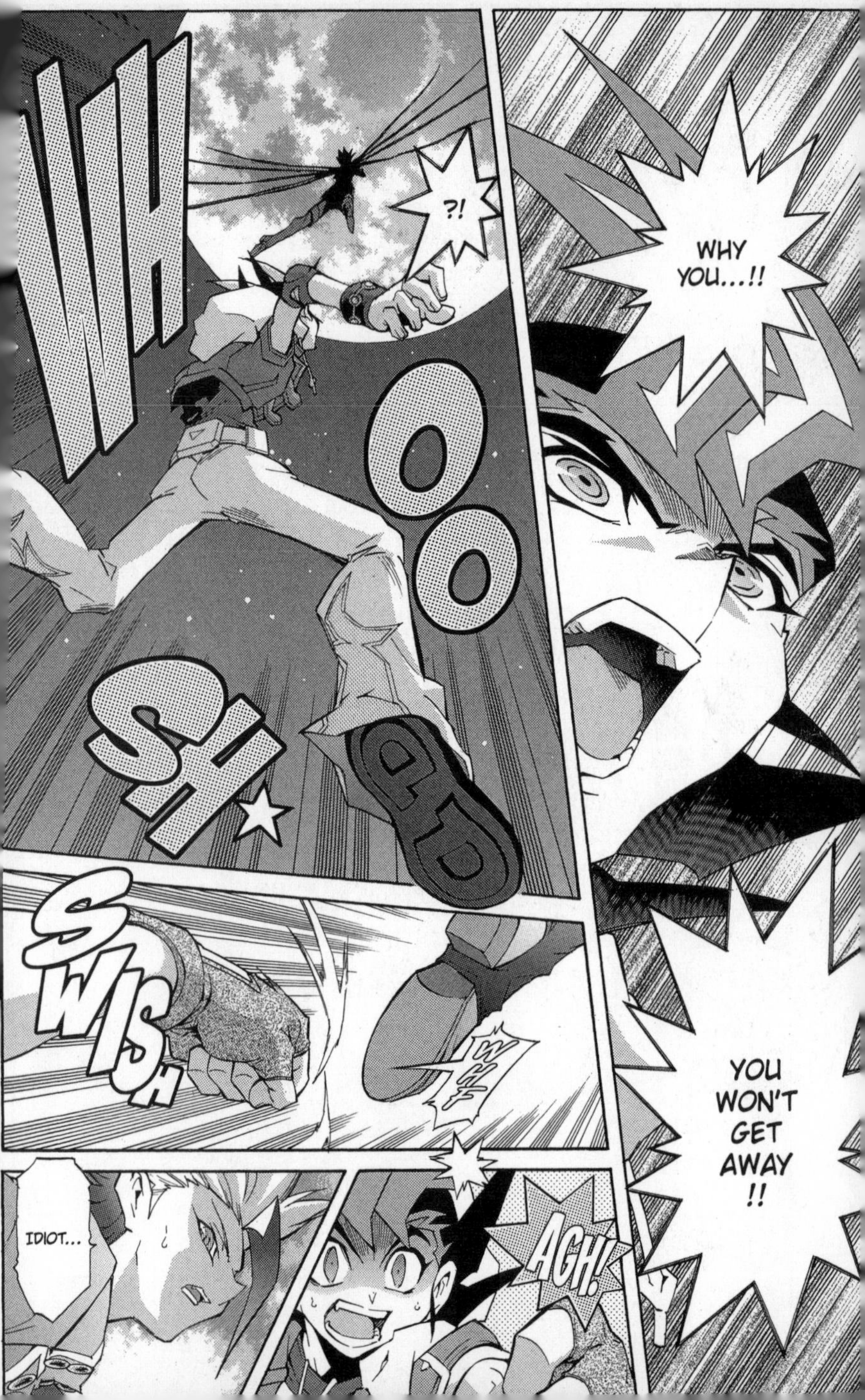
WHY YOU...!!
YOU WON'T GET AWAY!!
?!
WHHOOOSH
SWISH
WHIF
AGH!
IDIOT...

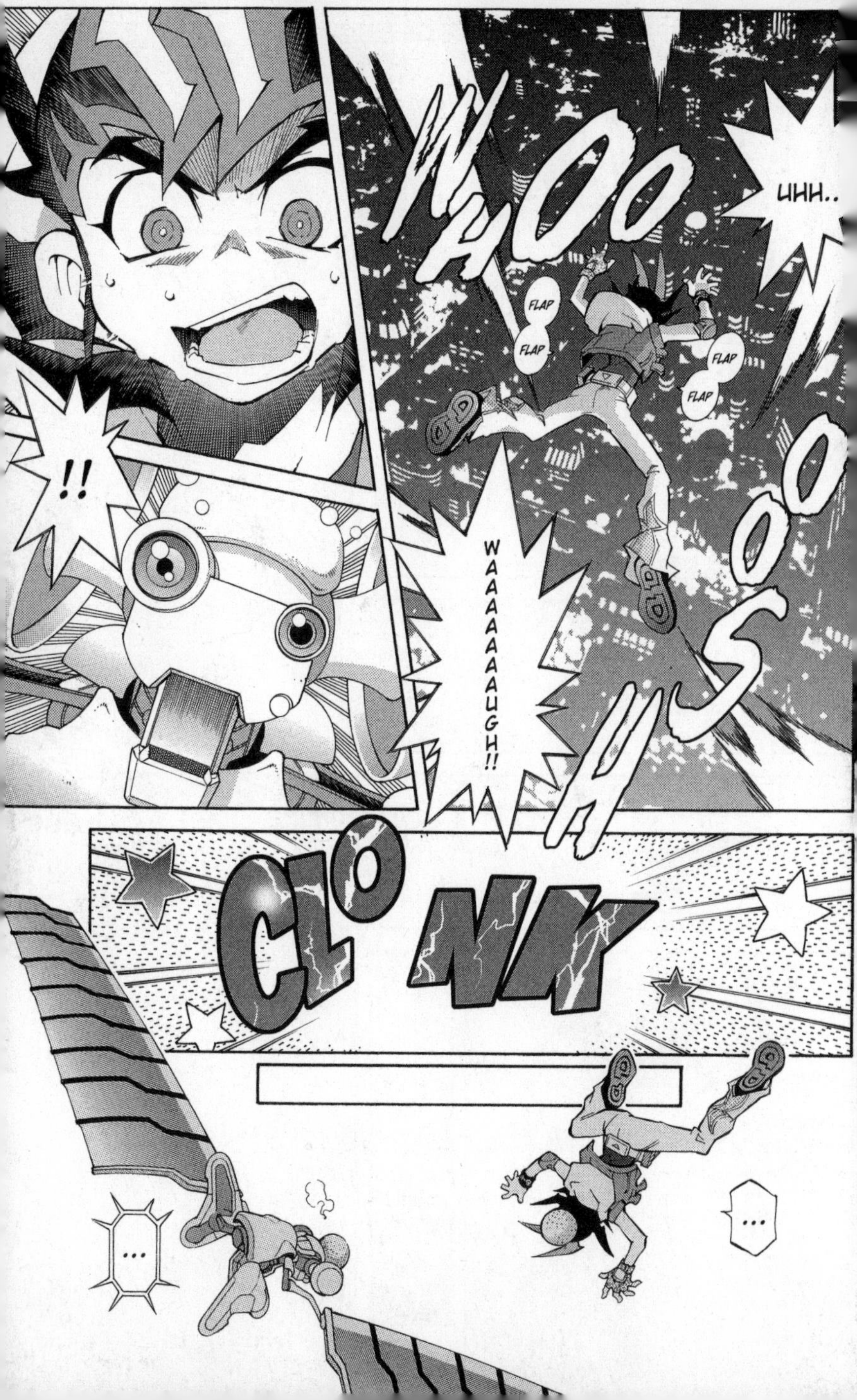

UHH..
WHOOOOOSH
FLAP
FLAP
FLAP
FLAP
WAAAAAAAAAUGH!!
!!
CLONK
...
...

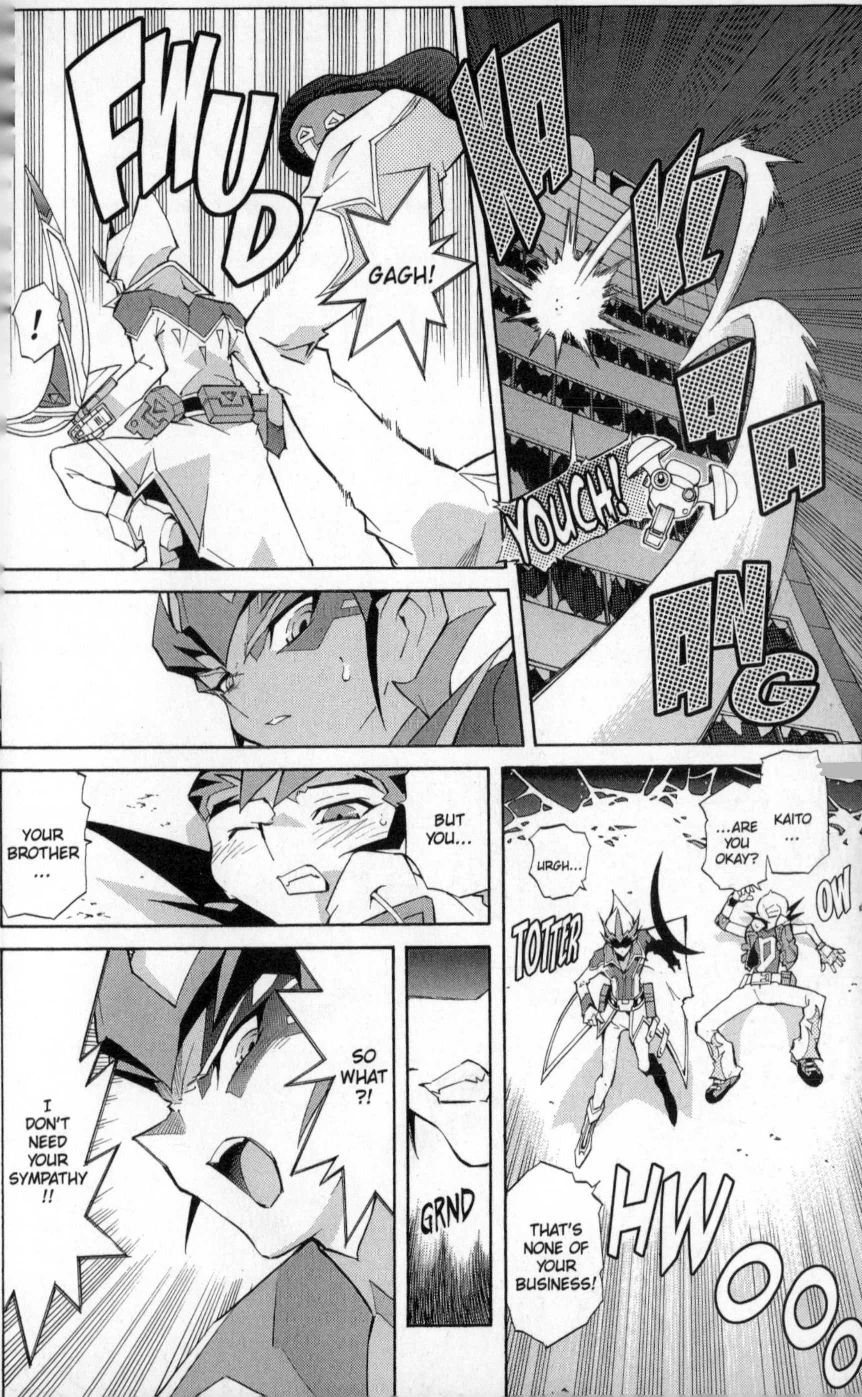
YOUCH!
FWUD
GAGH!
!
KAITO...
...ARE YOU OKAY?
URGH...
OW
TOTTER
THAT'S NONE OF YOUR BUSINESS!
HWOOO
BUT YOU...
YOUR BROTHER...
GRND
SO WHAT?!
I DON'T NEED YOUR SYMPATHY!!

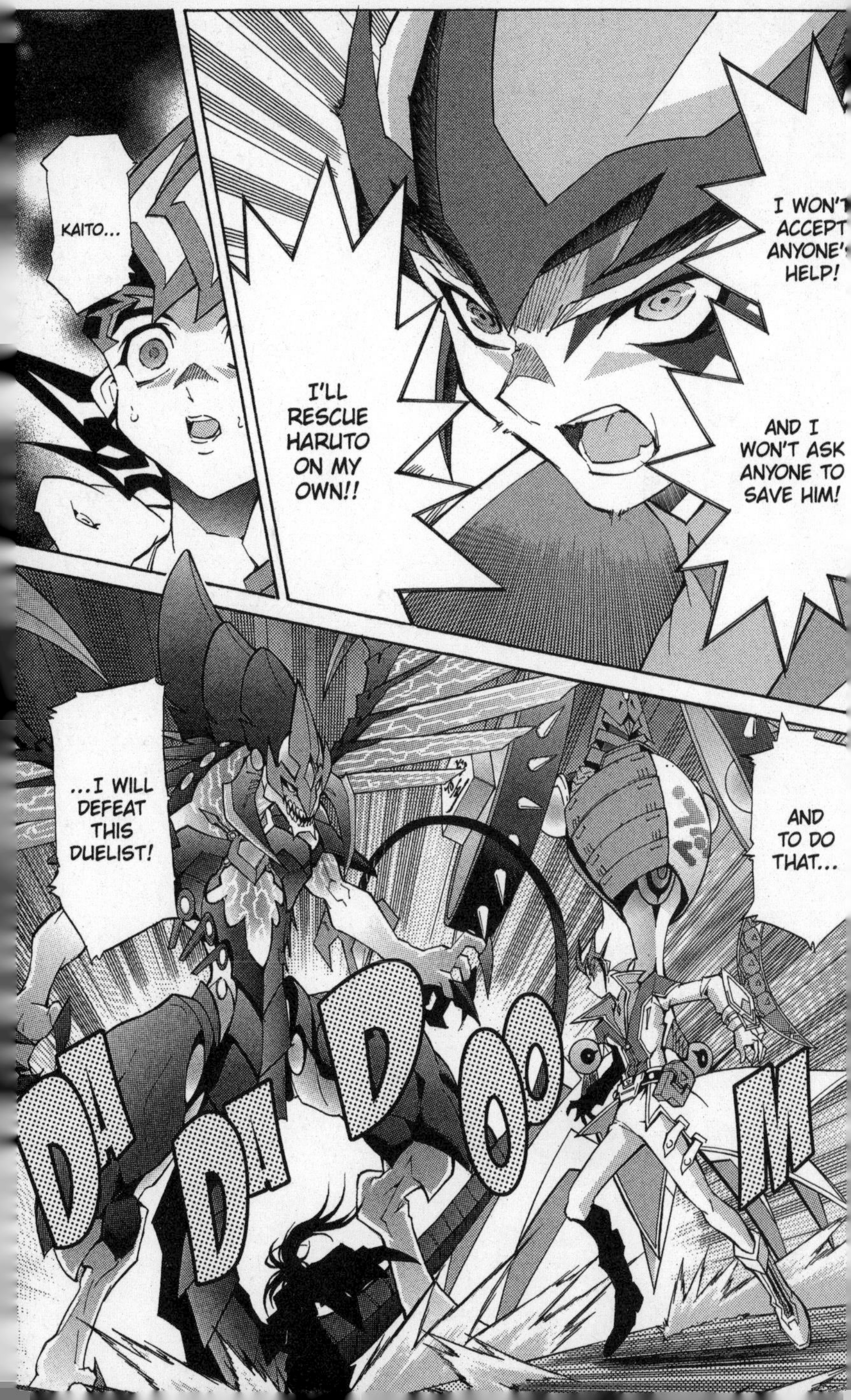
I WON'T ACCEPT ANYONE'S HELP!
AND I WON'T ASK ANYONE TO SAVE HIM!
I'LL RESCUE HARUTO ON MY OWN!!
KAITO...
AND TO DO THAT...
...I WILL DEFEAT THIS DUELIST!
DA DA DOOOOM

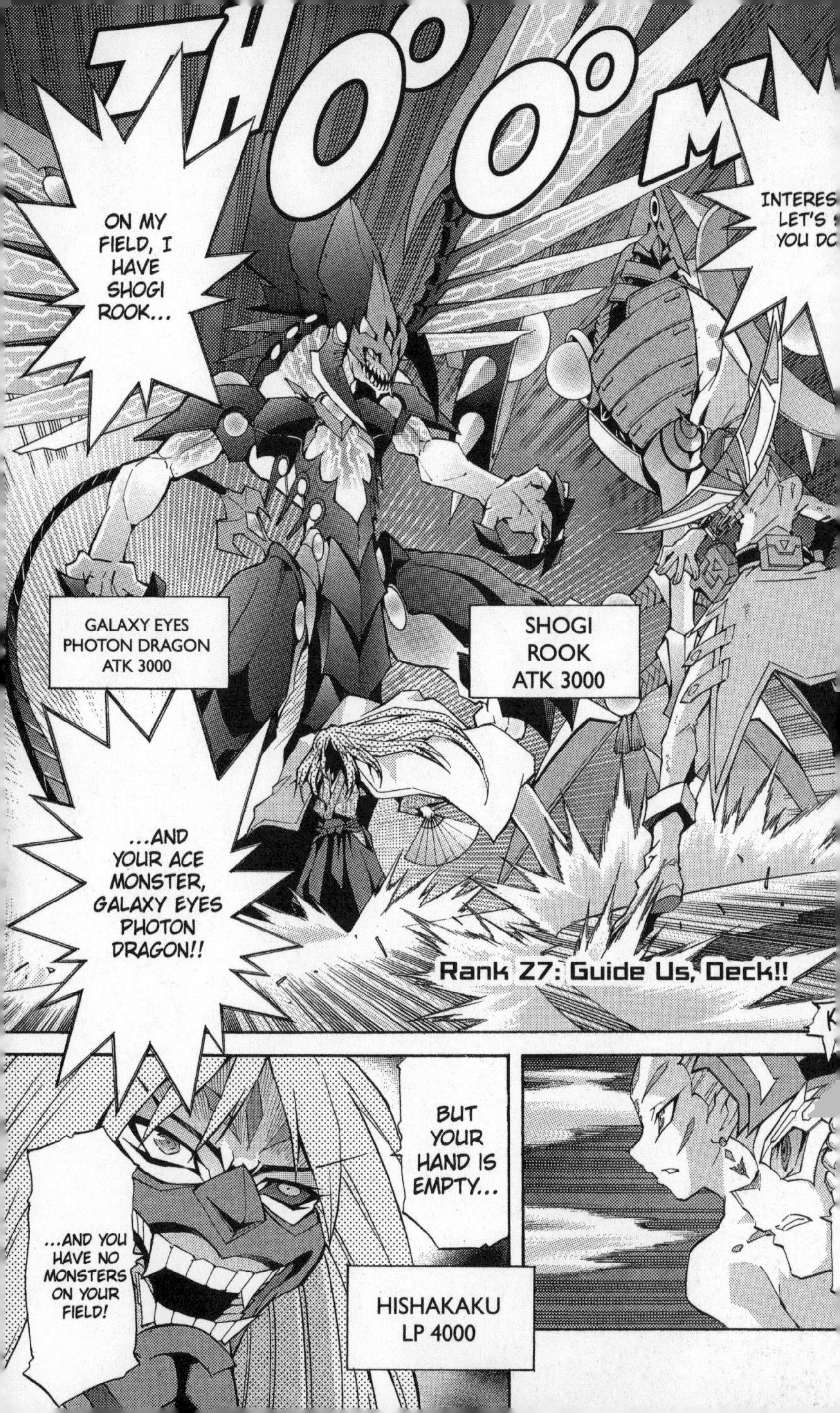
THOOOOM
INTERES
LET'S
YOU DC
ON MY FIELD, I HAVE SHOGI ROOK...
SHOGI ROOK ATK 3000
GALAXY EYES PHOTON DRAGON ATK 3000
...AND YOUR ACE MONSTER, GALAXY EYES PHOTON DRAGON!!
Rank 27: Guide Us, Deck!!
BUT YOUR HAND IS EMPTY...
HISHAKAKU LP 4000
...AND YOU HAVE NO MONSTERS ON YOUR FIELD!

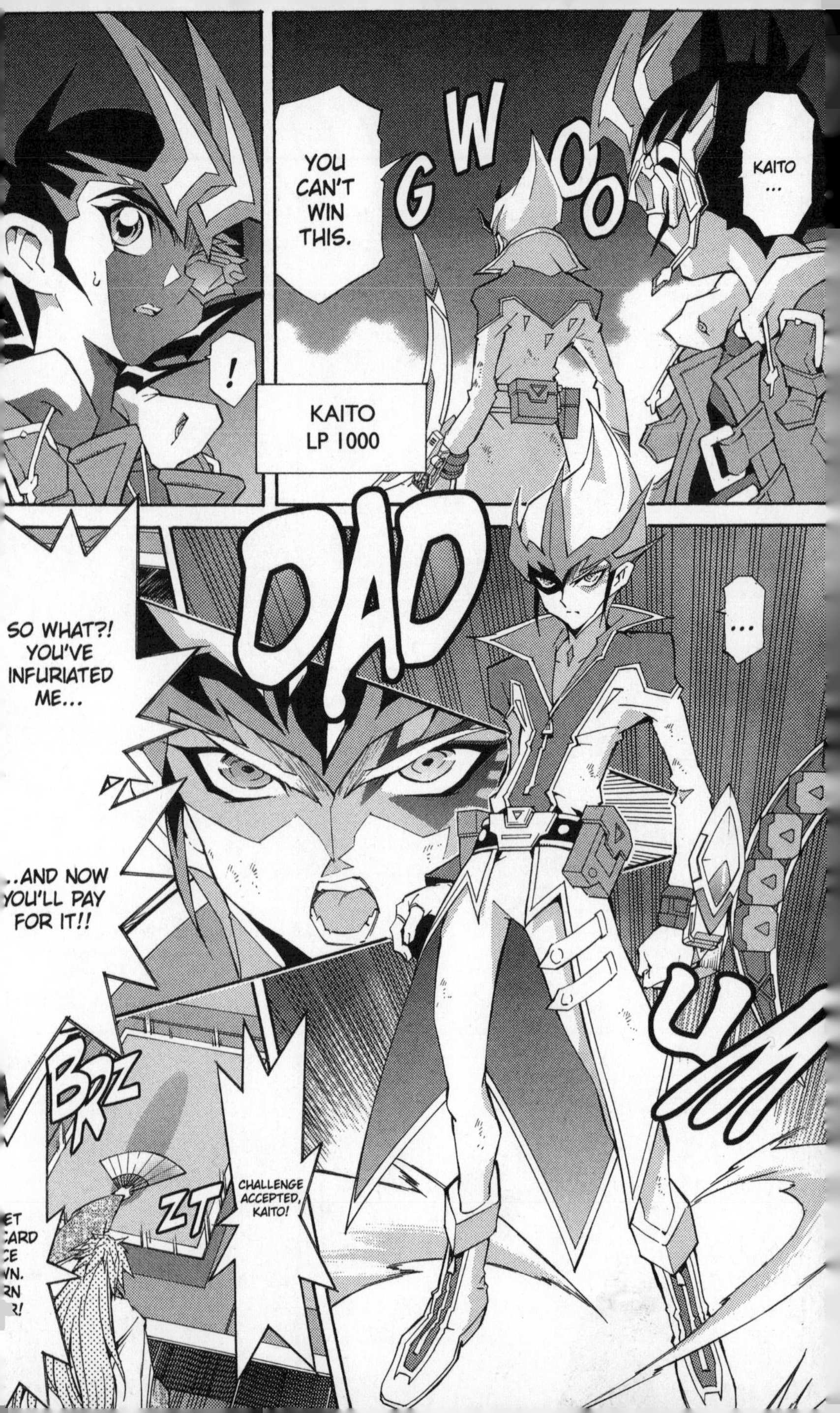
KAITO...
YOU CAN'T WIN THIS.
GWOOO
KAITO LP 1000
!
...
DAD
SO WHAT?! YOU'VE INFURIATED ME...
...AND NOW YOU'LL PAY FOR IT!!
BRZZ
ZT
CHALLENGE ACCEPTED, KAITO!

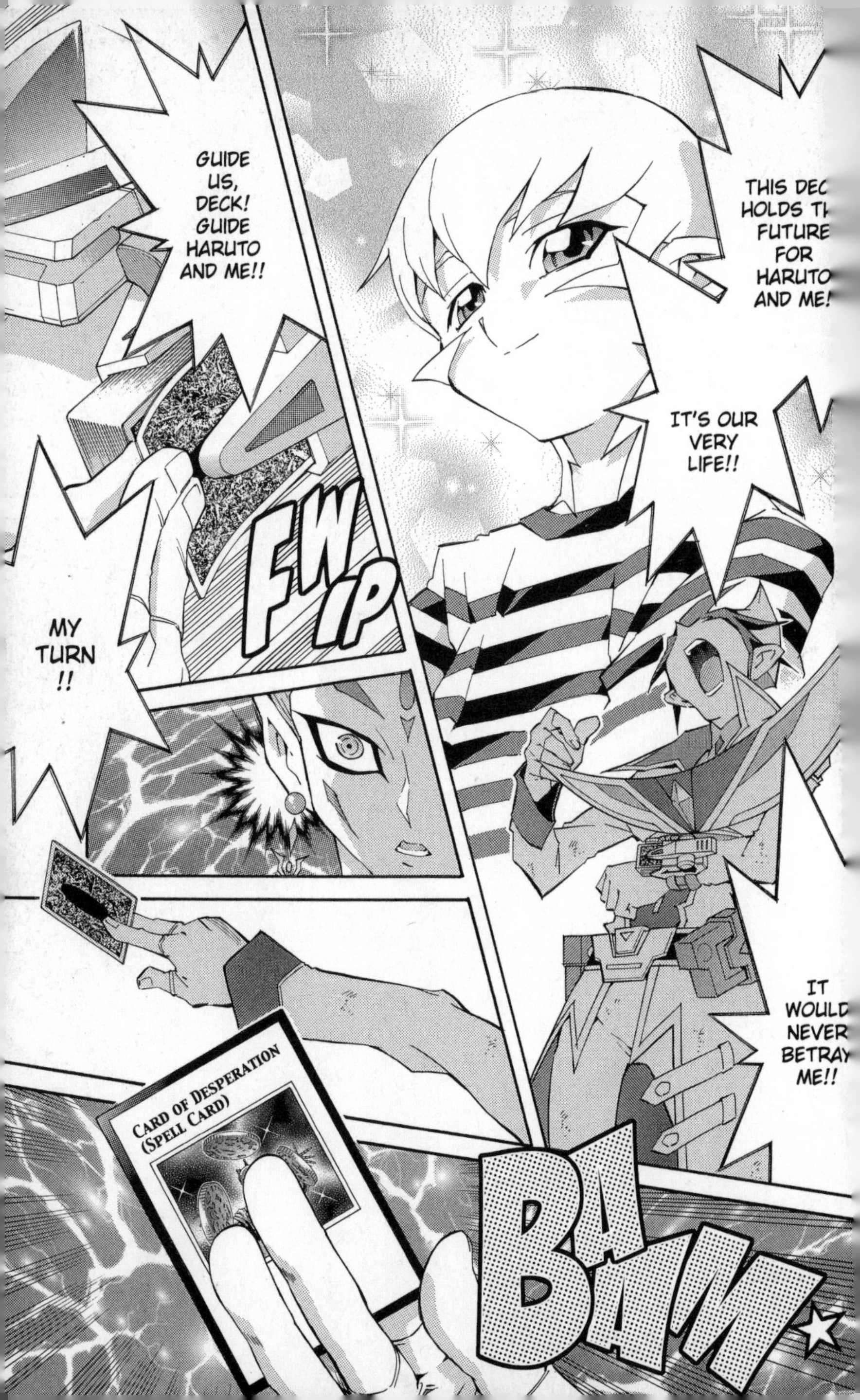

THIS DEC HOLDS TH FUTURE FOR HARUTO AND ME!
IT'S OUR VERY LIFE!!
IT WOULD NEVER BETRAY ME!!
GUIDE US, DECK! GUIDE HARUTO AND ME!!
F-WIP
MY TURN !!
CARD OF DESPERATION (SPELL CARD)
BA BAM

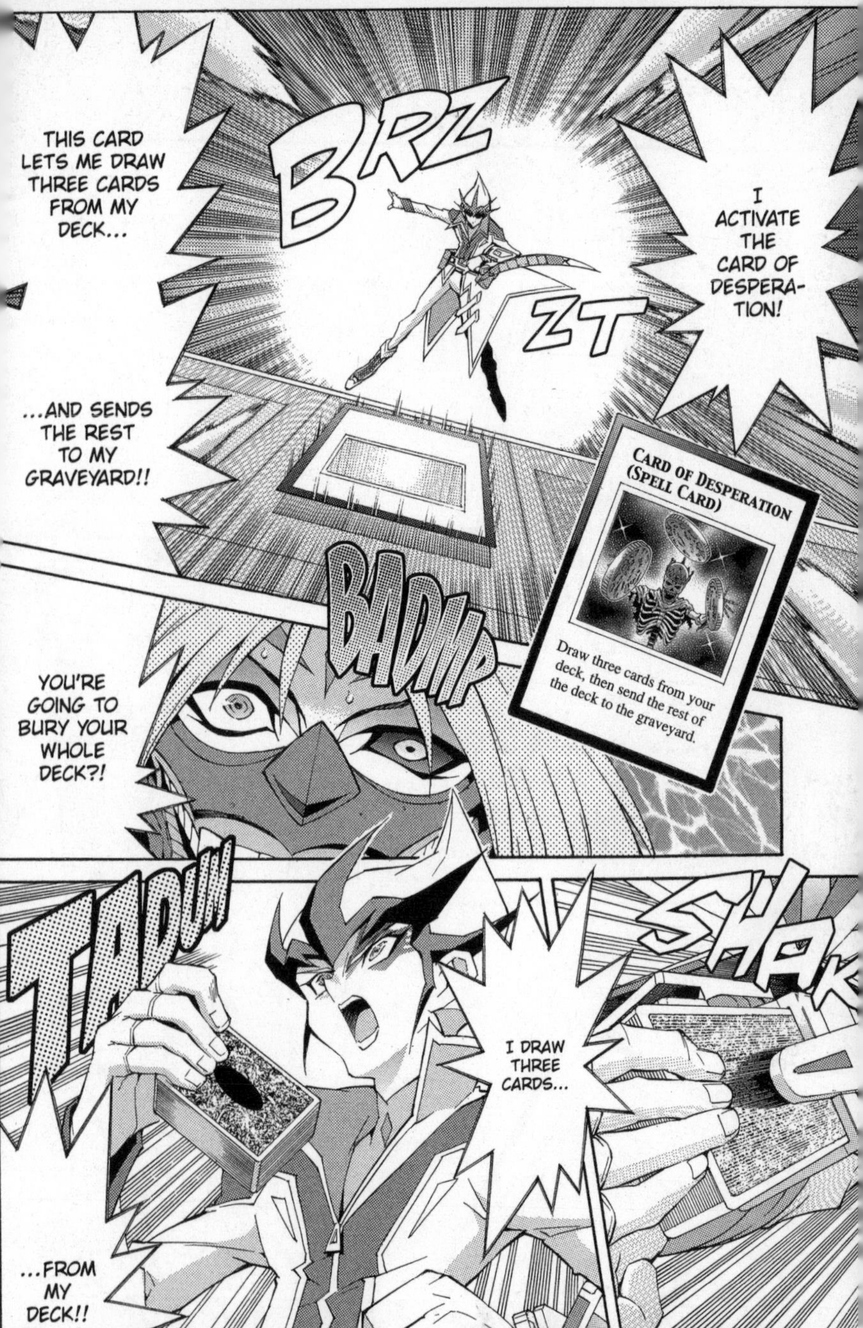
I ACTIVATE THE CARD OF DESPERATION!
BRZ
ZT
THIS CARD LETS ME DRAW THREE CARDS FROM MY DECK...
...AND SENDS THE REST TO MY GRAVEYARD!!
CARD OF DESPERATION (SPELL CARD)
Draw three cards from your deck, then send the rest of the deck to the graveyard.
BADMP
YOU'RE GOING TO BURY YOUR WHOLE DECK?!
SHAK
I DRAW THREE CARDS...
TADUM
...FROM MY DECK!!

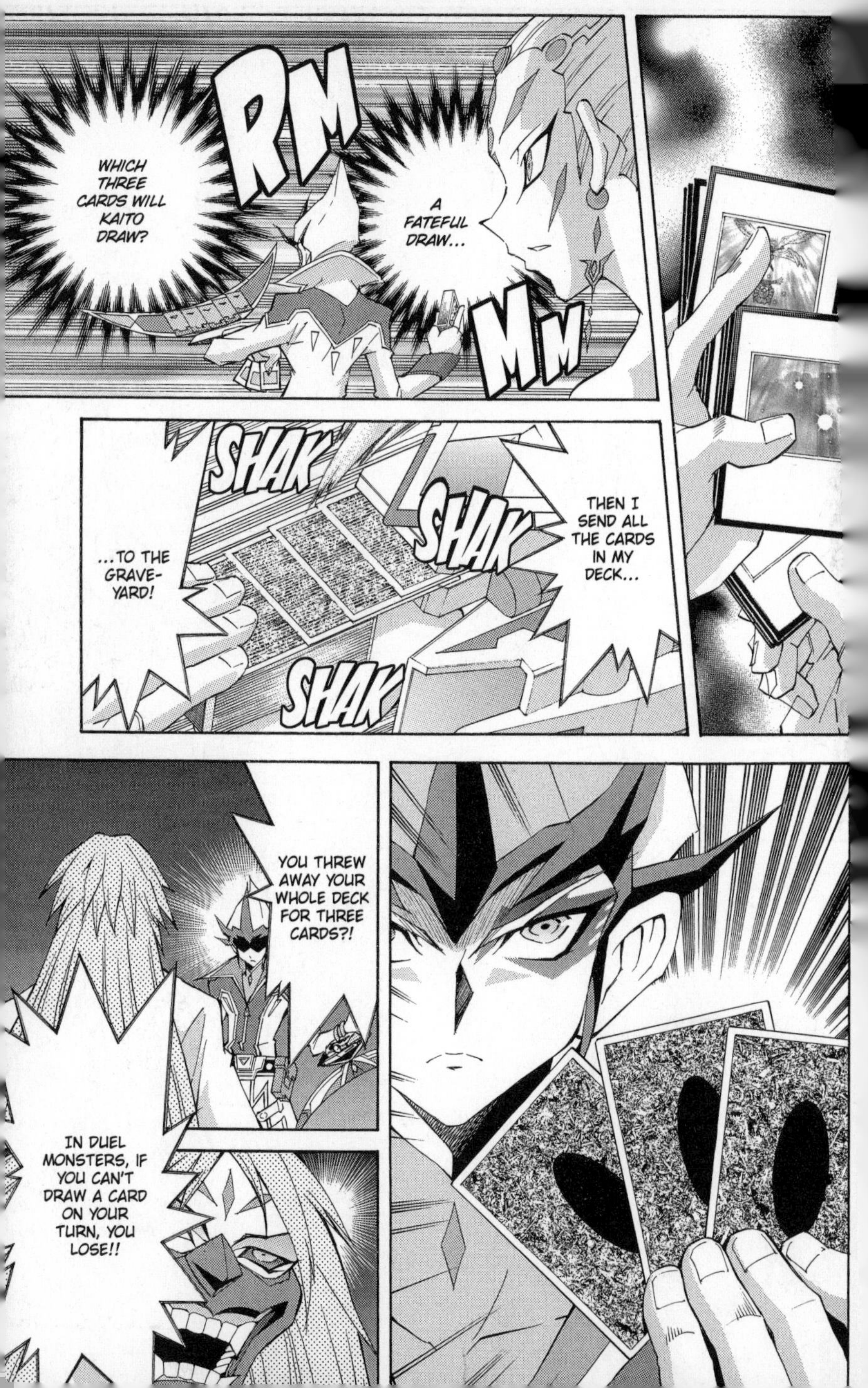
RM
A FATEFUL DRAW...
WHICH THREE CARDS WILL KAITO DRAW?
MM
SHAK
SHAK
THEN I SEND ALL THE CARDS IN MY DECK...
...TO THE GRAVEYARD!
SHAK
YOU THREW AWAY YOUR WHOLE DECK FOR THREE CARDS?!
IN DUEL MONSTERS, IF YOU CAN'T DRAW A CARD ON YOUR TURN, YOU LOSE!!

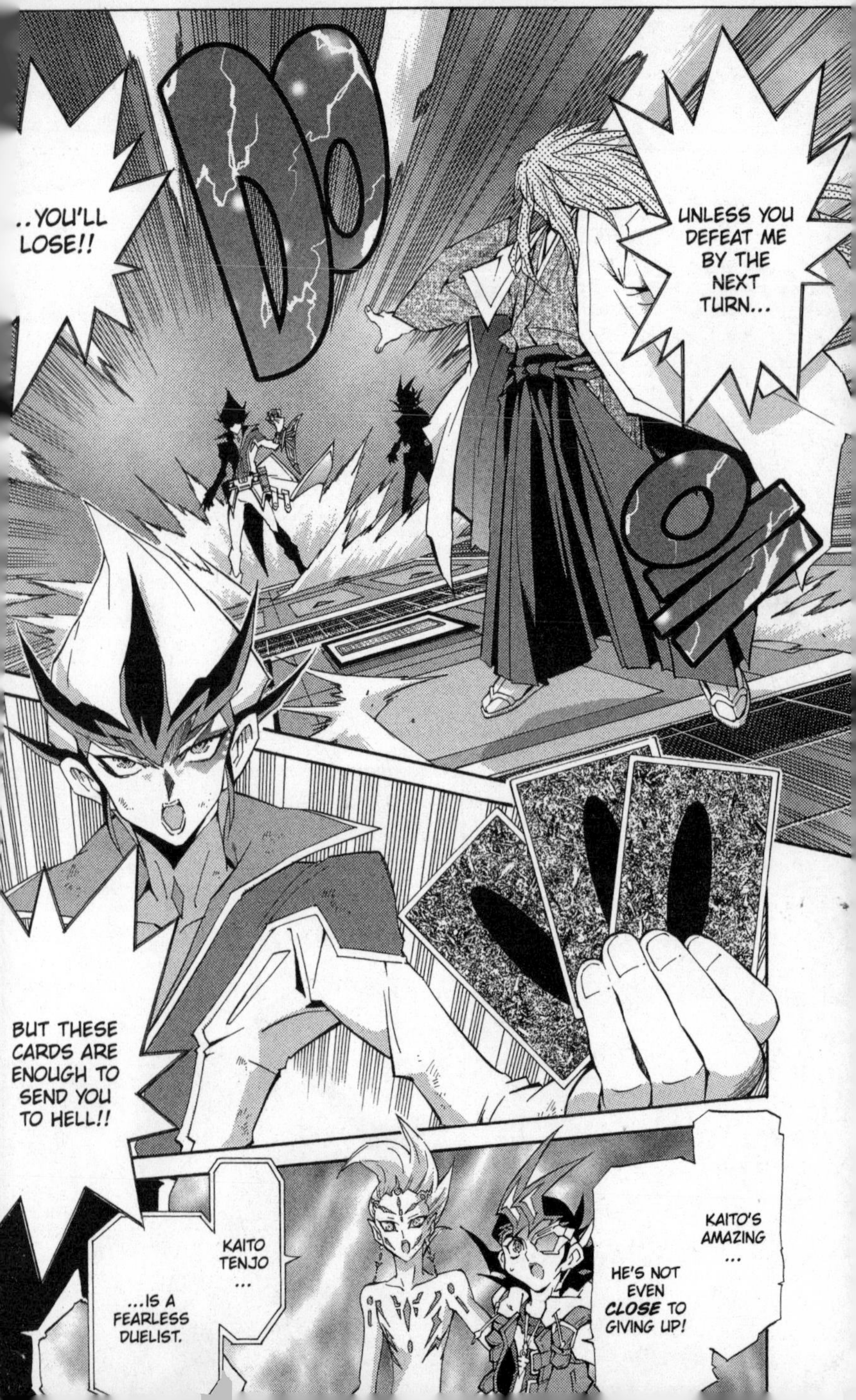
UNLESS YOU DEFEAT ME BY THE NEXT TURN...
..YOU'LL LOSE!!
DO
O!
BUT THESE CARDS ARE ENOUGH TO SEND YOU TO HELL!!
KAITO'S AMAZING...
HE'S NOT EVEN **CLOSE** TO GIVING UP!
KAITO TENJO...
...IS A FEARLESS DUELIST.

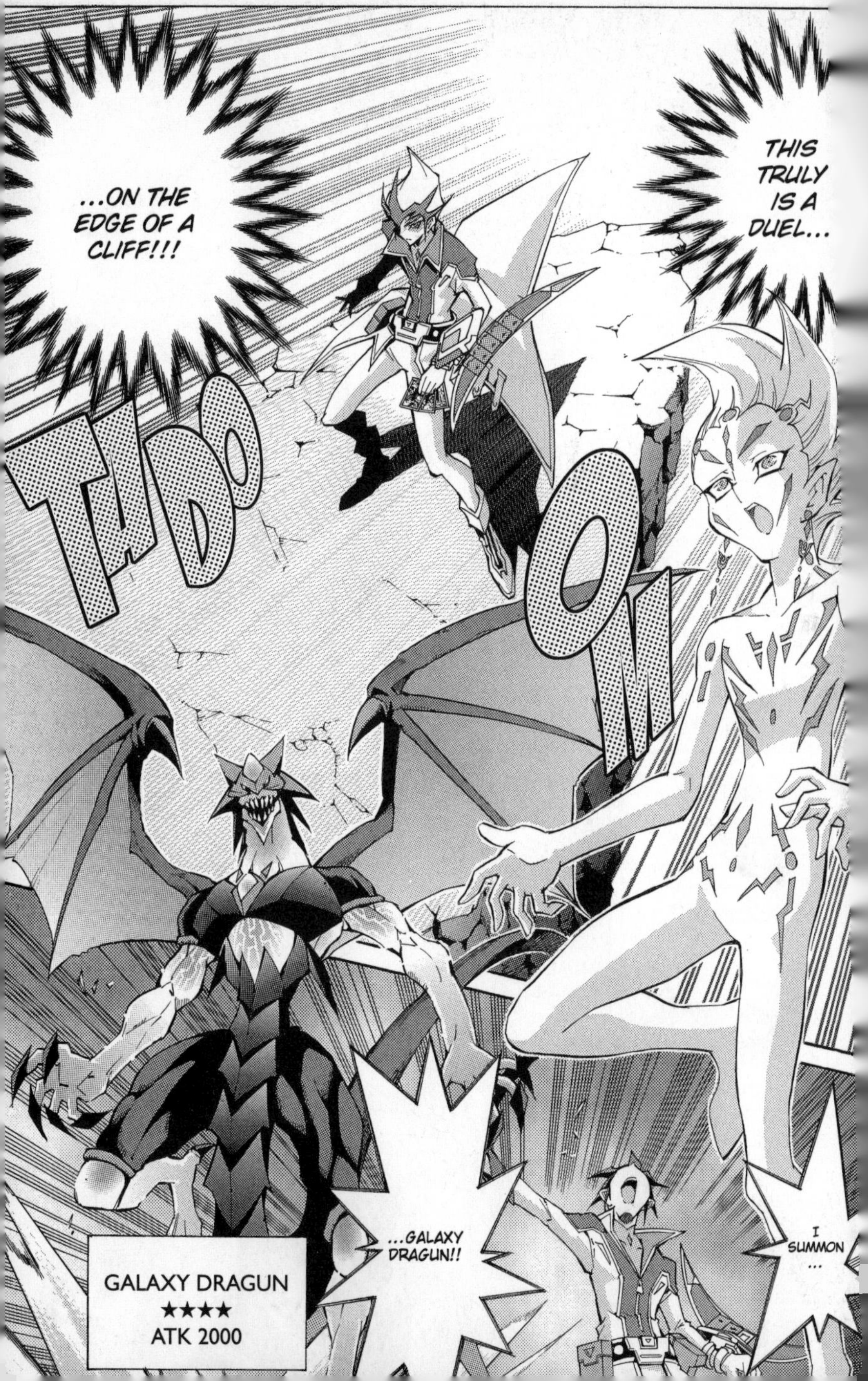
THIS TRULY IS A DUEL...
...ON THE EDGE OF A CLIFF!!!
THUDOOM
I SUMMON...
...GALAXY DRAGUN!!
GALAXY DRAGUN
★★★★
ATK 2000

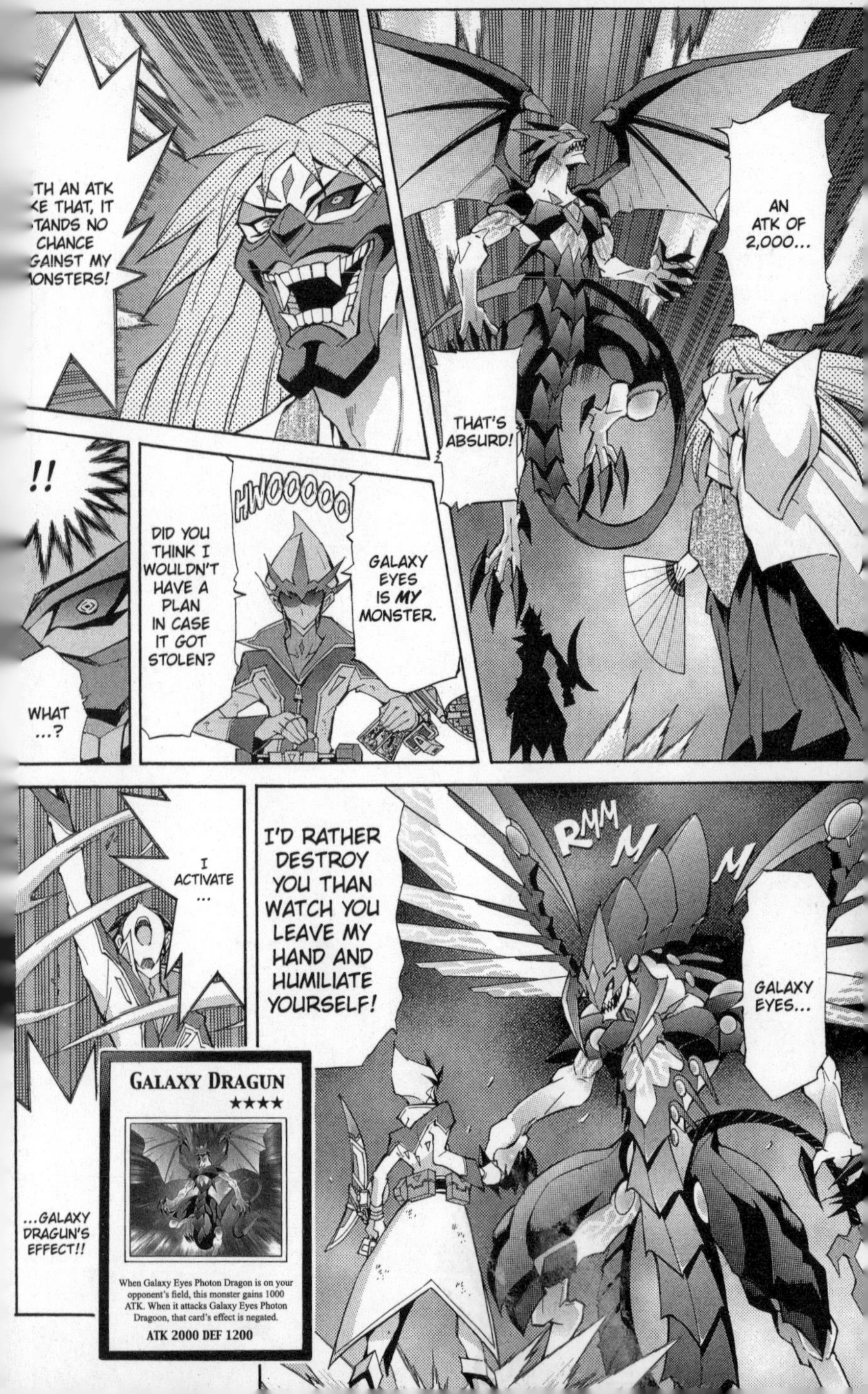

AN ATK OF 2,000...
THAT'S ABSURD!
TH AN ATK KE THAT, IT TANDS NO CHANCE GAINST MY ONSTERS!
HWOOOOOO
GALAXY EYES IS MY MONSTER.
DID YOU THINK I WOULDN'T HAVE A PLAN IN CASE IT GOT STOLEN?
!!
WHAT ...?
RMMM N N
GALAXY EYES...
I'D RATHER DESTROY YOU THAN WATCH YOU LEAVE MY HAND AND HUMILIATE YOURSELF!
I ACTIVATE ...
...GALAXY DRAGUN'S EFFECT!!
GALAXY DRAGUN
★★★★
When Galaxy Eyes Photon Dragon is on your opponent's field, this monster gains 1000 ATK. When it attacks Galaxy Eyes Photon Dragoon, that card's effect is negated.
ATK 2000 DEF 1200

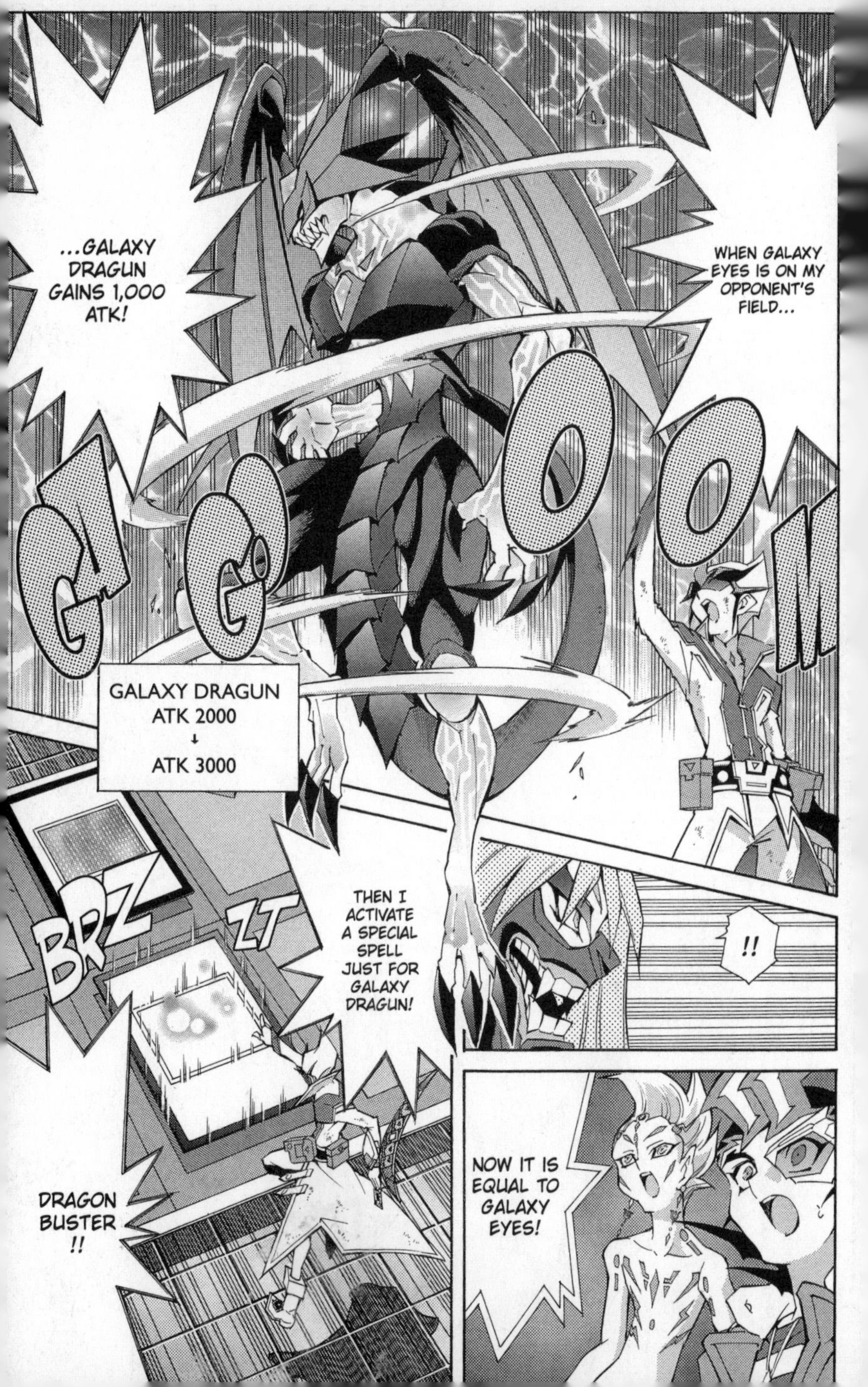
WHEN GALAXY EYES IS ON MY OPPONENT'S FIELD...
...GALAXY DRAGUN GAINS 1,000 ATK!
GAGOOOM
GALAXY DRAGUN ATK 2000 ↓ ATK 3000
!!
THEN I ACTIVATE A SPECIAL SPELL JUST FOR GALAXY DRAGUN!
NOW IT IS EQUAL TO GALAXY EYES!
BRZZT
DRAGON BUSTER !!

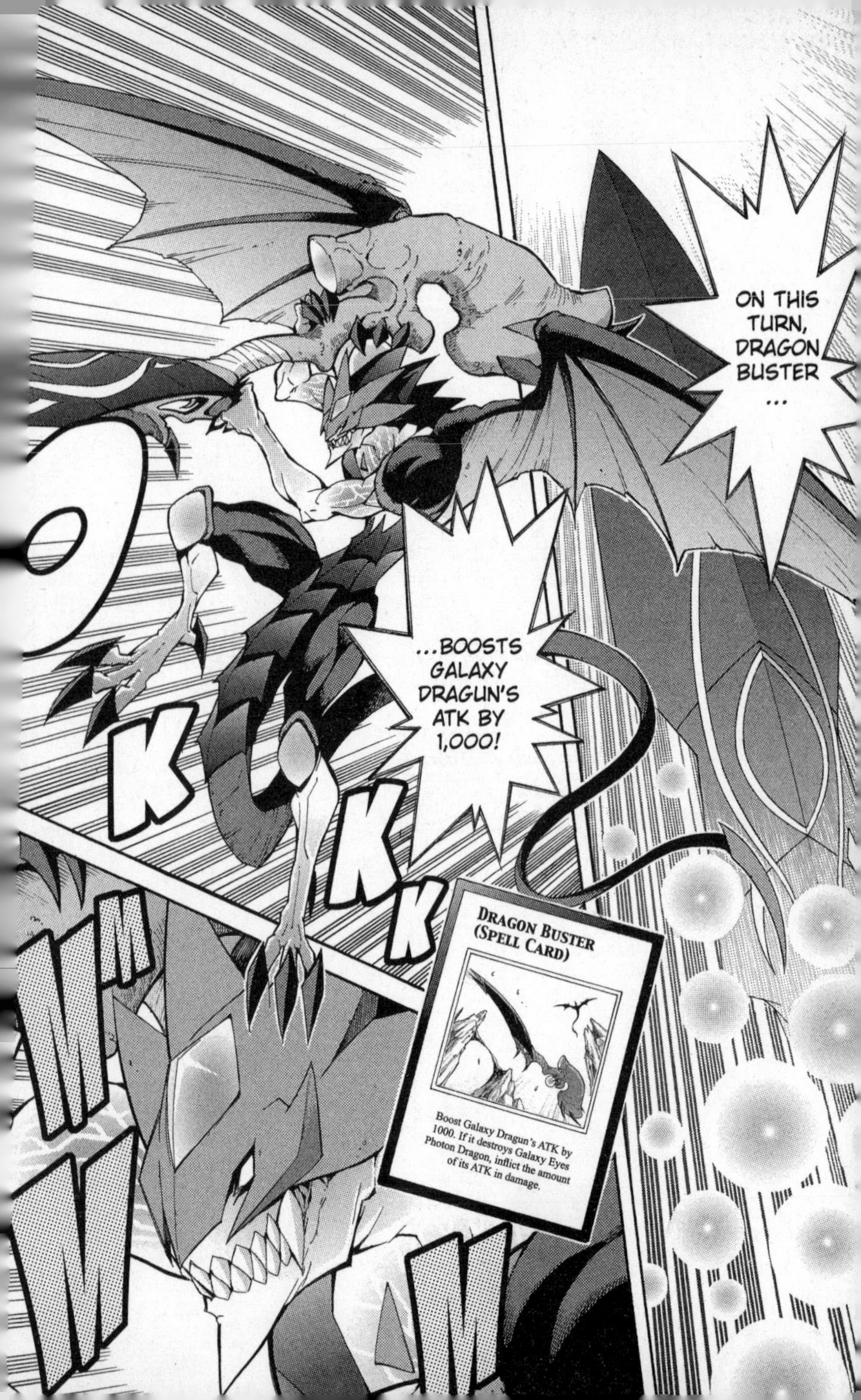
ON THIS TURN, DRAGON BUSTER ...
...BOOSTS GALAXY DRAGUN'S ATK BY 1,000!
K K K
DRAGON BUSTER (SPELL CARD)
Boost Galaxy Dragun's ATK by 1000. If it destroys Galaxy Eyes Photon Dragon, inflict the amount of its ATK in damage.

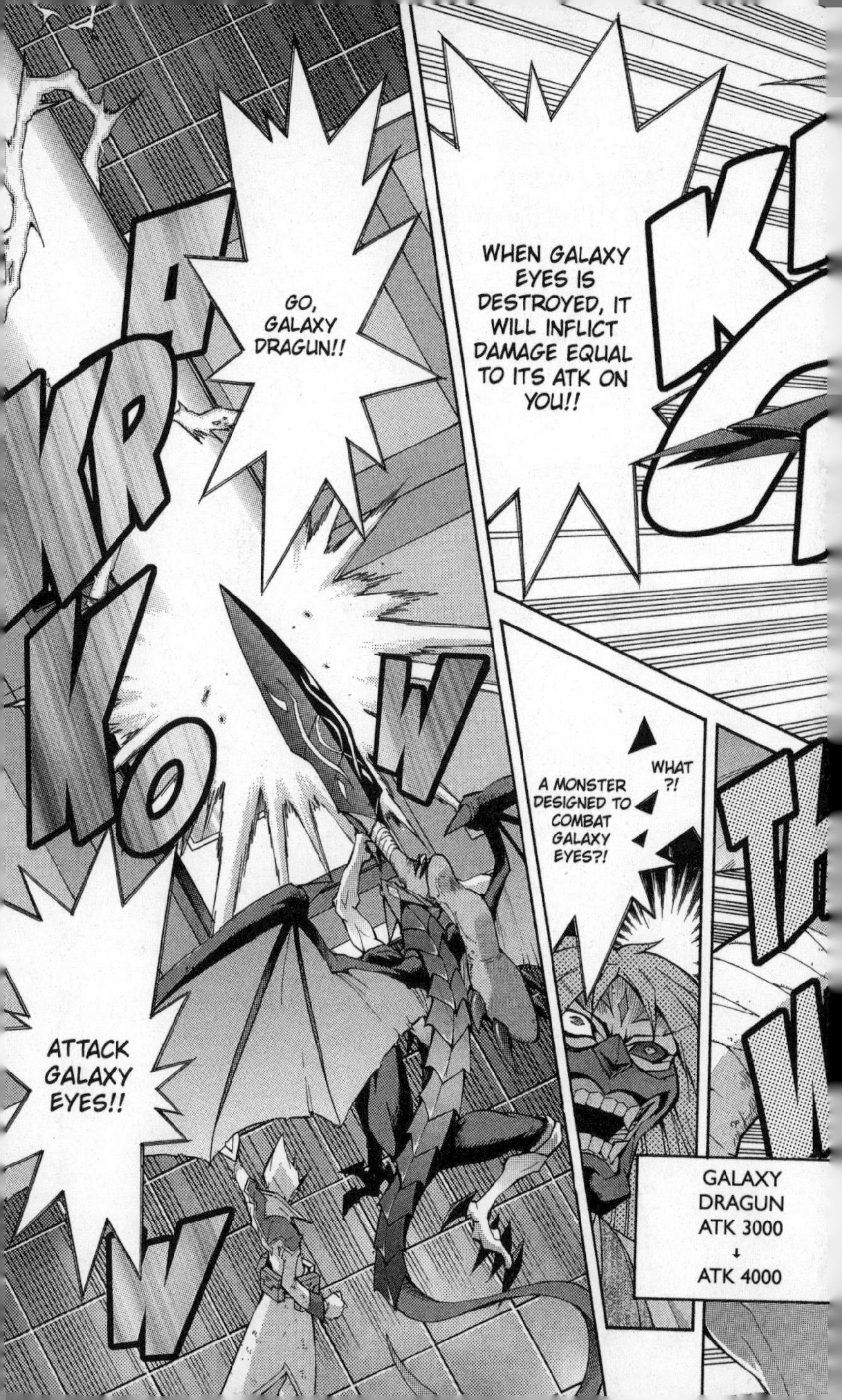
WHEN GALAXY EYES IS DESTROYED, IT WILL INFLICT DAMAGE EQUAL TO ITS ATK ON YOU!!
WHAT ?!
A MONSTER DESIGNED TO COMBAT GALAXY EYES?!
GALAXY DRAGUN ATK 3000 ↓ ATK 4000
GO, GALAXY DRAGUN!!
ATTACK GALAXY EYES!!

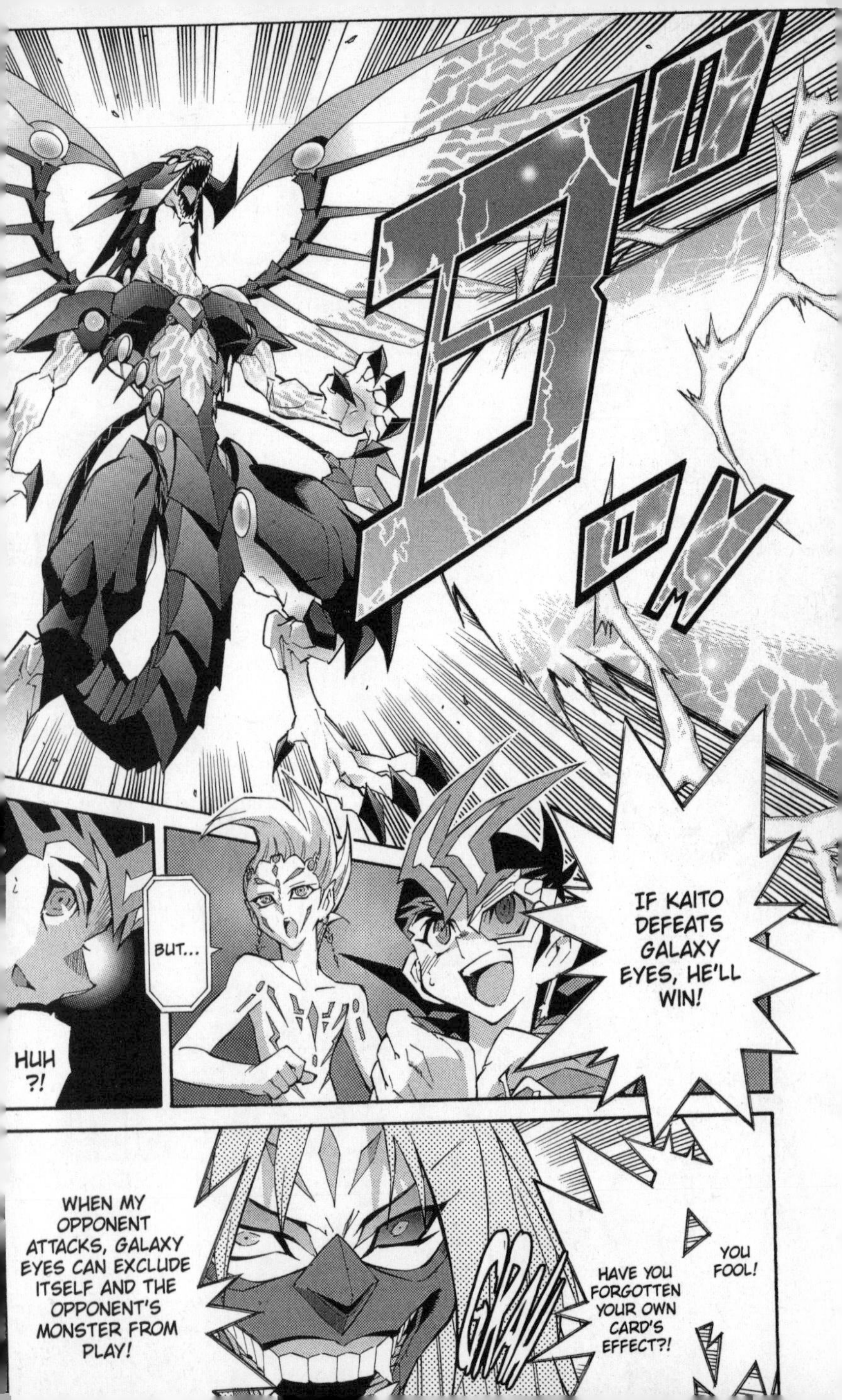
IF KAITO DEFEATS GALAXY EYES, HE'LL WIN!
BUT...
HUH ?!
YOU FOOL!
HAVE YOU FORGOTTEN YOUR OWN CARD'S EFFECT?!
WHEN MY OPPONENT ATTACKS, GALAXY EYES CAN EXCLUDE ITSELF AND THE OPPONENT'S MONSTER FROM PLAY!

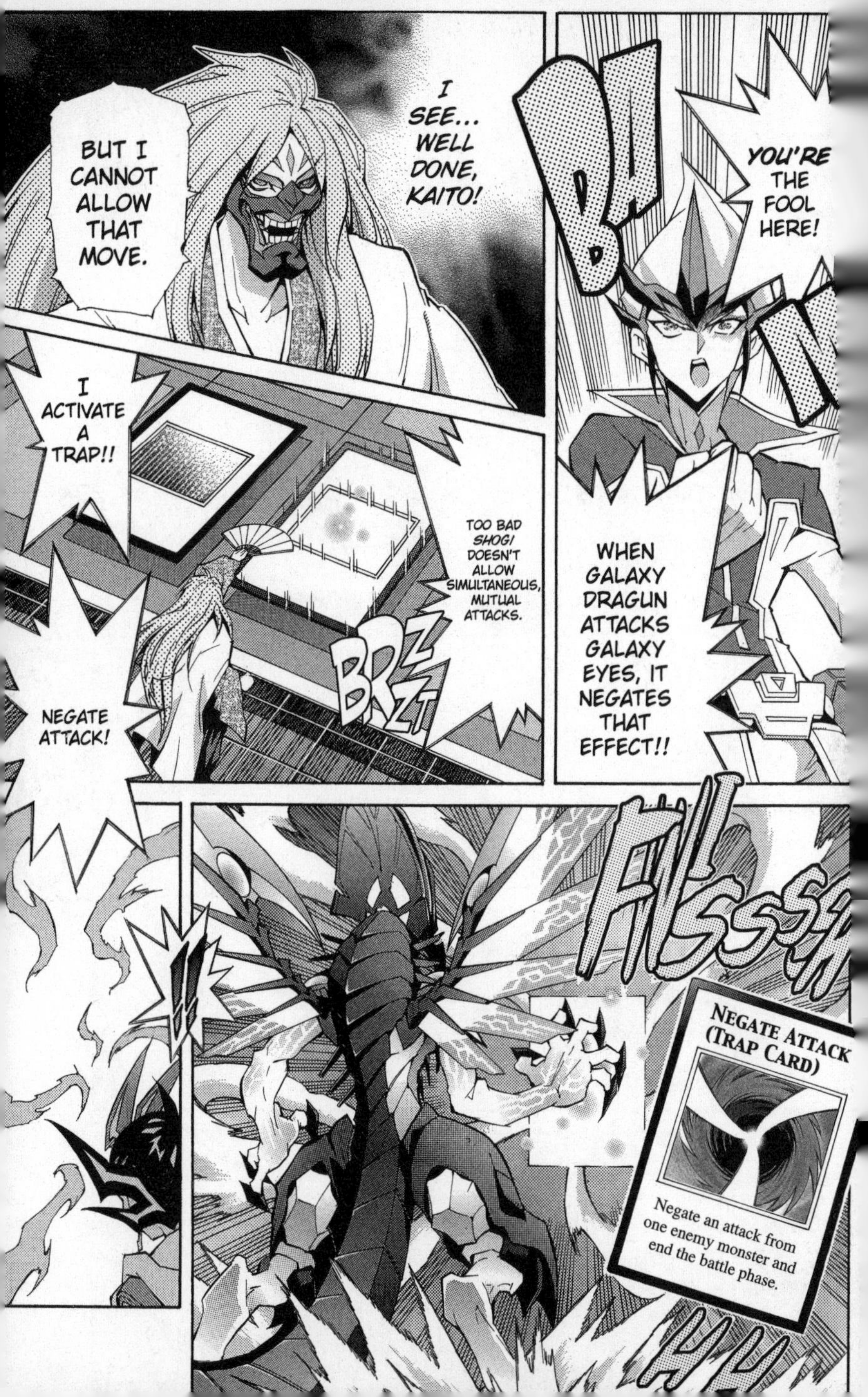
BAN
YOU'RE THE FOOL HERE!
WHEN GALAXY DRAGUN ATTACKS GALAXY EYES, IT NEGATES THAT EFFECT!!
I SEE... WELL DONE, KAITO!
BUT I CANNOT ALLOW THAT MOVE.
I ACTIVATE A TRAP!!
TOO BAD SHOGI DOESN'T ALLOW SIMULTANEOUS, MUTUAL ATTACKS.
BRZZT
NEGATE ATTACK!
FHSSSS
NEGATE ATTACK (TRAP CARD)
Negate an attack from one enemy monster and end the battle phase.
!!

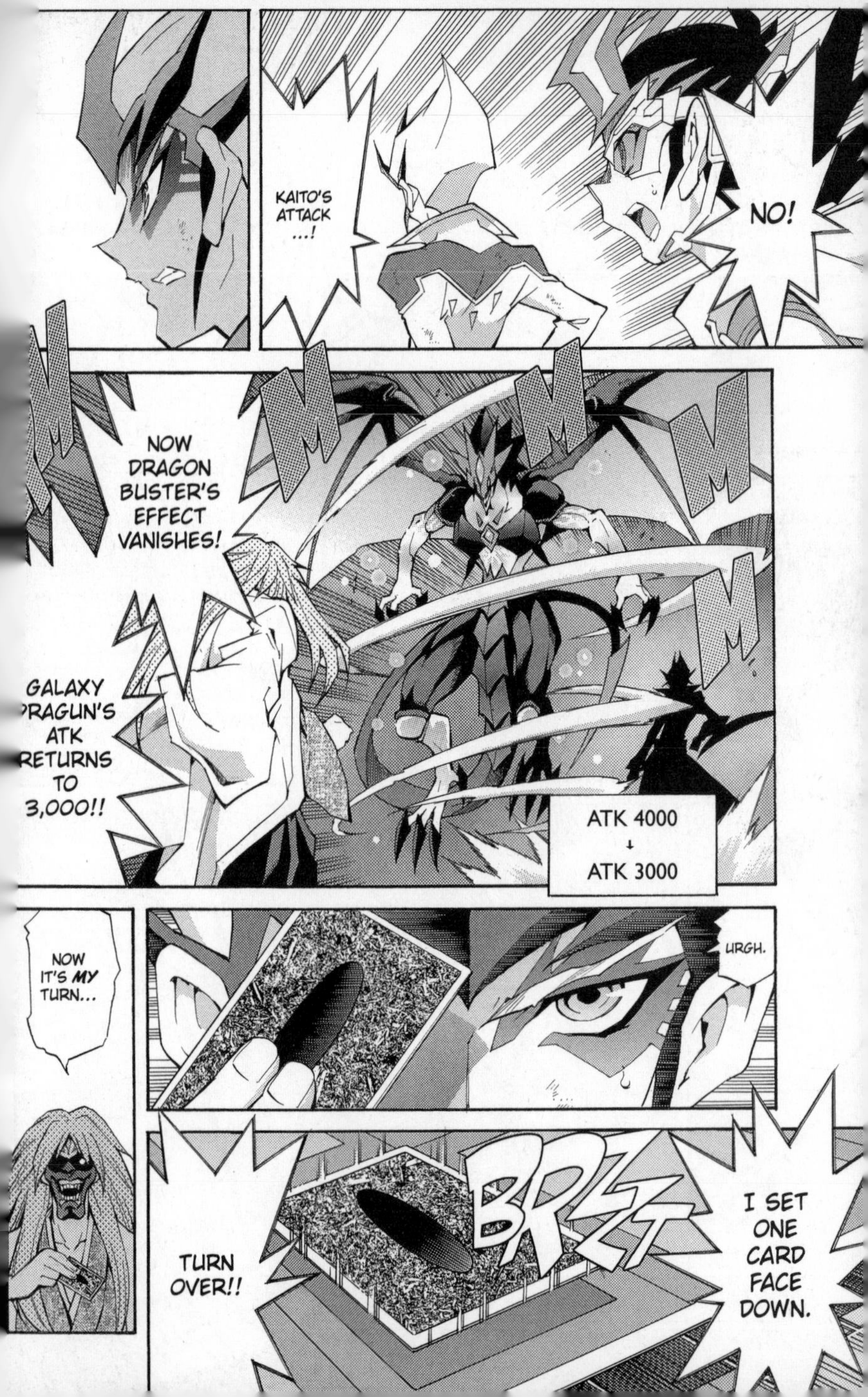
NO!
KAITO'S ATTACK ...!
NOW DRAGON BUSTER'S EFFECT VANISHES!
GALAXY PRAGUN'S ATK RETURNS TO 3,000!!
ATK 4000 ↓ ATK 3000
URGH.
NOW IT'S *MY* TURN...
BRZZT
I SET ONE CARD FACE DOWN.
TURN OVER!!

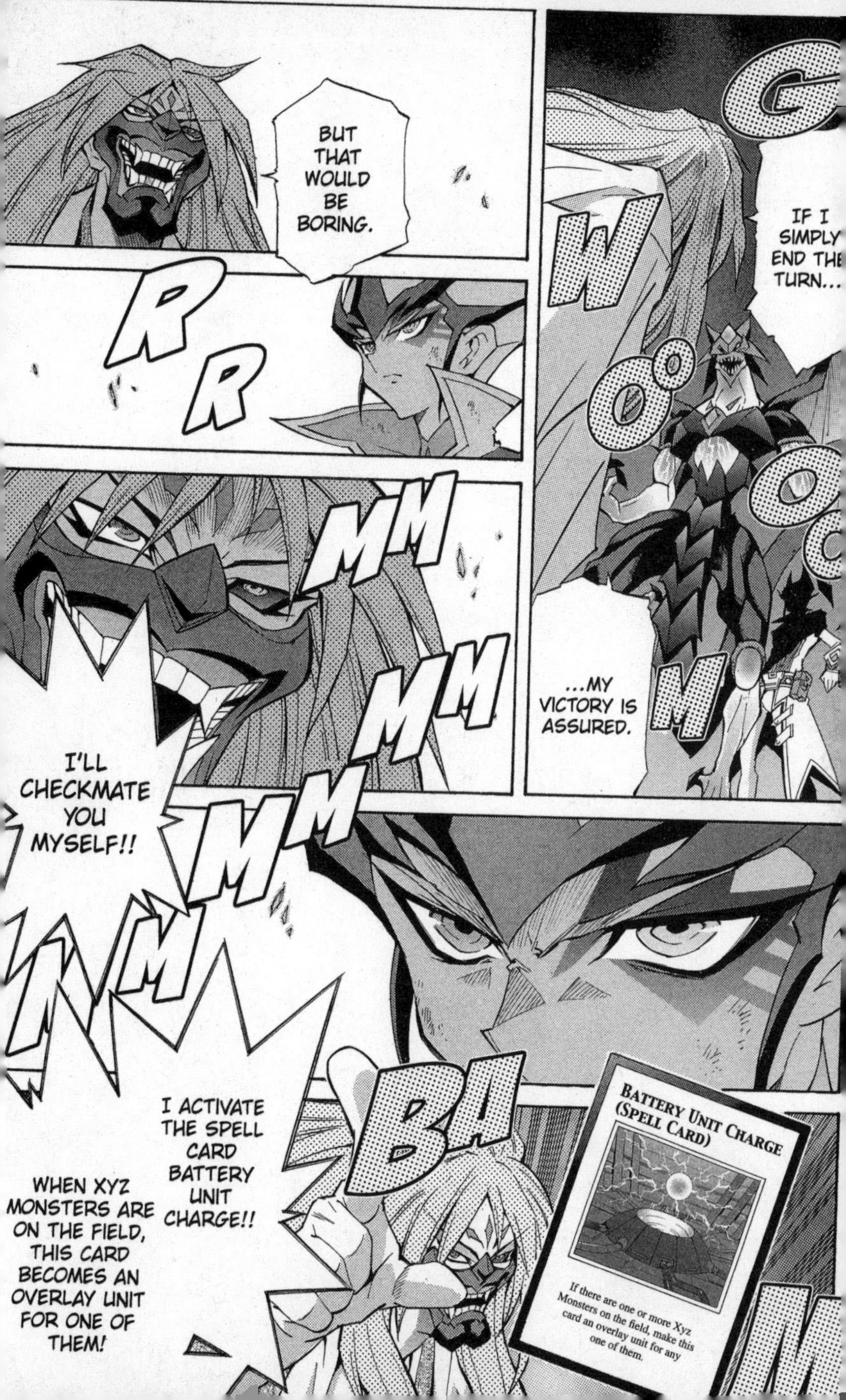

IF I SIMPLY END THE TURN...
GWOOOOM
...MY VICTORY IS ASSURED.
BUT THAT WOULD BE BORING.
RR
MMMMMMMMMM
I'LL CHECKMATE YOU MYSELF!!
BA
I ACTIVATE THE SPELL CARD BATTERY UNIT CHARGE!!
WHEN XYZ MONSTERS ARE ON THE FIELD, THIS CARD BECOMES AN OVERLAY UNIT FOR ONE OF THEM!
BATTERY UNIT CHARGE (SPELL CARD)
If there are one or more Xyz Monsters on the field, make this card an overlay unit for any one of them.

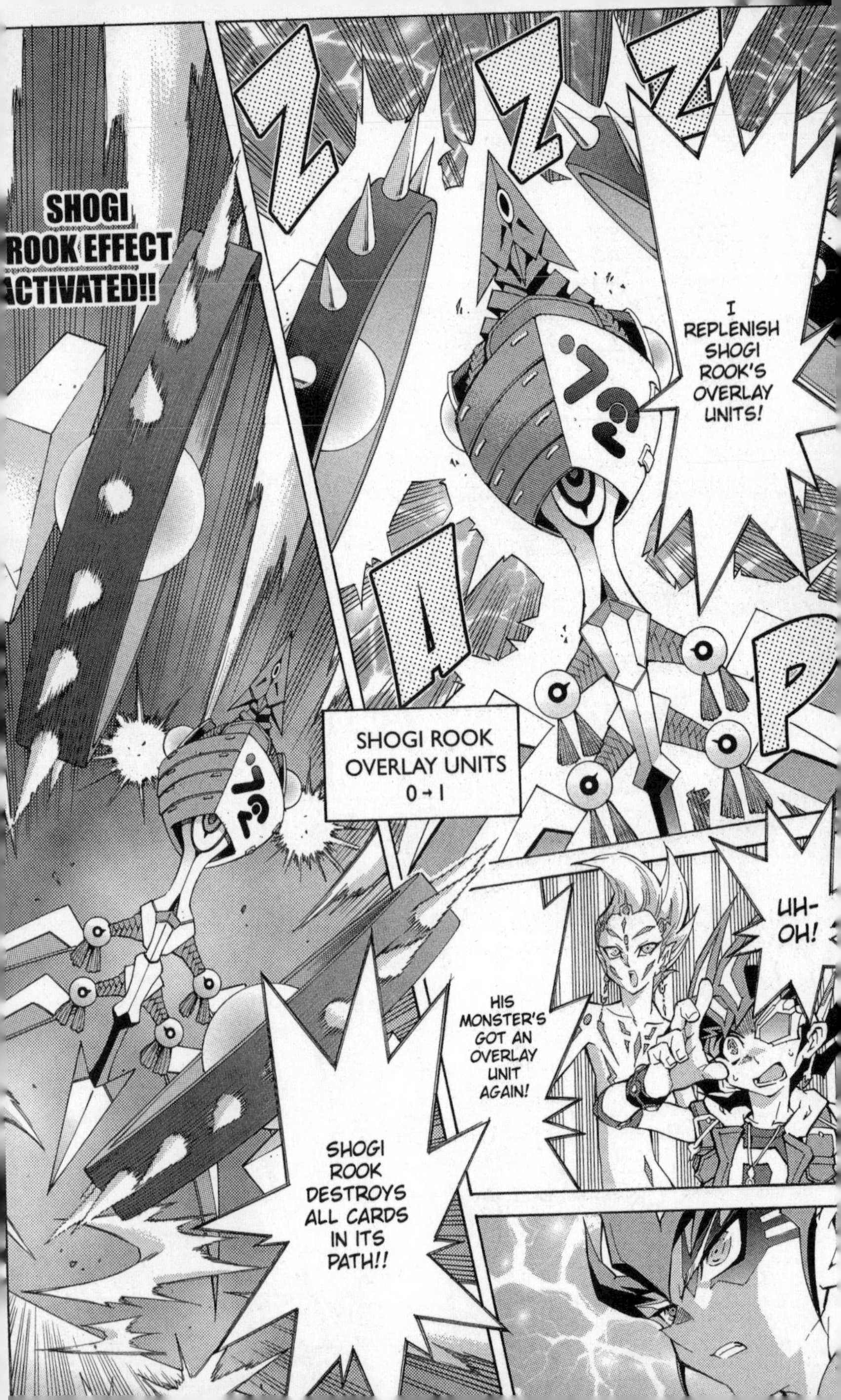

ZZZAP
I REPLENISH SHOGI ROOK'S OVERLAY UNITS!
SHOGI ROOK OVERLAY UNITS 0→1
UH-OH!
HIS MONSTER'S GOT AN OVERLAY UNIT AGAIN!
SHOGI ROOK EFFECT ACTIVATED!!
SHOGI ROOK DESTROYS ALL CARDS IN ITS PATH!!

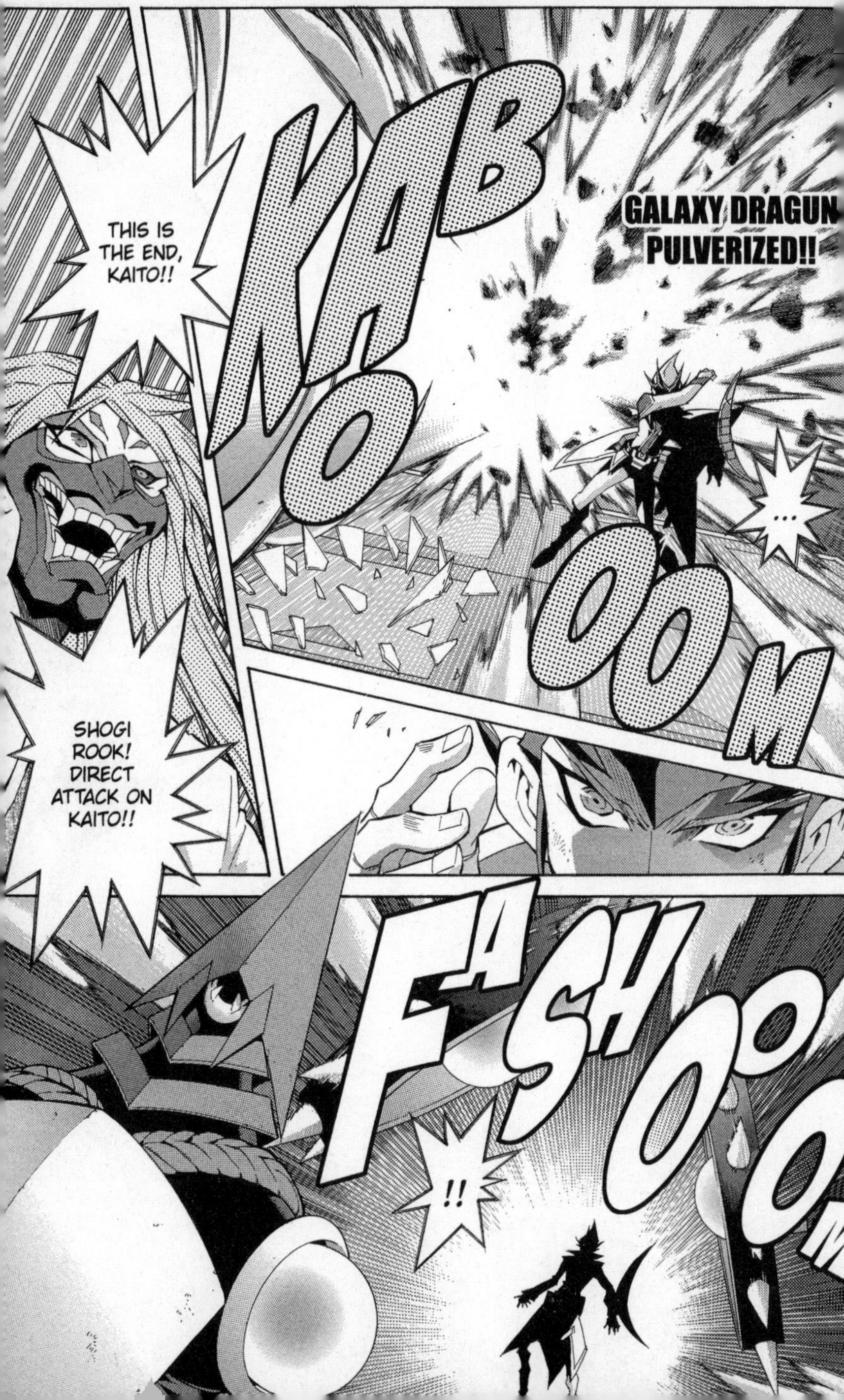
GALAXY DRAGUN PULVERIZED!!
KABOOOOOM
...
THIS IS THE END, KAITO!!
SHOGI ROOK! DIRECT ATTACK ON KAITO!!
FASHOOOOM
!!

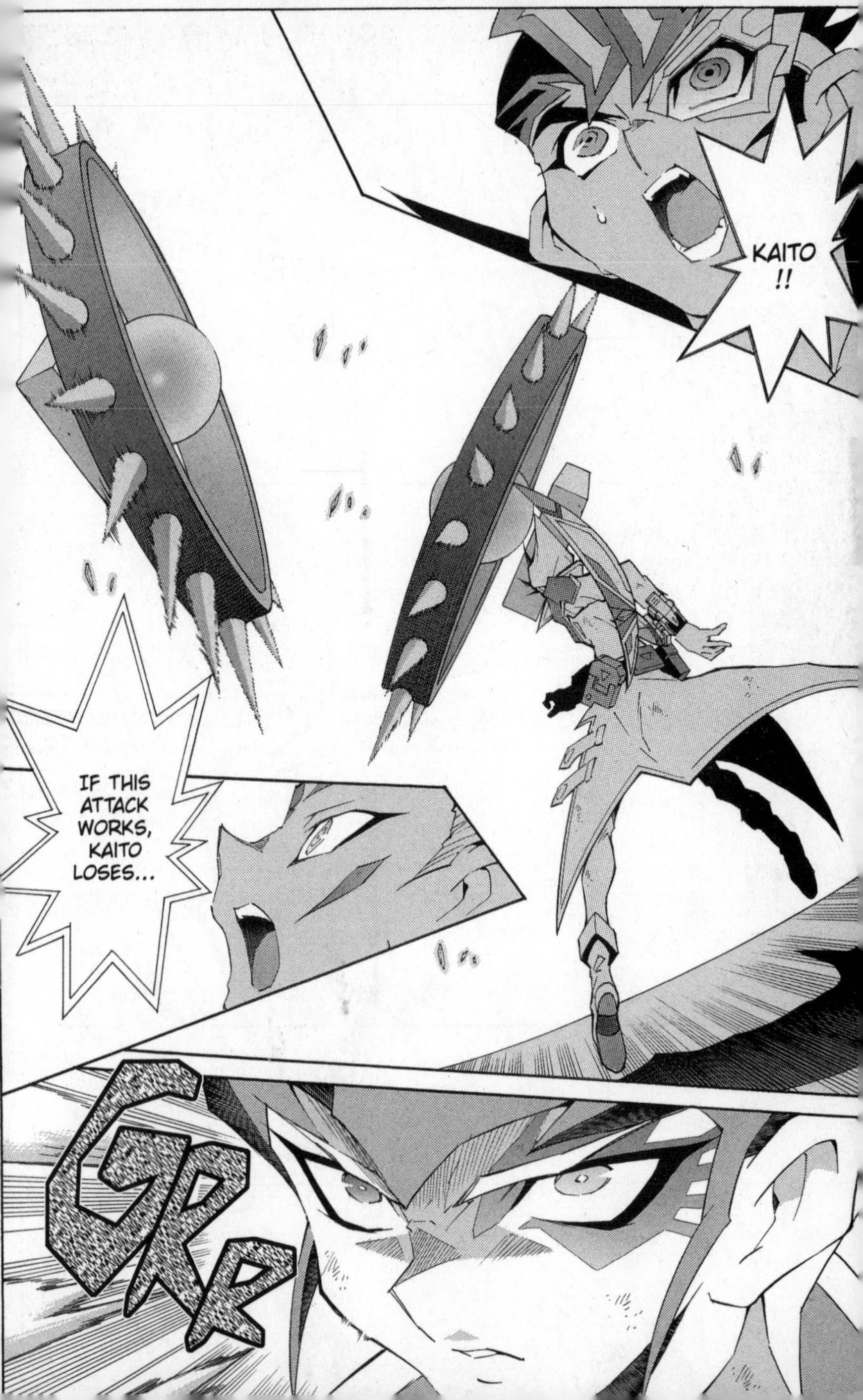
KAITO !!
IF THIS ATTACK WORKS, KAITO LOSES...
GRR

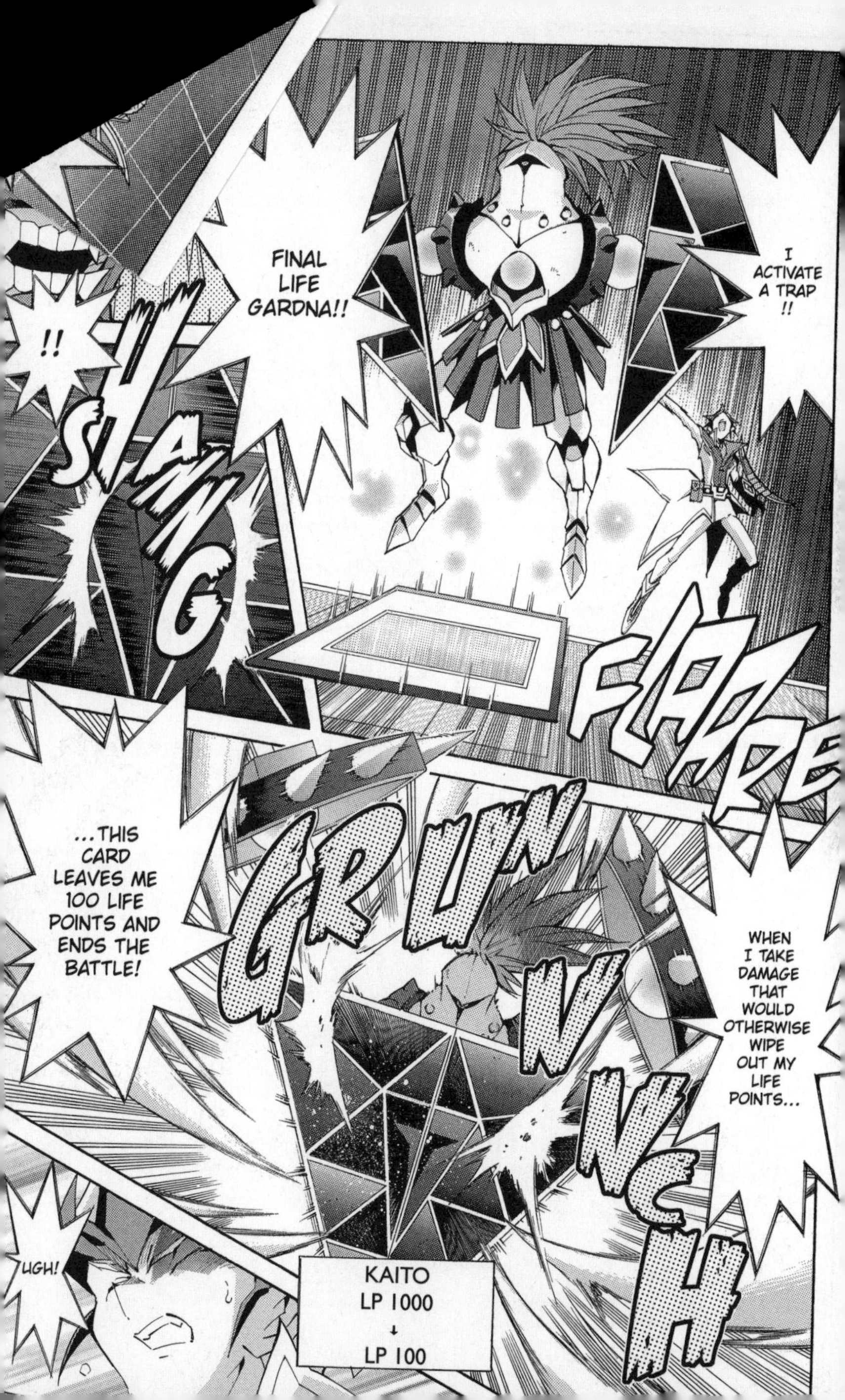
I ACTIVATE A TRAP!!
FINAL LIFE GARDNA!!
!!
SLANG
FLARE
WHEN I TAKE DAMAGE THAT WOULD OTHERWISE WIPE OUT MY LIFE POINTS...
...THIS CARD LEAVES ME 100 LIFE POINTS AND ENDS THE BATTLE!
GRUNNNCH
KAITO LP 1000 ↓ LP 100
UGH!

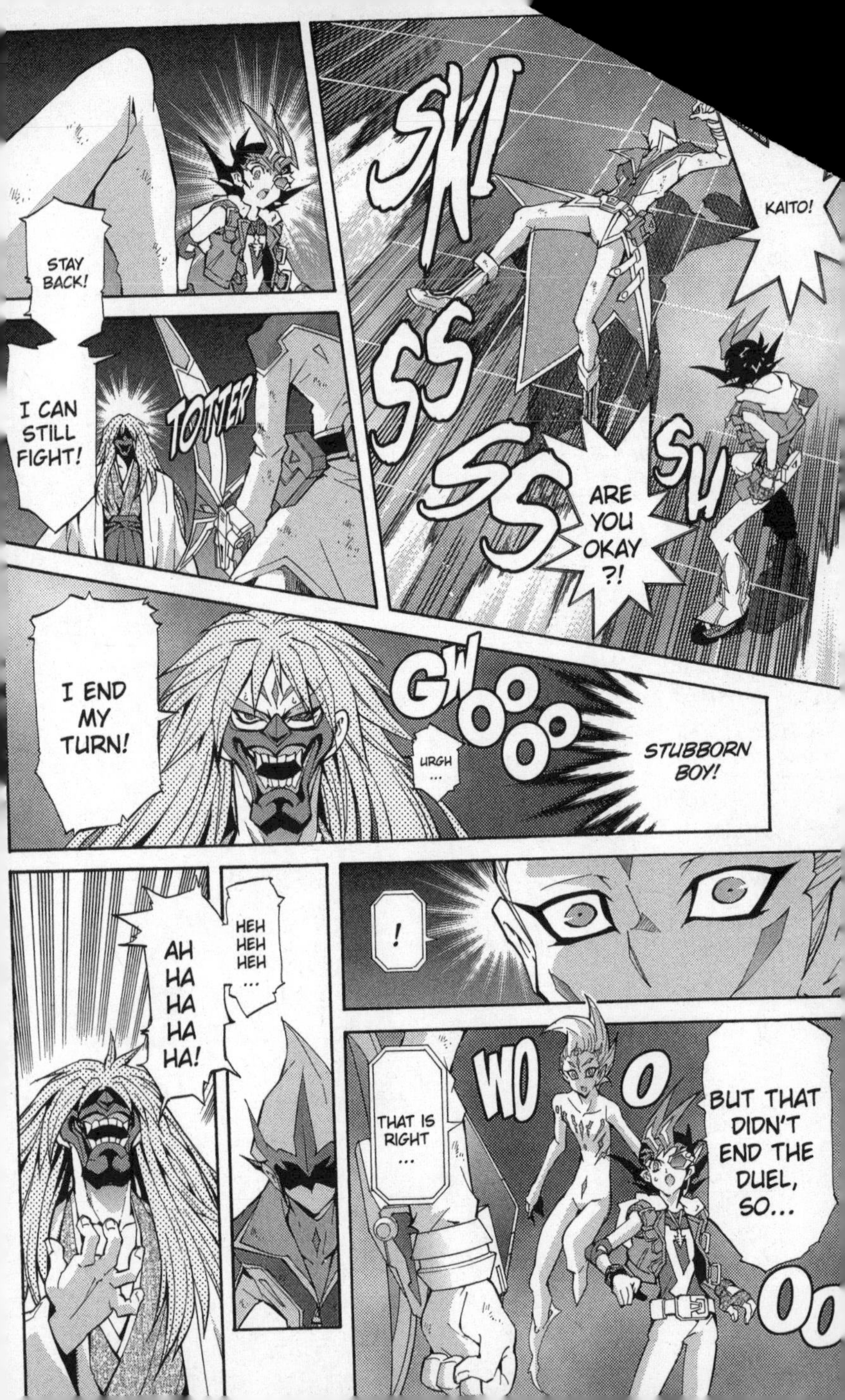
KAITO!
SWI
SS
SS
SU
ARE YOU OKAY?!
STAY BACK!
TOTTER
I CAN STILL FIGHT!
GWOOOOO
STUBBORN BOY!
URGH...
I END MY TURN!
!
BUT THAT DIDN'T END THE DUEL, SO...
WO
O
OO
THAT IS RIGHT...
HEH HEH HEH...
AH HA HA HA HA!

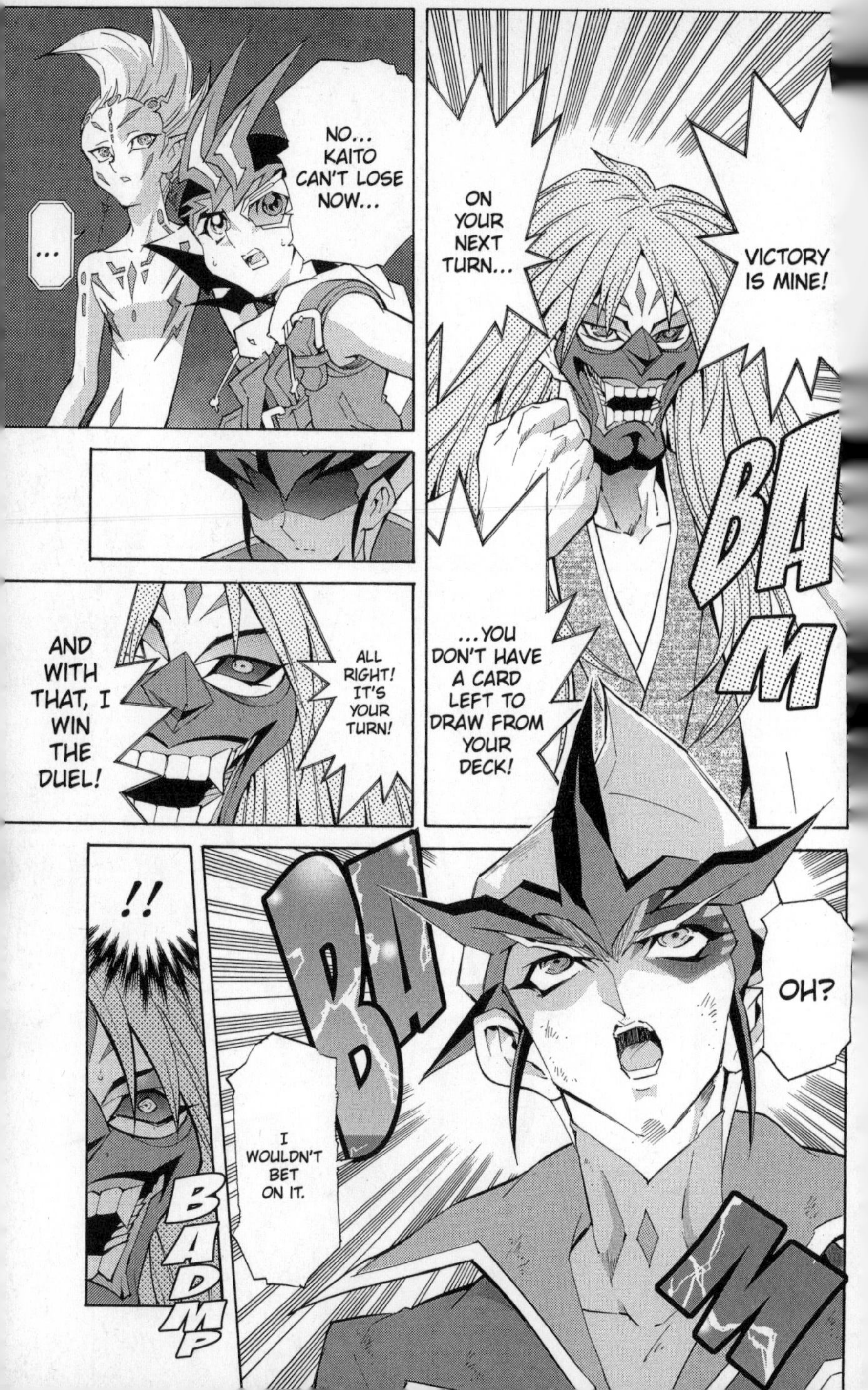
ON YOUR NEXT TURN...
...YOU DON'T HAVE A CARD LEFT TO DRAW FROM YOUR DECK!
VICTORY IS MINE!
BAM
NO... KAITO CAN'T LOSE NOW...
...
ALL RIGHT! IT'S YOUR TURN!
AND WITH THAT, I WIN THE DUEL!
OH?
BAM
I WOULDN'T BET ON IT.
!!
BADMP

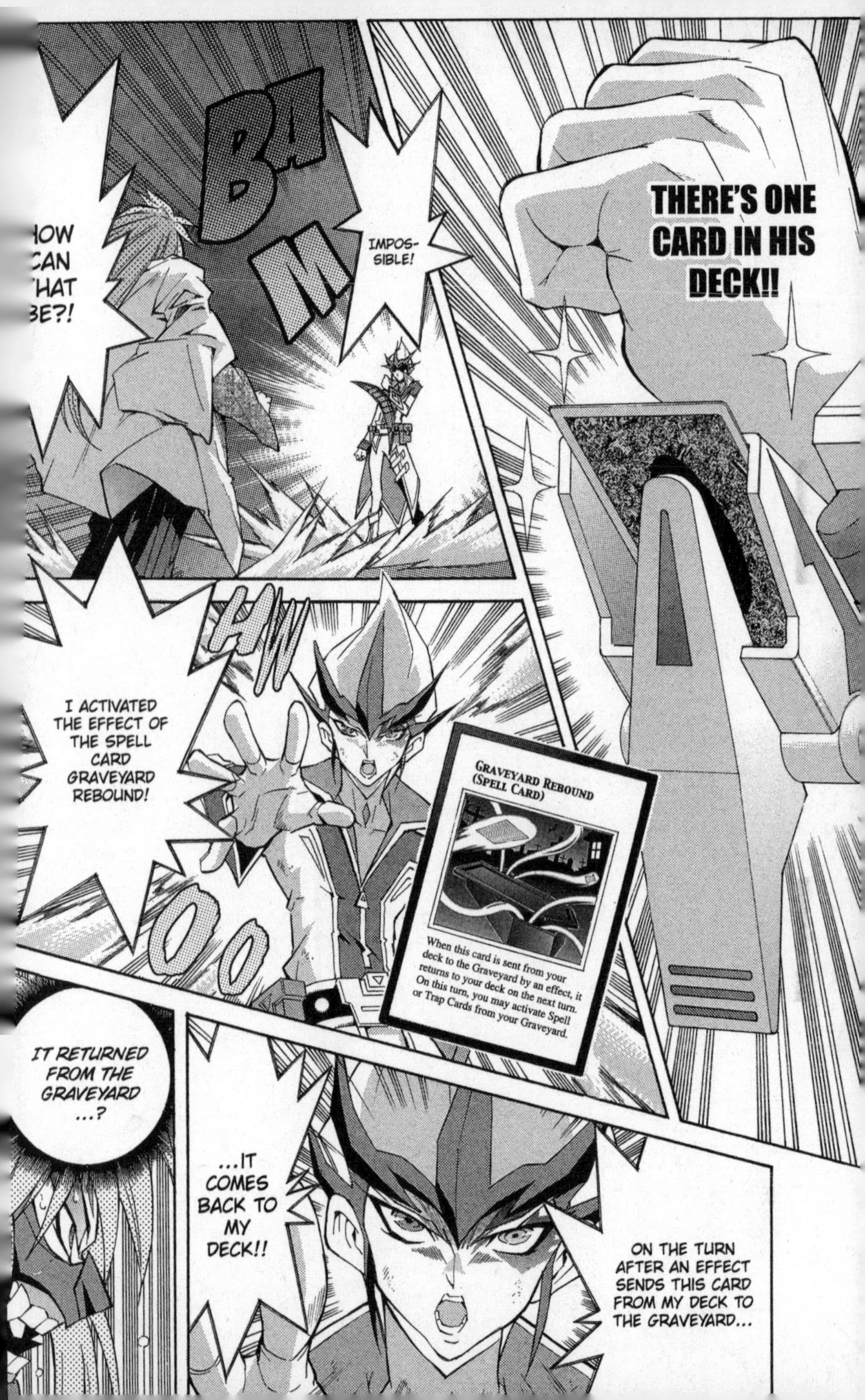
THERE'S ONE CARD IN HIS DECK!!
BAM
IMPOS-SIBLE!
HOW CAN THAT BE?!
I ACTIVATED THE EFFECT OF THE SPELL CARD GRAVEYARD REBOUND!
GRAVEYARD REBOUND (SPELL CARD)
When this card is sent from your deck to the Graveyard by an effect, it returns to your deck on the next turn. On this turn, you may activate Spell or Trap Cards from your Graveyard.
ON THE TURN AFTER AN EFFECT SENDS THIS CARD FROM MY DECK TO THE GRAVEYARD...
...IT COMES BACK TO MY DECK!!
IT RETURNED FROM THE GRAVEYARD...?

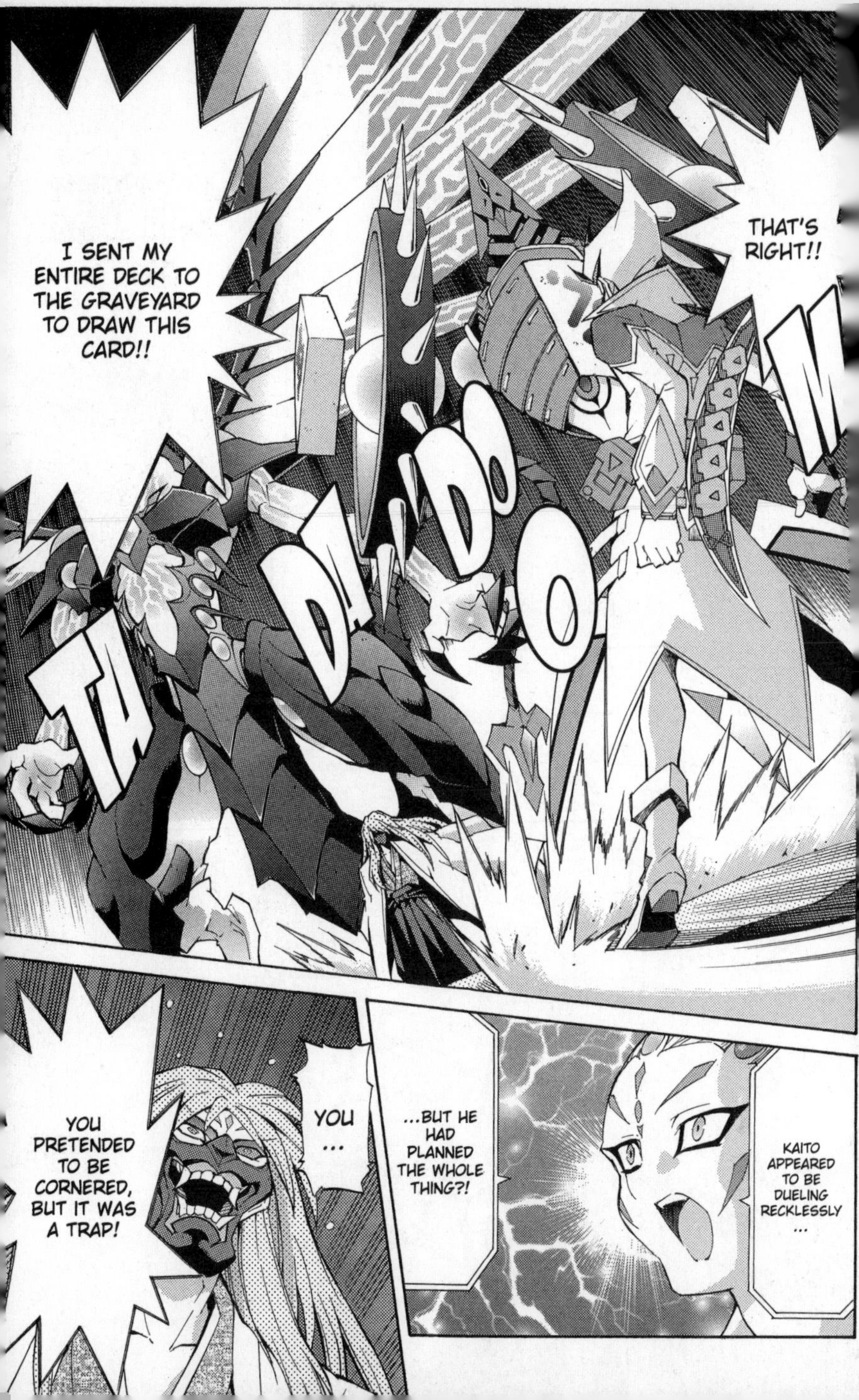
THAT'S RIGHT!!
I SENT MY ENTIRE DECK TO THE GRAVEYARD TO DRAW THIS CARD!!
KAITO APPEARED TO BE DUELING RECKLESSLY ...
...BUT HE HAD PLANNED THE WHOLE THING?!
YOU ...
YOU PRETENDED TO BE CORNERED, BUT IT WAS A TRAP!

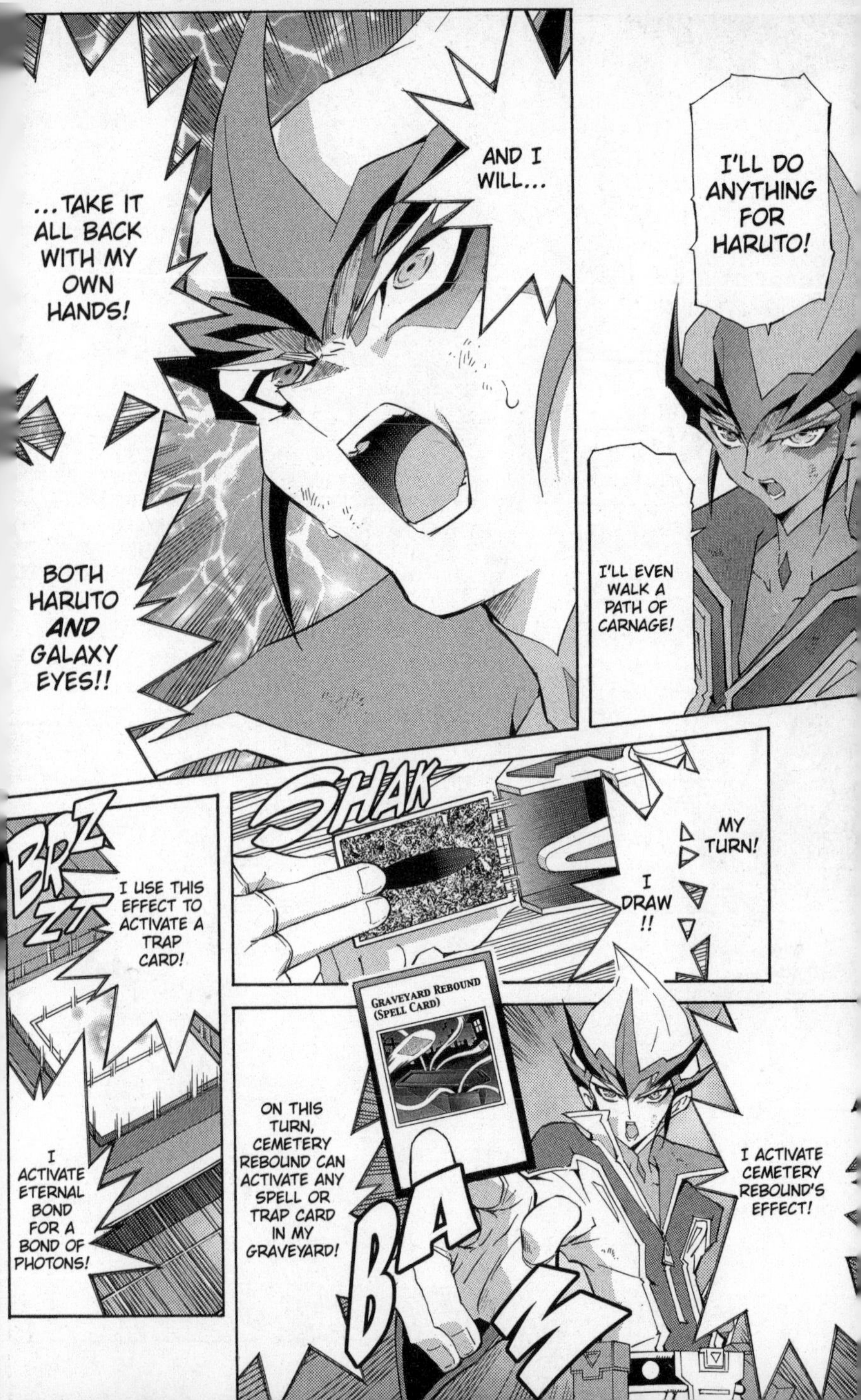
I'LL DO ANYTHING FOR HARUTO!
I'LL EVEN WALK A PATH OF CARNAGE!
AND I WILL...
...TAKE IT ALL BACK WITH MY OWN HANDS!
BOTH HARUTO AND GALAXY EYES!!
MY TURN!
I DRAW!!
SHAK
GRAVEYARD REBOUND (SPELL CARD)
I ACTIVATE CEMETERY REBOUND'S EFFECT!
ON THIS TURN, CEMETERY REBOUND CAN ACTIVATE ANY SPELL OR TRAP CARD IN MY GRAVEYARD!
BAM
BRZZT
I USE THIS EFFECT TO ACTIVATE A TRAP CARD!
I ACTIVATE ETERNAL BOND FOR A BOND OF PHOTONS!

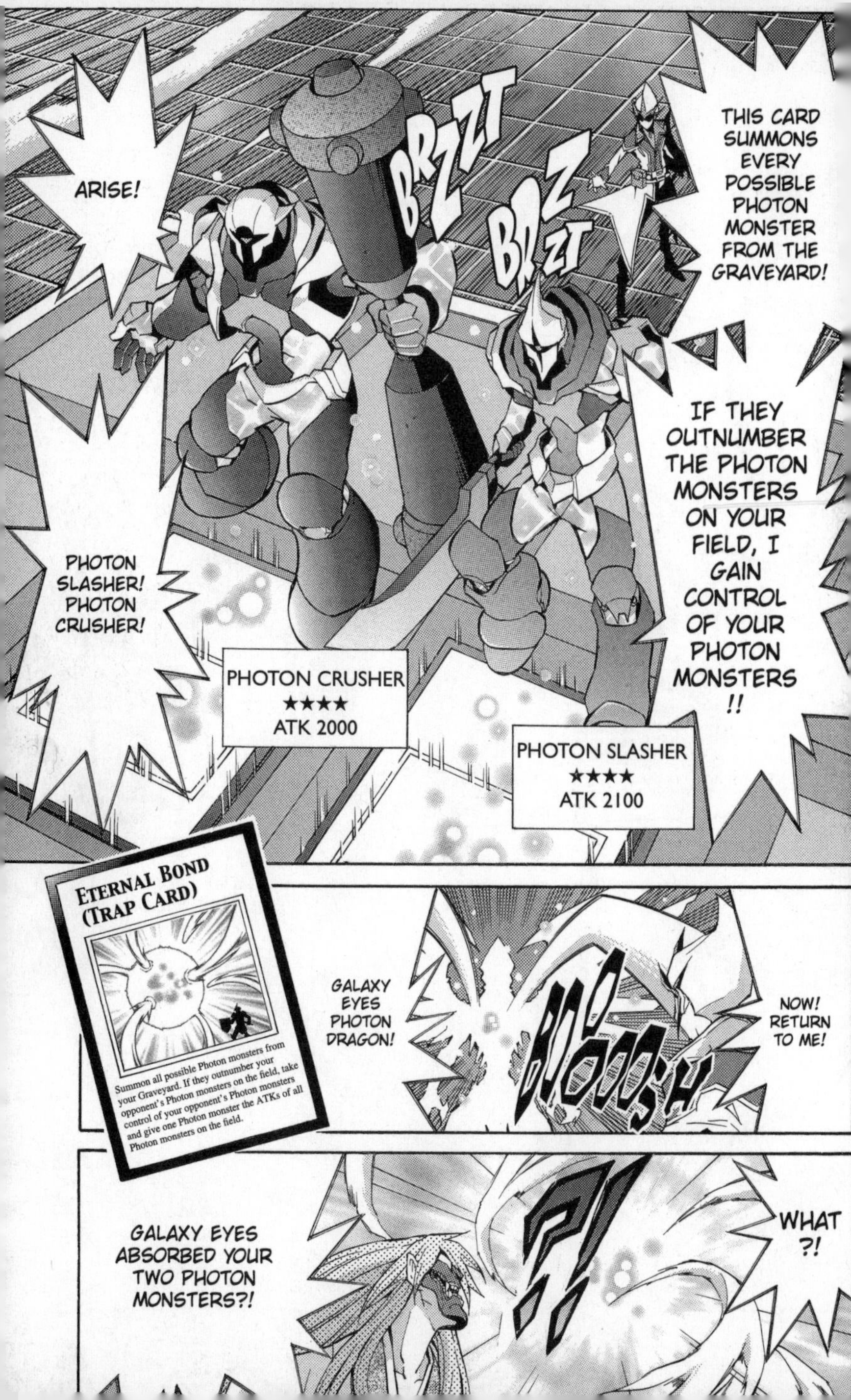
THIS CARD SUMMONS EVERY POSSIBLE PHOTON MONSTER FROM THE GRAVEYARD!
BRZZZT
BRZZT
ARISE!
IF THEY OUTNUMBER THE PHOTON MONSTERS ON YOUR FIELD, I GAIN CONTROL OF YOUR PHOTON MONSTERS!!
PHOTON SLASHER! PHOTON CRUSHER!
PHOTON SLASHER ★★★★ ATK 2100
PHOTON CRUSHER ★★★★ ATK 2000
ETERNAL BOND (TRAP CARD)
Summon all possible Photon monsters from your Graveyard. If they outnumber your opponent's Photon monsters on the field, take control of your opponent's Photon monsters and give one Photon monster the ATKs of all Photon monsters on the field.
NOW! RETURN TO ME!
GALAXY EYES PHOTON DRAGON!
WHAT?!
?!
GALAXY EYES ABSORBED YOUR TWO PHOTON MONSTERS?!

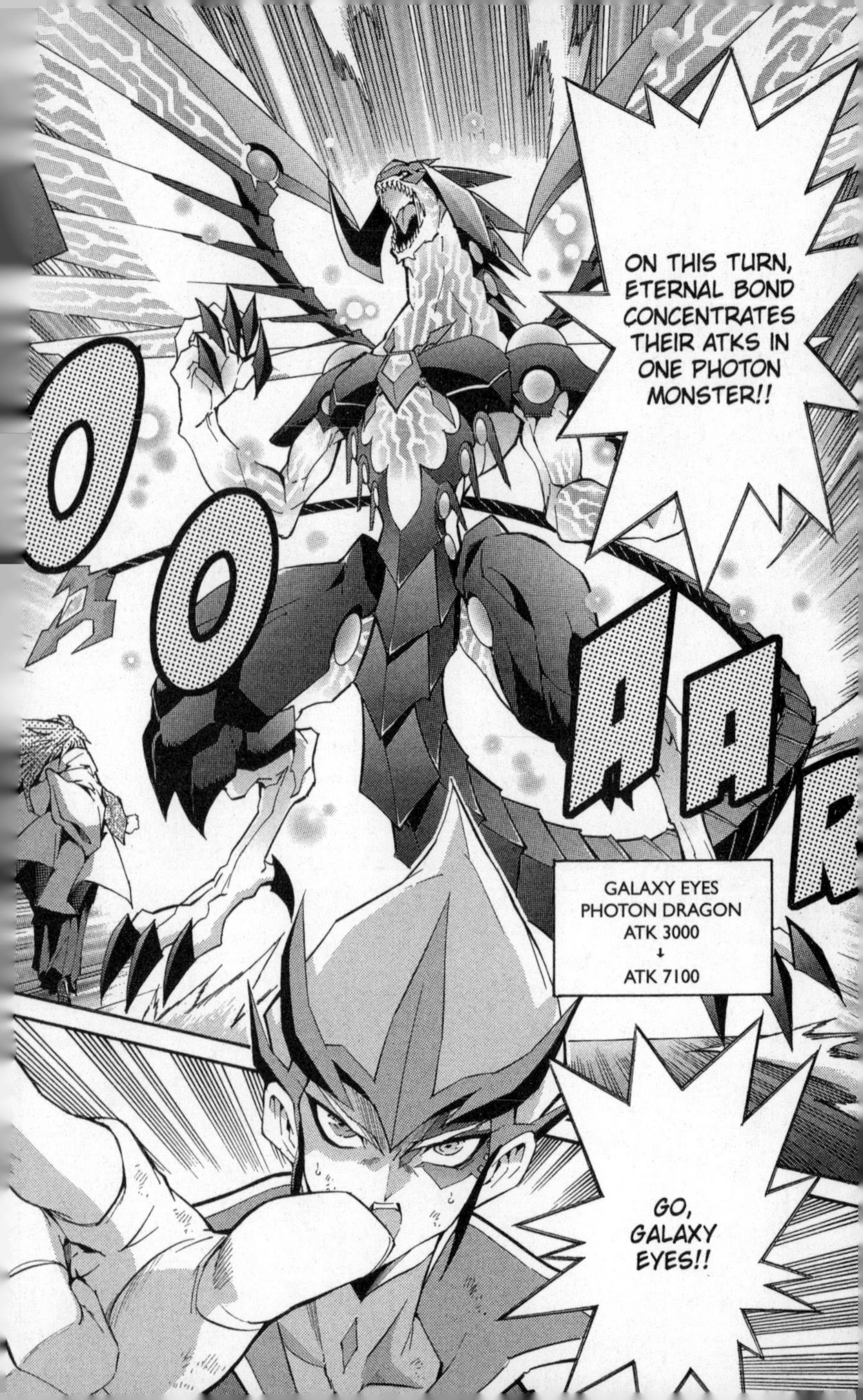
ON THIS TURN, ETERNAL BOND CONCENTRATES THEIR ATKS IN ONE PHOTON MONSTER!!
OO AAR
GALAXY EYES PHOTON DRAGON ATK 3000 ↓ ATK 7100
GO, GALAXY EYES!!

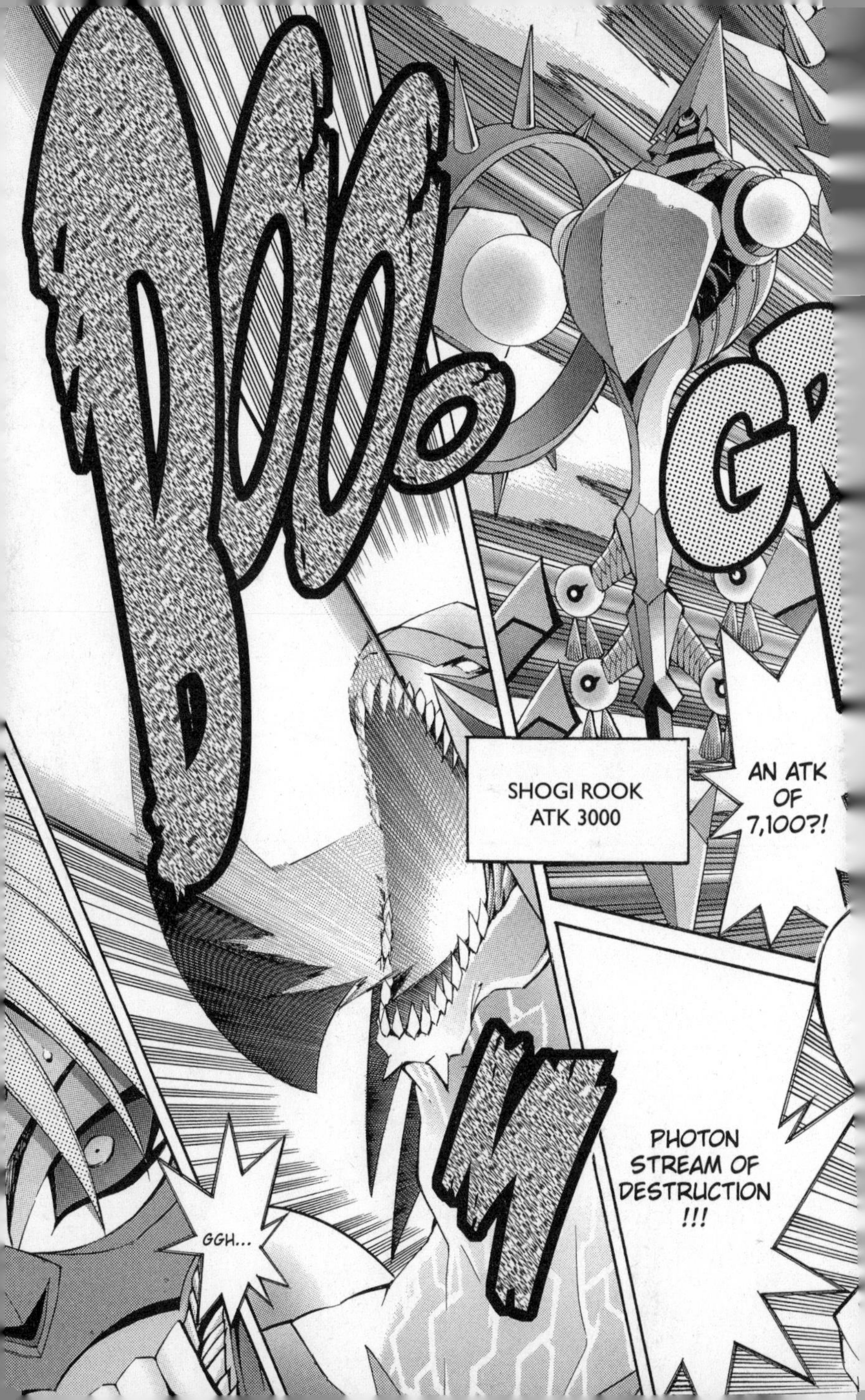
AN ATK OF 7,100?!
SHOGI ROOK ATK 3000
PHOTON STREAM OF DESTRUCTION !!!
GGH...

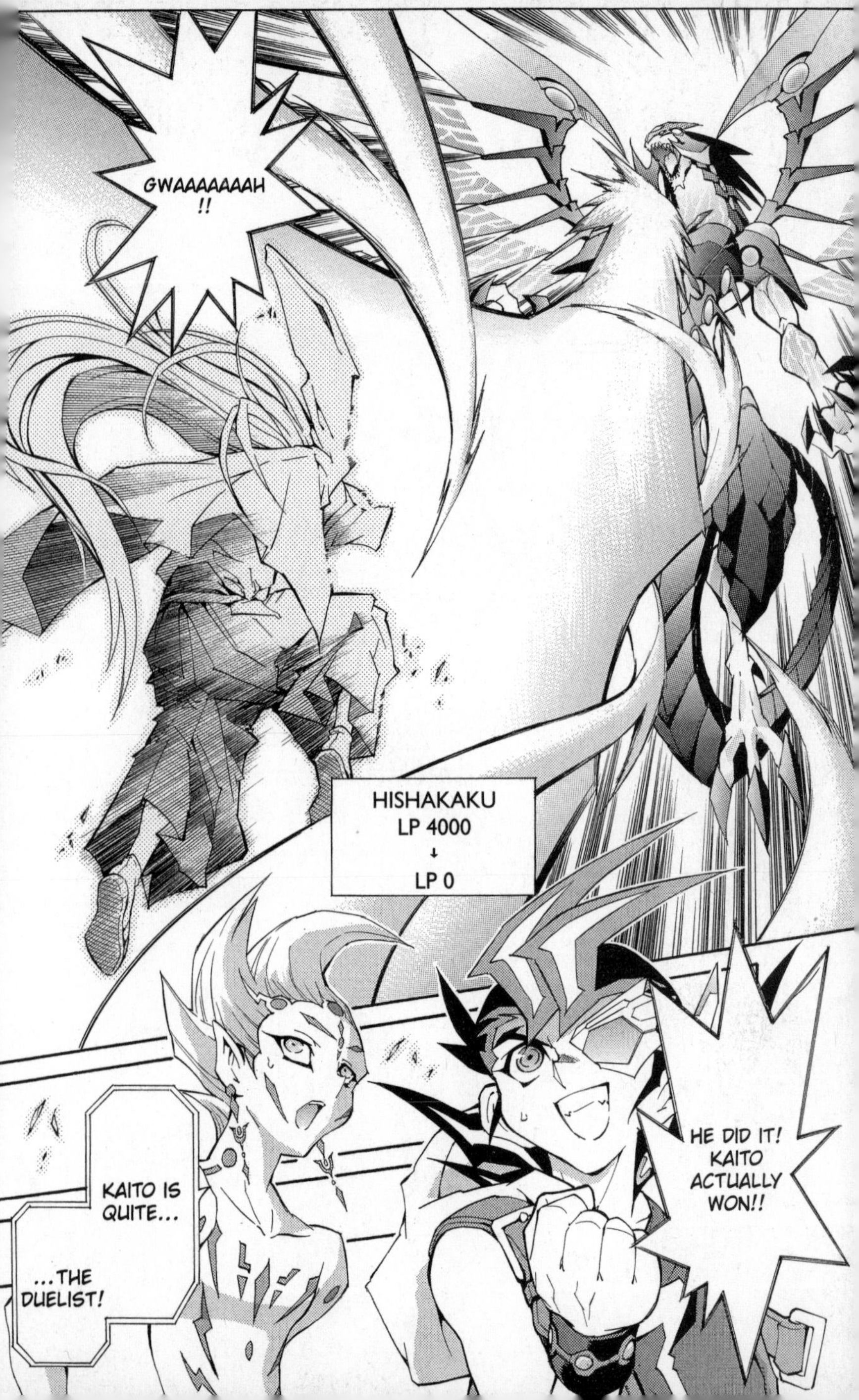
GWAAAAAAAH!!
HISHAKAKU LP 4000 ↓ LP 0
HE DID IT! KAITO ACTUALLY WON!!
KAITO IS QUITE...
...THE DUELIST!

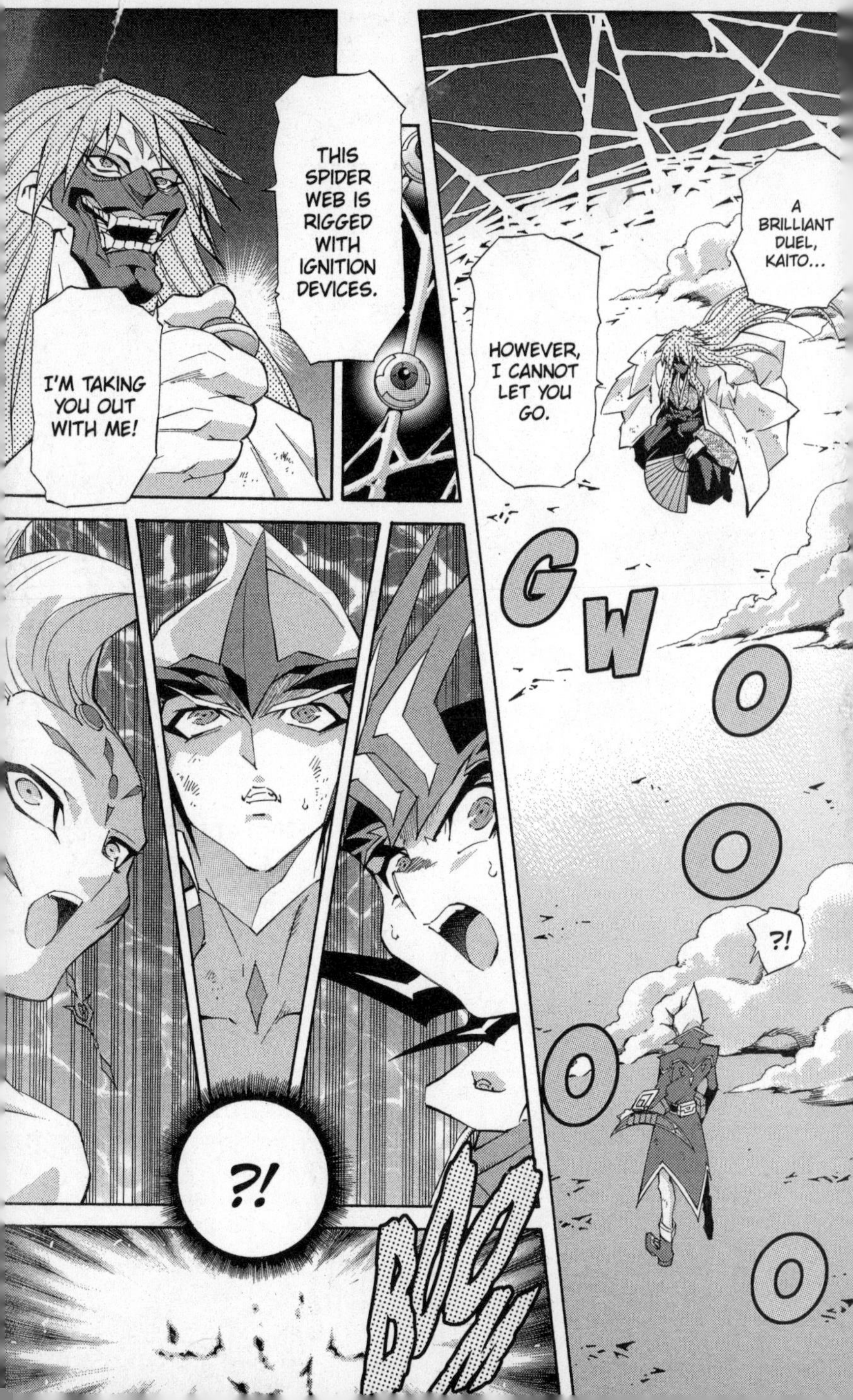
A BRILLIANT DUEL, KAITO...
HOWEVER, I CANNOT LET YOU GO.
GWOOOO
?!
THIS SPIDER WEB IS RIGGED WITH IGNITION DEVICES.
I'M TAKING YOU OUT WITH ME!
?!
BOOM

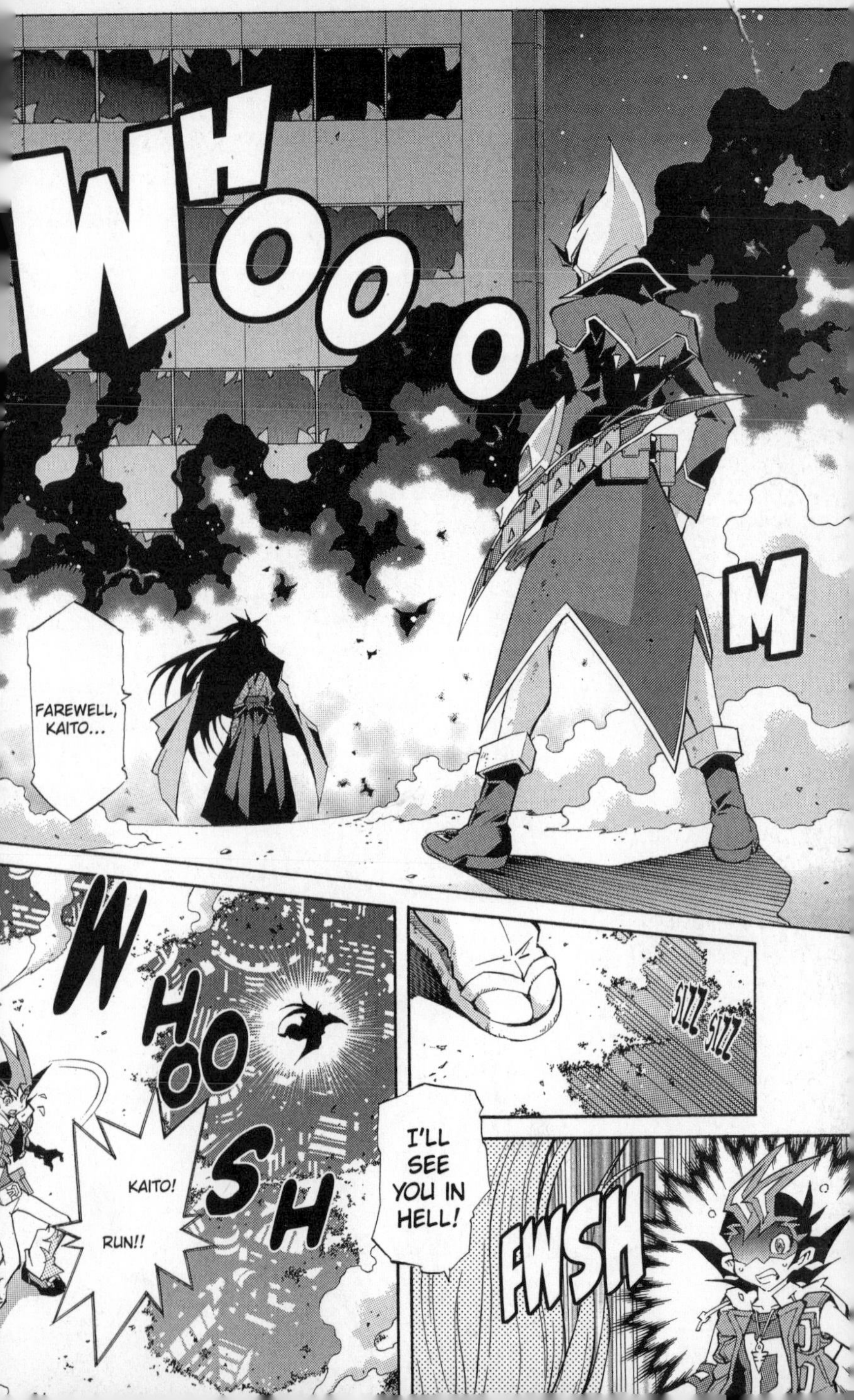
WHOOOOM
FAREWELL, KAITO...
SIZZ SIZZ
I'LL SEE YOU IN HELL!
FWSH
WHOOSH
KAITO!
RUN!!

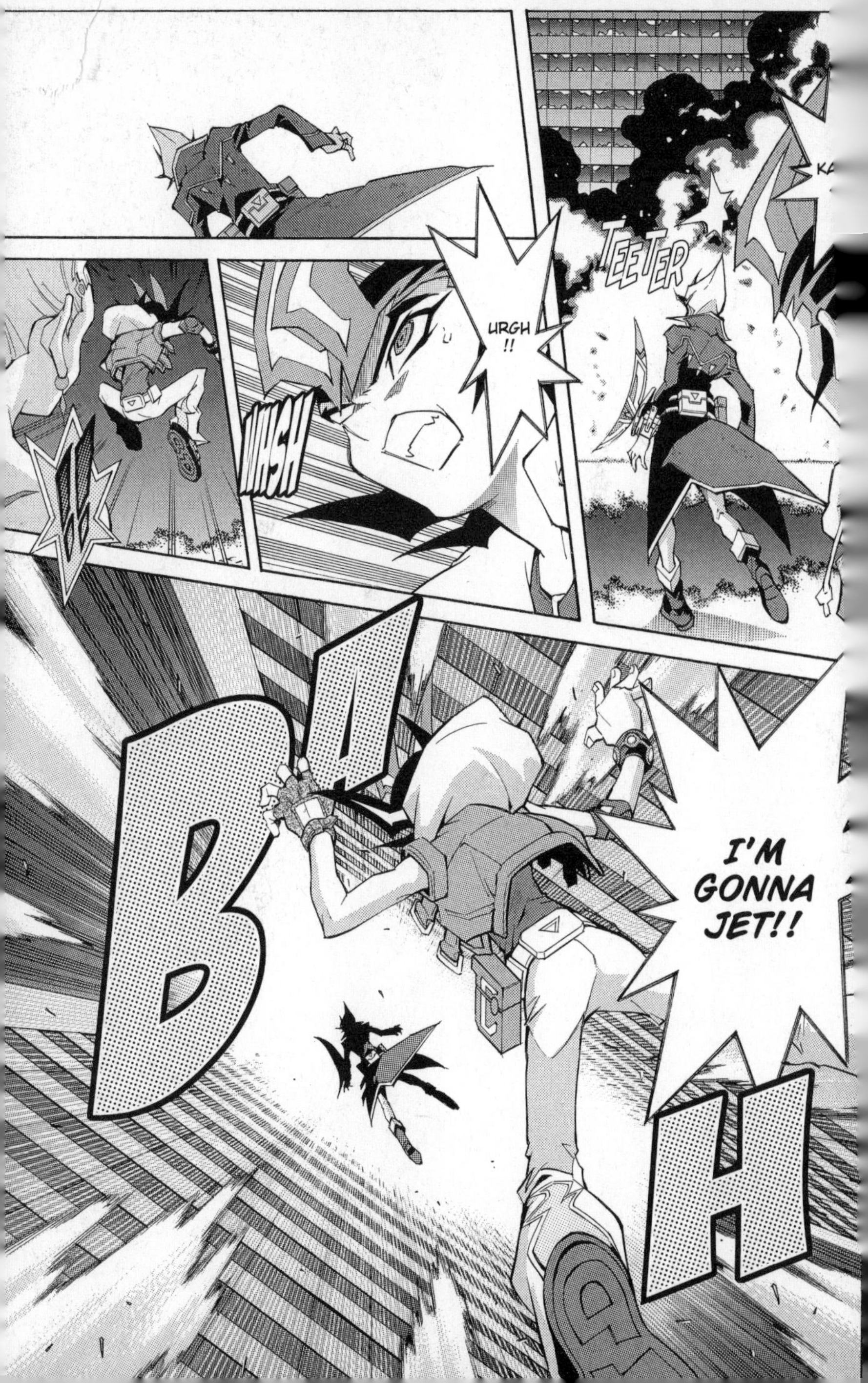
TEETER
URGH!!
WHSH
I'M GONNA JET!!
BAH

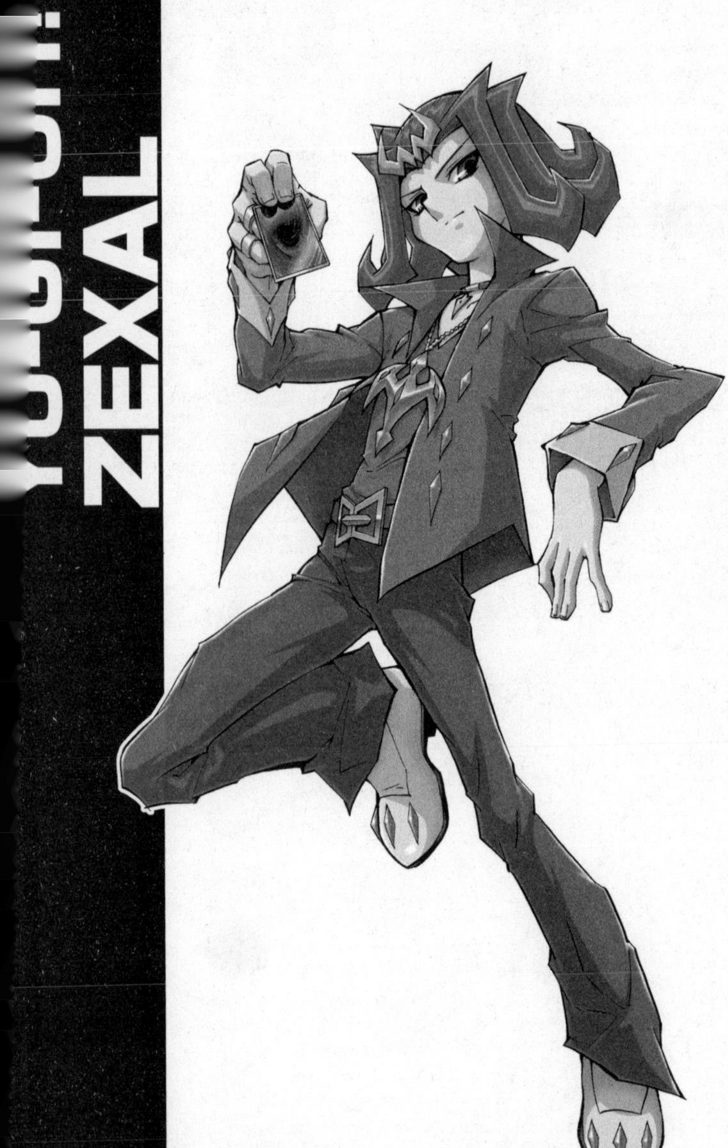
ZEXAL

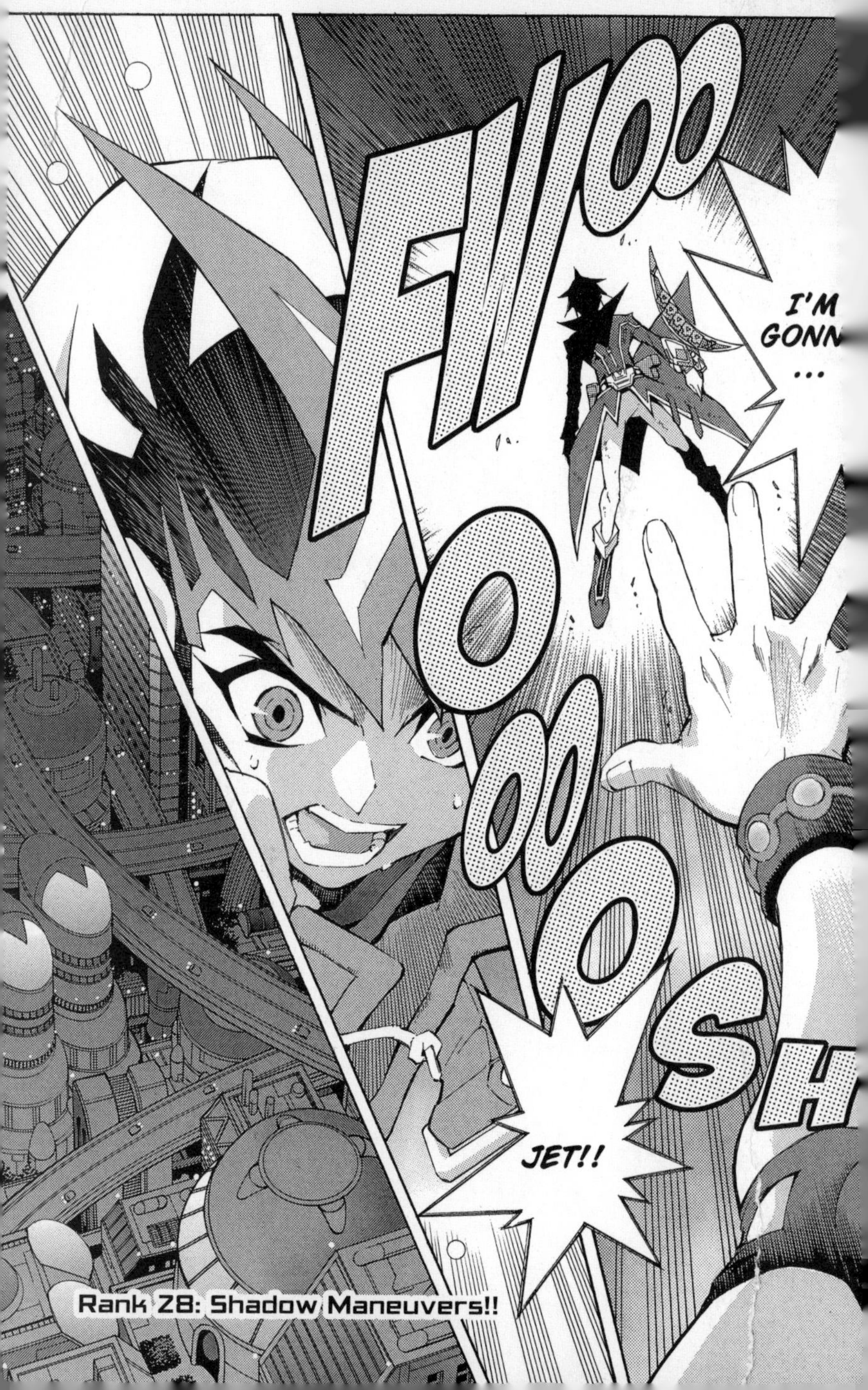
I'M GONN
...
FWOOOOOOSH
JET!!
Rank 28: Shadow Maneuvers!!

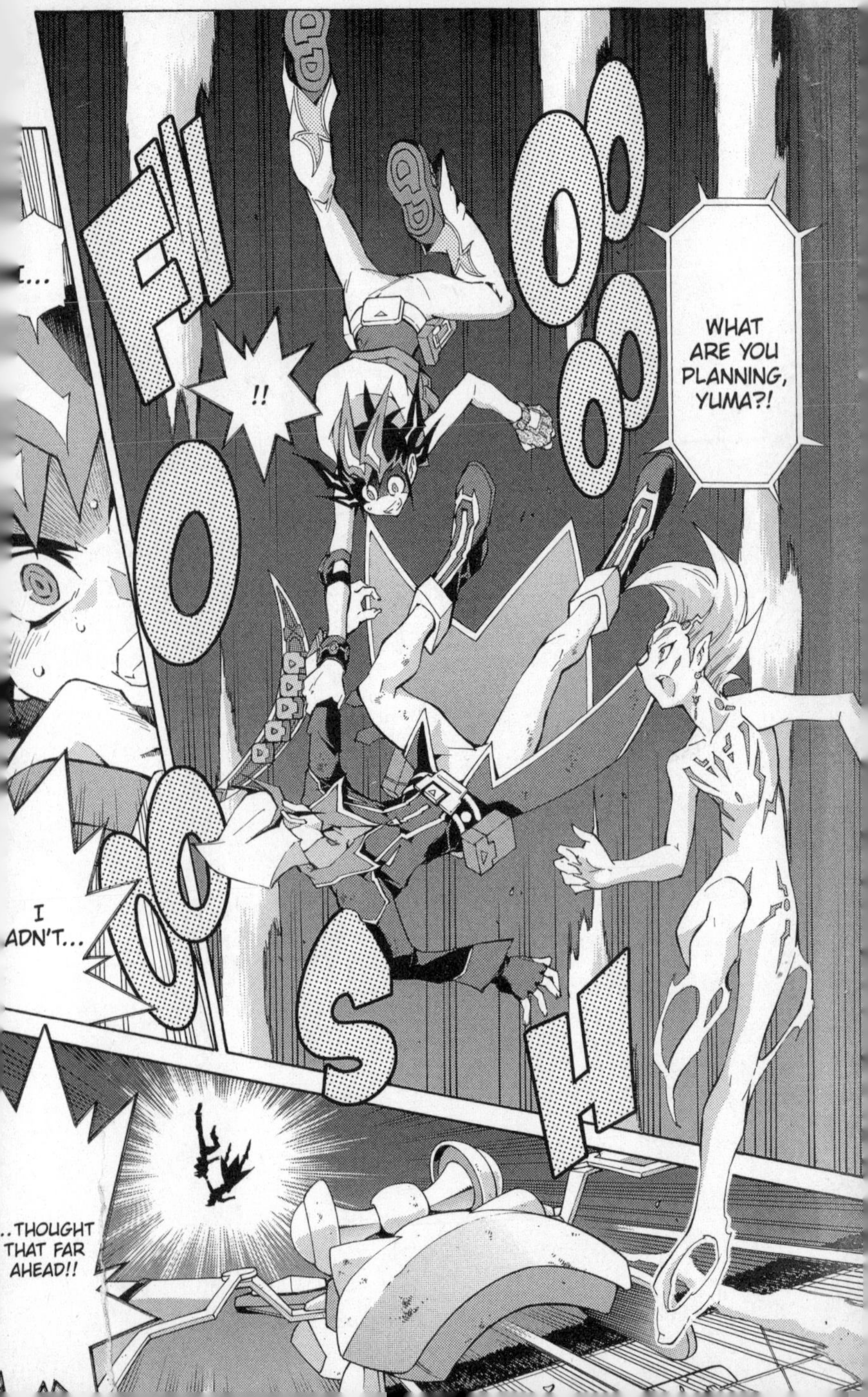
WHAT ARE YOU PLANNING, YUMA?!
!!
...
I ADN'T...
..THOUGHT THAT FAR AHEAD!!

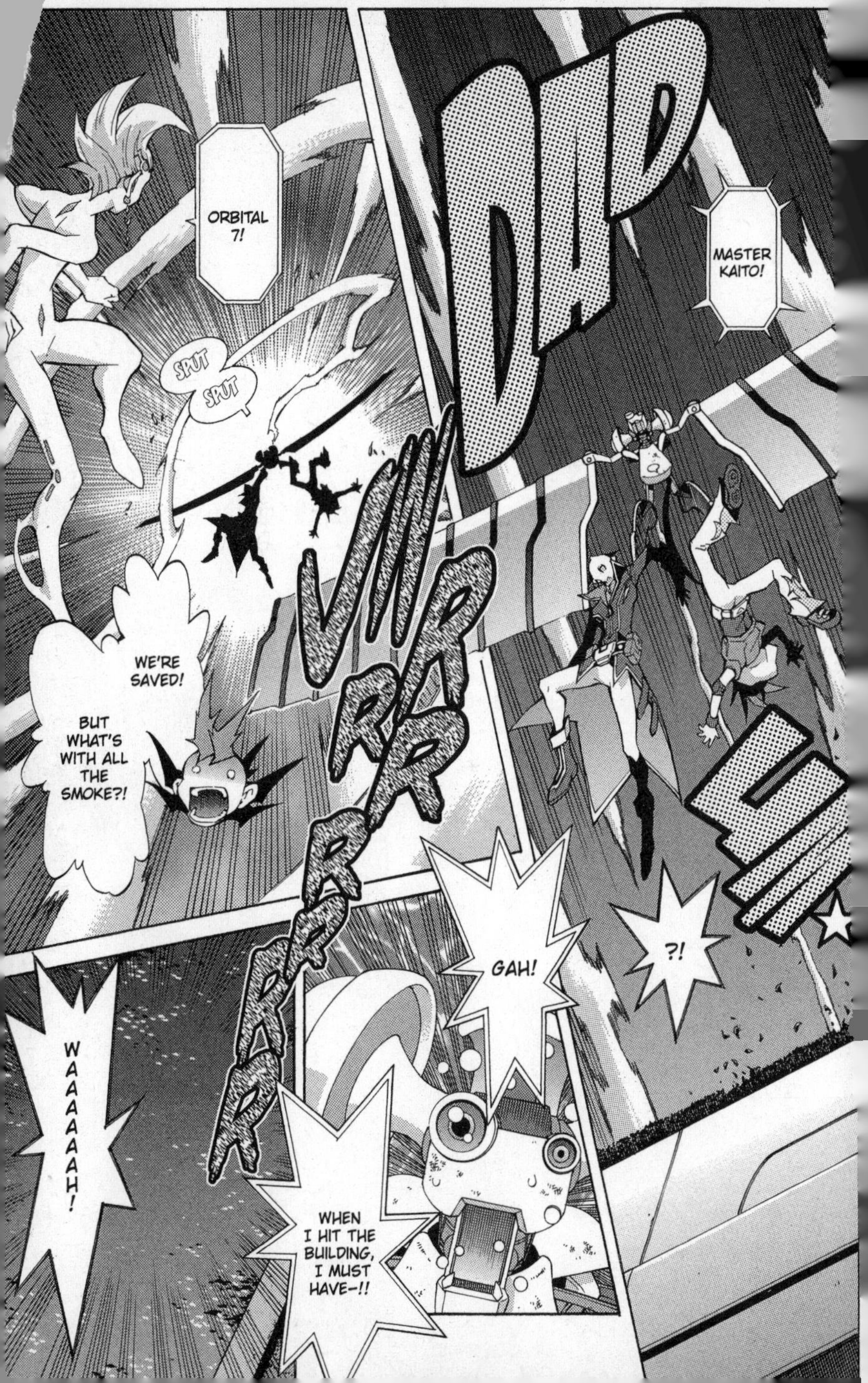
MASTER KAITO!
ORBITAL 7!
SPUT SPUT
WE'RE SAVED!
BUT WHAT'S WITH ALL THE SMOKE?!
?!
GAH!
WHEN I HIT THE BUILDING, I MUST HAVE-!!
WAAAAAAAAH!

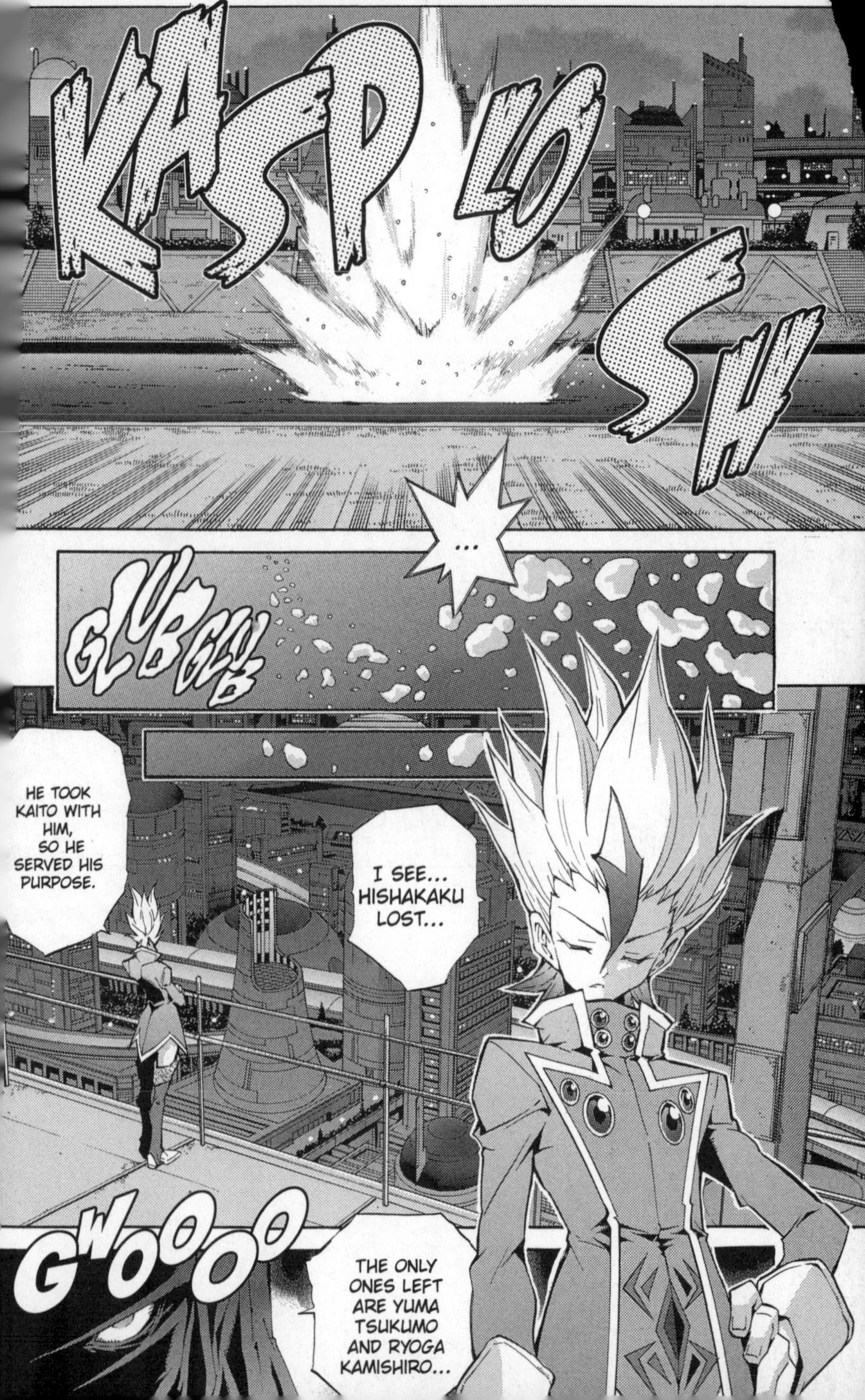
KASPLOOSH
...
GLUBGLUB
I SEE... HISHAKAKU LOST...
HE TOOK KAITO WITH HIM, SO HE SERVED HIS PURPOSE.
THE ONLY ONES LEFT ARE YUMA TSUKUMO AND RYOGA KAMISHIRO...
GWOOOO

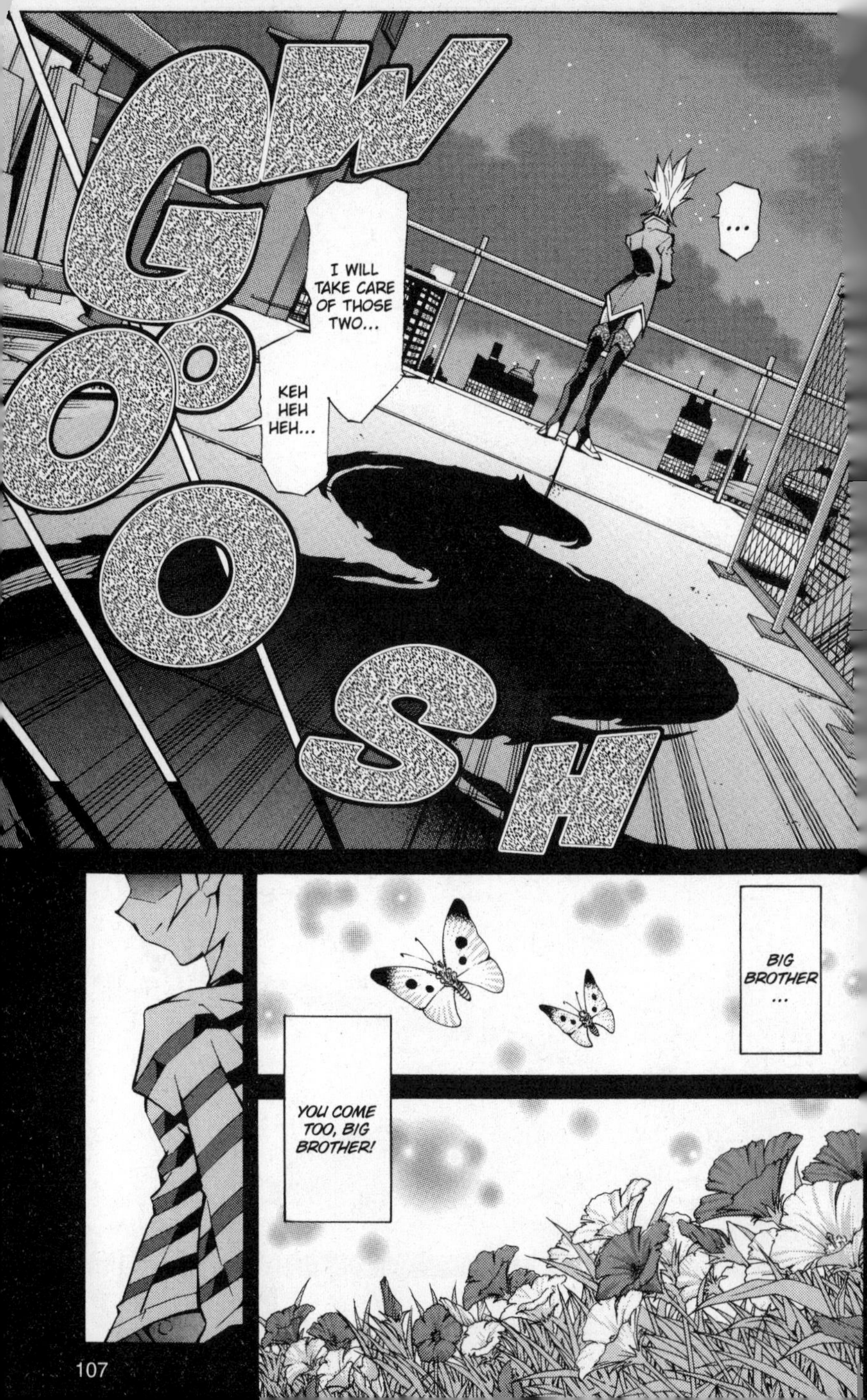
...
I WILL TAKE CARE OF THOSE TWO...
KEH HEH HEH...
GWOOOSH
BIG BROTHER ...
YOU COME TOO, BIG BROTHER!

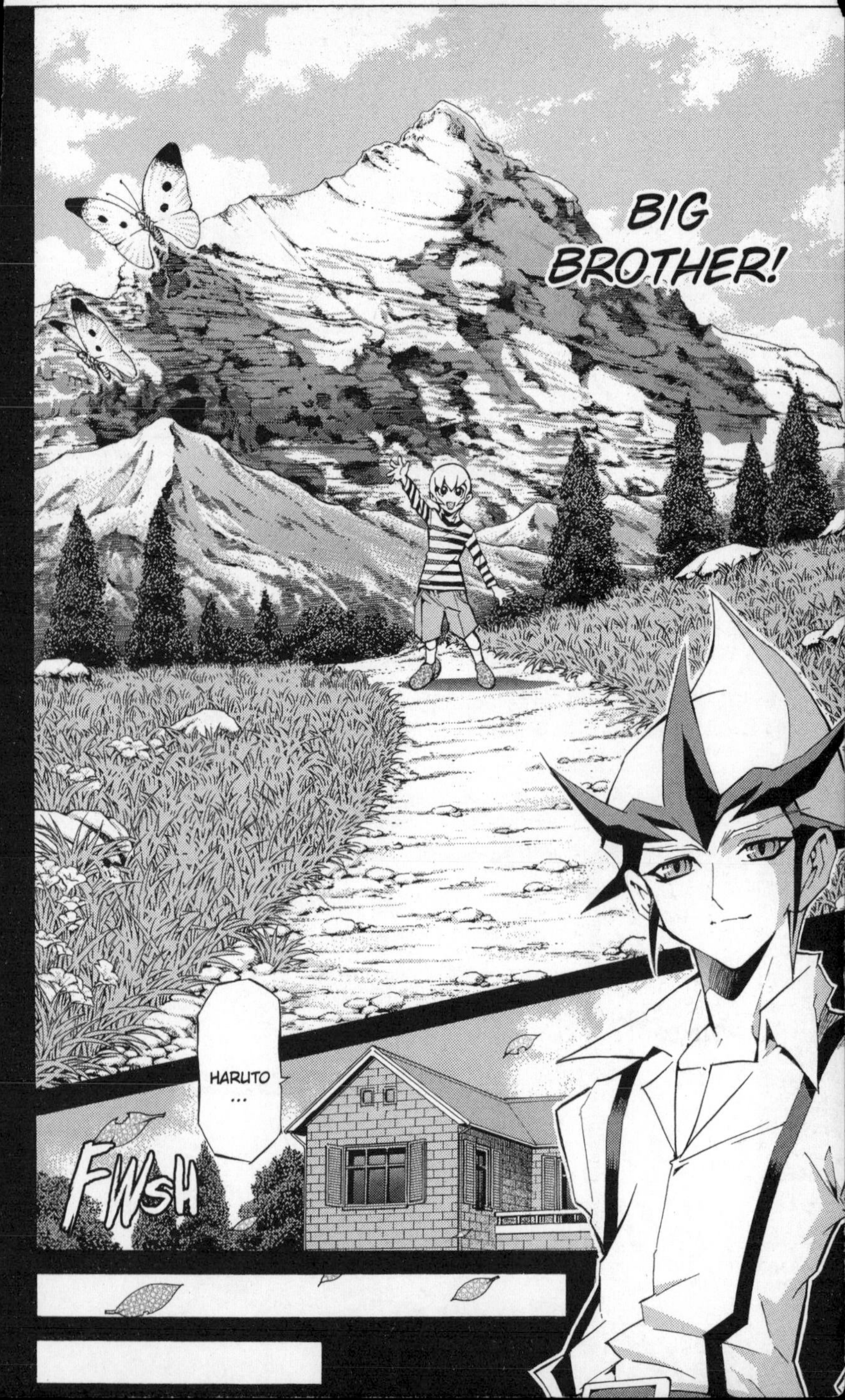
BIG BROTHER!
HARUTO ...
FWSH

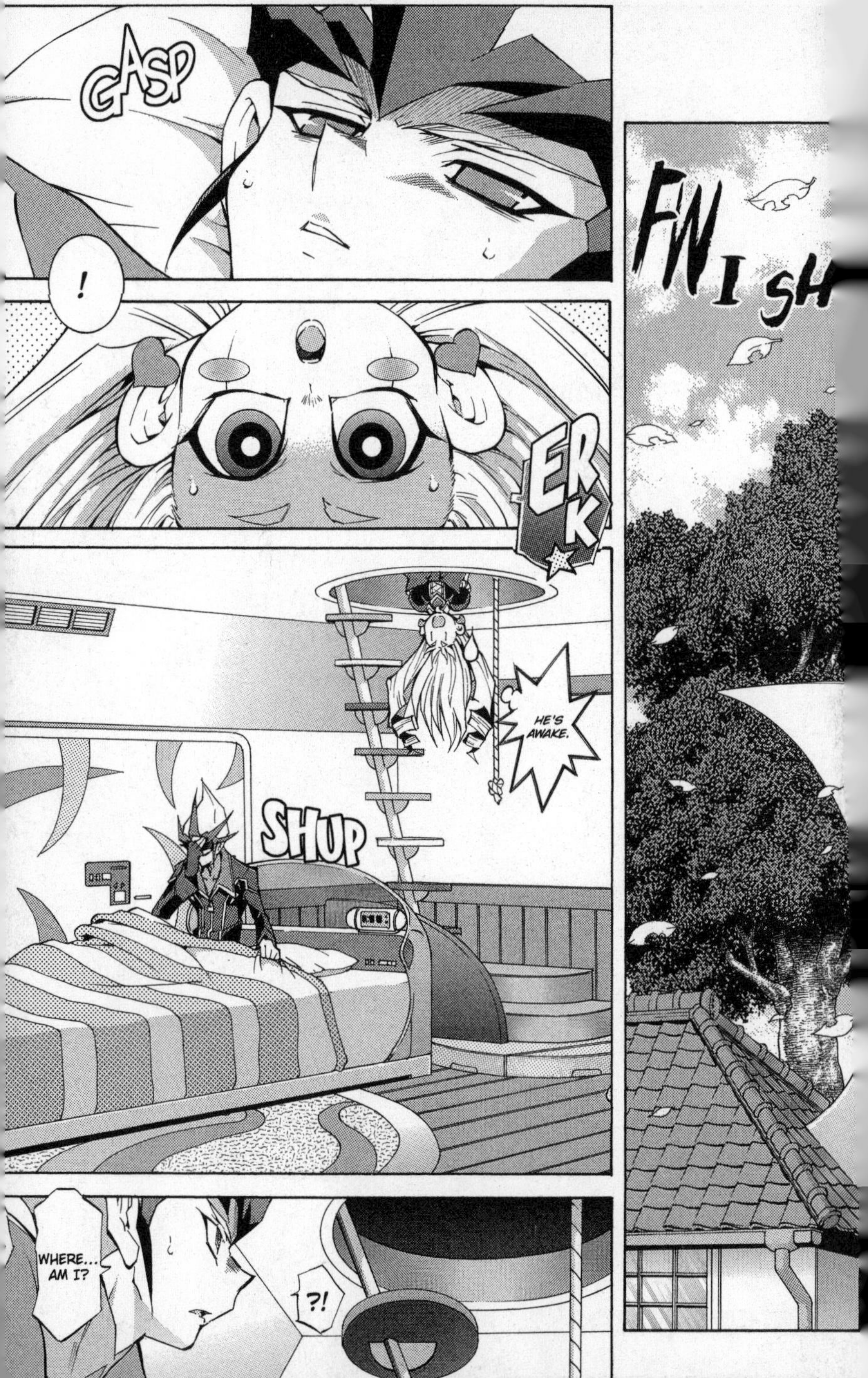
FWISH
GASP
!
ERK
HE'S AWAKE.
SHUP
WHERE... AM I?
?!

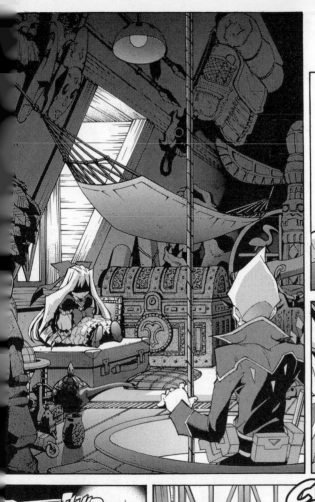

GRB

WHAT A MESSY ROOM...

UH-OH...

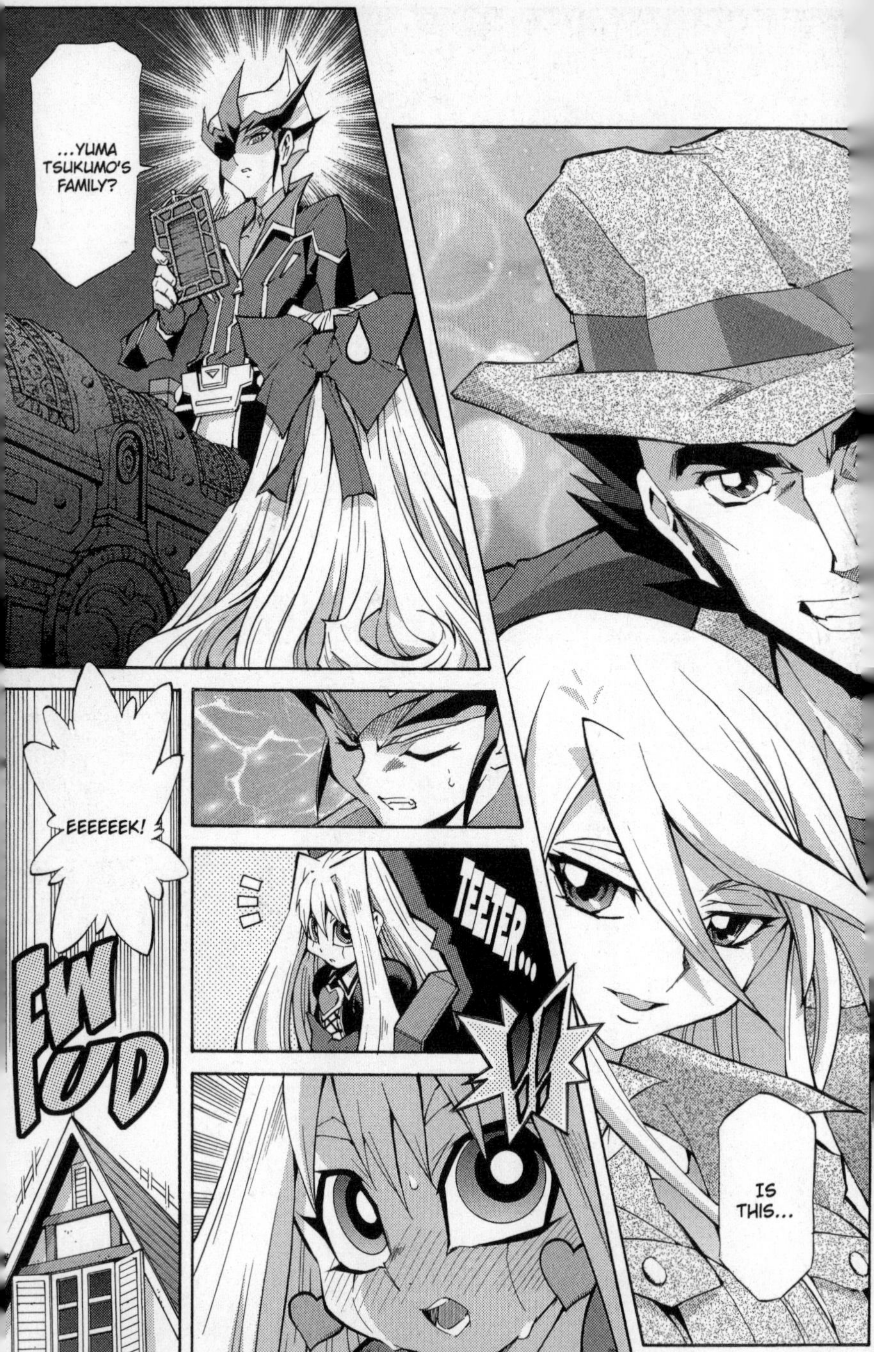
IS THIS...
...YUMA TSUKUMO'S FAMILY?
TEETER...
EEEEEEK!

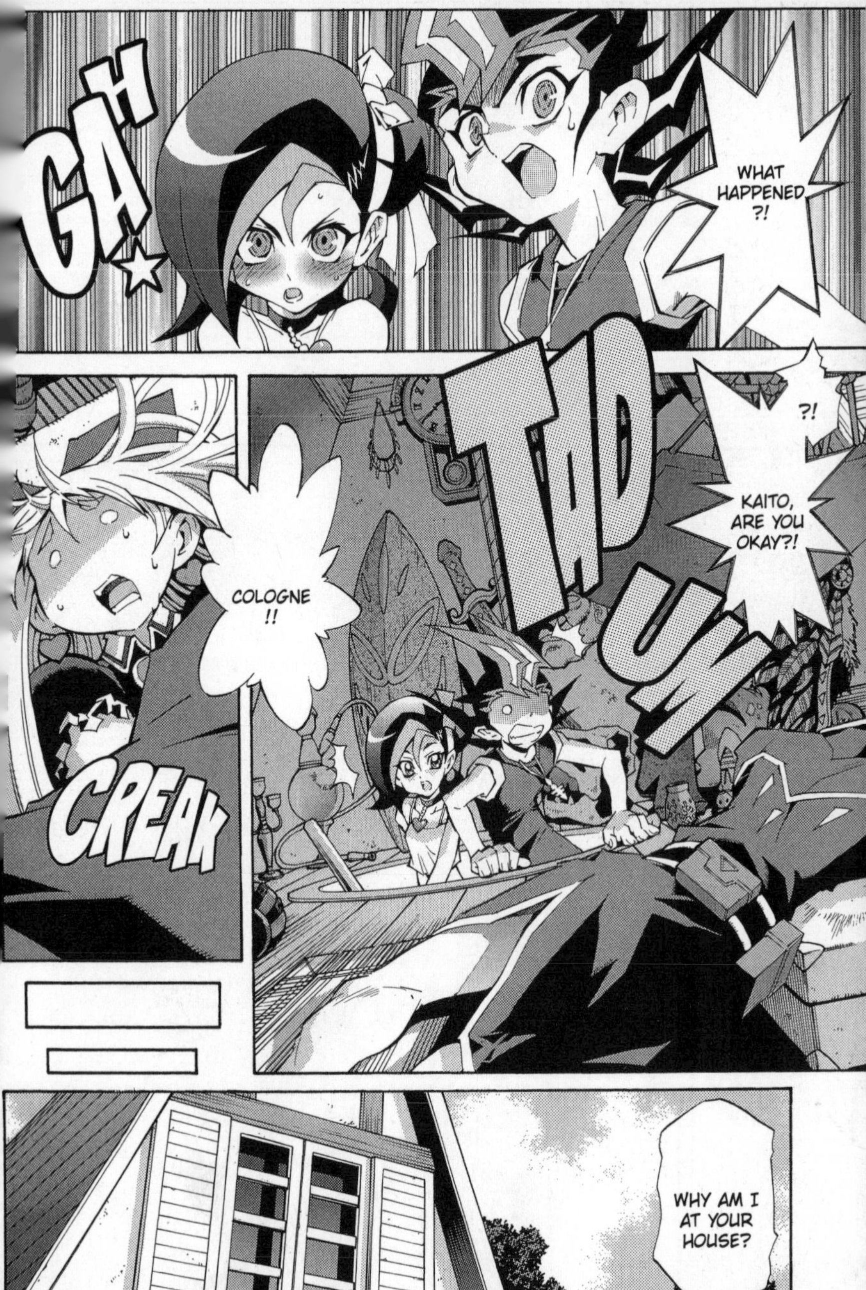
WHAT HAPPENED ?!
GAH
?!
KAITO, ARE YOU OKAY?!
TADUM
COLOGNE !!
CREAK
WHY AM I AT YOUR HOUSE?

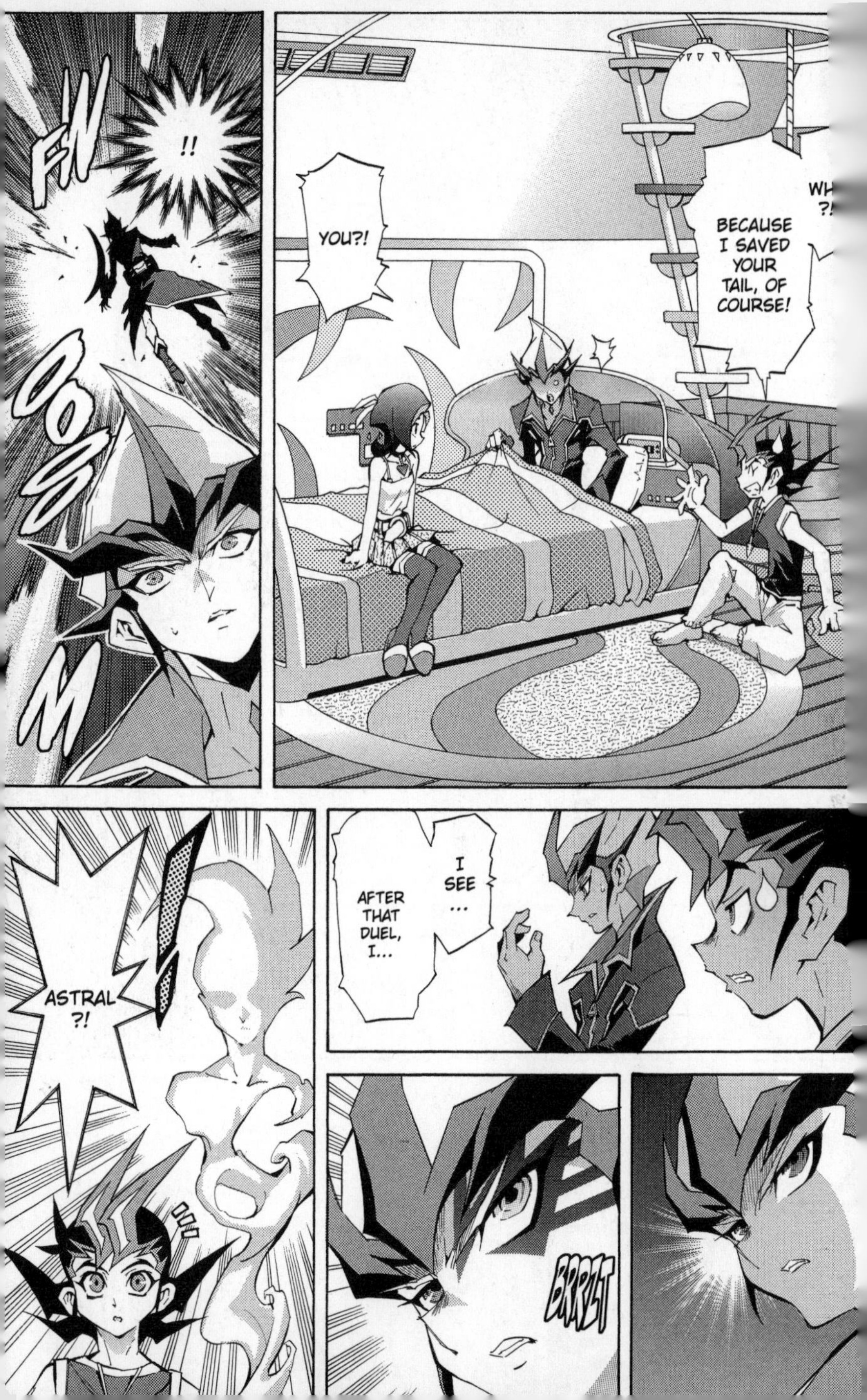
WH ?!
BECAUSE I SAVED YOUR TAIL, OF COURSE!
YOU?!
!!
FWOOOOM
I SEE ...
AFTER THAT DUEL, I...
BRRZLT
!
ASTRAL ?!

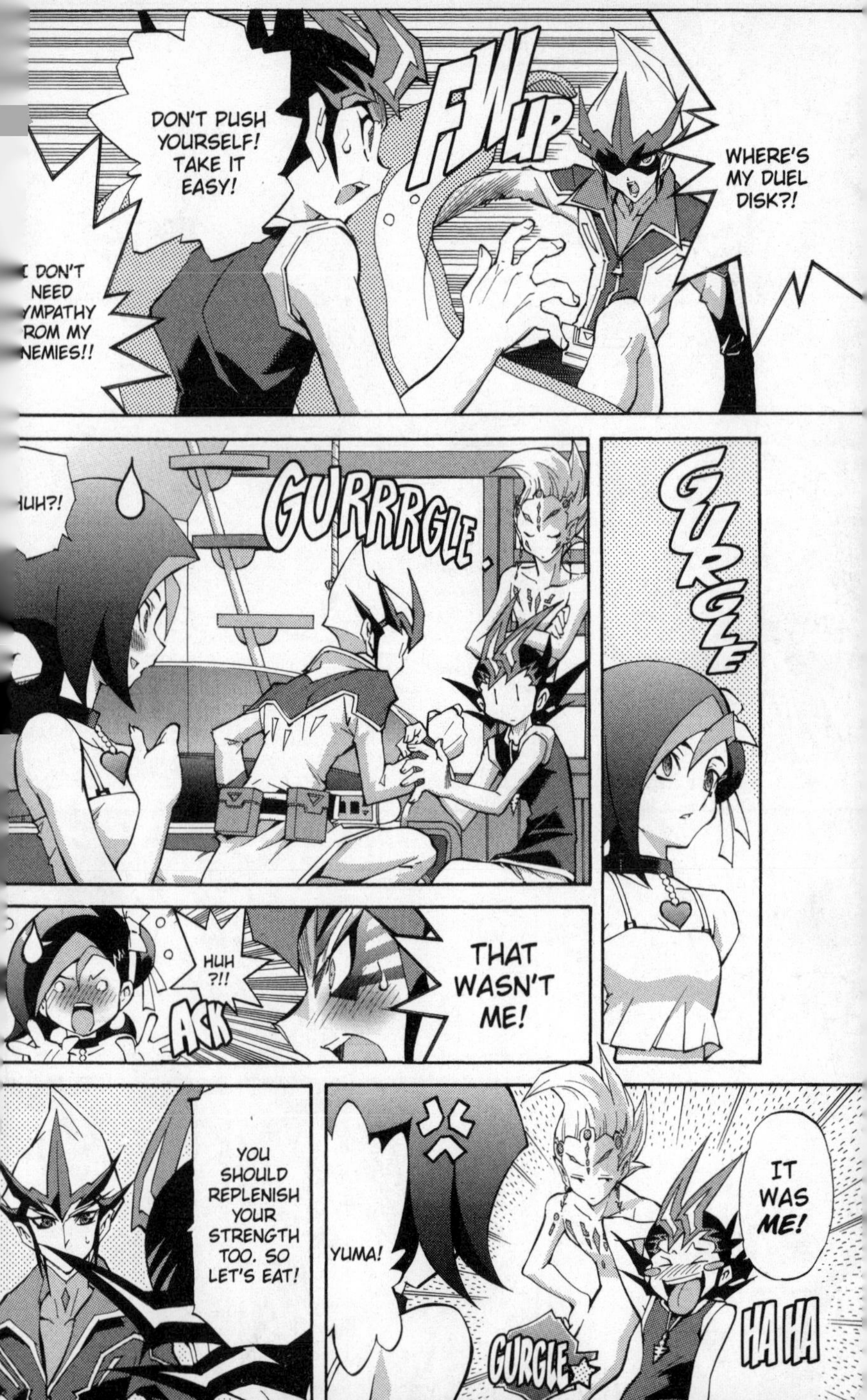
WHERE'S MY DUEL DISK?!
FWUP
DON'T PUSH YOURSELF! TAKE IT EASY!
DON'T NEED
YMPATHY ROM MY NEMIES!!
GURGLE
GURRRGLE
UH?!
THAT WASN'T ME!
HUH ?!!
ACK
IT WAS ME!
HA HA
GURGLE
YUMA!
YOU SHOULD REPLENISH YOUR STRENGTH TOO. SO LET'S EAT!

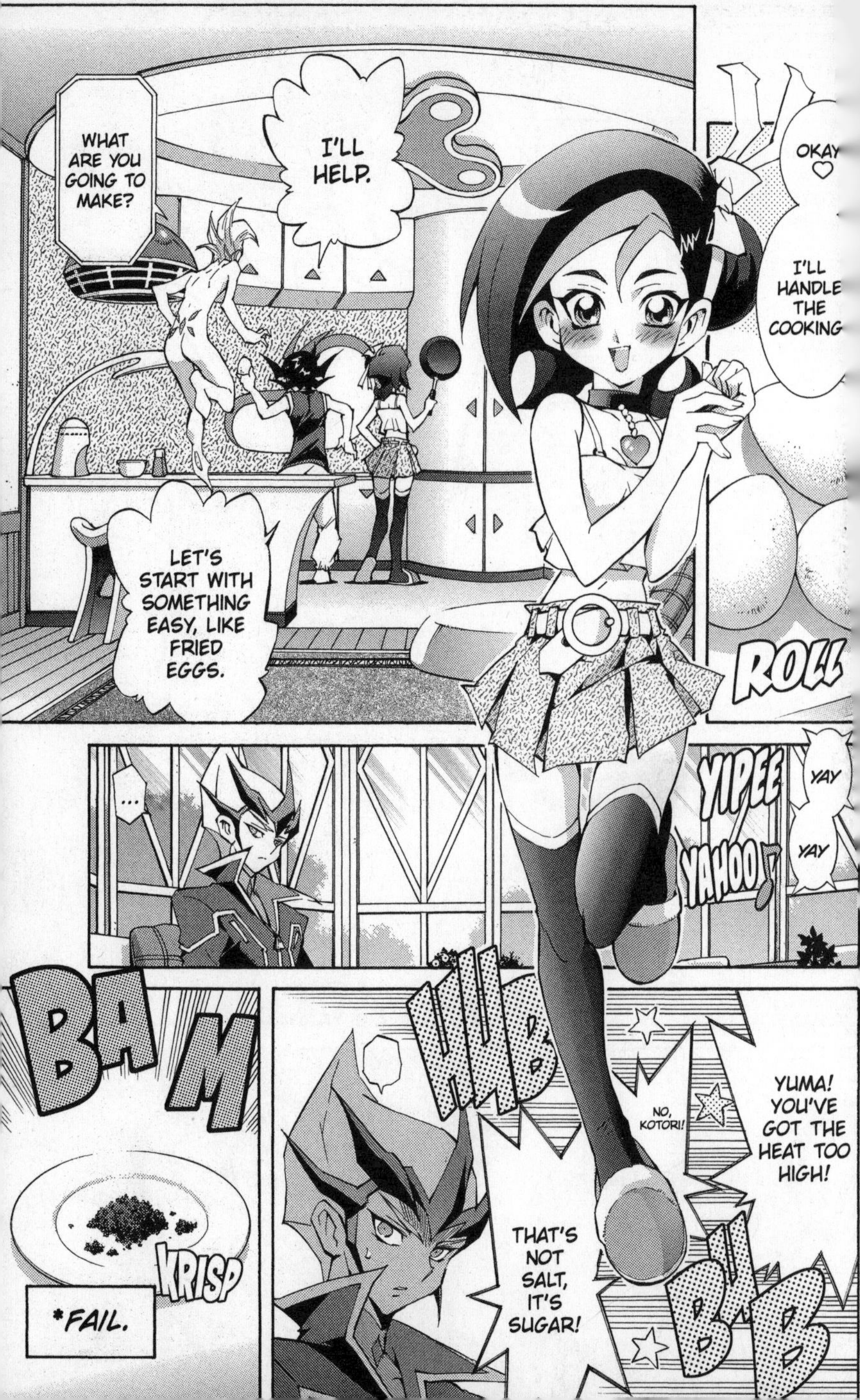
OKAY ♡
I'LL HANDLE THE COOKING
ROLL
I'LL HELP.
WHAT ARE YOU GOING TO MAKE?
LET'S START WITH SOMETHING EASY, LIKE FRIED EGGS.
YAY
YIPEE
YAY
YAHOO
...
YUMA! YOU'VE GOT THE HEAT TOO HIGH!
NO, KOTORI!
THAT'S NOT SALT, IT'S SUGAR!
BAM
KRISP
*FAIL.

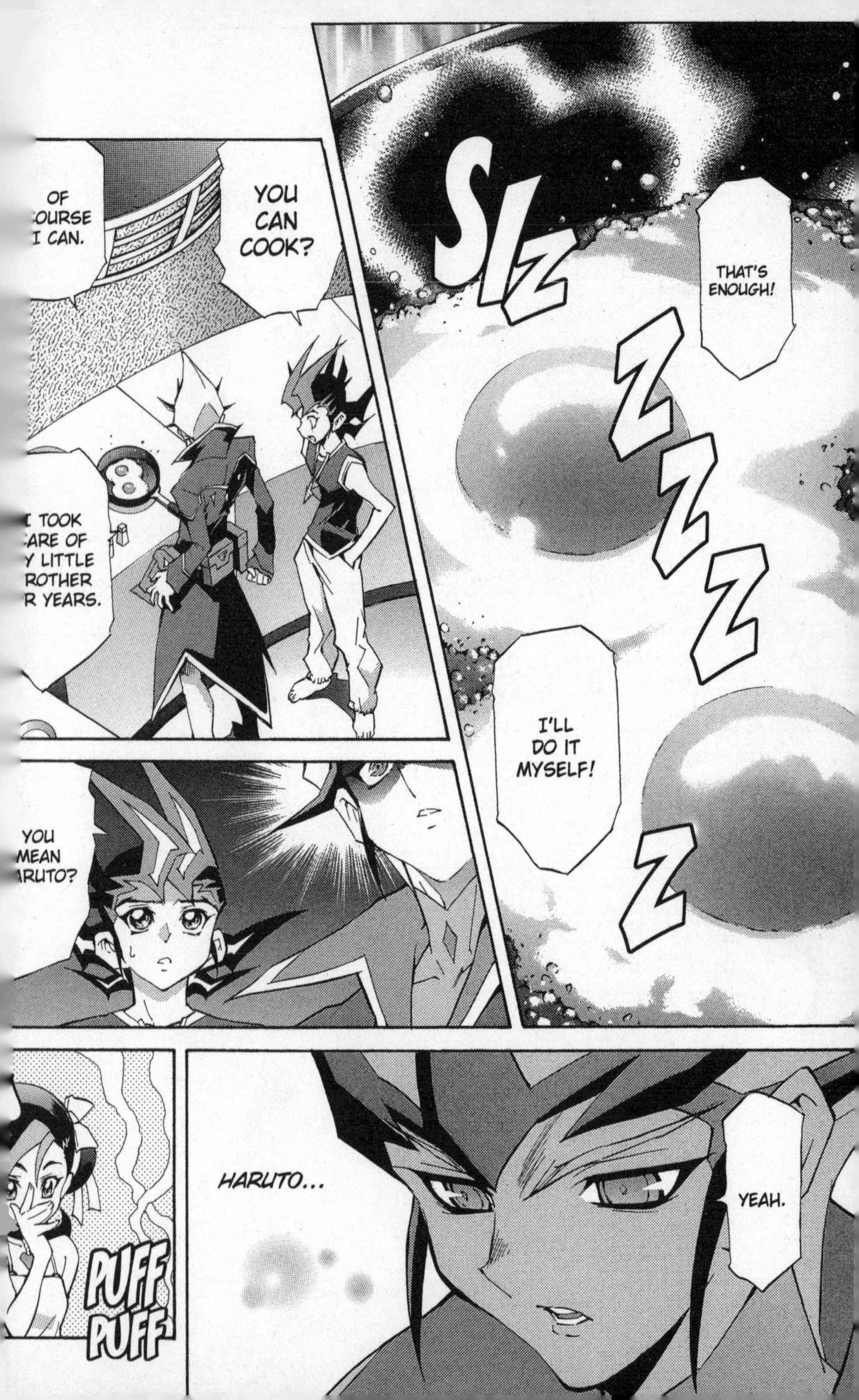
SIZZZZZZ
THAT'S ENOUGH!
I'LL DO IT MYSELF!
YOU CAN COOK?
OF COURSE I CAN.
I TOOK CARE OF Y LITTLE ROTHER R YEARS.
YOU MEAN ARUTO?
HARUTO...
YEAH.
PUFF PUFF

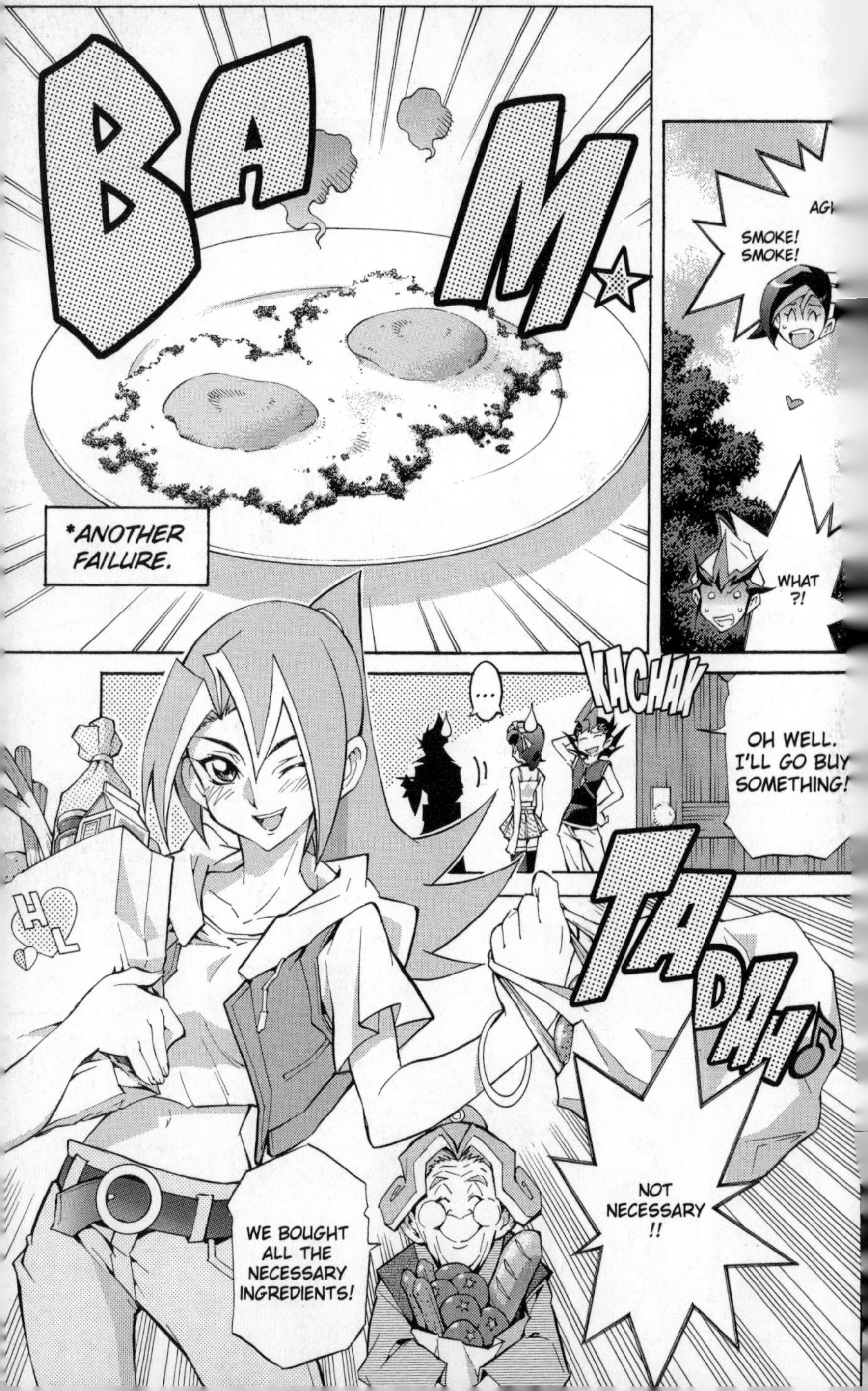
SMOKE! SMOKE!
WHAT ?!
BAM
*ANOTHER FAILURE.
KACHAK
OH WELL. I'LL GO BUY SOMETHING!
...
TADAH
NOT NECESSARY !!
WE BOUGHT ALL THE NECESSARY INGREDIENTS!

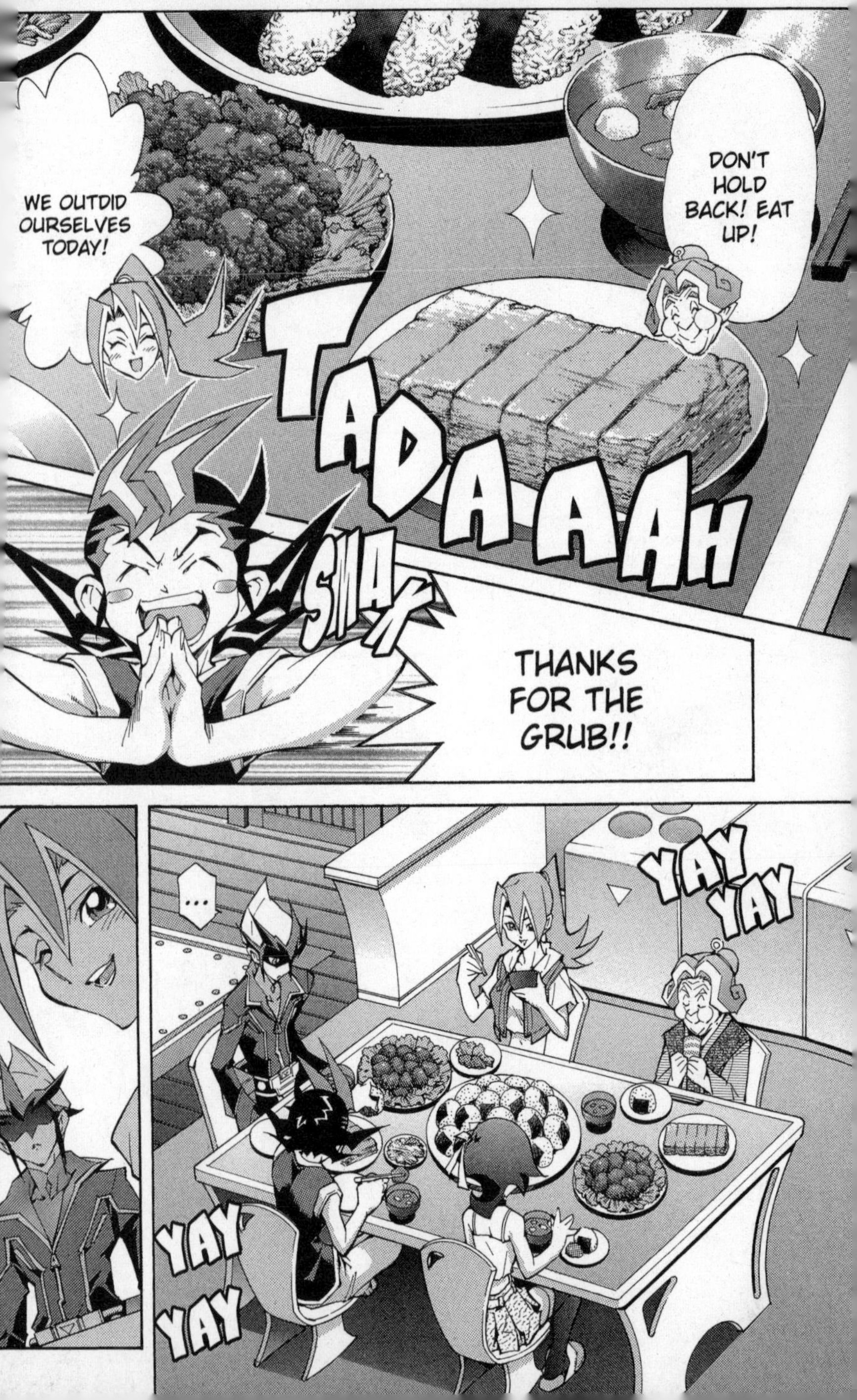

DON'T HOLD BACK! EAT UP!
WE OUTDID OURSELVES TODAY!
TADAAAAH
SMAK
THANKS FOR THE GRUB!!
YAY YAY
...
YAY YAY

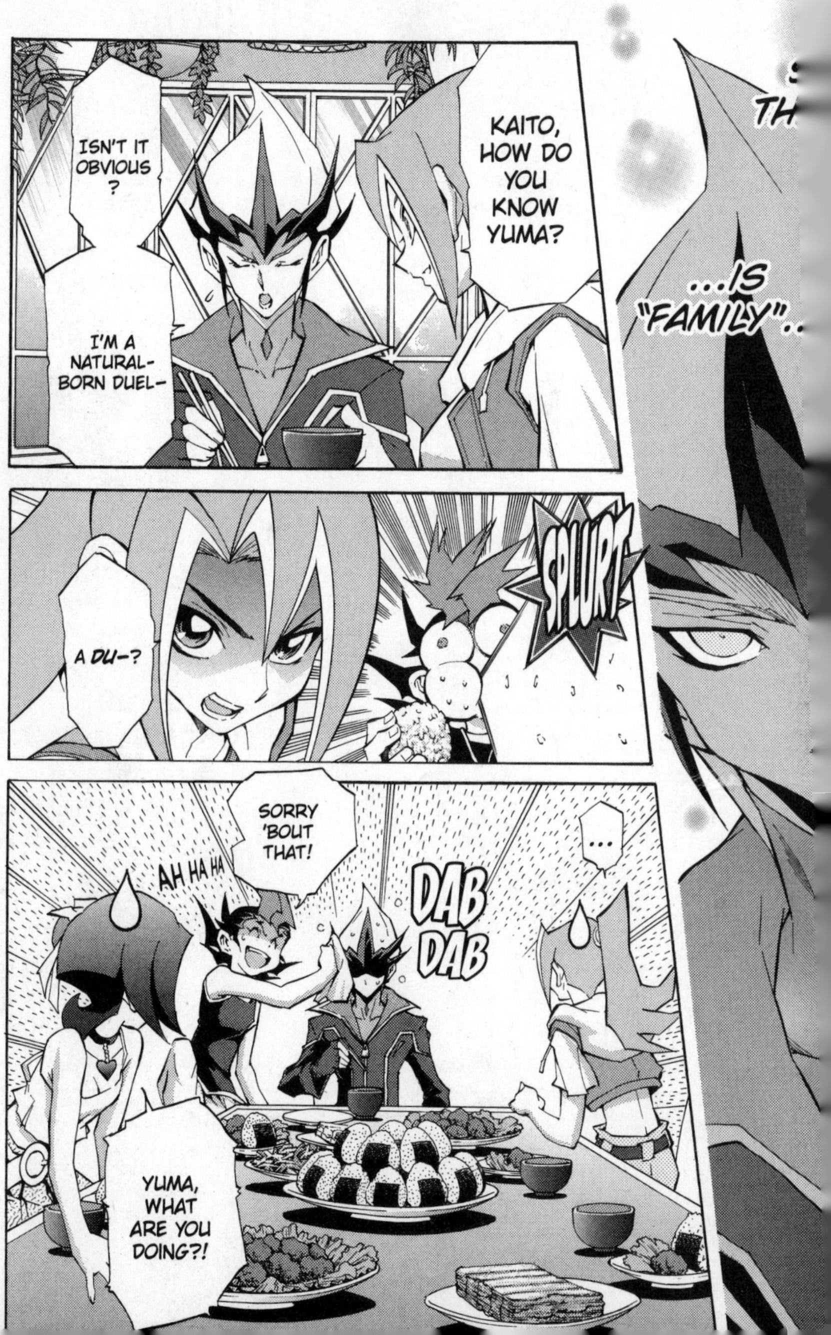
..."IS "FAMILY"...
KAITO, HOW DO YOU KNOW YUMA?
ISN'T IT OBVIOUS?
I'M A NATURAL-BORN DUEL-
SPLURT
A DU-?
...
DAB DAB
SORRY 'BOUT THAT!
AH HA HA
YUMA, WHAT ARE YOU DOING?!

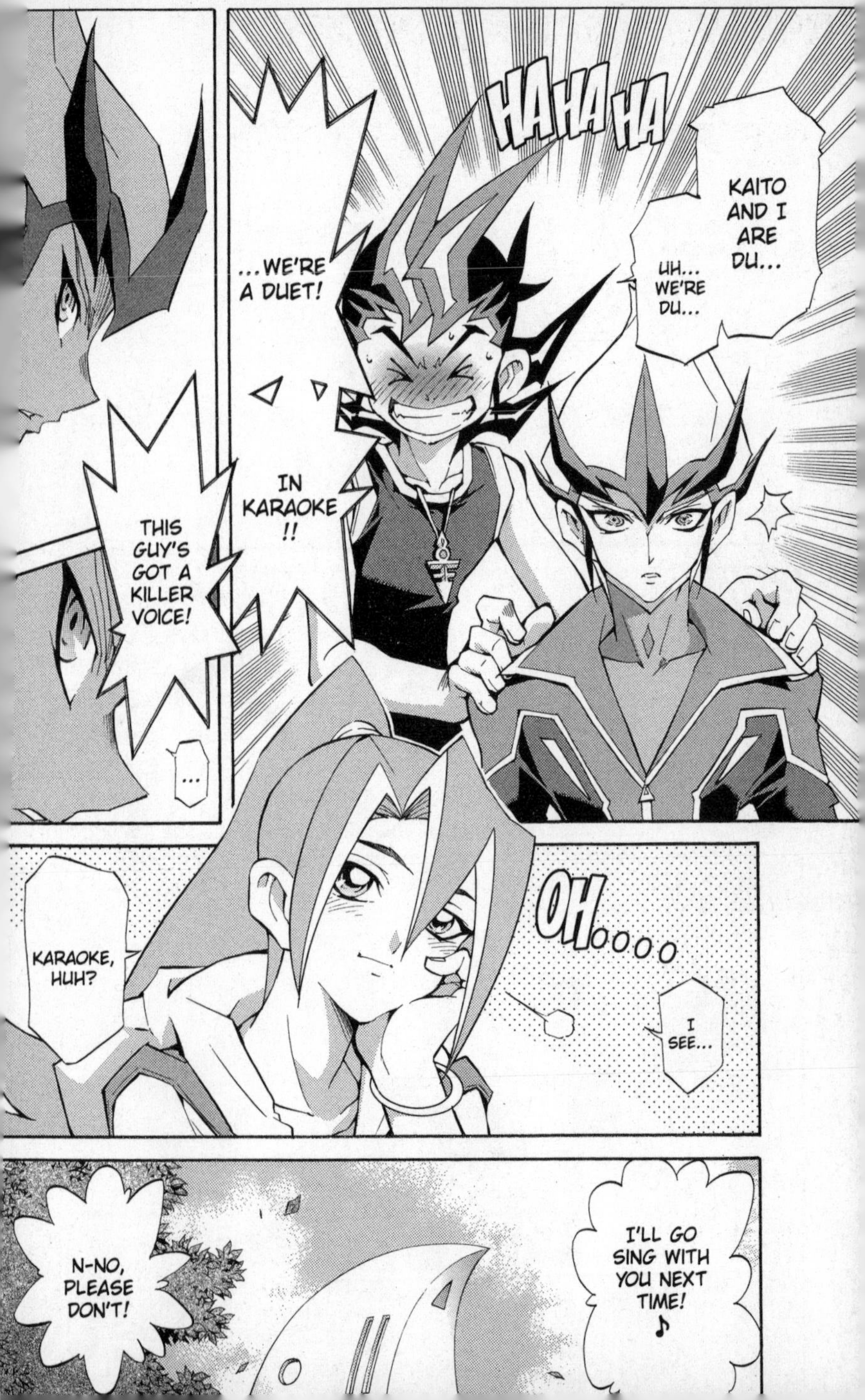
KAITO AND I ARE DU...
UH... WE'RE DU...
HAHAHA
...WE'RE A DUET!
IN KARAOKE!!
THIS GUY'S GOT A KILLER VOICE!
...
OHOOOO
I SEE...
KARAOKE, HUH?
I'LL GO SING WITH YOU NEXT TIME! ♪
N-NO, PLEASE DON'T!

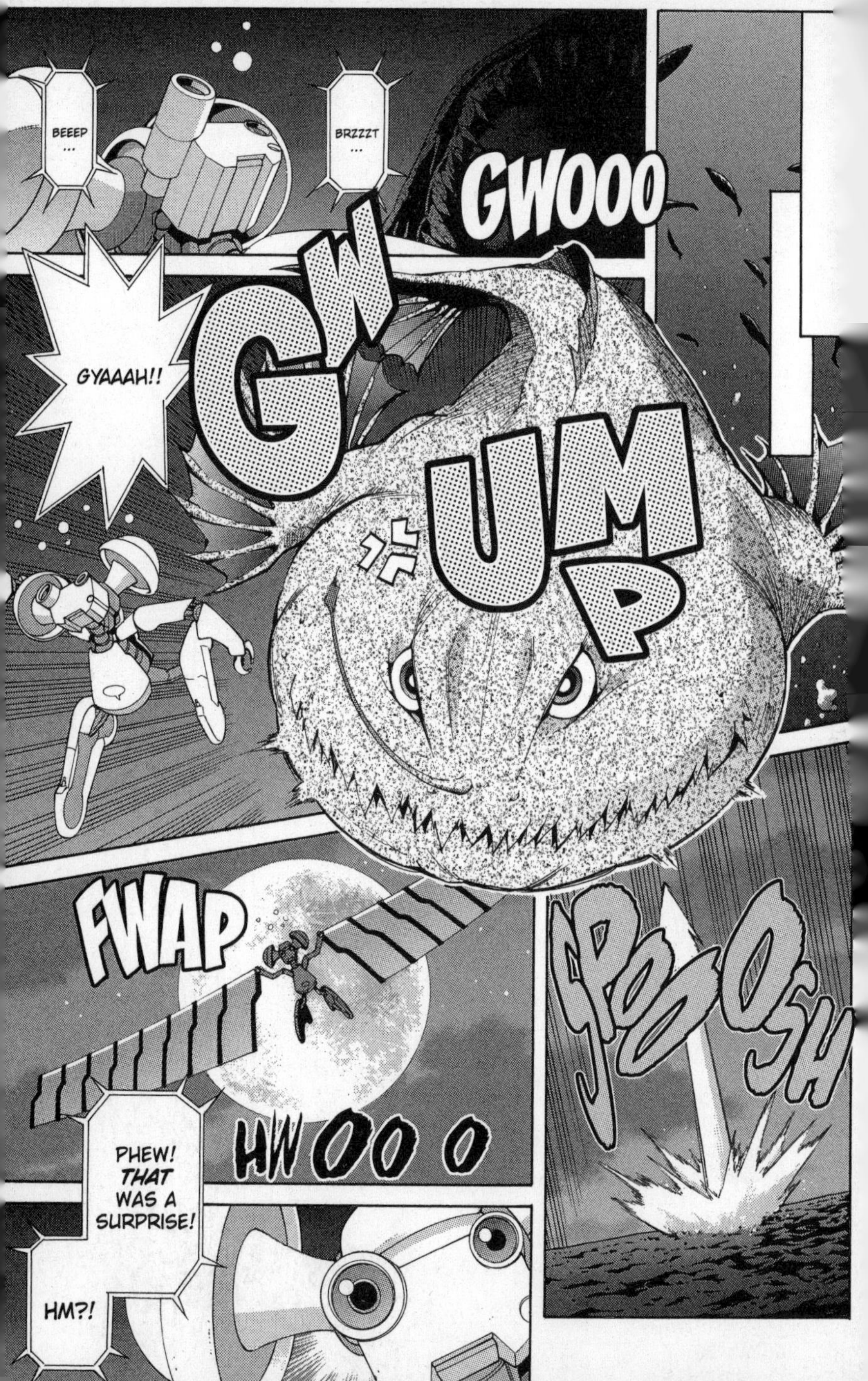
GWOOO
BRZZZT ...
BEEEP ...
GWUMP
GYAAAH!!
GPSOSH
FWAP
HWOOO
PHEW! *THAT* WAS A SURPRISE!
HM?!

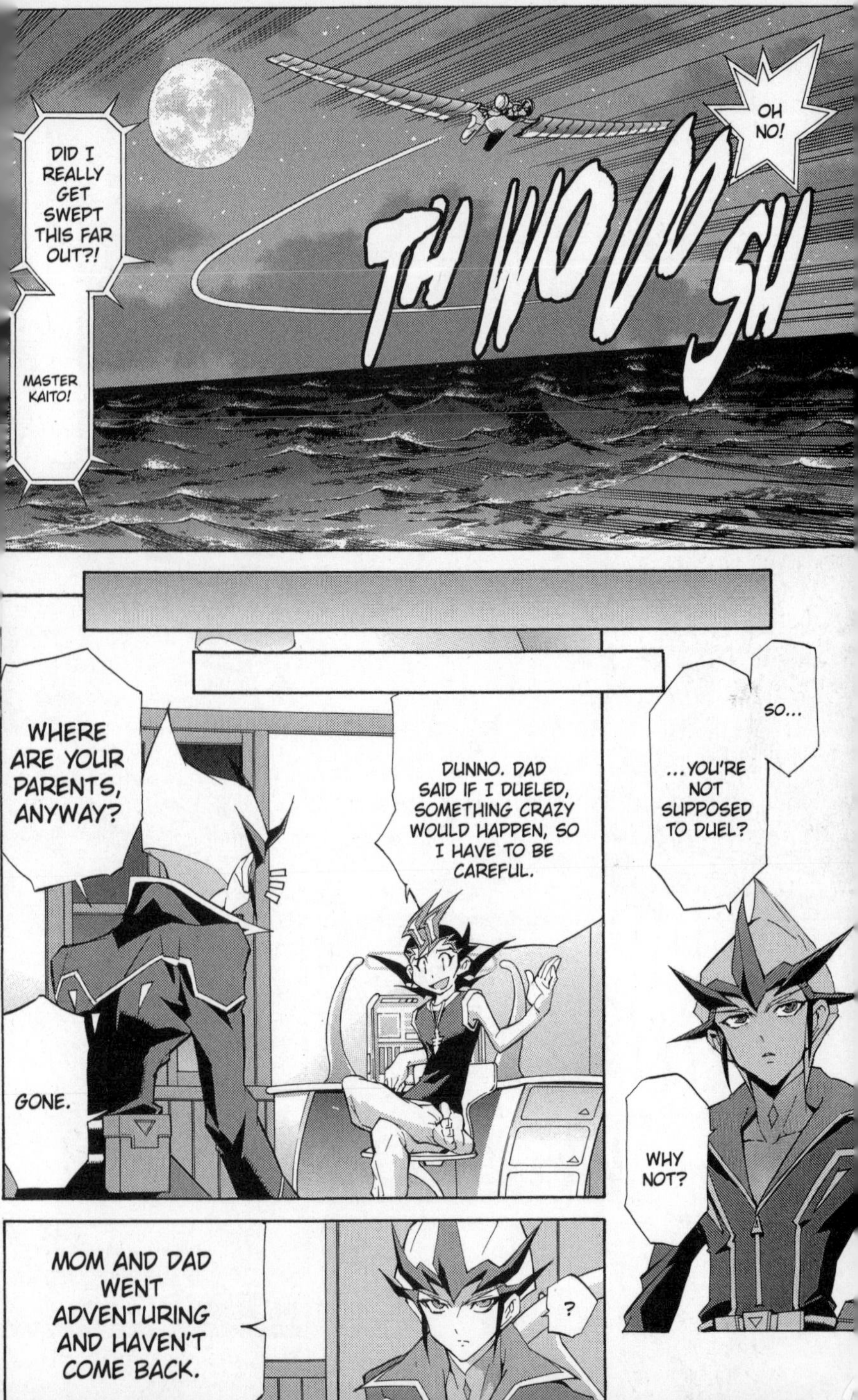
OH NO!
THWOOOSH
DID I REALLY GET SWEPT THIS FAR OUT?!
MASTER KAITO!
SO...
...YOU'RE NOT SUPPOSED TO DUEL?
WHY NOT?
DUNNO. DAD SAID IF I DUELED, SOMETHING CRAZY WOULD HAPPEN, SO I HAVE TO BE CAREFUL.
WHERE ARE YOUR PARENTS, ANYWAY?
GONE.
MOM AND DAD WENT ADVENTURING AND HAVEN'T COME BACK.
?

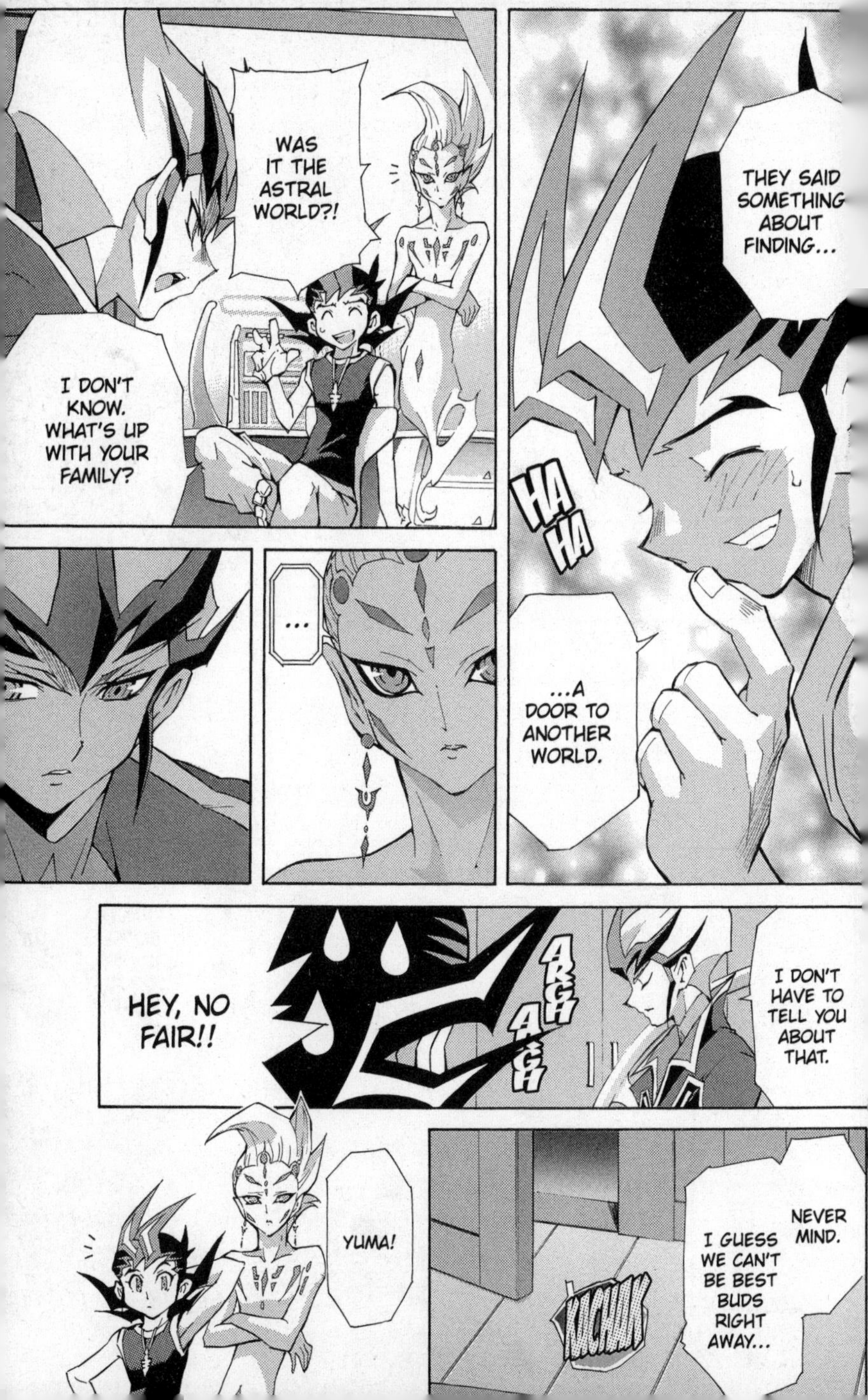
THEY SAID SOMETHING ABOUT FINDING...
HA HA
...A DOOR TO ANOTHER WORLD.
WAS IT THE ASTRAL WORLD?!
I DON'T KNOW. WHAT'S UP WITH YOUR FAMILY?
...
I DON'T HAVE TO TELL YOU ABOUT THAT.
ARGH ARGH
HEY, NO FAIR!!
NEVER MIND.
I GUESS WE CAN'T BE BEST BUDS RIGHT AWAY...
KACHAK
YUMA!

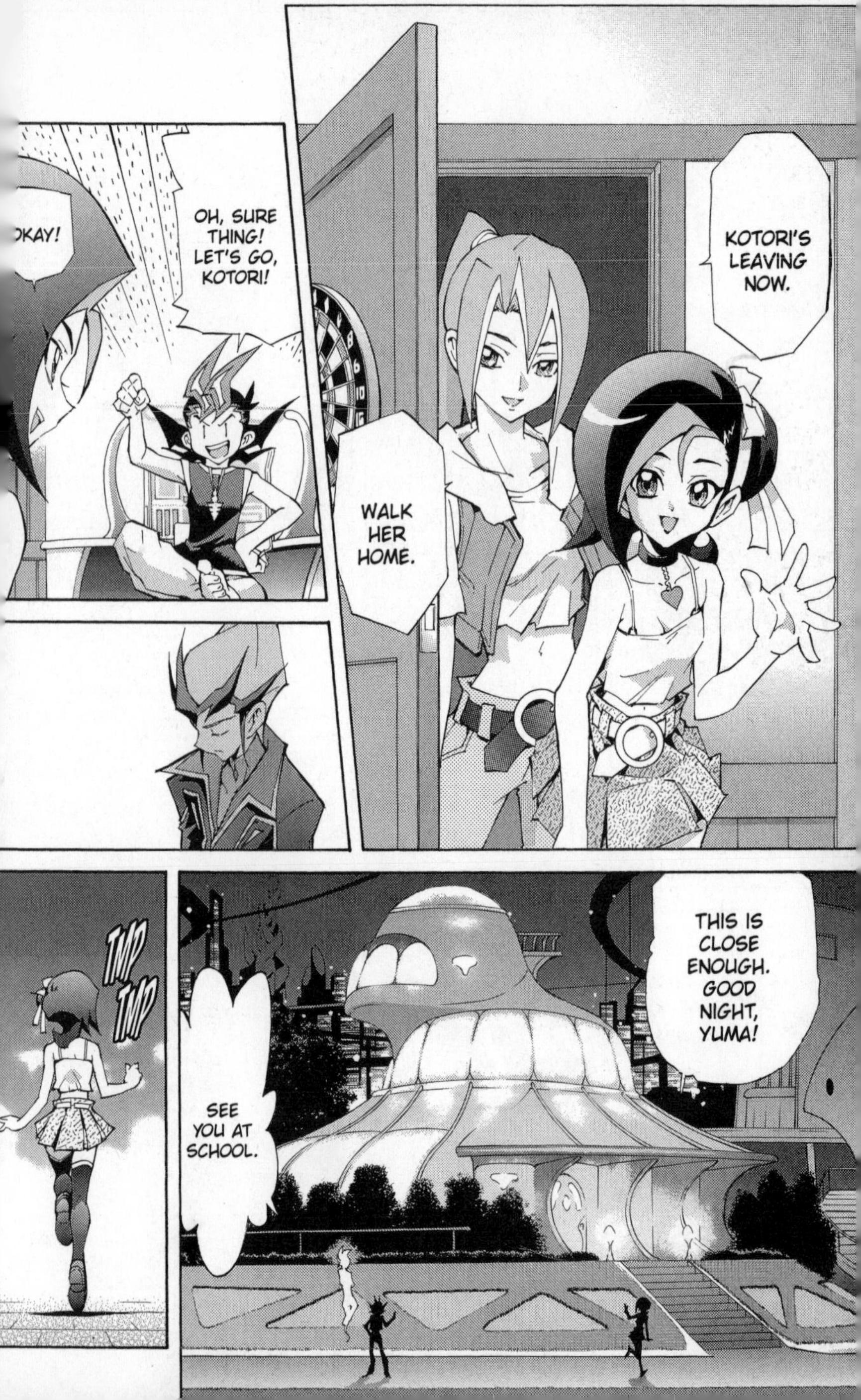
KOTORI'S LEAVING NOW.
WALK HER HOME.
OH, SURE THING! LET'S GO, KOTORI!
OKAY!
THIS IS CLOSE ENOUGH. GOOD NIGHT, YUMA!
SEE YOU AT SCHOOL.
TMP TMP

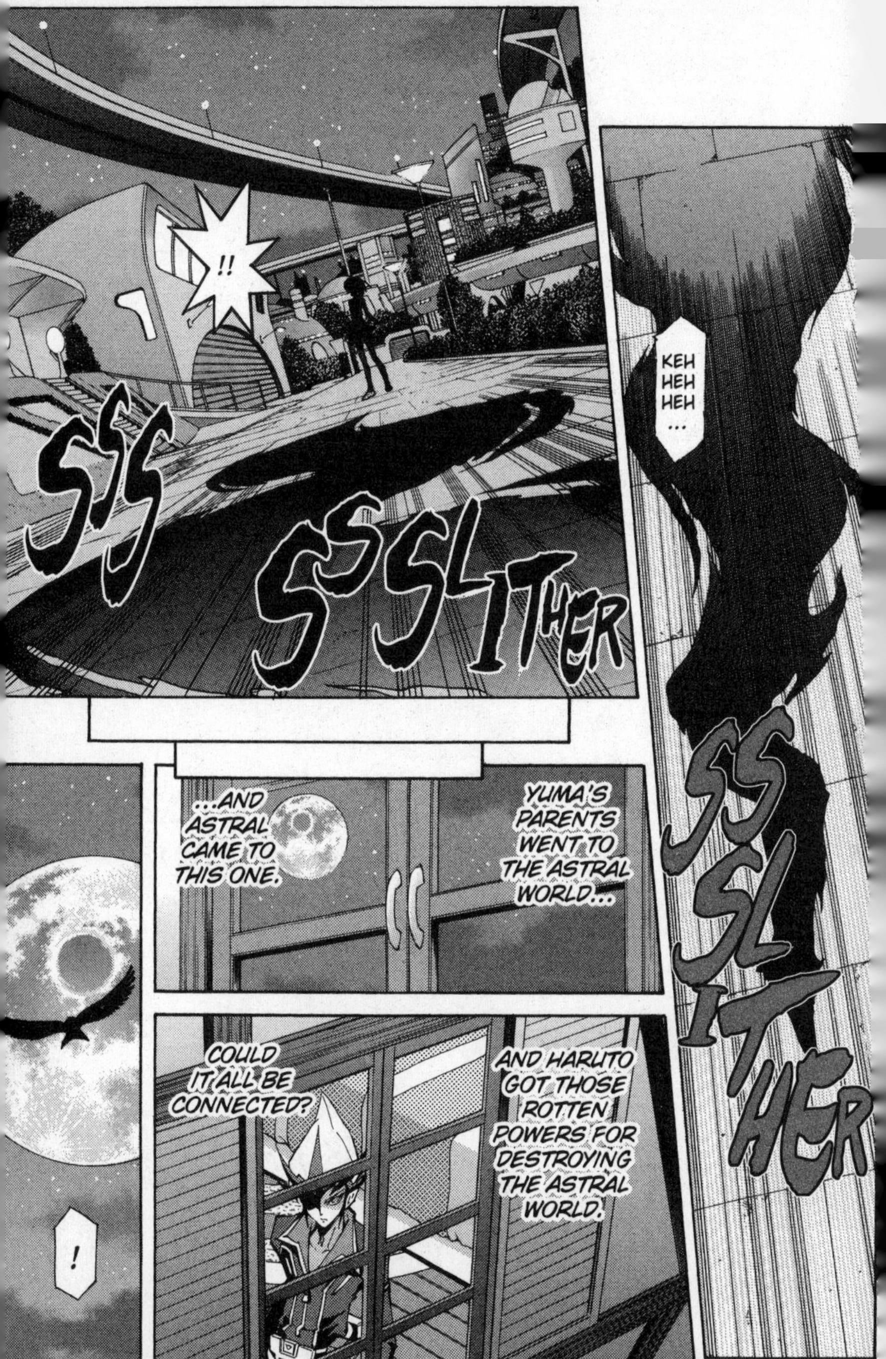
!!
SSS
SSSLITHER
KEH HEH HEH...
SSSLITHER
YUMA'S PARENTS WENT TO THE ASTRAL WORLD...
...AND ASTRAL CAME TO THIS ONE.
AND HARUTO GOT THOSE ROTTEN POWERS FOR DESTROYING THE ASTRAL WORLD.
COULD IT ALL BE CONNECTED?
!

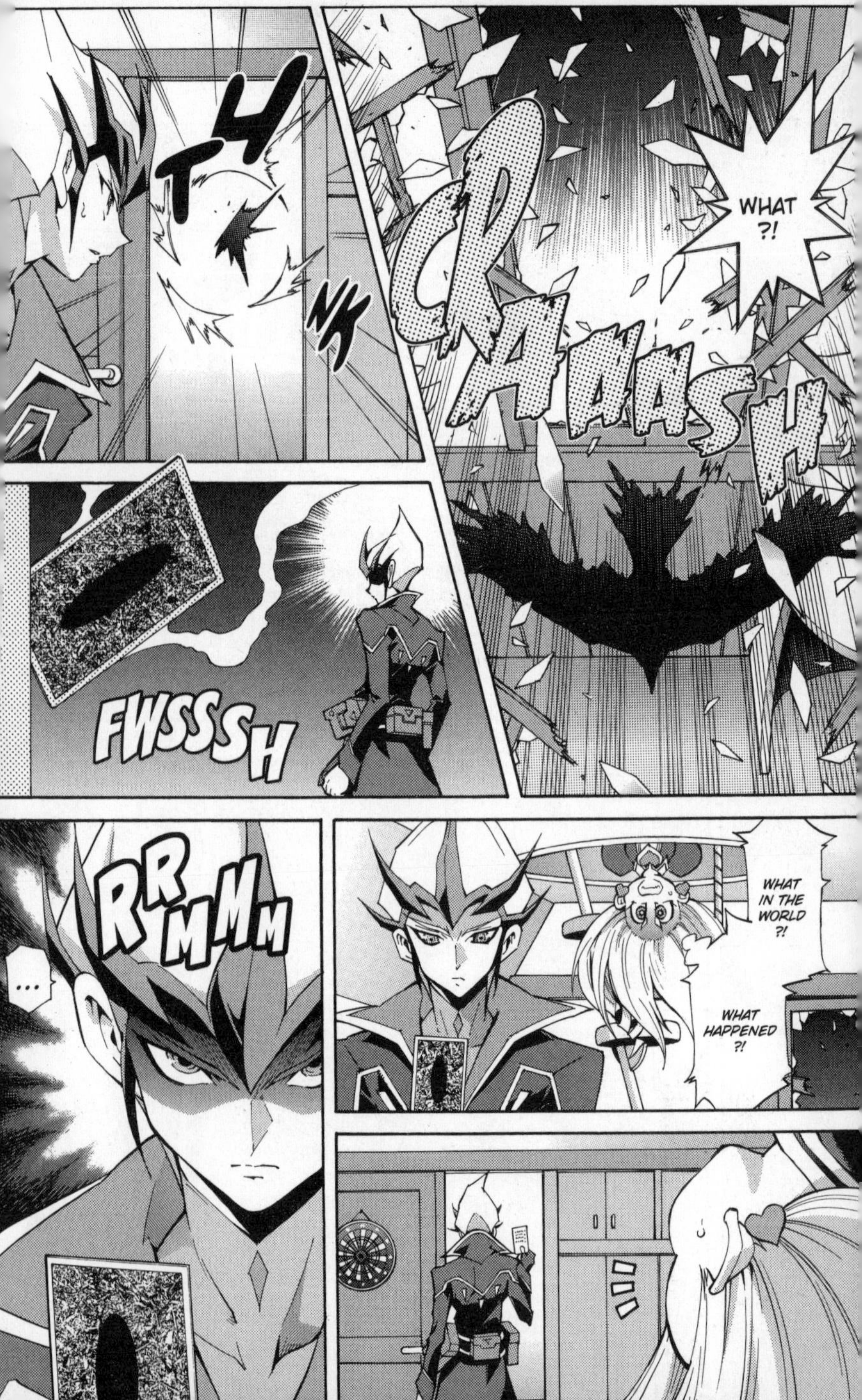
CRAAASH
WHAT ?!
FWSSSH
WHAT IN THE WORLD ?!
WHAT HAPPENED ?!
RRMMMM
...

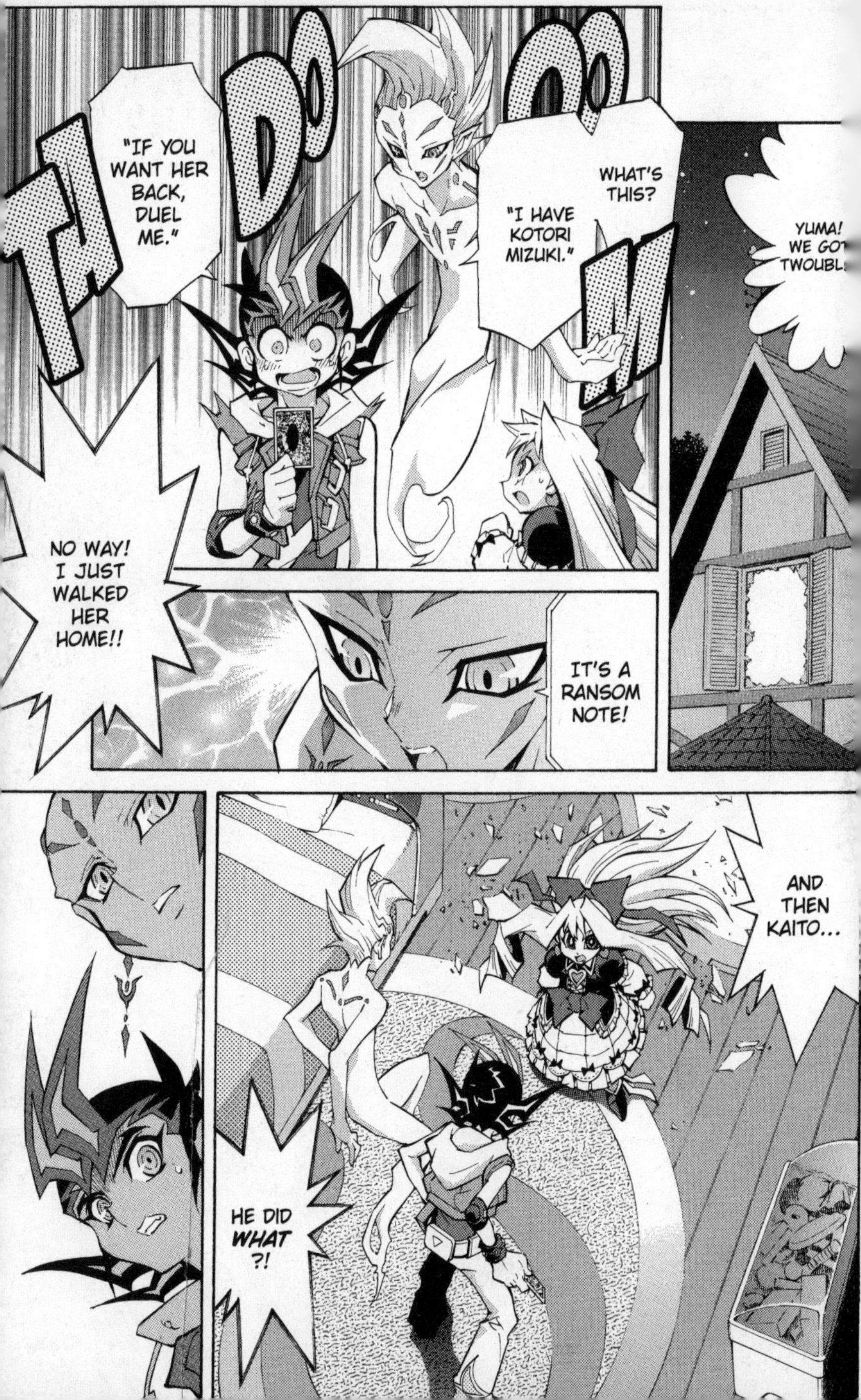
YUMA! WE GOT TWOUBL
WHAT'S THIS?
"I HAVE KOTORI MIZUKI."
"IF YOU WANT HER BACK, DUEL ME."
THDOOM
IT'S A RANSOM NOTE!
NO WAY! I JUST WALKED HER HOME!!
AND THEN KAITO...
HE DID *WHAT* ?!

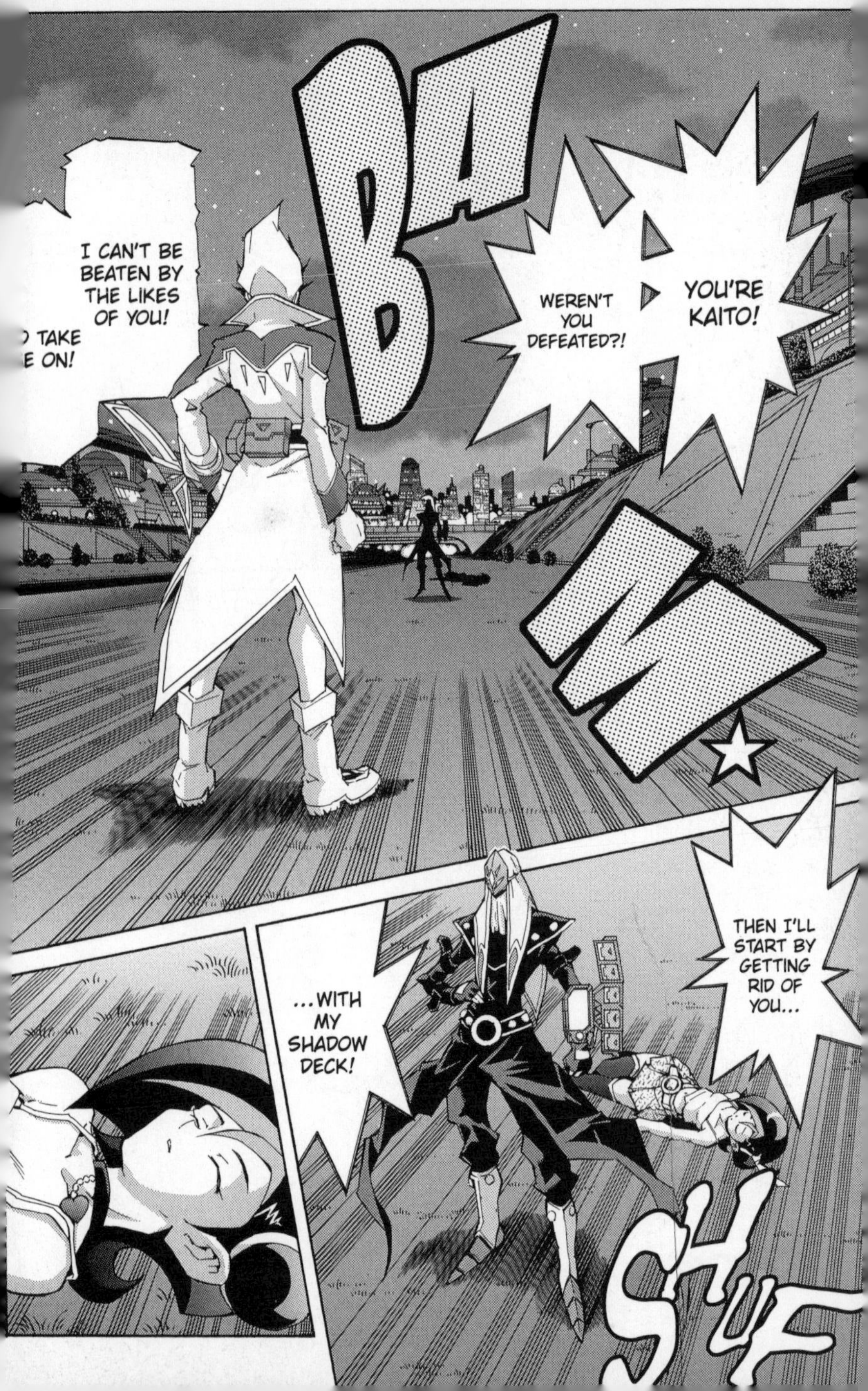
BAM
YOU'RE KAITO!
WEREN'T YOU DEFEATED?!
I CAN'T BE BEATEN BY THE LIKES OF YOU!
THEN I'LL START BY GETTING RID OF YOU...
...WITH MY SHADOW DECK!
SHUF

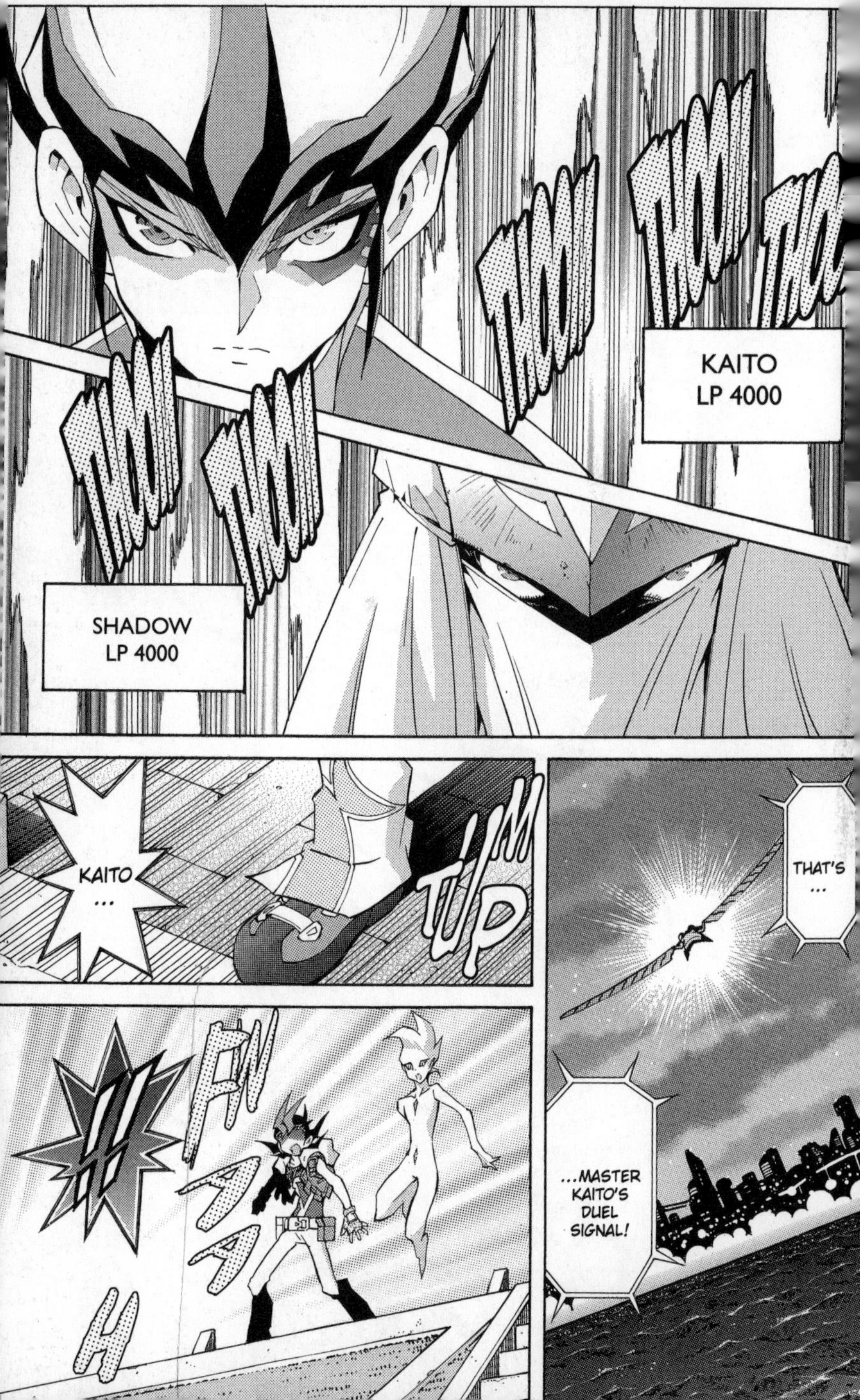
THOOM THOOM THO
KAITO
LP 4000
THOOM THOOM
SHADOW
LP 4000
THAT'S ...
...MASTER KAITO'S DUEL SIGNAL!
KAITO ...
TUP
!!

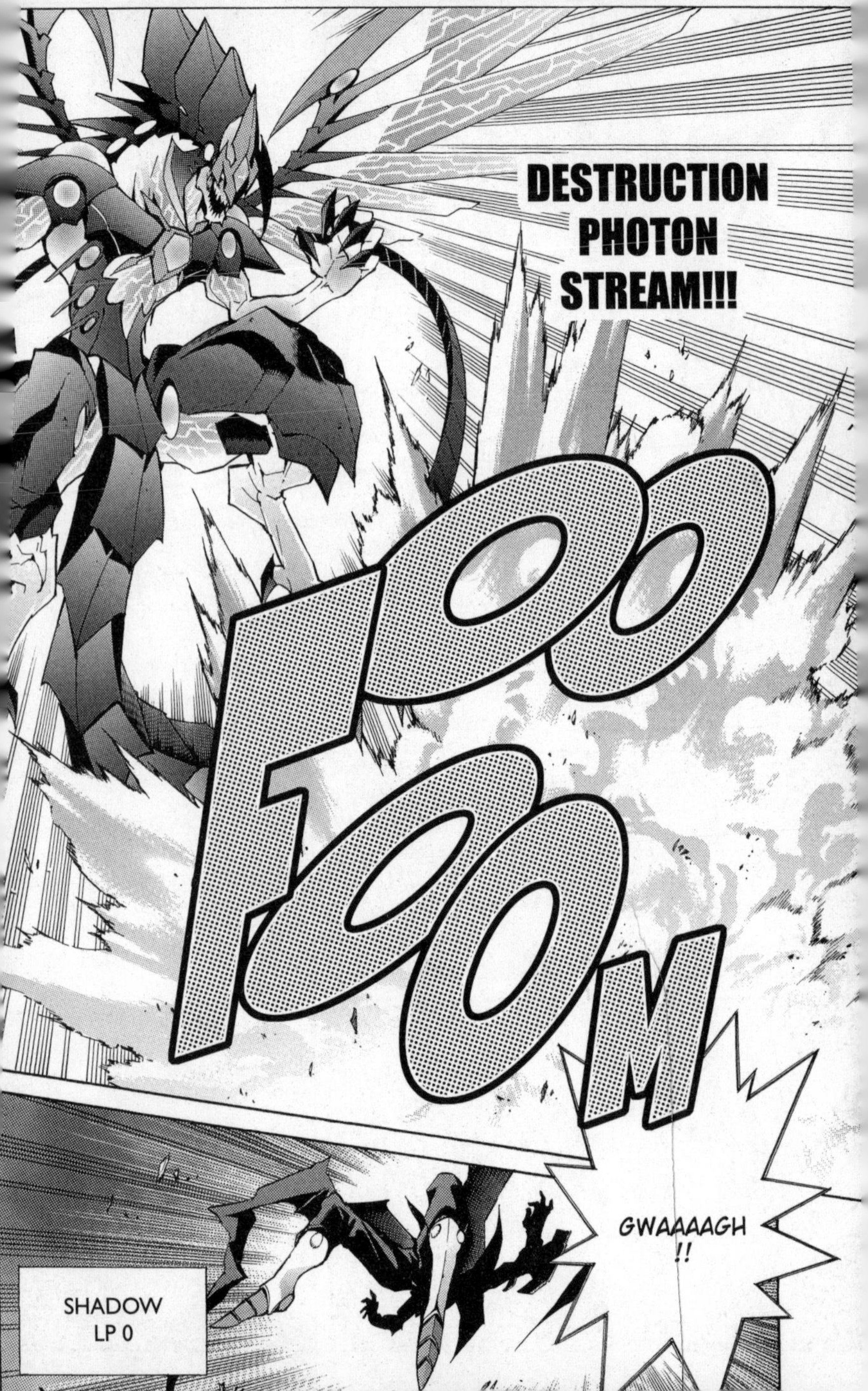
DESTRUCTION PHOTON STREAM!!!
FOOOOOM
GWAAAAGH !!
SHADOW LP 0

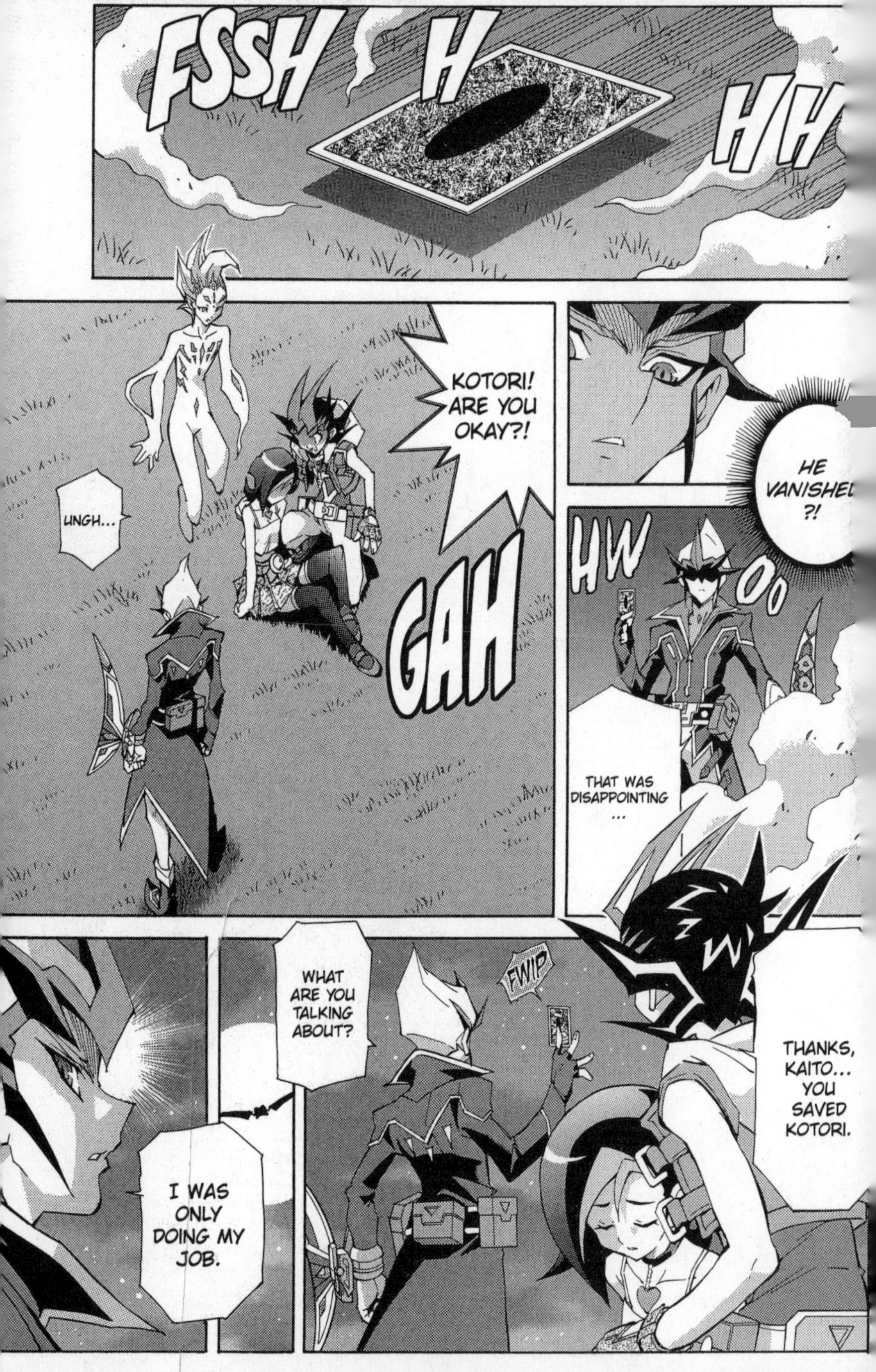
FSSH
H
HH
HE VANISHED ?!
HWOO
THAT WAS DISAPPOINTING ...
KOTORI! ARE YOU OKAY?!
GAH
UNGH...
THANKS, KAITO... YOU SAVED KOTORI.
FWIP
WHAT ARE YOU TALKING ABOUT?
I WAS ONLY DOING MY JOB.

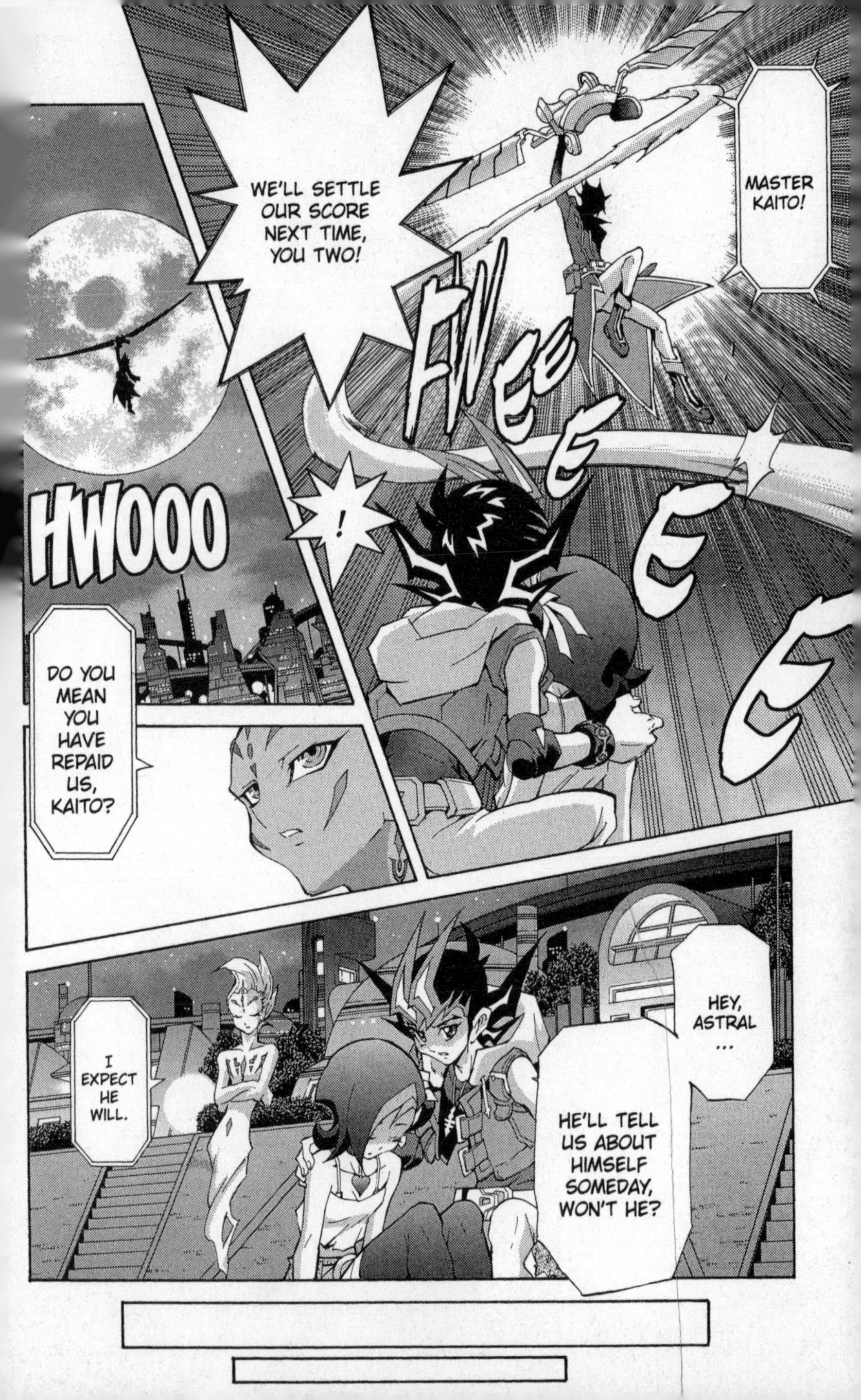
MASTER KAITO!
WE'LL SETTLE OUR SCORE NEXT TIME, YOU TWO!
FWEEEEEE
HWOOO
!
DO YOU MEAN YOU HAVE REPAID US, KAITO?
HEY, ASTRAL...
HE'LL TELL US ABOUT HIMSELF SOMEDAY, WON'T HE?
I EXPECT HE WILL.

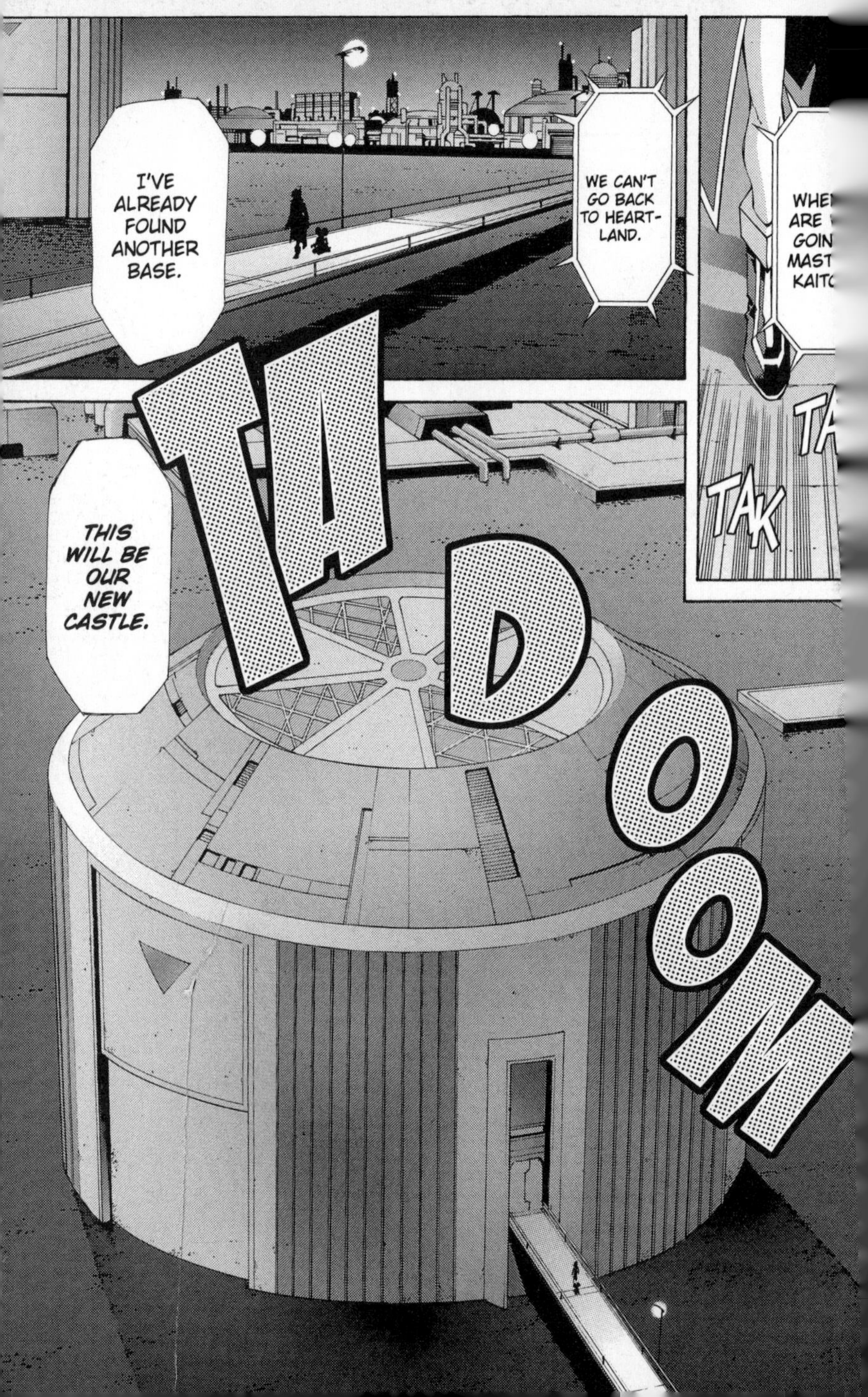
WHE
ARE
GOIN
MAST
KAITO
TA
TAK
WE CAN'T GO BACK TO HEART-LAND.
I'VE ALREADY FOUND ANOTHER BASE.
TA DOOM
THIS WILL BE OUR NEW CASTLE.

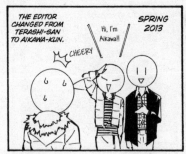

astral's journal - terashi-san
absent

SPRING 2013
Hi, I'm Aikawa!!
THE EDITOR CHANGED FROM TERASHI-SAN TO AIKAWA-KUN.
CHEERY
TERASHI-SAN, I'VE KNOWN YOU SINCE I WORKED ON THE OCTOBER 2003 ISSUE OF VJ.
Handsome
THAT JOB WAS A SUPPLEMENT MANGA FOR SWORD OF MANA.
IN THE FALL OF 2010, AN ABRUPT PHONE CALL FROM YOU CHANGED MY LIFE.
MIYOSHI-SAN? HI, IT'S BEEN A WHILE.
THIS IS SUDDEN, BUT WE'RE GATHERING WRITERS FOR YU-GI-OH! MANGA.
WANNA JOIN THE COMPETITION?
I OWE YOU SO VERY, VERY MUCH FOR THAT!
WAVE
WAVE
BYE!

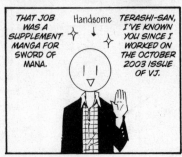

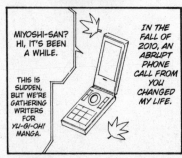

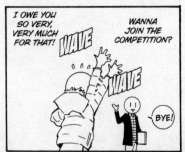

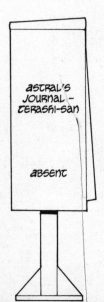

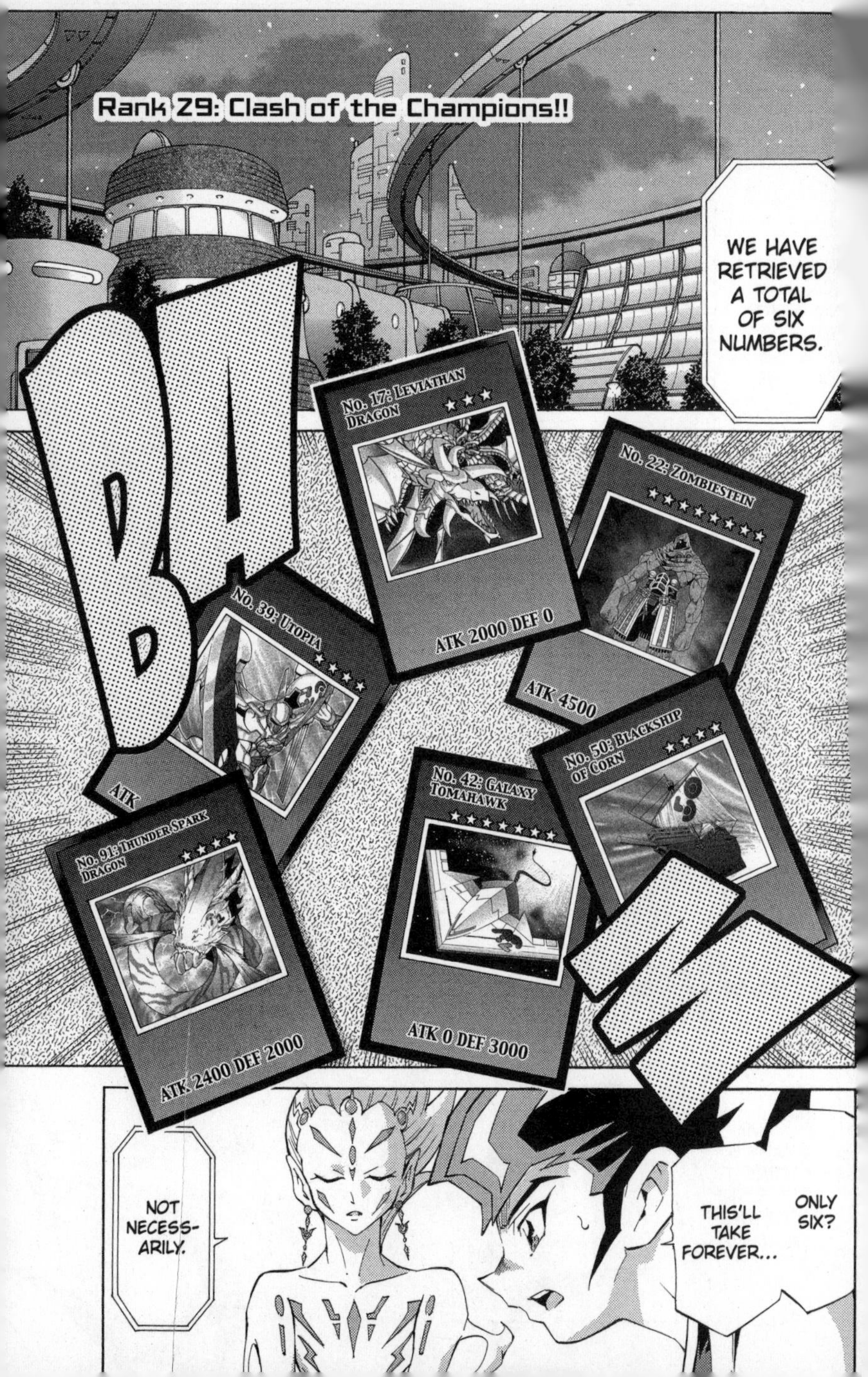
Rank 29: Clash of the Champions!!
WE HAVE RETRIEVED A TOTAL OF SIX NUMBERS.
BAM
No. 17: Leviathan Dragon
ATK 2000 DEF 0
No. 22: Zombiestein
ATK 4500
No. 39: Utopia
ATK
No. 50: Blackship of Corn
No. 42: Galaxy Tomahawk
ATK 0 DEF 3000
No. 91: Thunder Spark Dragon
ATK 2400 DEF 2000
ONLY SIX?
THIS'LL TAKE FOREVER...
NOT NECESS-ARILY.

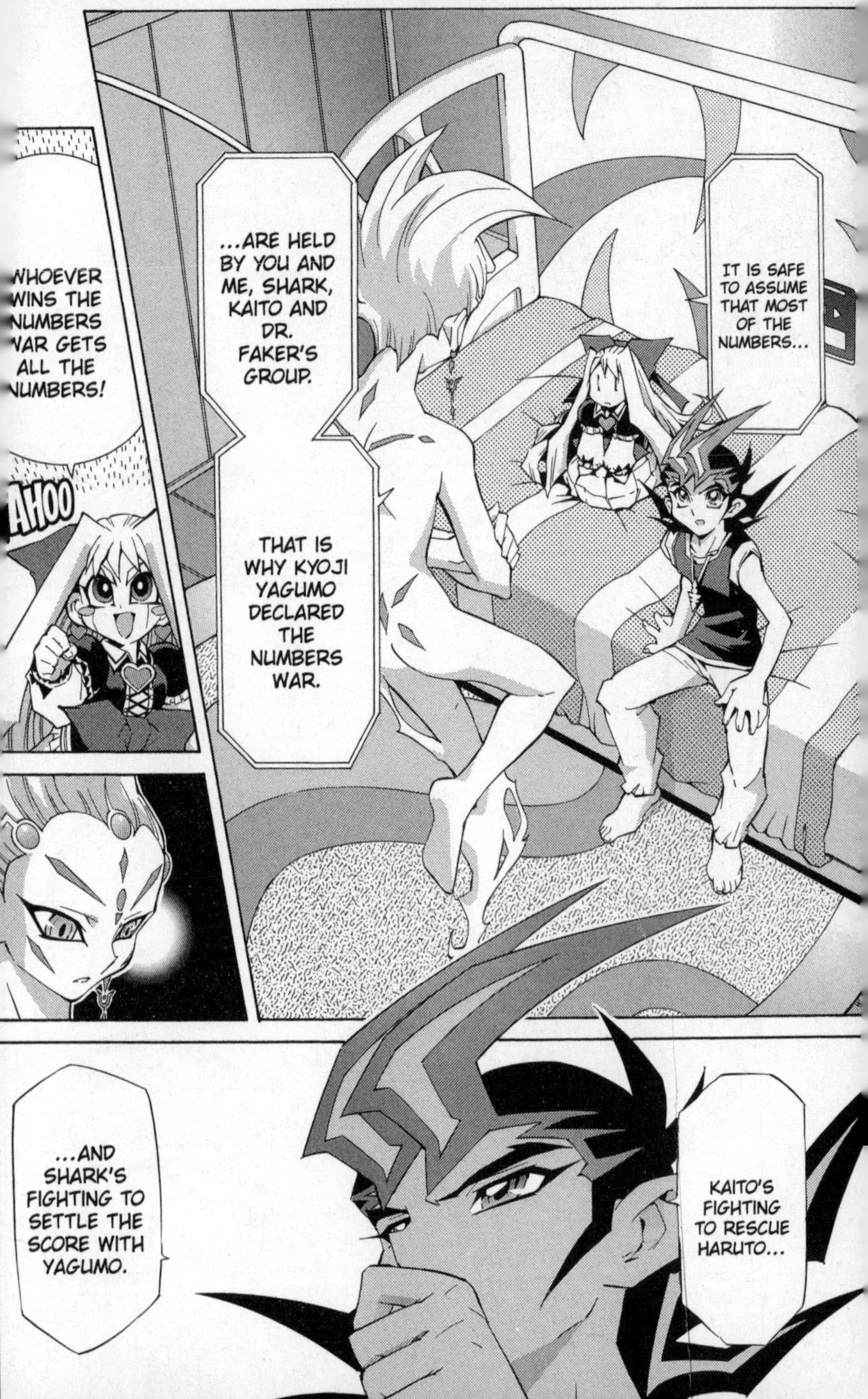
IT IS SAFE TO ASSUME THAT MOST OF THE NUMBERS...
...ARE HELD BY YOU AND ME, SHARK, KAITO AND DR. FAKER'S GROUP.
THAT IS WHY KYOJI YAGUMO DECLARED THE NUMBERS WAR.
WHOEVER WINS THE NUMBERS WAR GETS ALL THE NUMBERS!
AHOO
KAITO'S FIGHTING TO RESCUE HARUTO...
...AND SHARK'S FIGHTING TO SETTLE THE SCORE WITH YAGUMO.

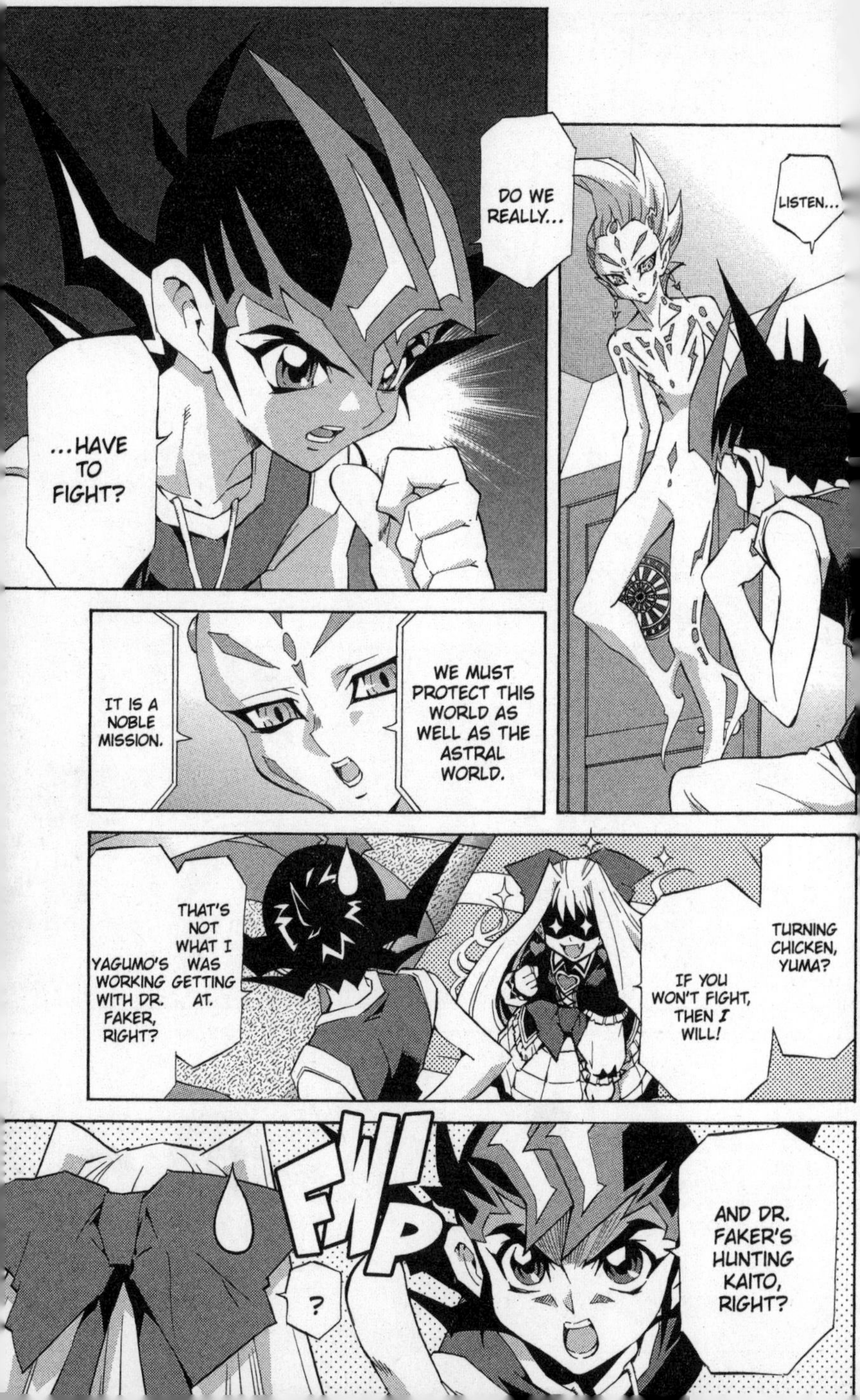
LISTEN...
DO WE REALLY...
...HAVE TO FIGHT?
WE MUST PROTECT THIS WORLD AS WELL AS THE ASTRAL WORLD.
IT IS A NOBLE MISSION.
TURNING CHICKEN, YUMA?
IF YOU WON'T FIGHT, THEN *I* WILL!
THAT'S NOT WHAT I WAS GETTING AT.
YAGUMO'S WORKING WITH DR. FAKER, RIGHT?
AND DR. FAKER'S HUNTING KAITO, RIGHT?
FWIP
?

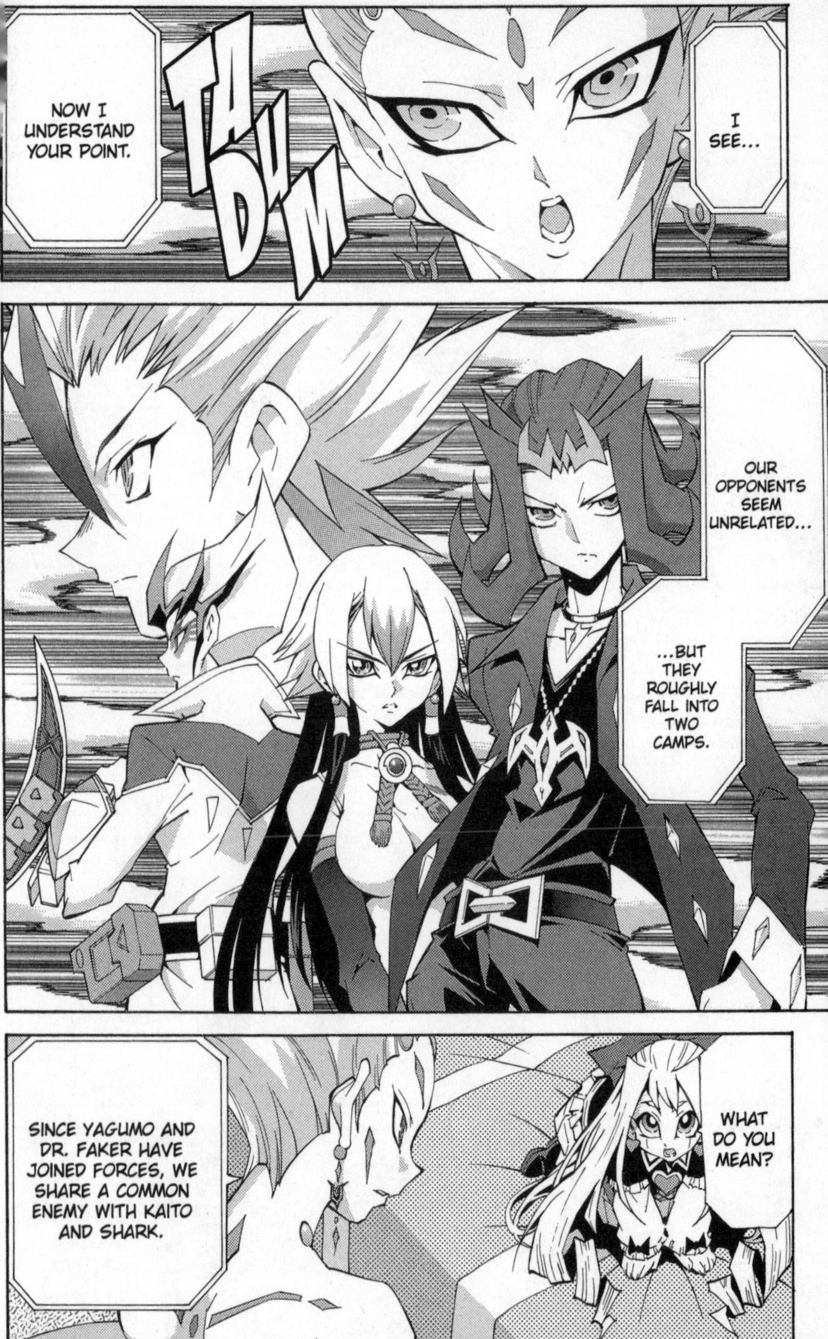
I SEE...
TA DUM
NOW I UNDERSTAND YOUR POINT.
OUR OPPONENTS SEEM UNRELATED...
...BUT THEY ROUGHLY FALL INTO TWO CAMPS.
WHAT DO YOU MEAN?
SINCE YAGUMO AND DR. FAKER HAVE JOINED FORCES, WE SHARE A COMMON ENEMY WITH KAITO AND SHARK.

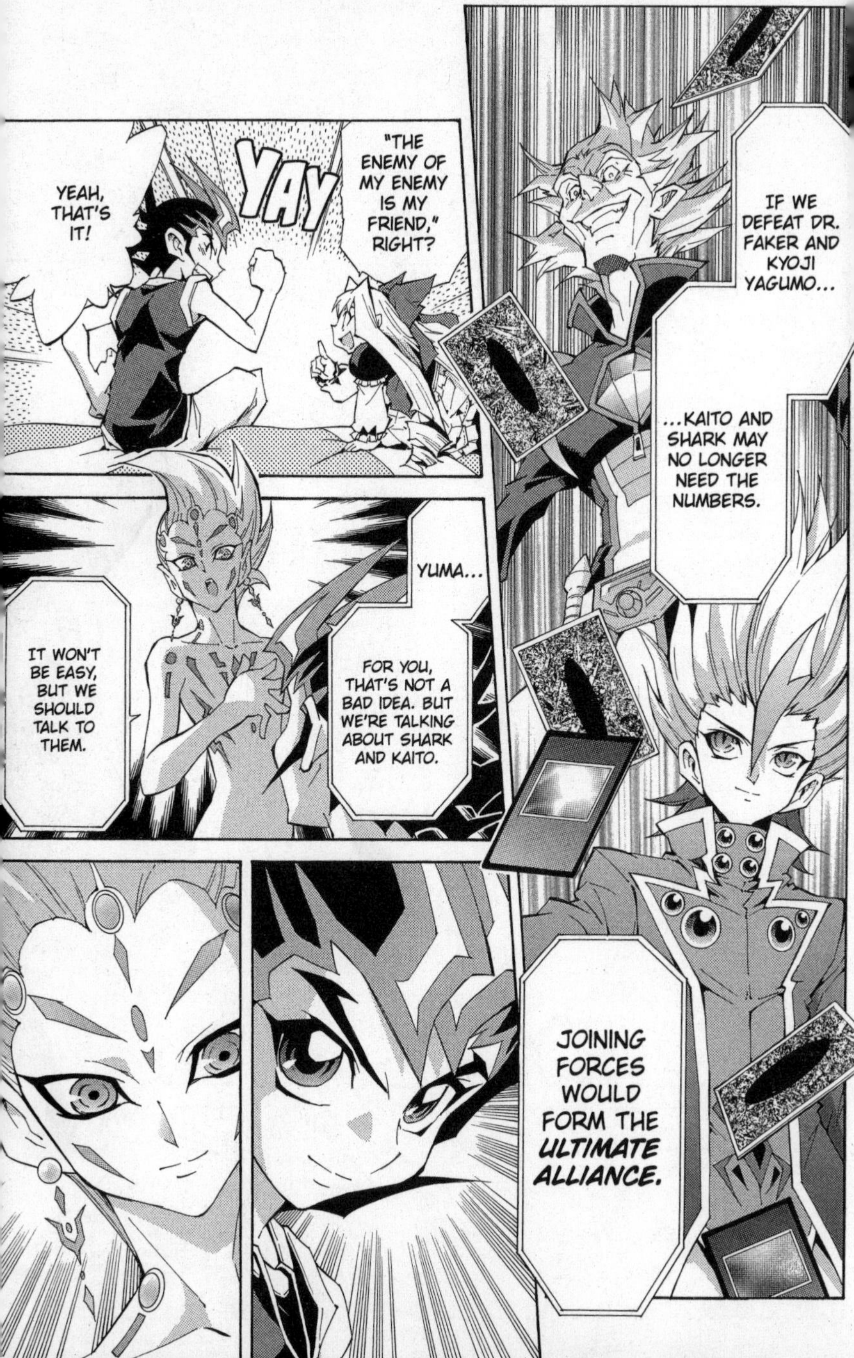
IF WE DEFEAT DR. FAKER AND KYOJI YAGUMO...
...KAITO AND SHARK MAY NO LONGER NEED THE NUMBERS.
JOINING FORCES WOULD FORM THE *ULTIMATE ALLIANCE.*
"THE ENEMY OF MY ENEMY IS MY FRIEND," RIGHT?
YAY
YEAH, THAT'S IT!
YUMA...
FOR YOU, THAT'S NOT A BAD IDEA. BUT WE'RE TALKING ABOUT SHARK AND KAITO.
IT WON'T BE EASY, BUT WE SHOULD TALK TO THEM.

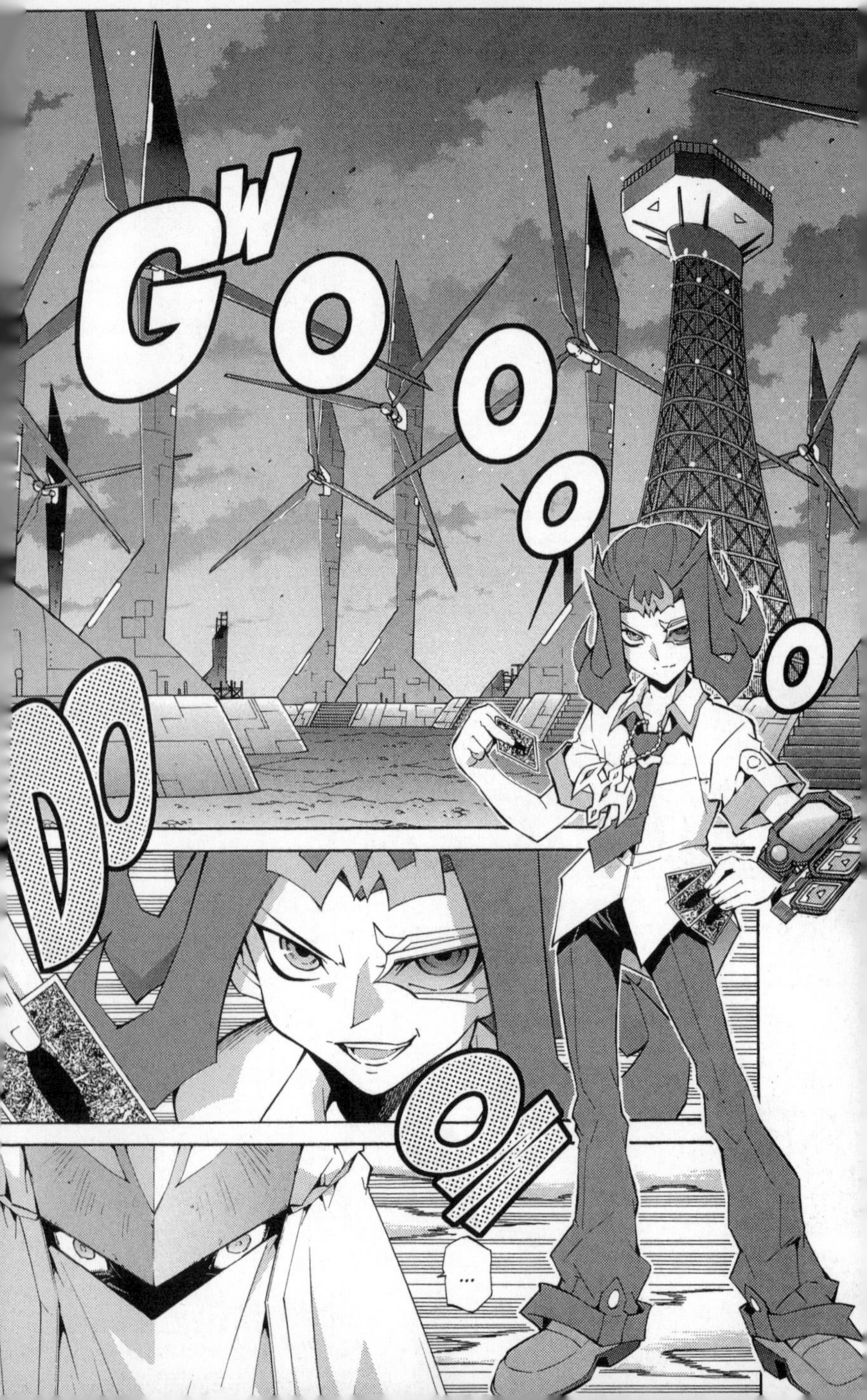
GWOOOOO
DOOON
...

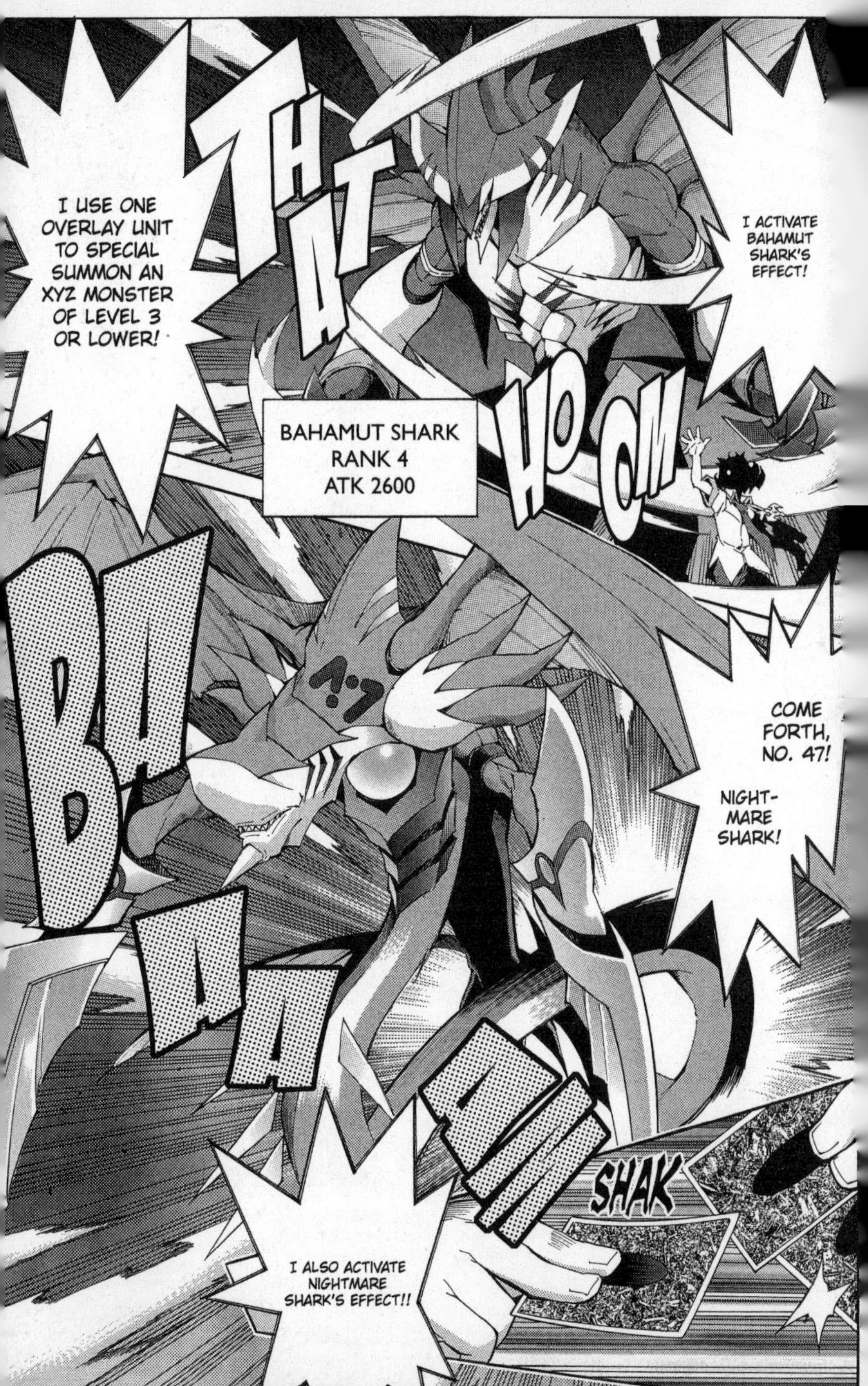
I ACTIVATE BAHAMUT SHARK'S EFFECT!
I USE ONE OVERLAY UNIT TO SPECIAL SUMMON AN XYZ MONSTER OF LEVEL 3 OR LOWER!
BAHAMUT SHARK
RANK 4
ATK 2600
COME FORTH, NO. 47!
NIGHT-MARE SHARK!
SHAK
I ALSO ACTIVATE NIGHTMARE SHARK'S EFFECT!!

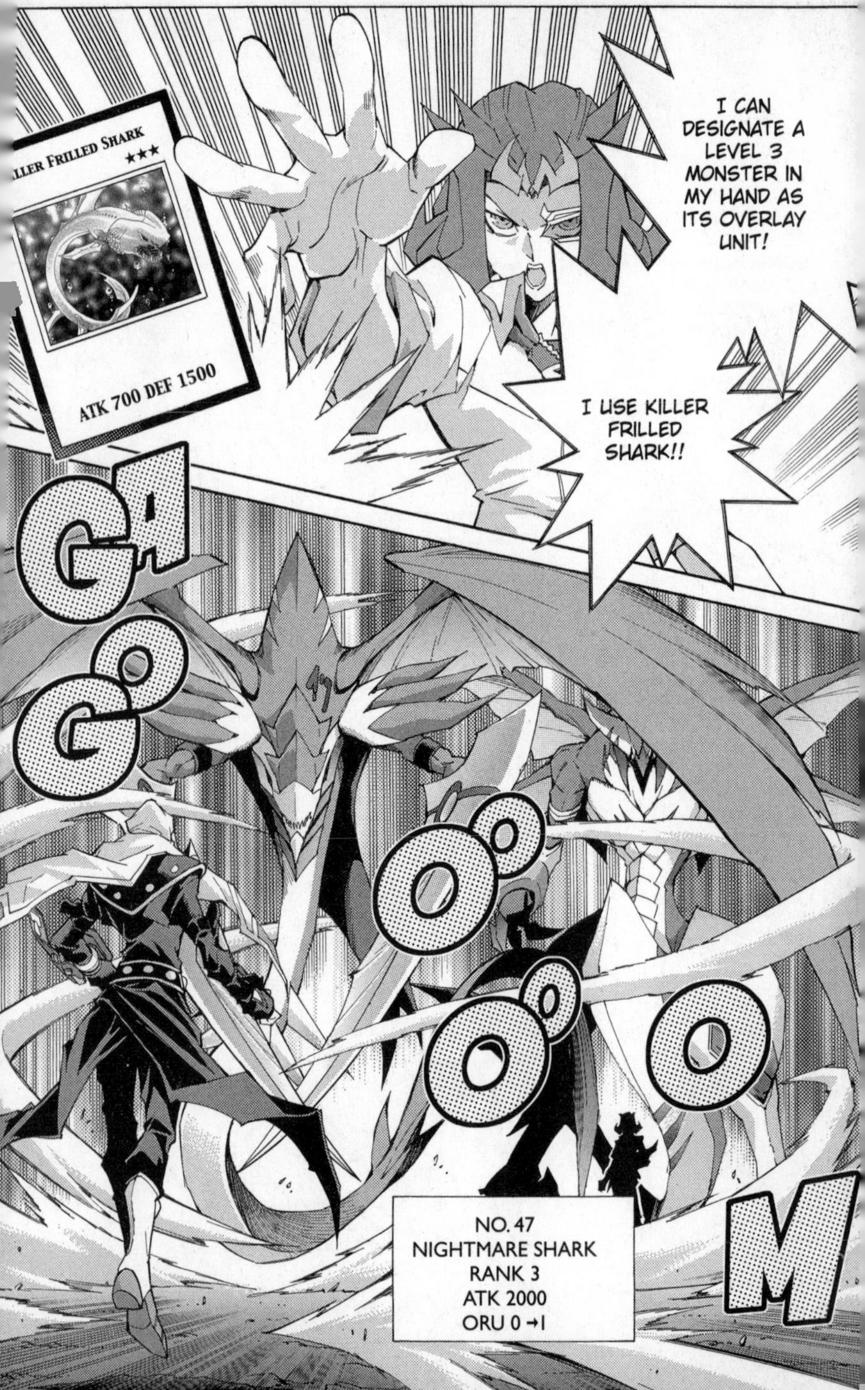
I CAN DESIGNATE A LEVEL 3 MONSTER IN MY HAND AS ITS OVERLAY UNIT!
I USE KILLER FRILLED SHARK!!
LLER FRILLED SHARK ★★★
ATK 700 DEF 1500
GAGOOOOOOM
NO. 47
NIGHTMARE SHARK
RANK 3
ATK 2000
ORU 0 →1

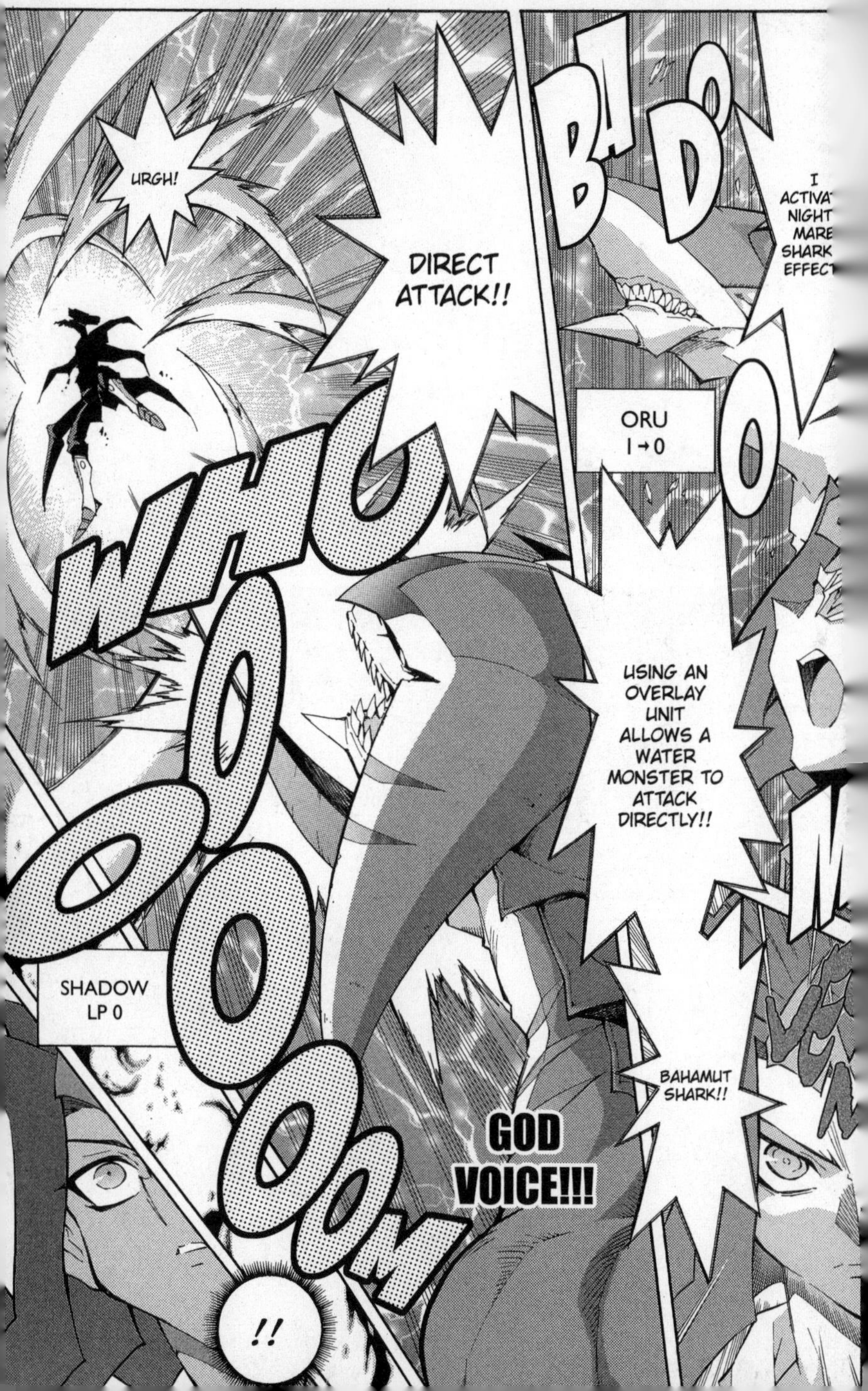
BADOOM
I
ACTIVAT
NIGHT
MARE
SHARK
EFFECT
ORU
1→0
USING AN OVERLAY UNIT ALLOWS A WATER MONSTER TO ATTACK DIRECTLY!!
BAHAMUT SHARK!!
DIRECT ATTACK!!
URGH!
WHOOOOOOM
SHADOW
LP 0
GOD VOICE!!!
!!

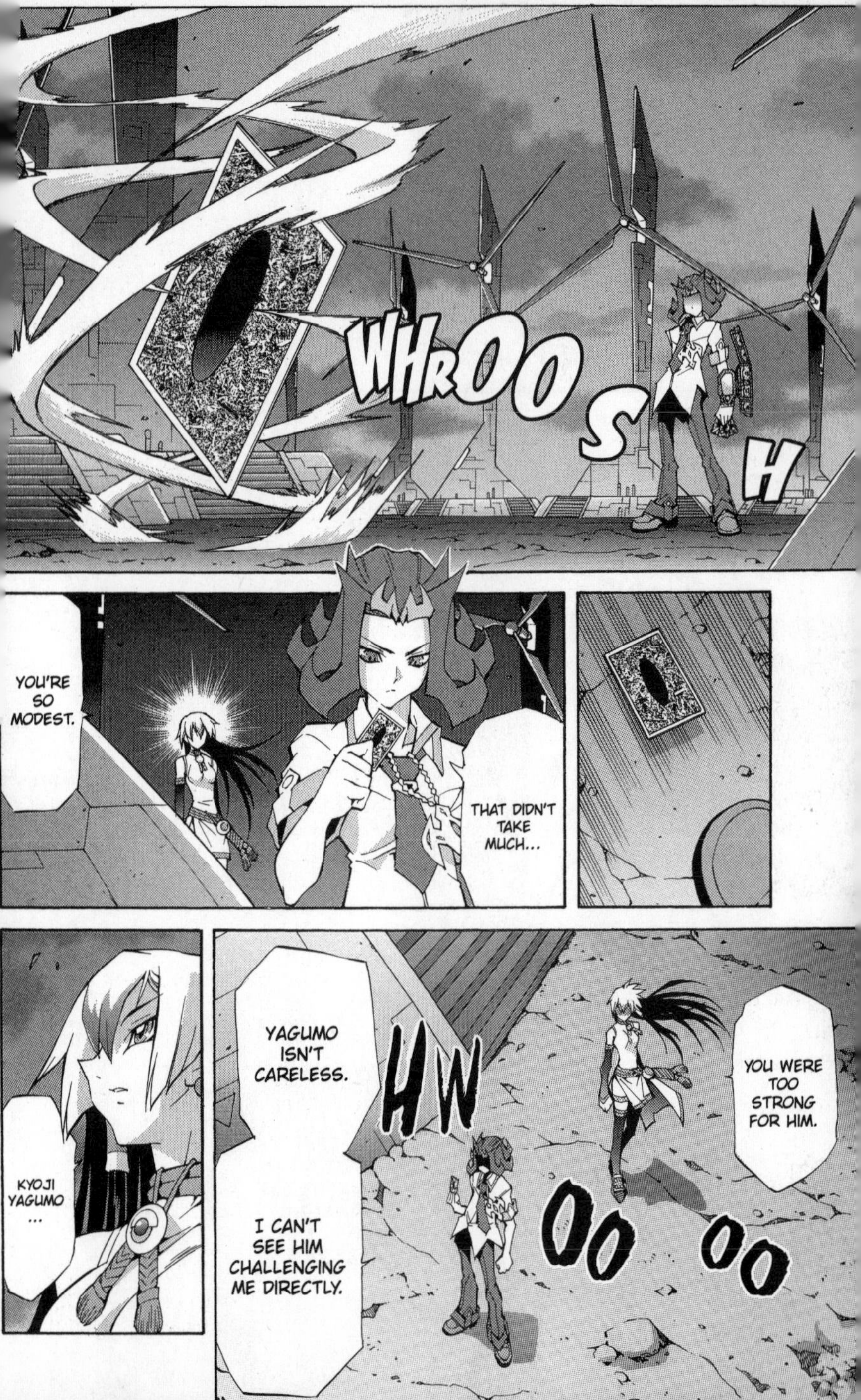
WHROOOSH
THAT DIDN'T TAKE MUCH...
YOU'RE SO MODEST.
YOU WERE TOO STRONG FOR HIM.
HWOOOO
YAGUMO ISN'T CARELESS.
I CAN'T SEE HIM CHALLENGING ME DIRECTLY.
KYOJI YAGUMO ...

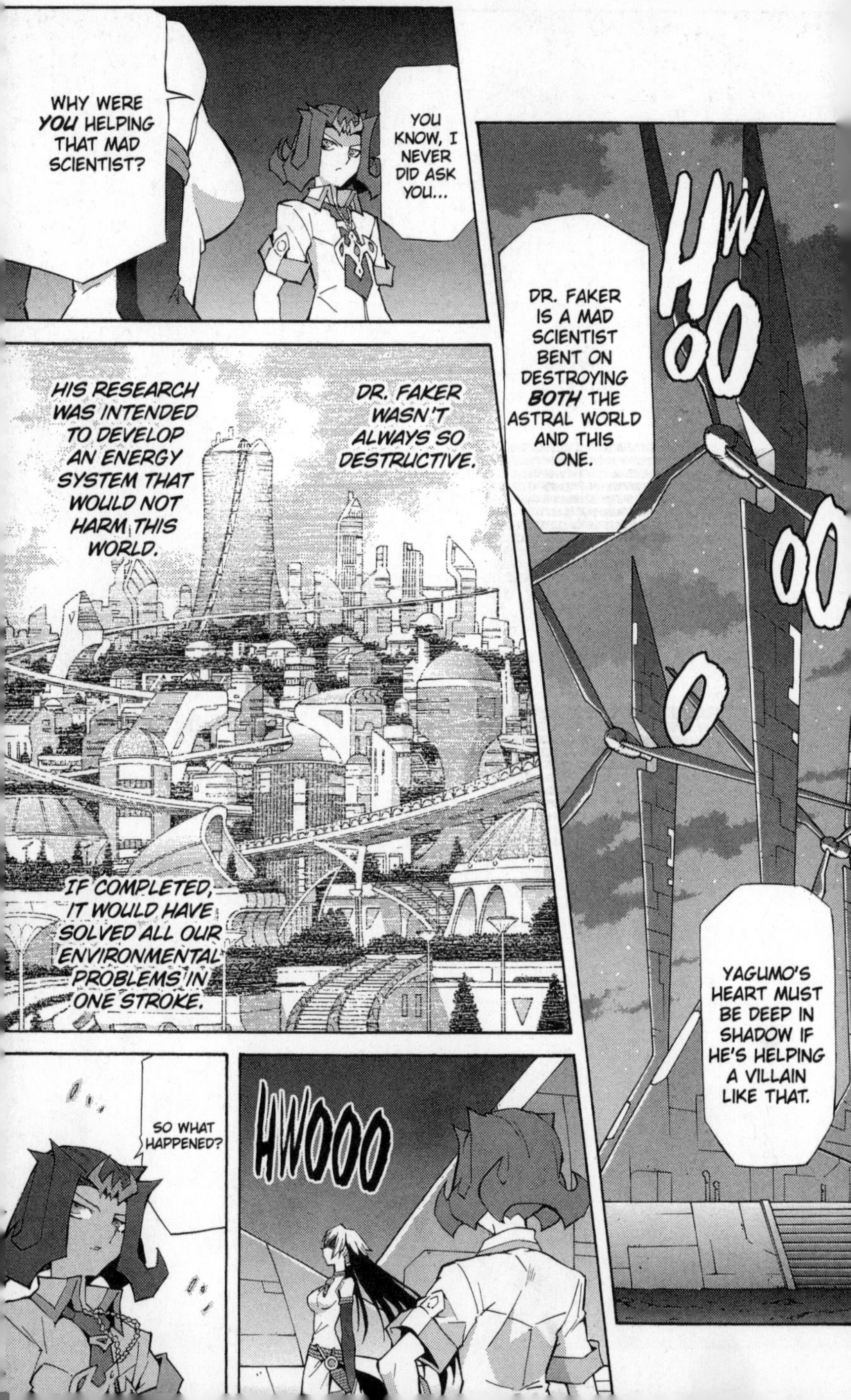
HWOOOOO
DR. FAKER IS A MAD SCIENTIST BENT ON DESTROYING *BOTH* THE ASTRAL WORLD AND THIS ONE.
YAGUMO'S HEART MUST BE DEEP IN SHADOW IF HE'S HELPING A VILLAIN LIKE THAT.
YOU KNOW, I NEVER DID ASK YOU...
WHY WERE *YOU* HELPING THAT MAD SCIENTIST?
DR. FAKER WASN'T ALWAYS SO DESTRUCTIVE.
HIS RESEARCH WAS INTENDED TO DEVELOP AN ENERGY SYSTEM THAT WOULD NOT HARM THIS WORLD.
IF COMPLETED, IT WOULD HAVE SOLVED ALL OUR ENVIRONMENTAL PROBLEMS IN ONE STROKE.
HWOOO
SO WHAT HAPPENED?

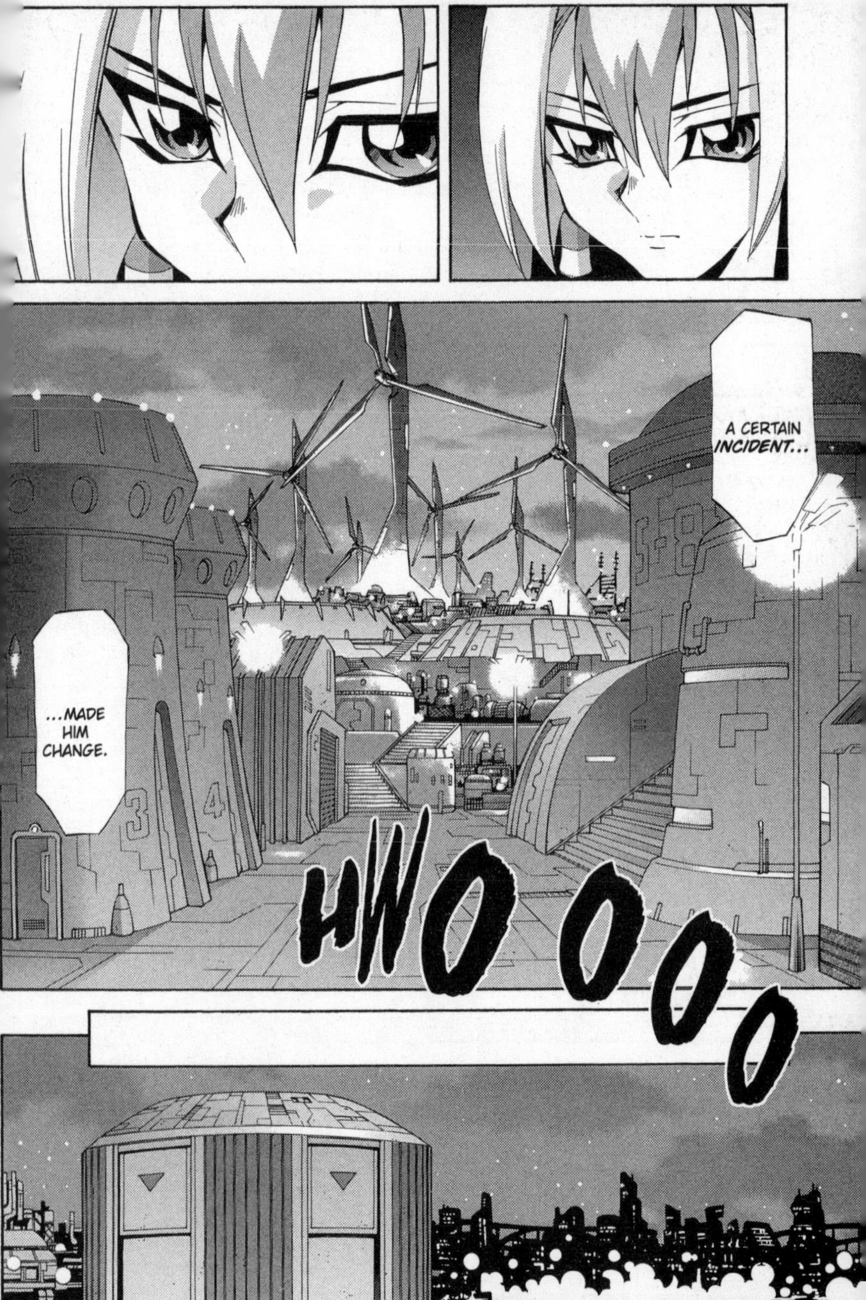
A CERTAIN INCIDENT...
...MADE HIM CHANGE.
HWOOOO

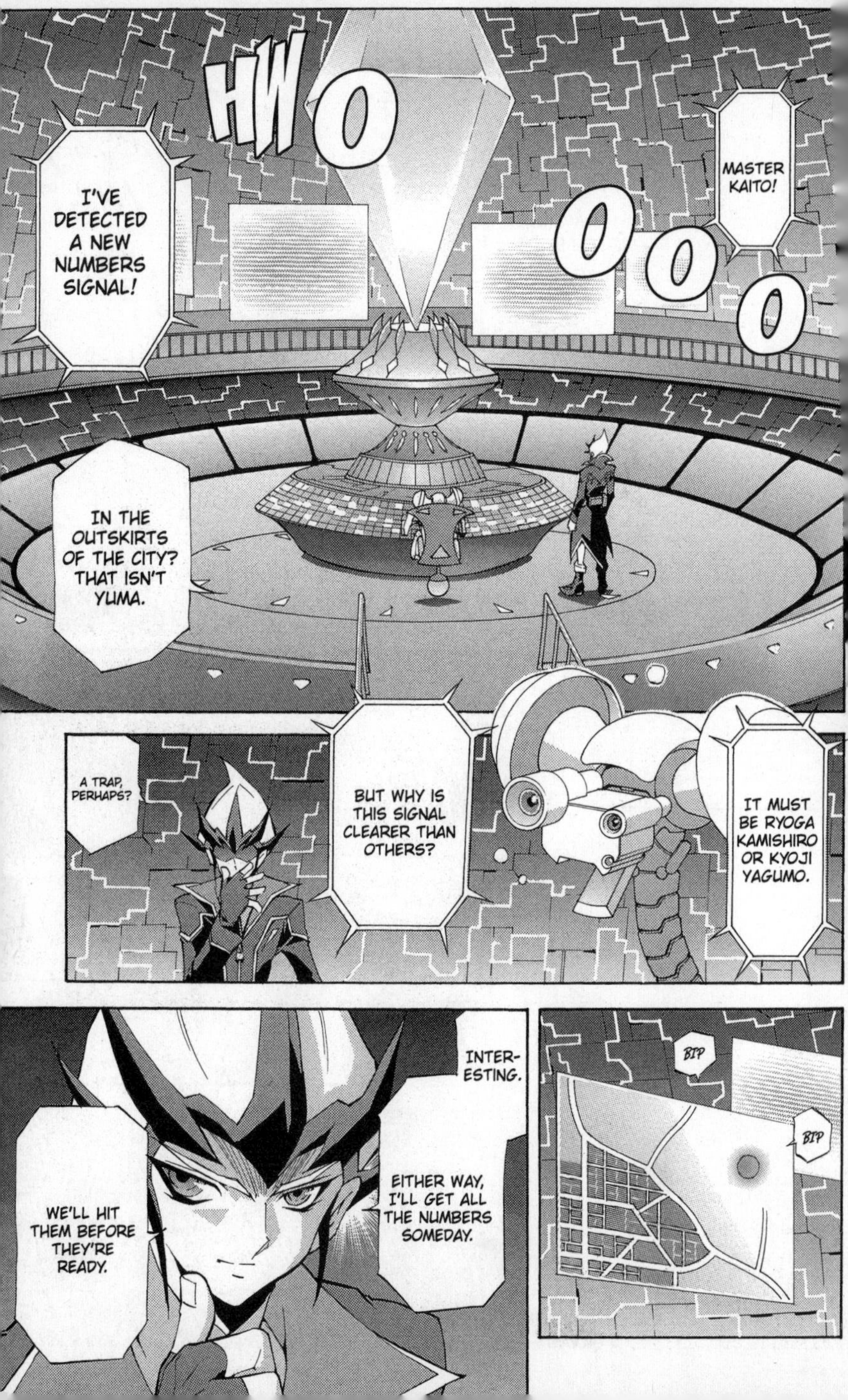
MASTER KAITO!
HWOOOO
I'VE DETECTED A NEW NUMBERS SIGNAL!
IN THE OUTSKIRTS OF THE CITY? THAT ISN'T YUMA.
IT MUST BE RYOGA KAMISHIRO OR KYOJI YAGUMO.
BUT WHY IS THIS SIGNAL CLEARER THAN OTHERS?
A TRAP, PERHAPS?
BIP
BIP
INTER-ESTING.
EITHER WAY, I'LL GET ALL THE NUMBERS SOMEDAY.
WE'LL HIT THEM BEFORE THEY'RE READY.

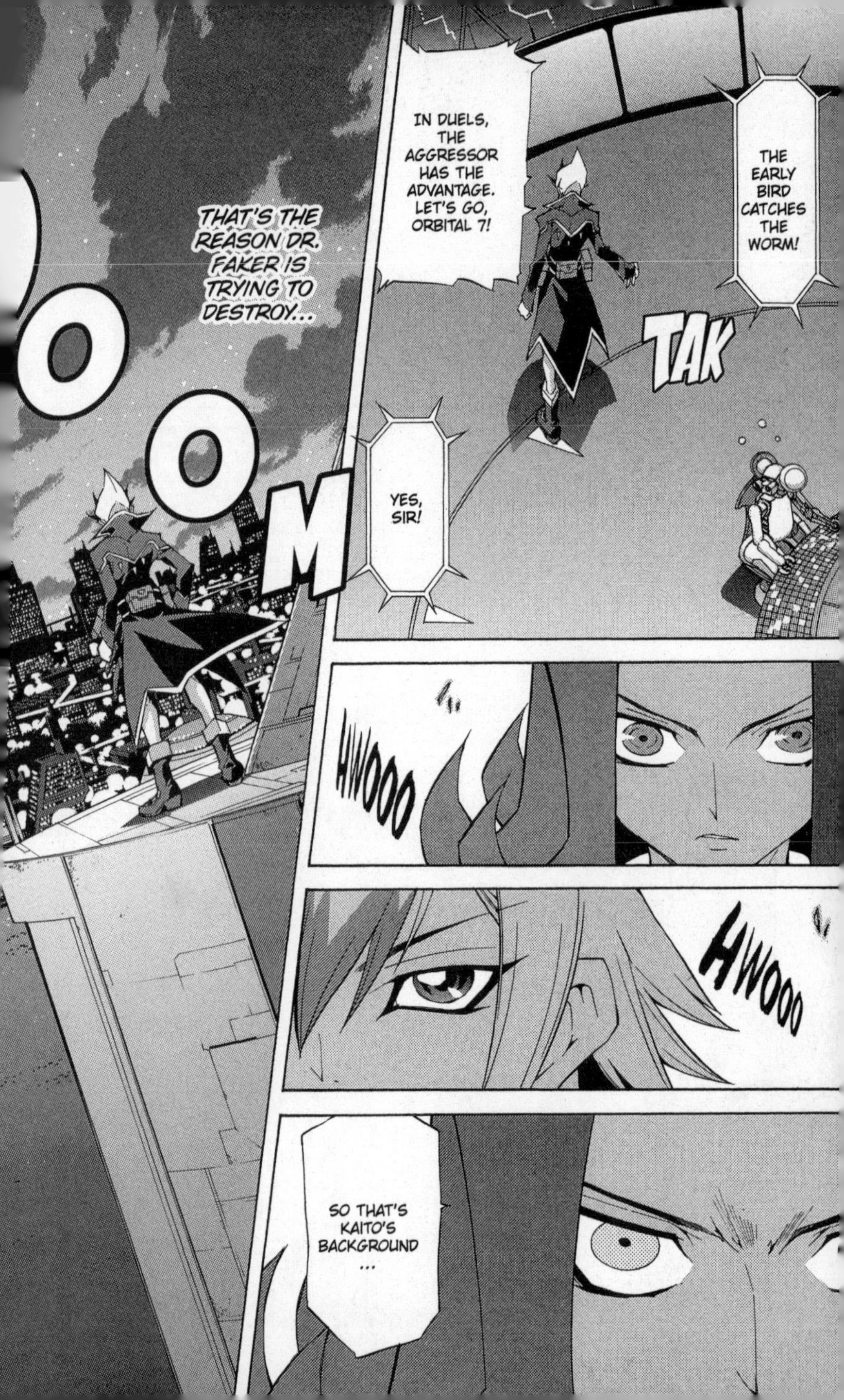
THE EARLY BIRD CATCHES THE WORM!
IN DUELS, THE AGGRESSOR HAS THE ADVANTAGE. LET'S GO, ORBITAL 7!
TAK
YES, SIR!
HWOOO
HWOOO
SO THAT'S KAITO'S BACKGROUND ...
THAT'S THE REASON DR. FAKER IS TRYING TO DESTROY...
OOOM

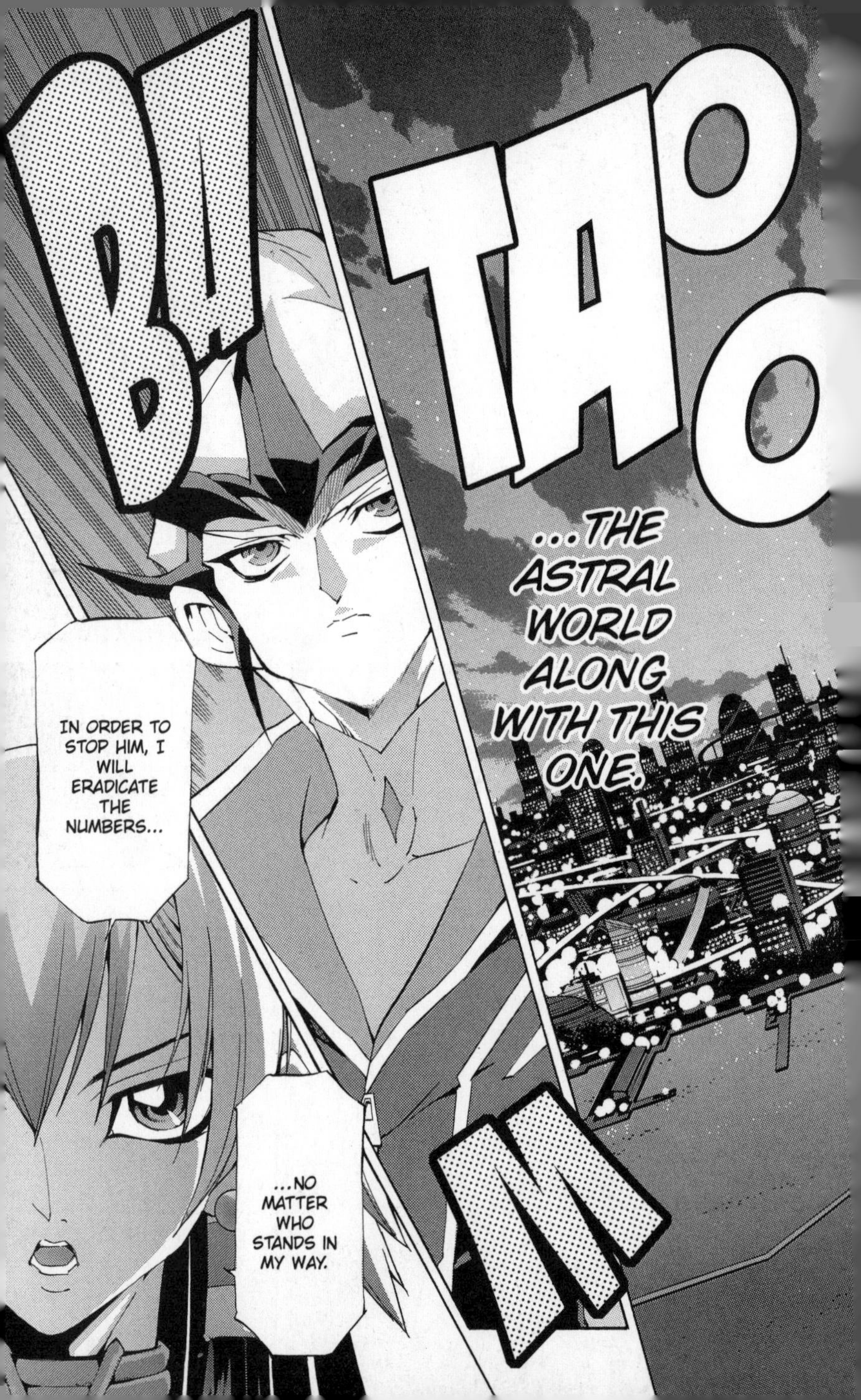
TAO
...THE ASTRAL WORLD ALONG WITH THIS ONE.
BA
IN ORDER TO STOP HIM, I WILL ERADICATE THE NUMBERS...
...NO MATTER WHO STANDS IN MY WAY.

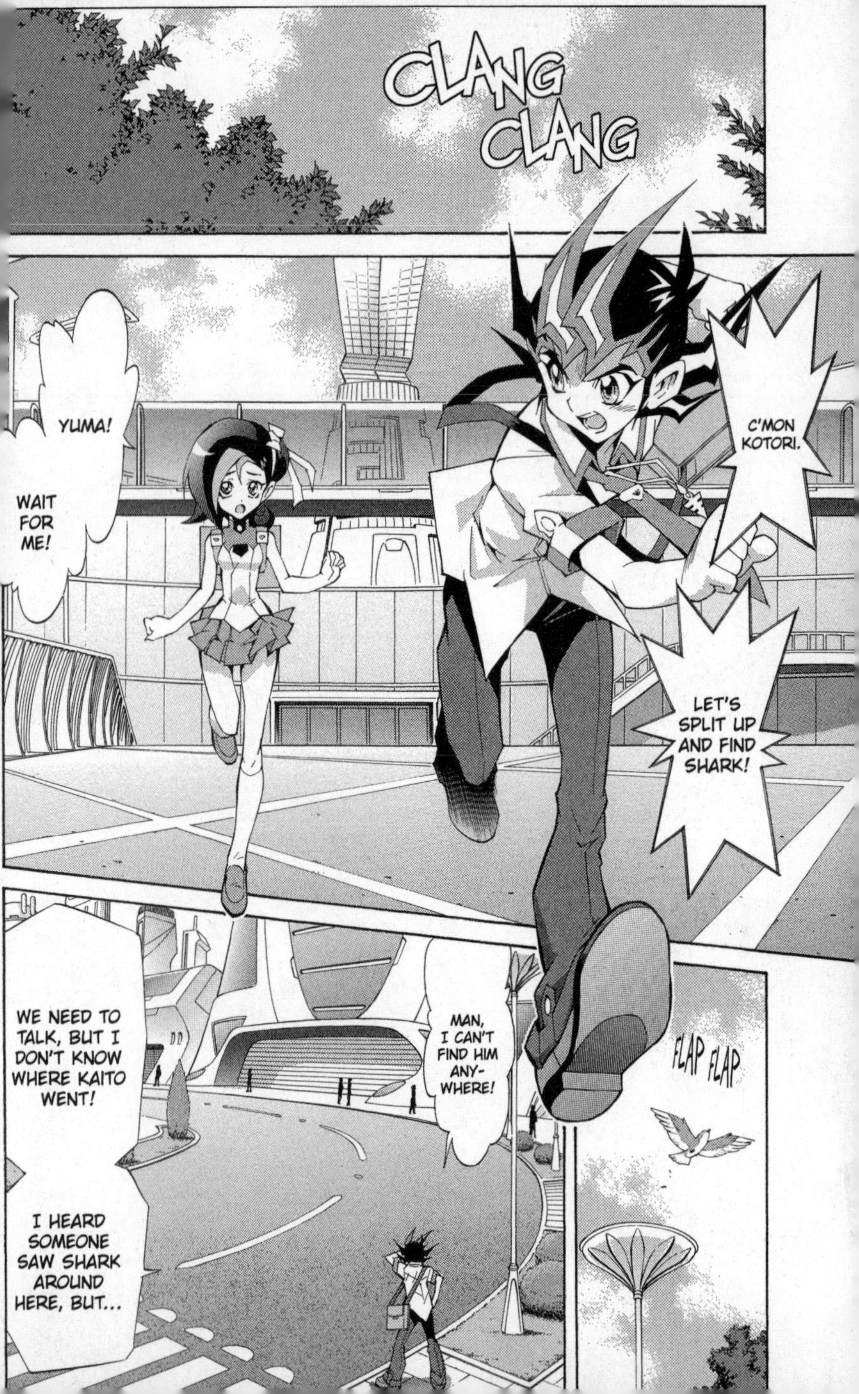
CLANG CLANG
C'MON KOTORI.
LET'S SPLIT UP AND FIND SHARK!
YUMA!
WAIT FOR ME!
FLAP FLAP
MAN, I CAN'T FIND HIM ANY-WHERE!
WE NEED TO TALK, BUT I DON'T KNOW WHERE KAITO WENT!
I HEARD SOMEONE SAW SHARK AROUND HERE, BUT...

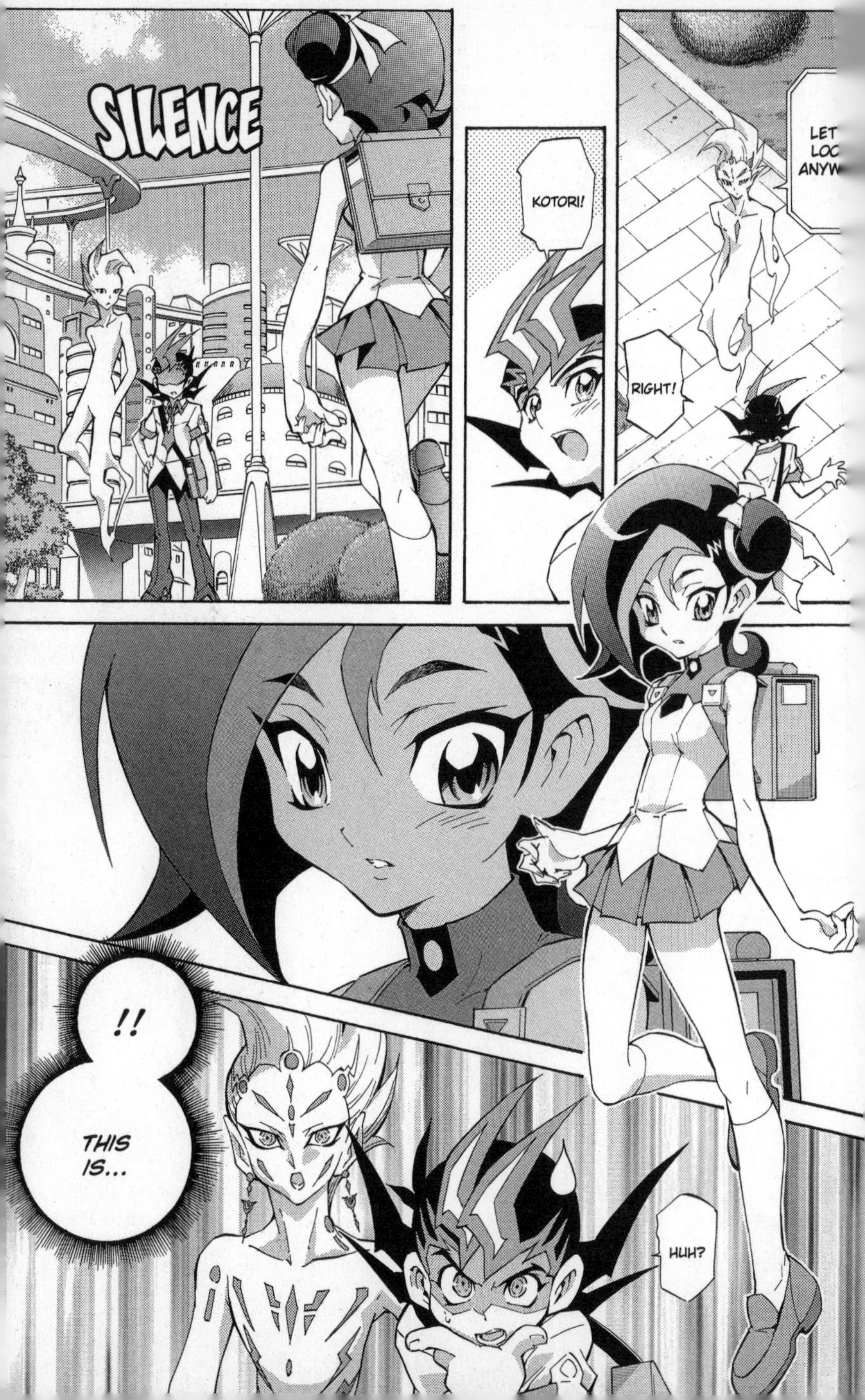
LET LOO ANYW
RIGHT!
KOTORI!
SILENCE
!!
THIS IS...
HUH?

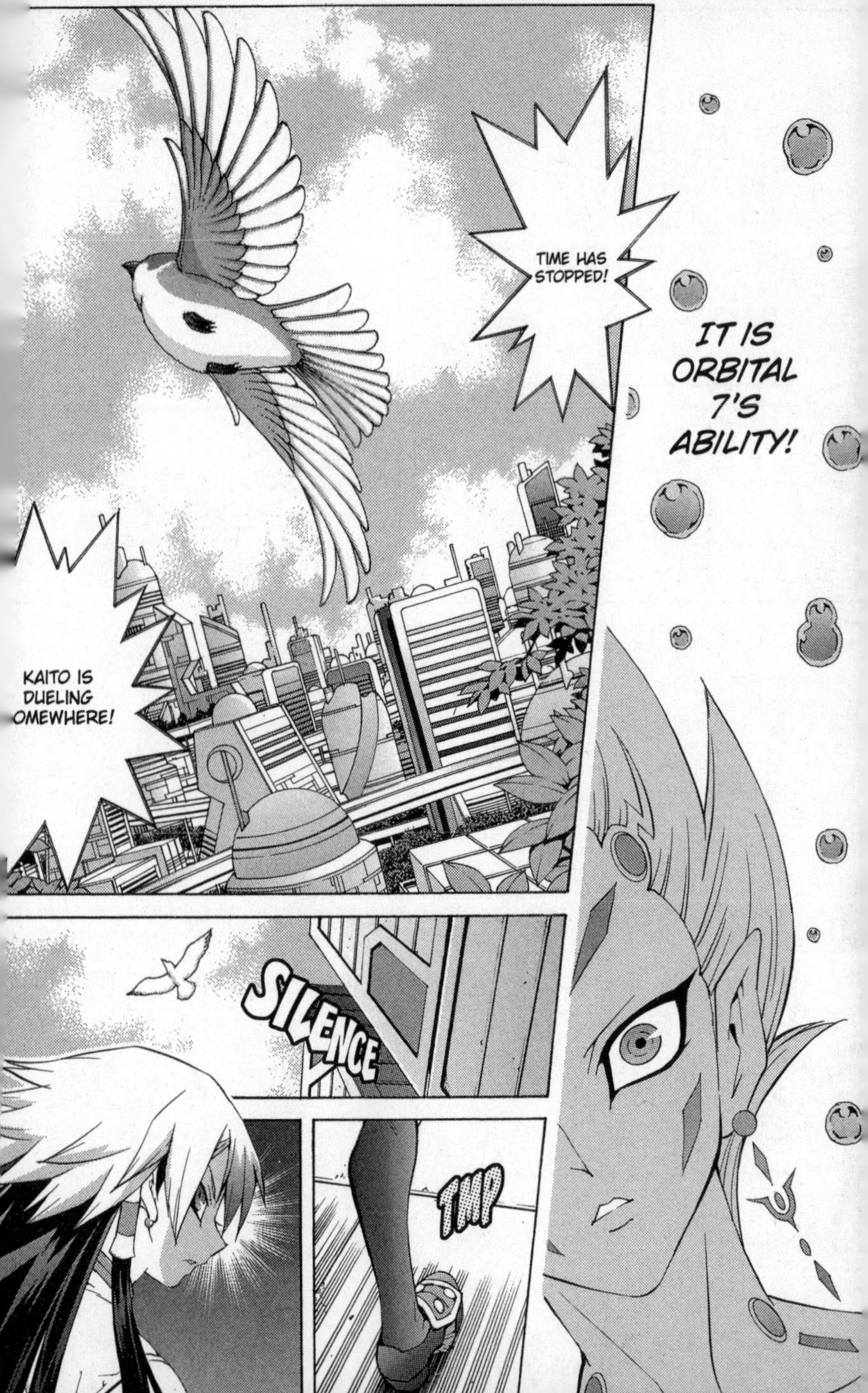
IT IS ORBITAL 7'S ABILITY!
TIME HAS STOPPED!
KAITO IS DUELING OMEWHERE!
SILENCE
TMP

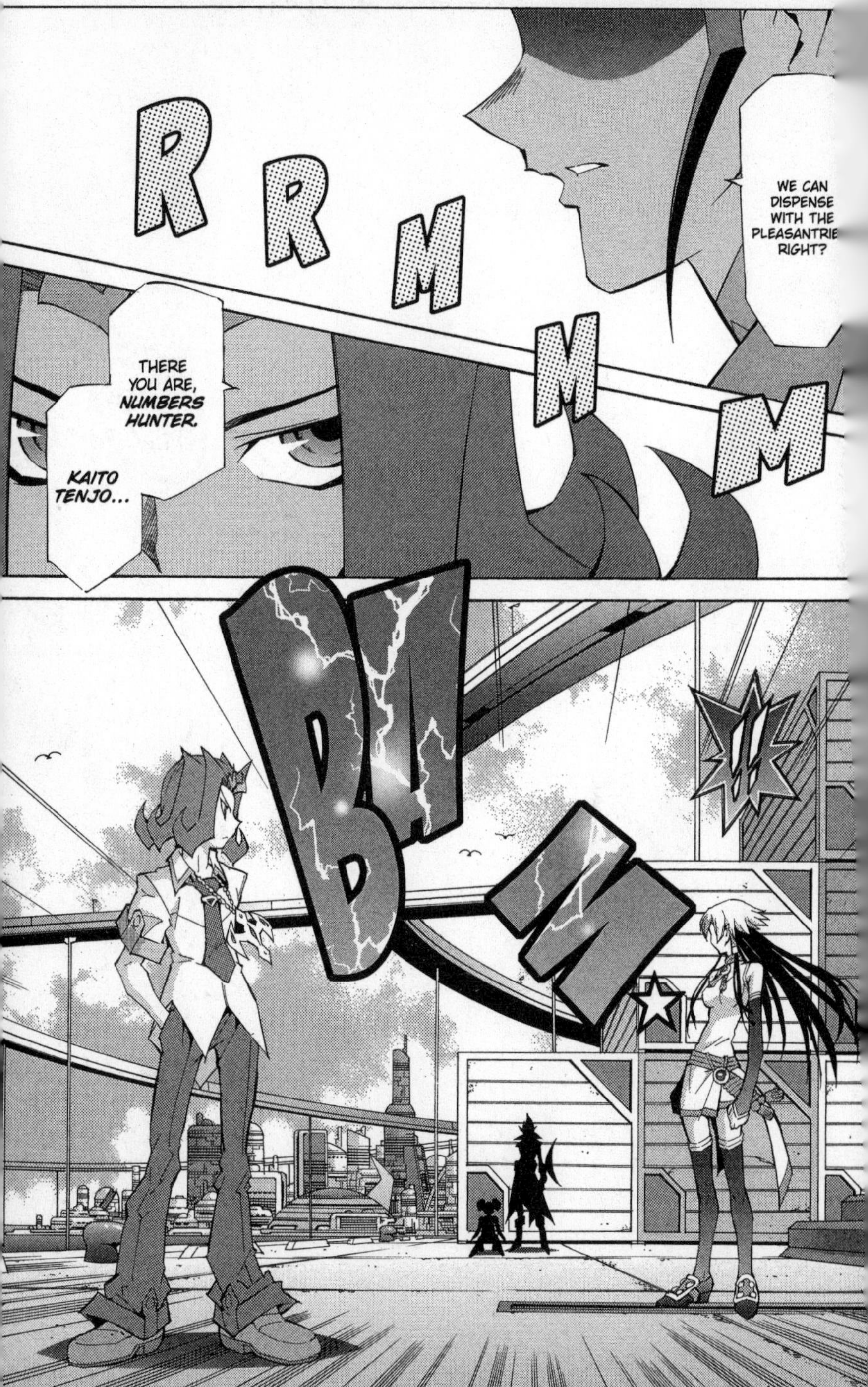
WE CAN DISPENSE WITH THE PLEASANTRIES, RIGHT?
RRMMMM
THERE YOU ARE, NUMBERS HUNTER.
KAITO TENJO...
!!
BAM

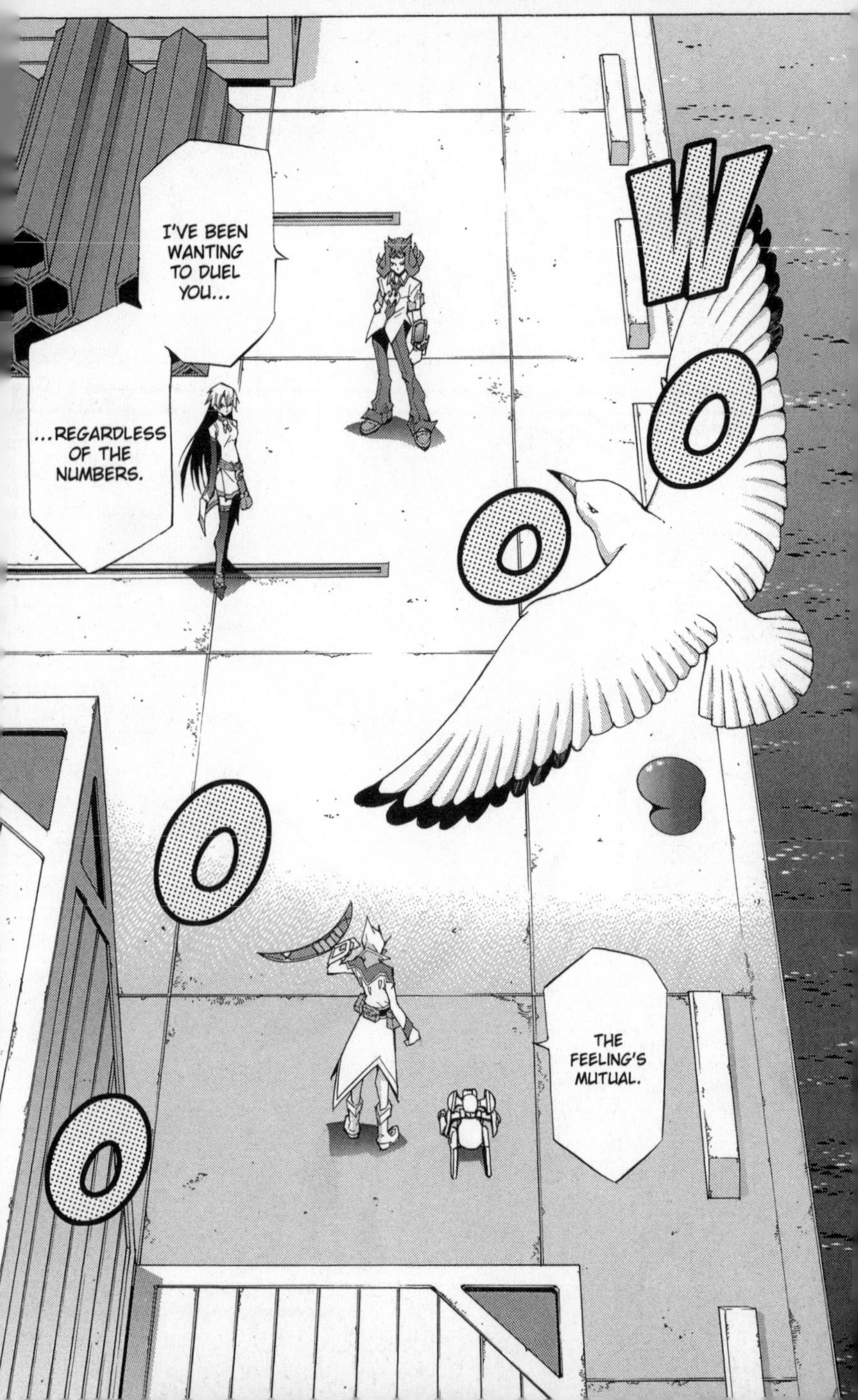
WOOOO
I'VE BEEN WANTING TO DUEL YOU...
...REGARDLESS OF THE NUMBERS.
THE FEELING'S MUTUAL.

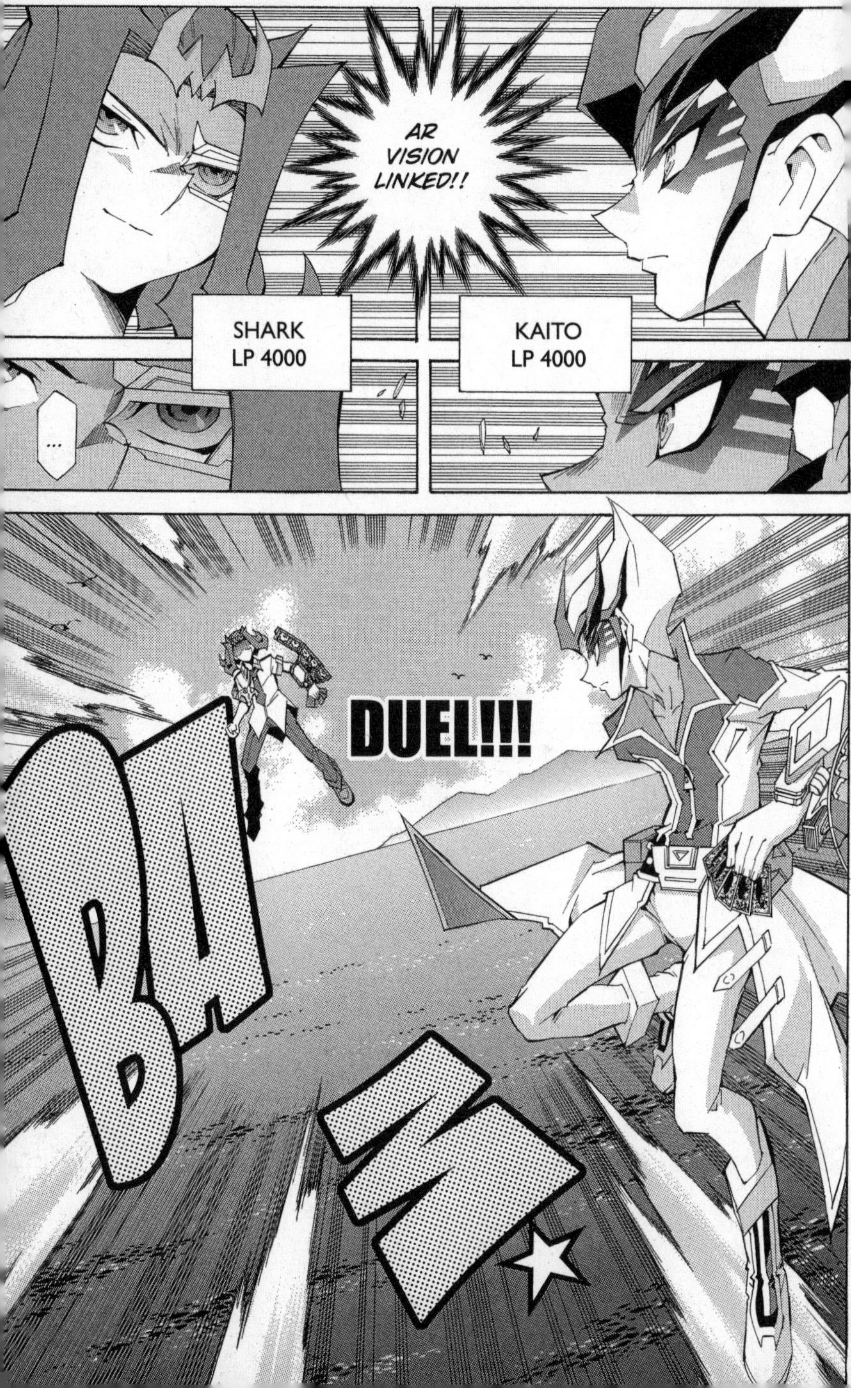

AR VISION LINKED!!
KAITO LP 4000
SHARK LP 4000
...
DUEL!!!
BAM

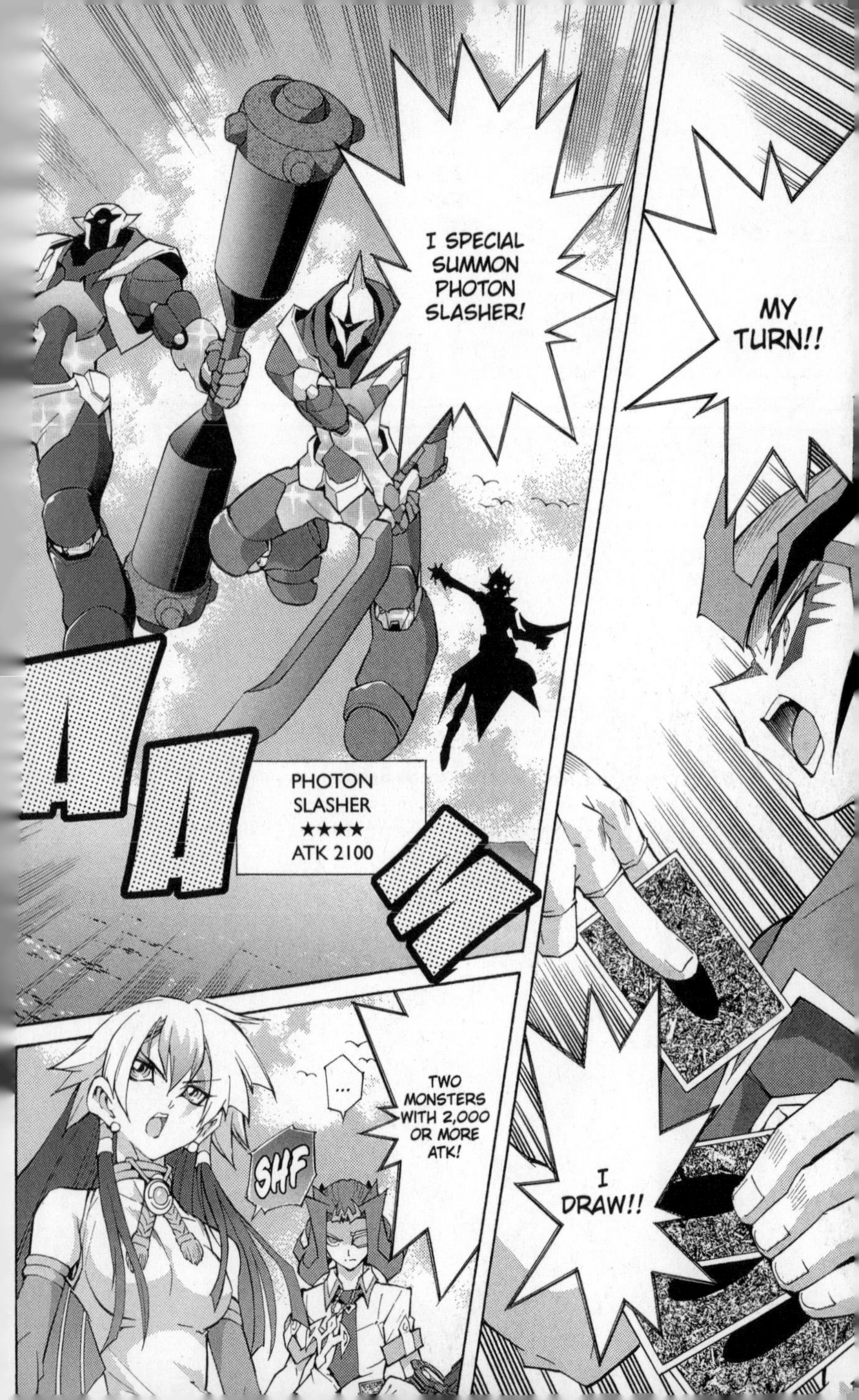
MY TURN!!
I DRAW!!
I SPECIAL SUMMON PHOTON SLASHER!
PHOTON SLASHER ★★★★ ATK 2100
TWO MONSTERS WITH 2,000 OR MORE ATK!
...
SHF

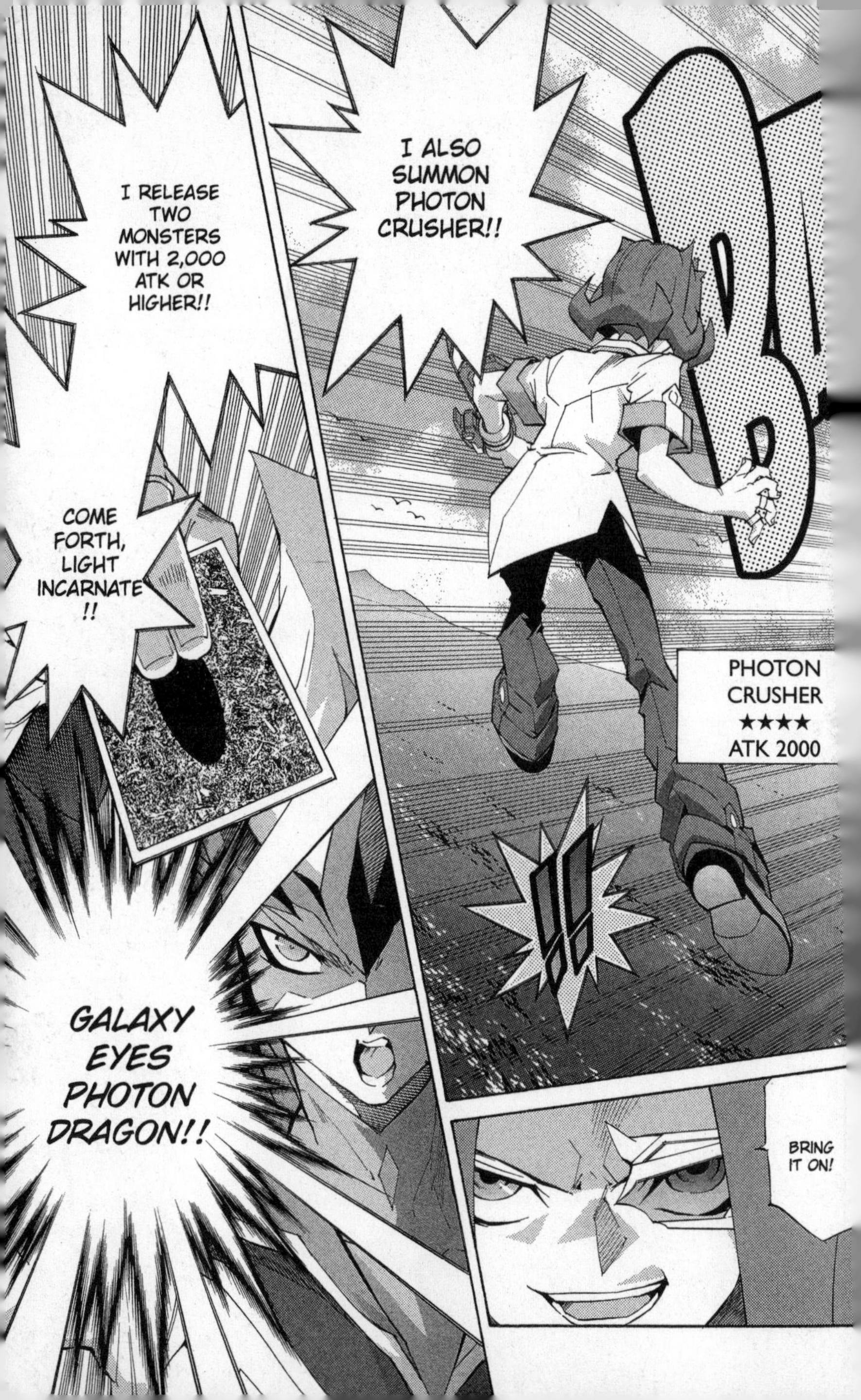
I ALSO SUMMON PHOTON CRUSHER!!
PHOTON CRUSHER ★★★★ ATK 2000
!!
BRING IT ON!
I RELEASE TWO MONSTERS WITH 2,000 ATK OR HIGHER!!
COME FORTH, LIGHT INCARNATE!!
GALAXY EYES PHOTON DRAGON!!

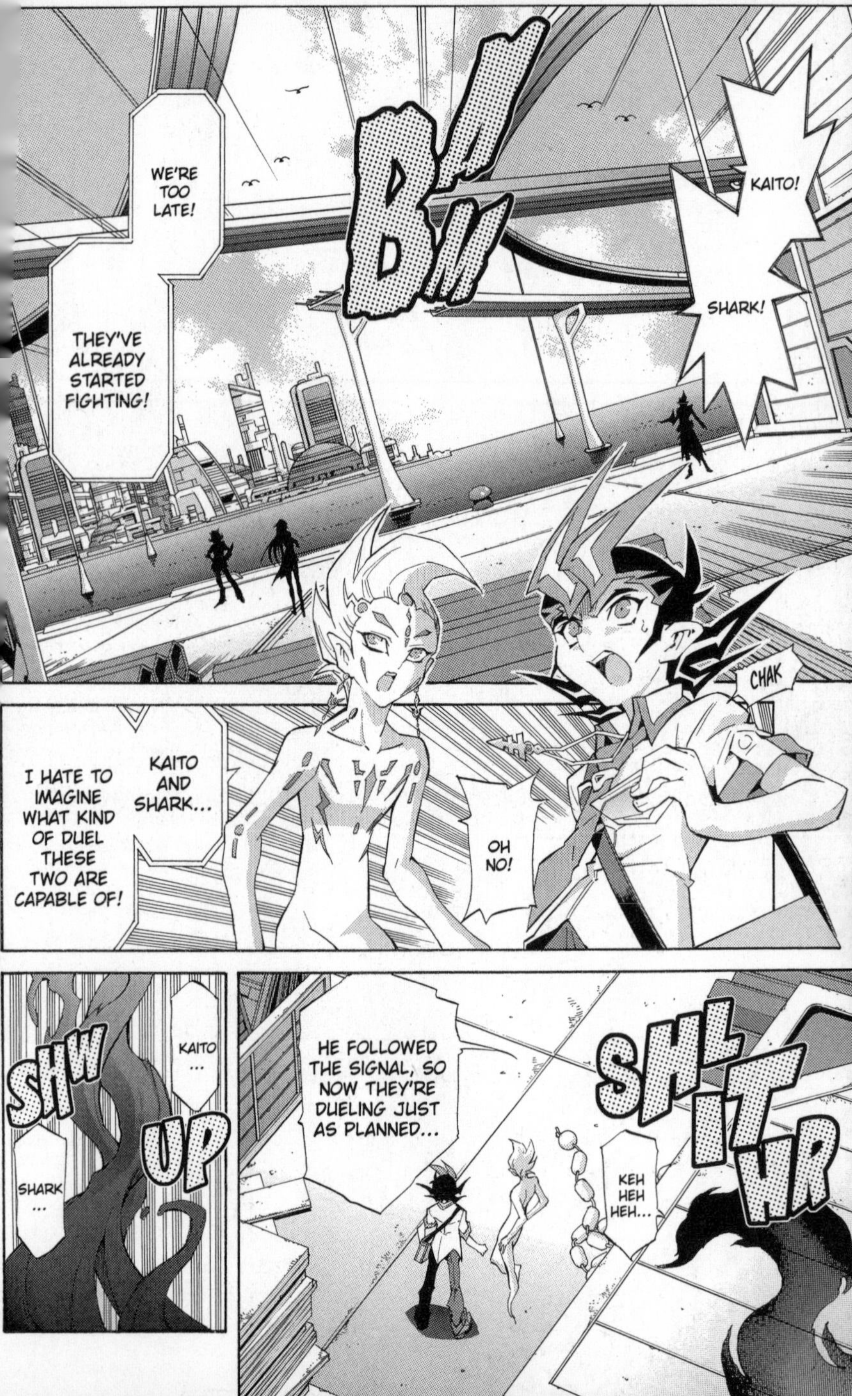
KAITO!
SHARK!
WE'RE TOO LATE!
THEY'VE ALREADY STARTED FIGHTING!
CHAK
OH NO!
KAITO AND SHARK...
I HATE TO IMAGINE WHAT KIND OF DUEL THESE TWO ARE CAPABLE OF!
HE FOLLOWED THE SIGNAL, SO NOW THEY'RE DUELING JUST AS PLANNED...
KEH HEH HEH...
SHW UP
KAITO...
SHARK...

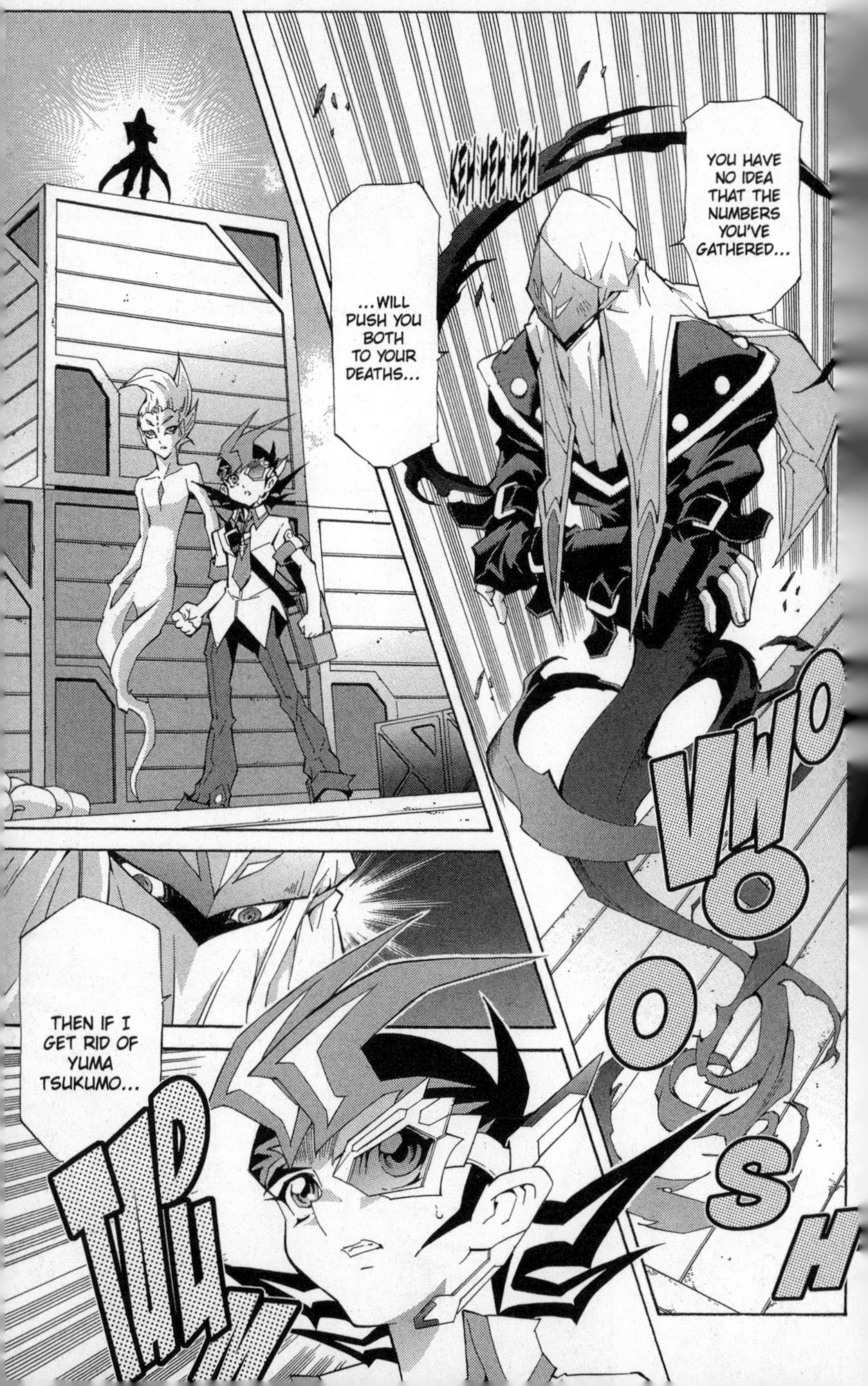
KEH HEH HEH
YOU HAVE NO IDEA THAT THE NUMBERS YOU'VE GATHERED...
...WILL PUSH YOU BOTH TO YOUR DEATHS...
VWOOOOSH
THEN IF I GET RID OF YUMA TSUKUMO...

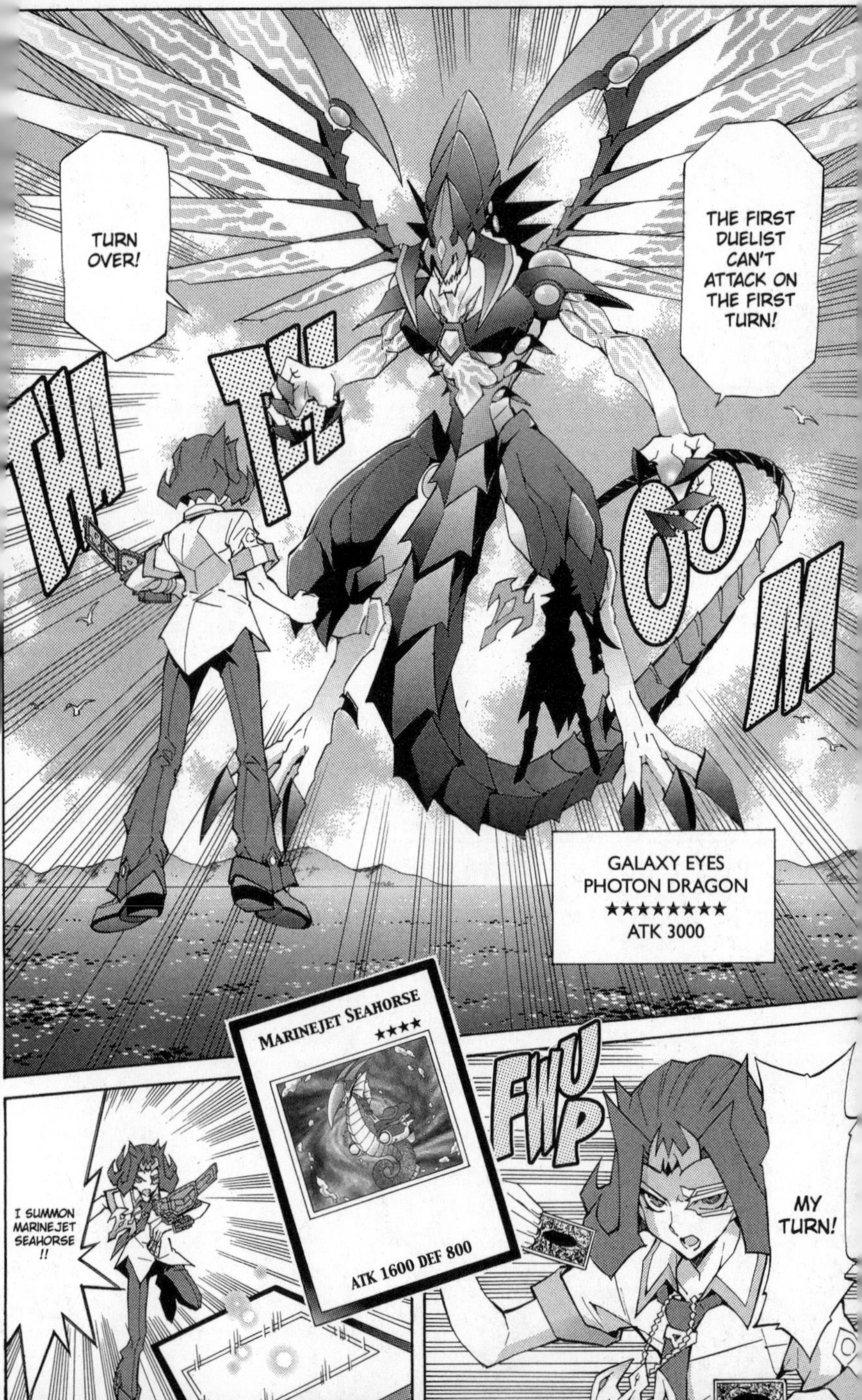
THE FIRST DUELIST CAN'T ATTACK ON THE FIRST TURN!
TURN OVER!
GALAXY EYES PHOTON DRAGON ★★★★★★★★ ATK 3000
MY TURN!
FWUP
MARINEJET SEAHORSE ★★★★
ATK 1600 DEF 800
I SUMMON MARINEJET SEAHORSE !!

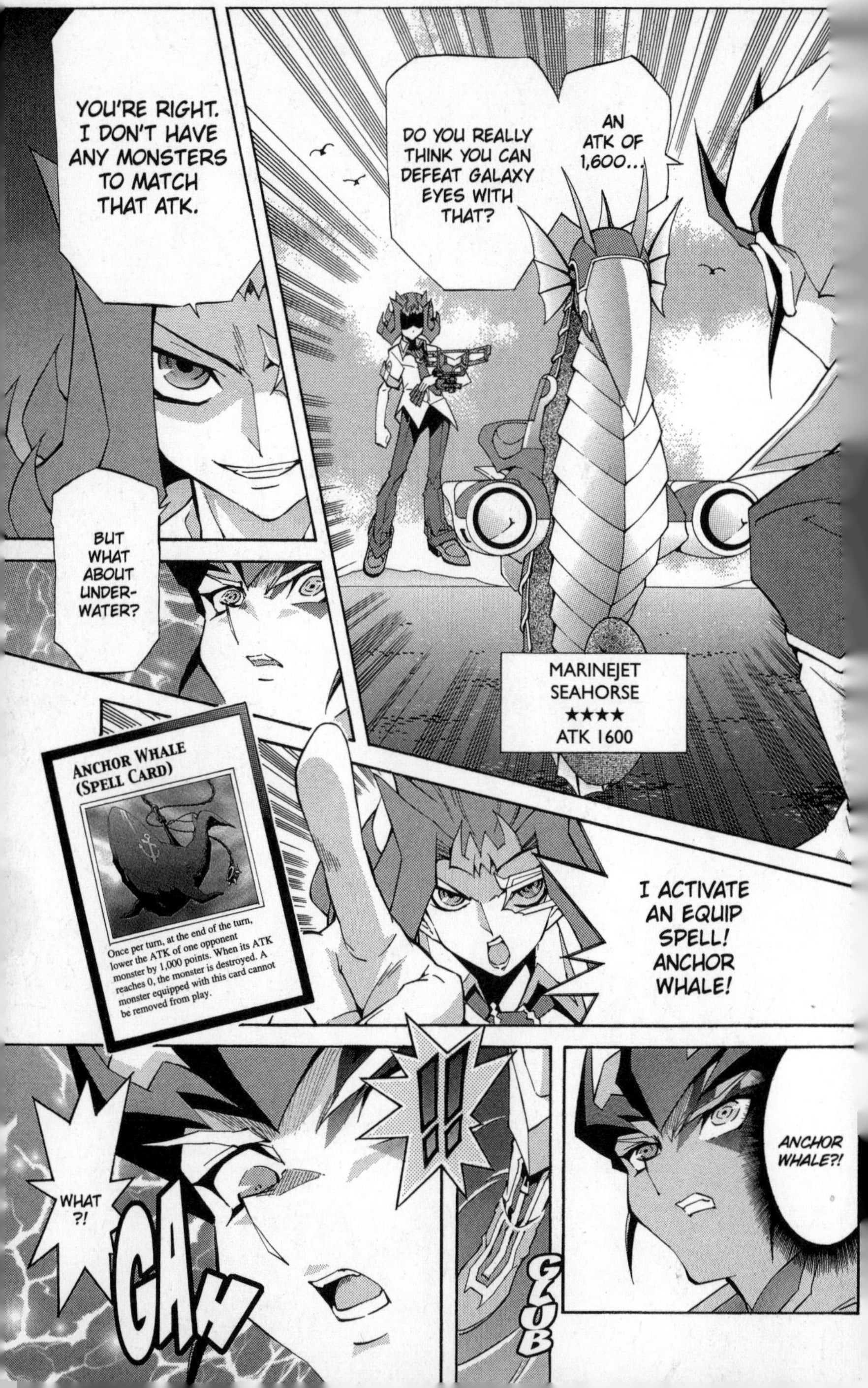
AN ATK OF 1,600...
DO YOU REALLY THINK YOU CAN DEFEAT GALAXY EYES WITH THAT?
MARINEJET SEAHORSE ★★★★ ATK 1600
YOU'RE RIGHT. I DON'T HAVE ANY MONSTERS TO MATCH THAT ATK.
BUT WHAT ABOUT UNDER-WATER?
I ACTIVATE AN EQUIP SPELL! ANCHOR WHALE!
ANCHOR WHALE (SPELL CARD)
Once per turn, at the end of the turn, lower the ATK of one opponent monster by 1,000 points. When its ATK reaches 0, the monster is destroyed. A monster equipped with this card cannot be removed from play.
ANCHOR WHALE?!
GLUB
!!
WHAT?!
GAH

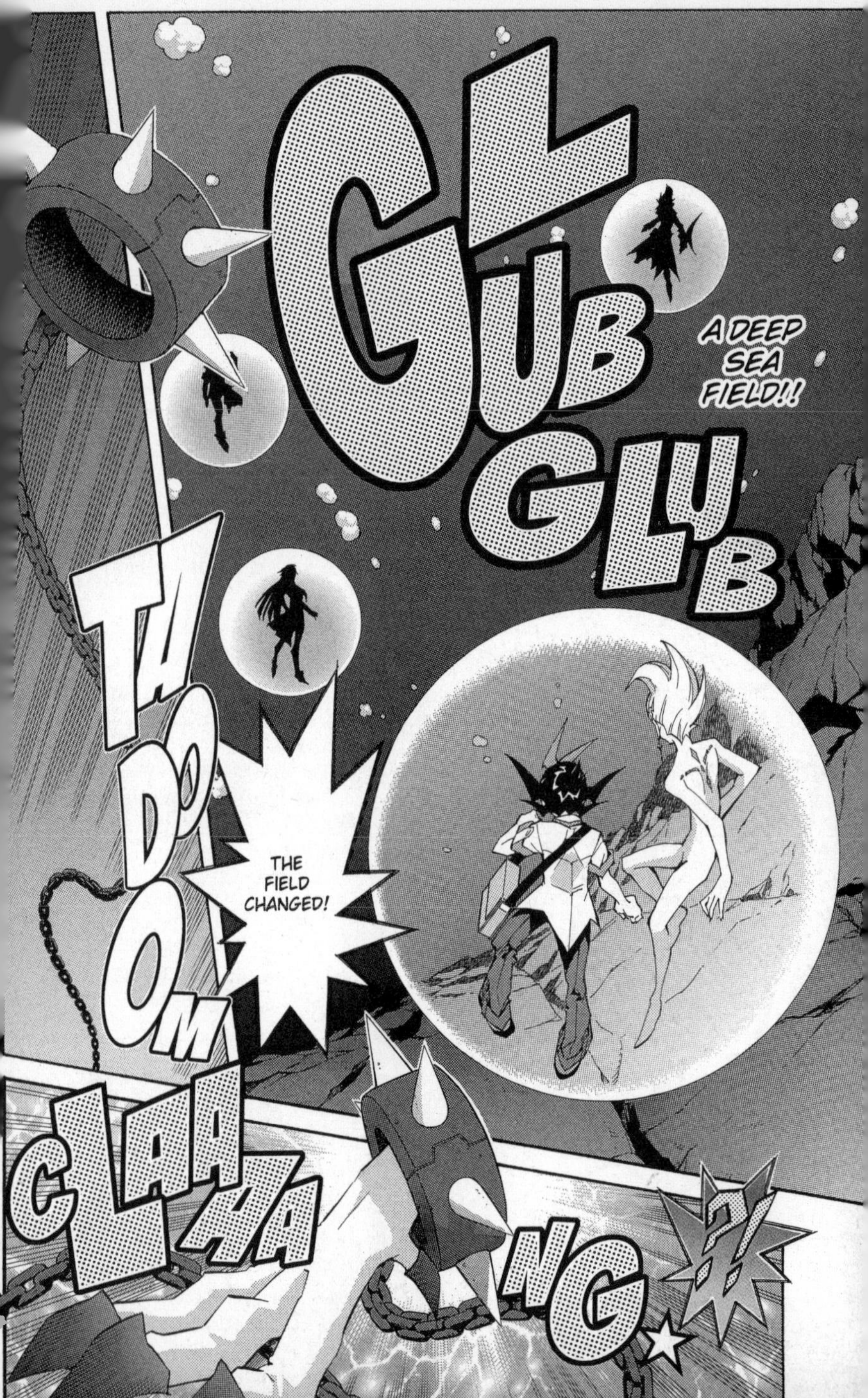
GLUB GLUB
A DEEP SEA FIELD!!
TADOOM
THE FIELD CHANGED!
?!
CLAAAANG

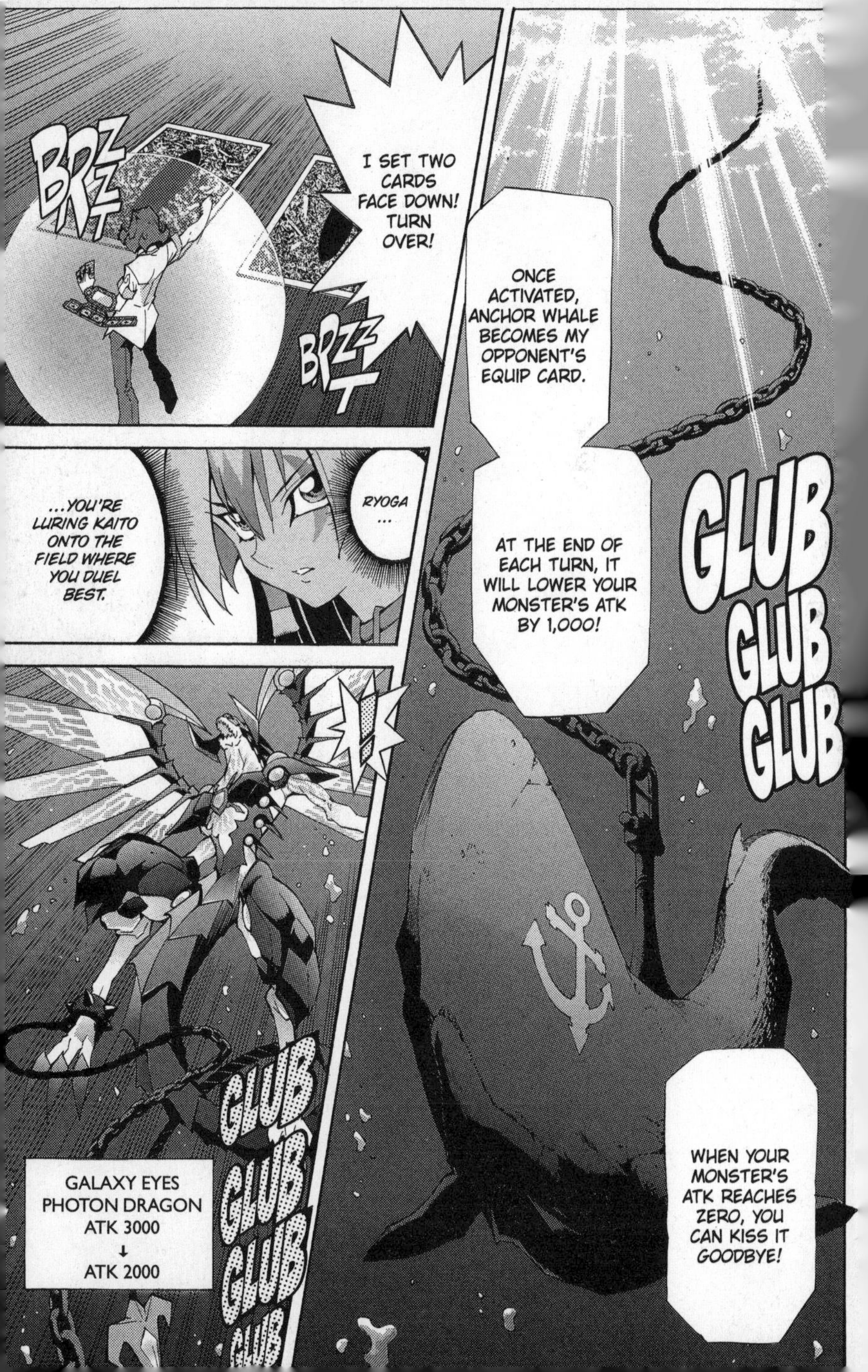
ONCE ACTIVATED, ANCHOR WHALE BECOMES MY OPPONENT'S EQUIP CARD.
AT THE END OF EACH TURN, IT WILL LOWER YOUR MONSTER'S ATK BY 1,000!
GLUB GLUB GLUB
WHEN YOUR MONSTER'S ATK REACHES ZERO, YOU CAN KISS IT GOODBYE!
I SET TWO CARDS FACE DOWN! TURN OVER!
BRZZT
BRZZT
RYOGA...
...YOU'RE LURING KAITO ONTO THE FIELD WHERE YOU DUEL BEST.
!
GLUB GLUB GLUB GLUB
GALAXY EYES PHOTON DRAGON ATK 3000 ↓ ATK 2000

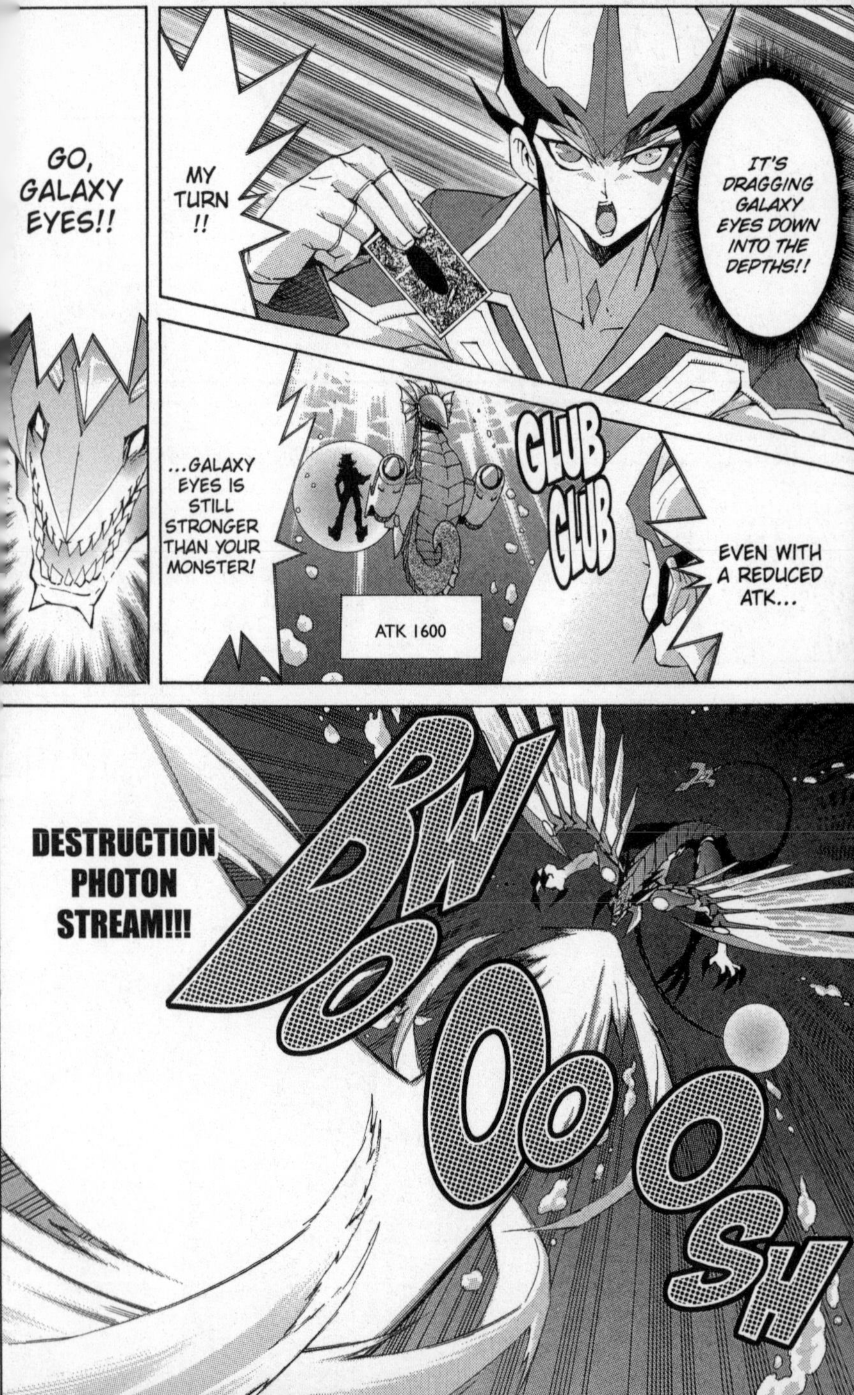
IT'S DRAGGING GALAXY EYES DOWN INTO THE DEPTHS!!
MY TURN!!
EVEN WITH A REDUCED ATK...
GLUB GLUB
...GALAXY EYES IS STILL STRONGER THAN YOUR MONSTER!
ATK 1600
GO, GALAXY EYES!!
DESTRUCTION PHOTON STREAM!!!
BWOOOOOSH

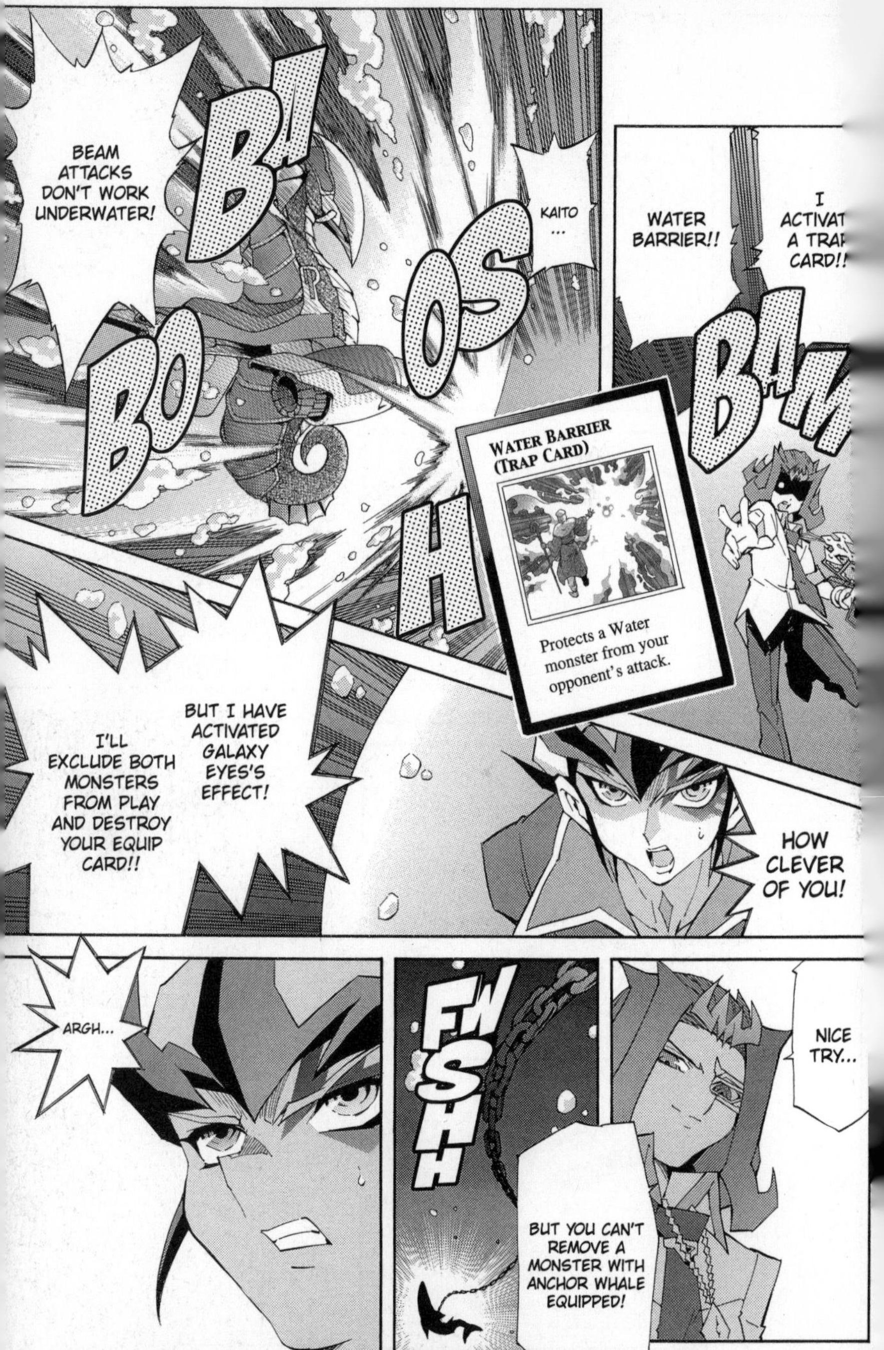

I ACTIVAT A TRA CARD!!
WATER BARRIER!!
BAM
WATER BARRIER (TRAP CARD)
Protects a Water monster from your opponent's attack.
KAITO ...
BOOSH
BEAM ATTACKS DON'T WORK UNDERWATER!
HOW CLEVER OF YOU!
BUT I HAVE ACTIVATED GALAXY EYES'S EFFECT!
I'LL EXCLUDE BOTH MONSTERS FROM PLAY AND DESTROY YOUR EQUIP CARD!!
NICE TRY...
BUT YOU CAN'T REMOVE A MONSTER WITH ANCHOR WHALE EQUIPPED!
FWSHH
ARGH...

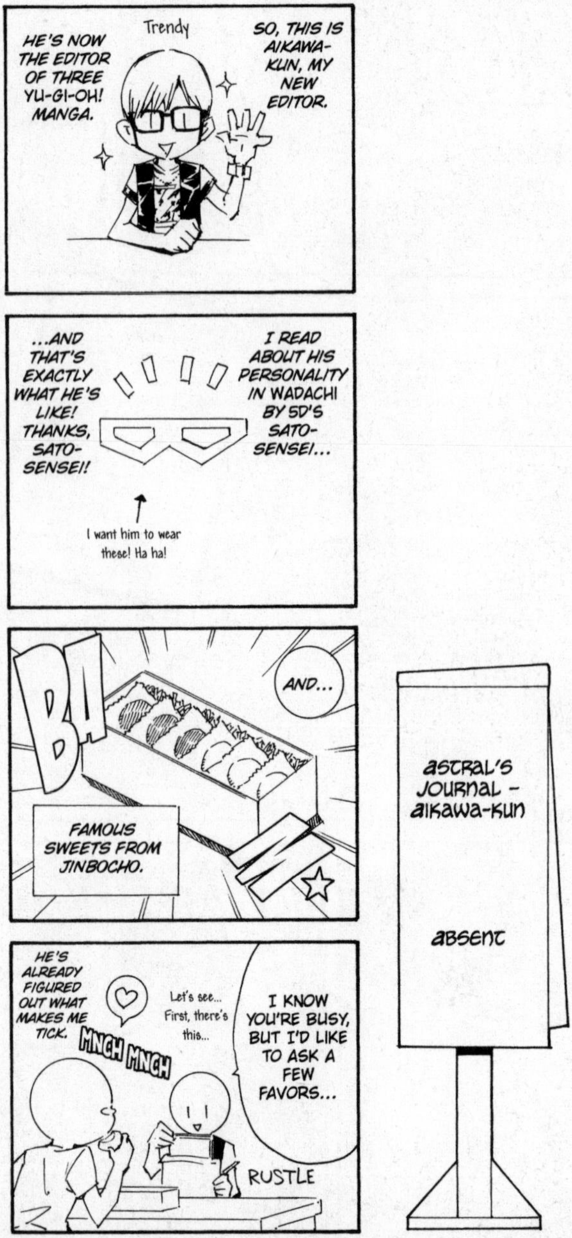
astral's journal - aikawa-kun
absent
SO, THIS IS AIKAWA-KUN, MY NEW EDITOR.
Trendy
HE'S NOW THE EDITOR OF THREE YU-GI-OH! MANGA.
I READ ABOUT HIS PERSONALITY IN WADACHI BY 5D'S SATO-SENSEI...
...AND THAT'S EXACTLY WHAT HE'S LIKE! THANKS, SATO-SENSEI!
I want him to wear these! Ha ha!
AND...
BA
FAMOUS SWEETS FROM JINBOCHO.
I KNOW YOU'RE BUSY, BUT I'D LIKE TO ASK A FEW FAVORS...
RUSTLE
Let's see... First, there's this...
HE'S ALREADY FIGURED OUT WHAT MAKES ME TICK.
MNCH MNCH

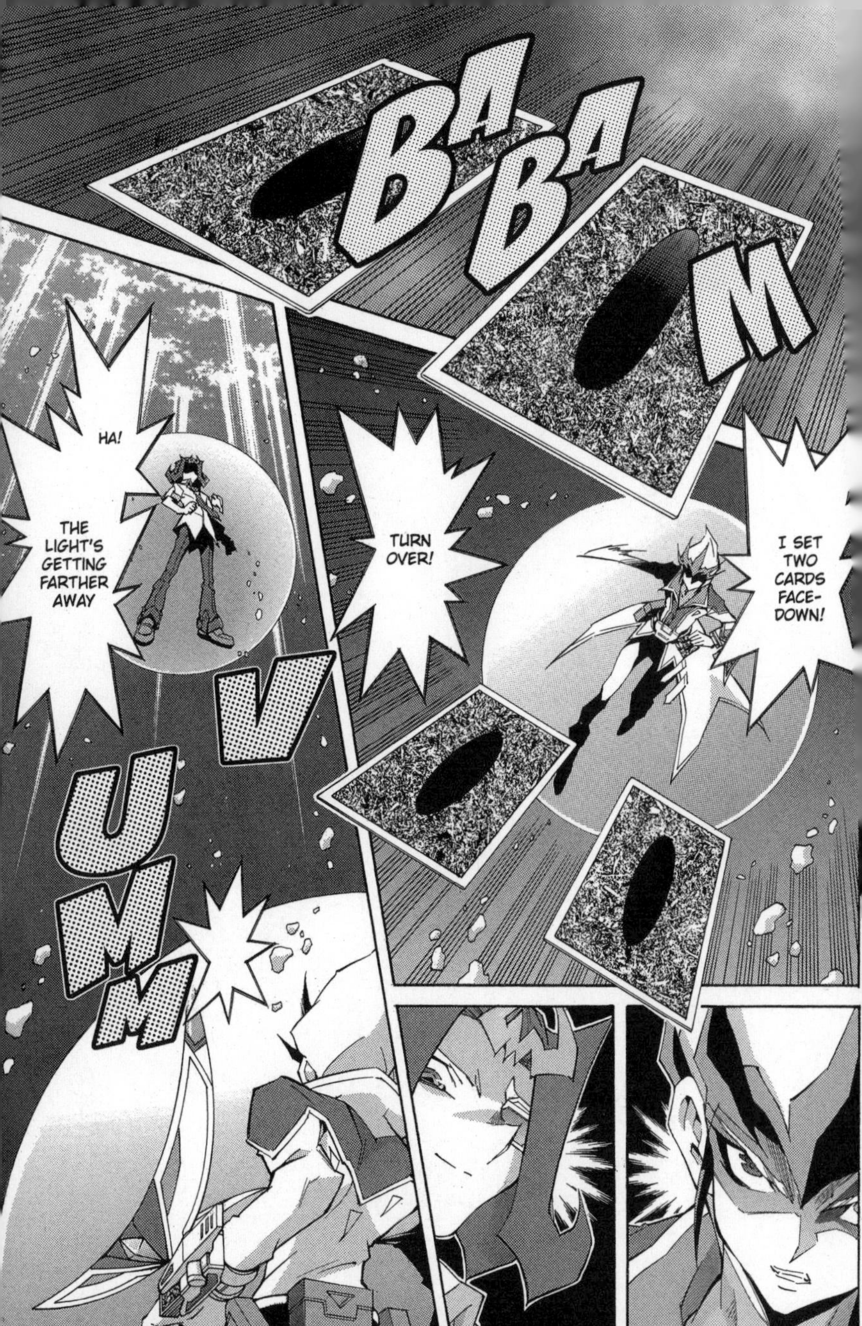
BABABOOM
I SET TWO CARDS FACE-DOWN!
TURN OVER!
HA!
THE LIGHT'S GETTING FARTHER AWAY
VUMMM

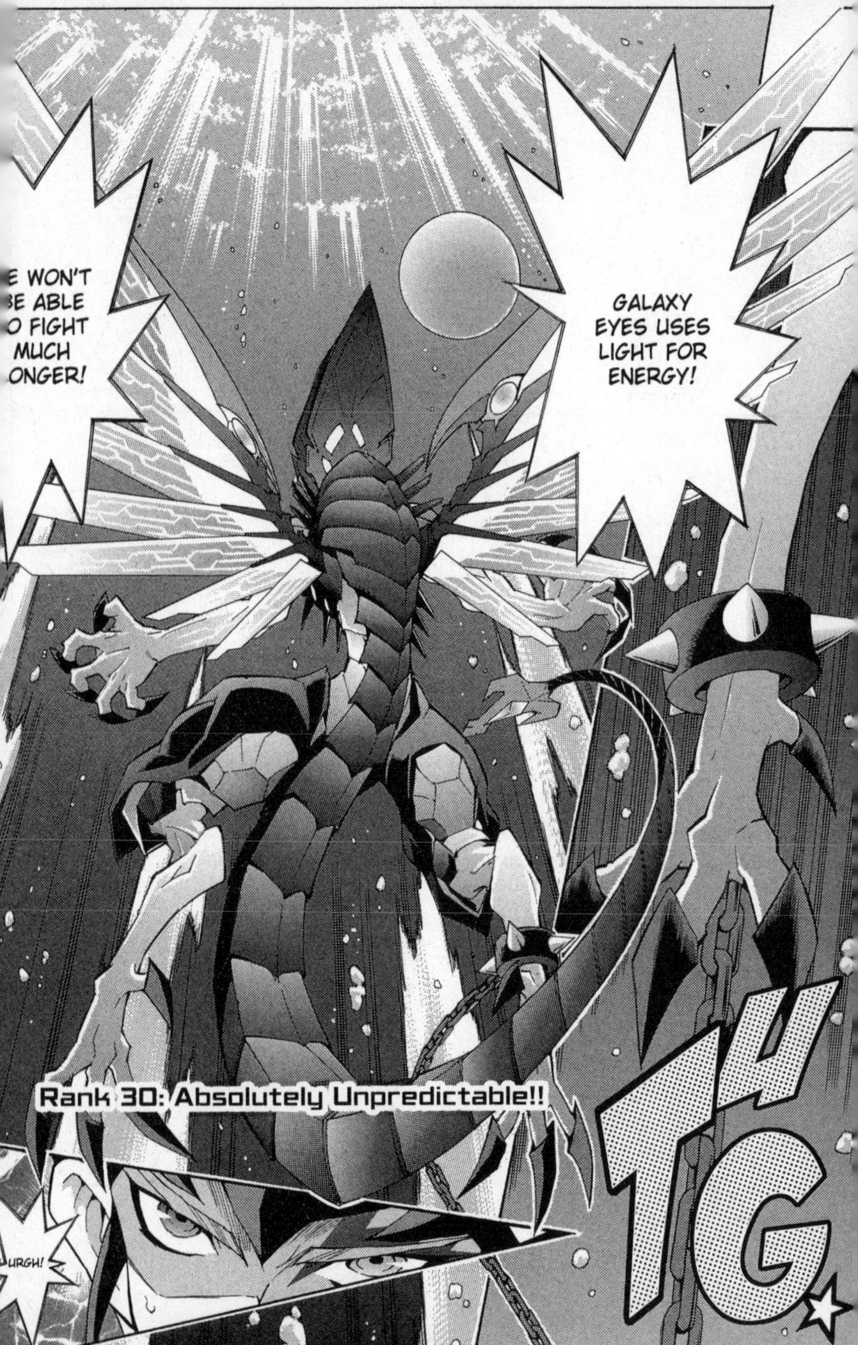
GALAXY EYES USES LIGHT FOR ENERGY!
E WON'T BE ABLE O FIGHT MUCH ONGER!
Rank 30: Absolutely Unpredictable!!
URGH!

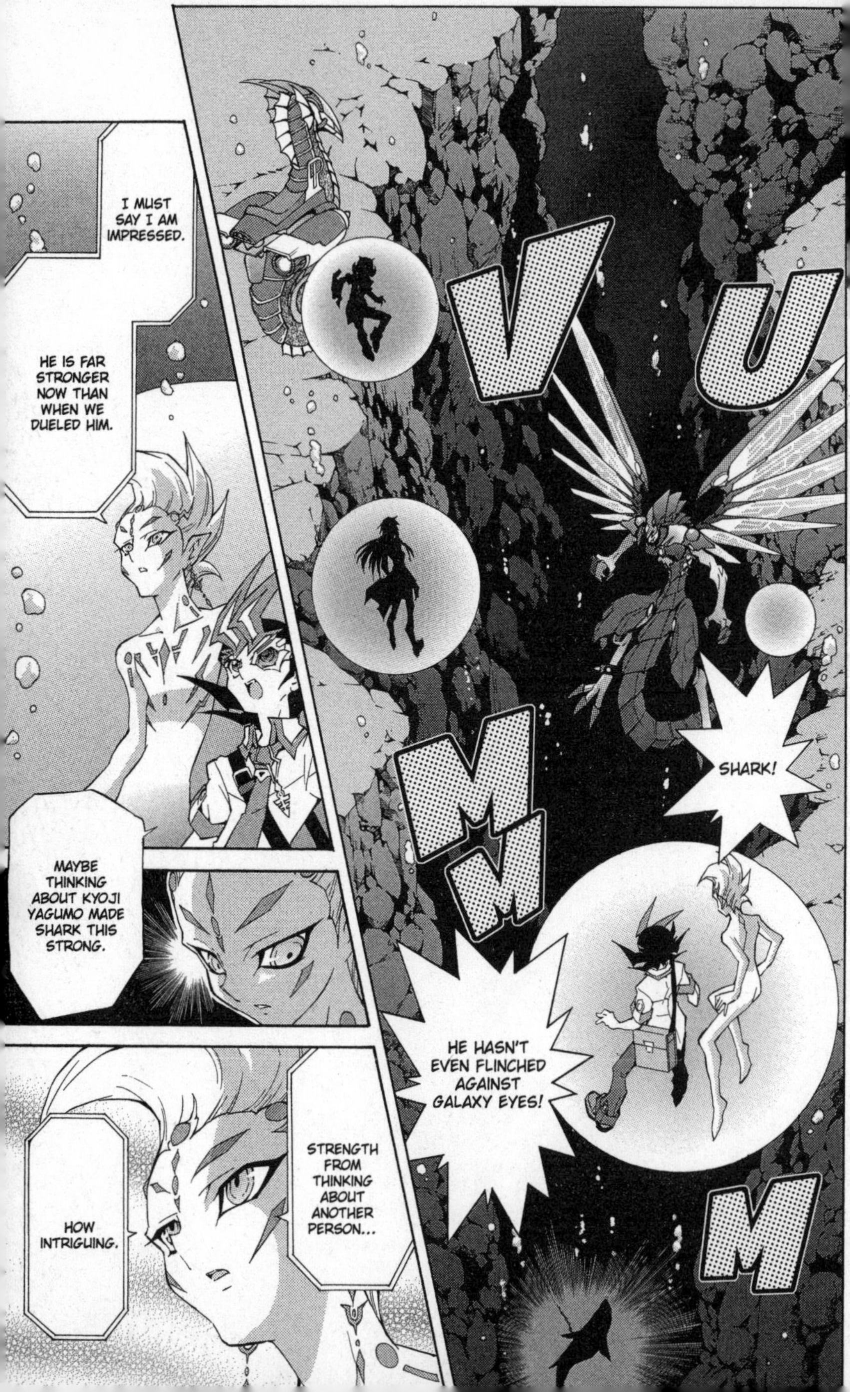
VUMMM
SHARK!
HE HASN'T EVEN FLINCHED AGAINST GALAXY EYES!
I MUST SAY I AM IMPRESSED.
HE IS FAR STRONGER NOW THAN WHEN WE DUELED HIM.
MAYBE THINKING ABOUT KYOJI YAGUMO MADE SHARK THIS STRONG.
STRENGTH FROM THINKING ABOUT ANOTHER PERSON...
HOW INTRIGUING.

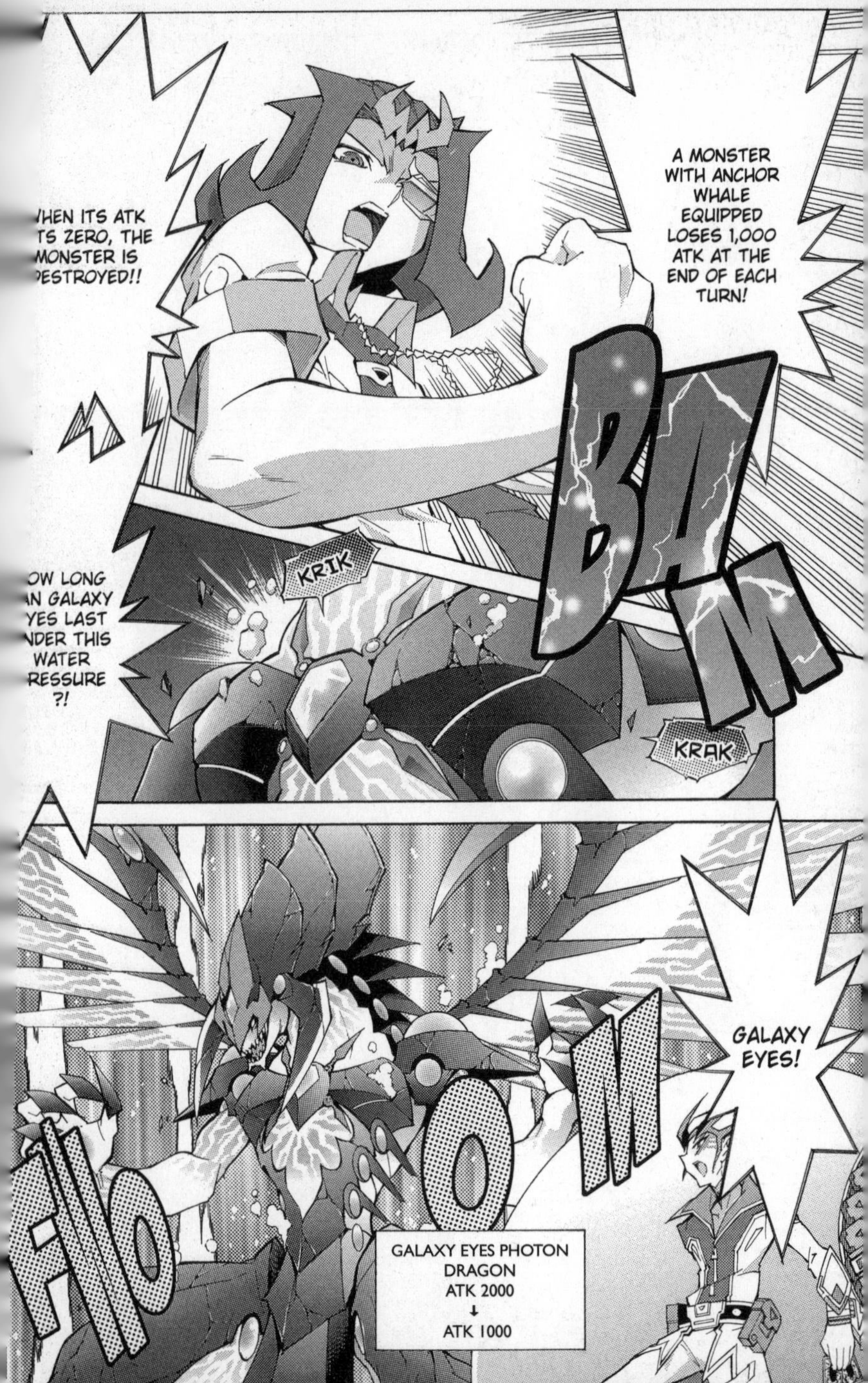
A MONSTER WITH ANCHOR WHALE EQUIPPED LOSES 1,000 ATK AT THE END OF EACH TURN!
HEN ITS ATK TS ZERO, THE MONSTER IS ESTROYED!!
BAM
KRAK
KRIK
OW LONG AN GALAXY YES LAST NDER THIS WATER RESSURE ?!
GALAXY EYES!
OOM
GALAXY EYES PHOTON DRAGON
ATK 2000
↓
ATK 1000

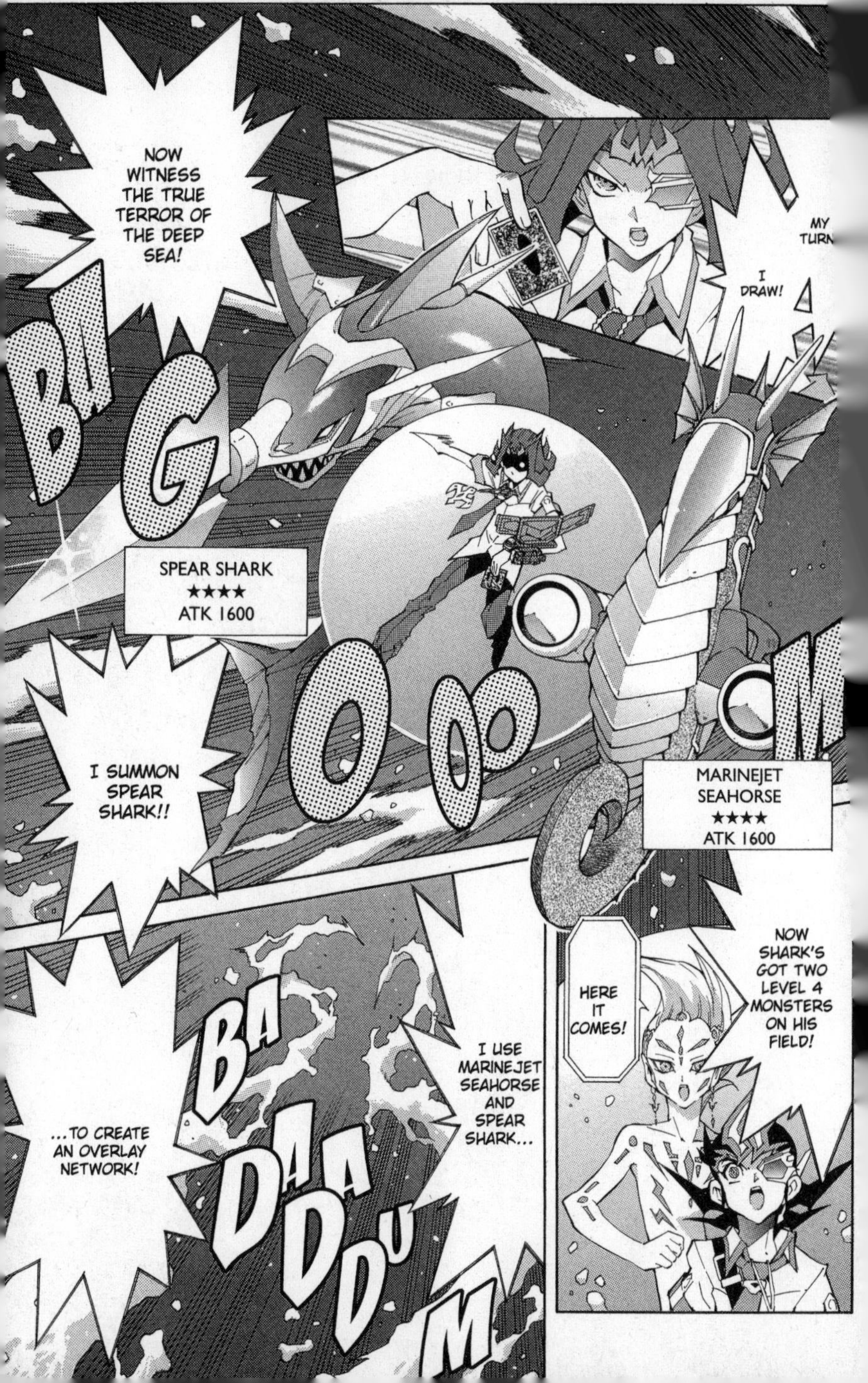
MY TURN
I DRAW!
NOW WITNESS THE TRUE TERROR OF THE DEEP SEA!
BUG
MARINEJET SEAHORSE ★★★★ ATK 1600
OOOOM
SPEAR SHARK ★★★★ ATK 1600
I SUMMON SPEAR SHARK!!
NOW SHARK'S GOT TWO LEVEL 4 MONSTERS ON HIS FIELD!
HERE IT COMES!
I USE MARINEJET SEAHORSE AND SPEAR SHARK...
...TO CREATE AN OVERLAY NETWORK!
BADADADUM

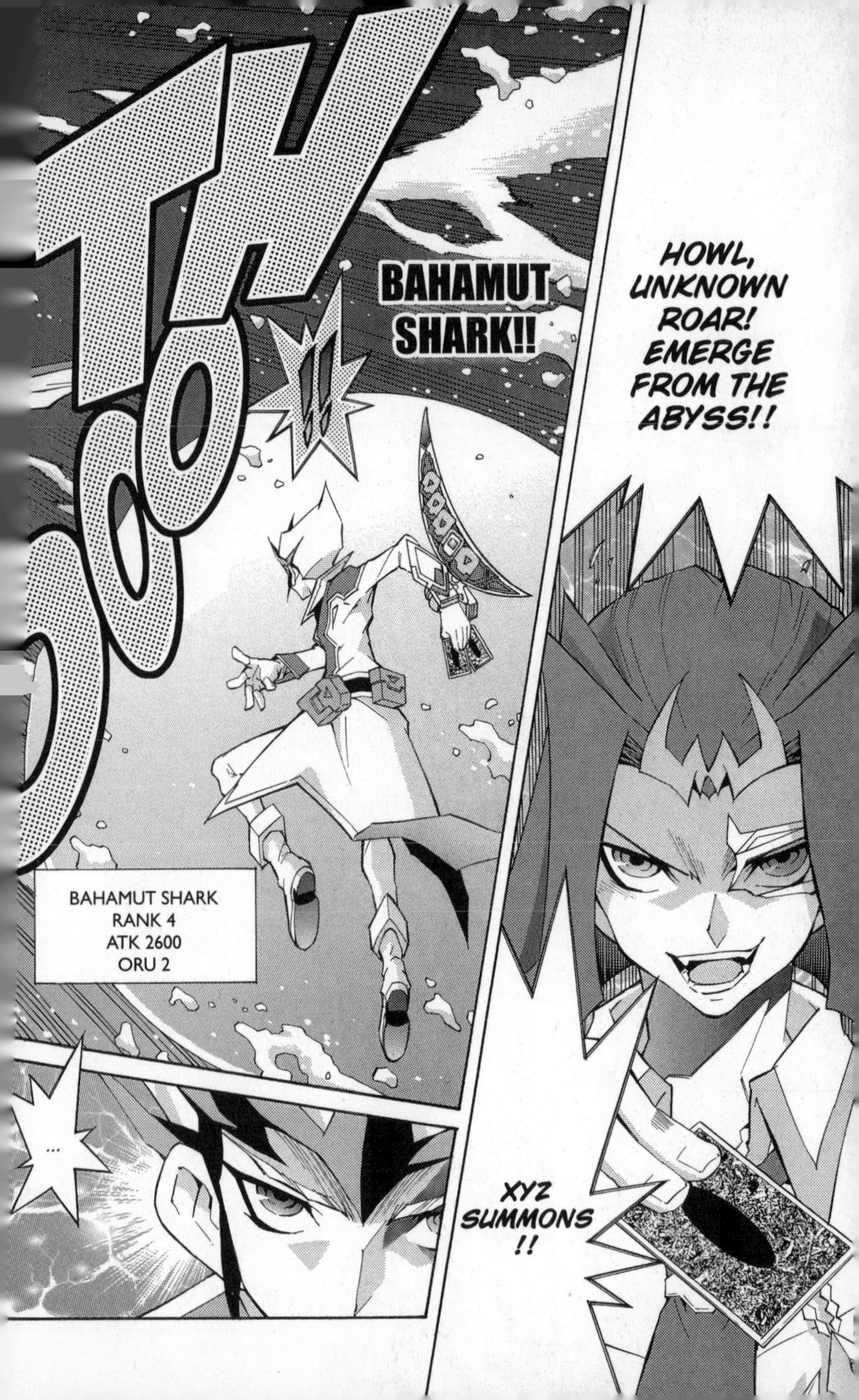
HOWL, UNKNOWN ROAR! EMERGE FROM THE ABYSS!!
XYZ SUMMONS !!
BAHAMUT SHARK!!
!!
BAHAMUT SHARK
RANK 4
ATK 2600
ORU 2
...

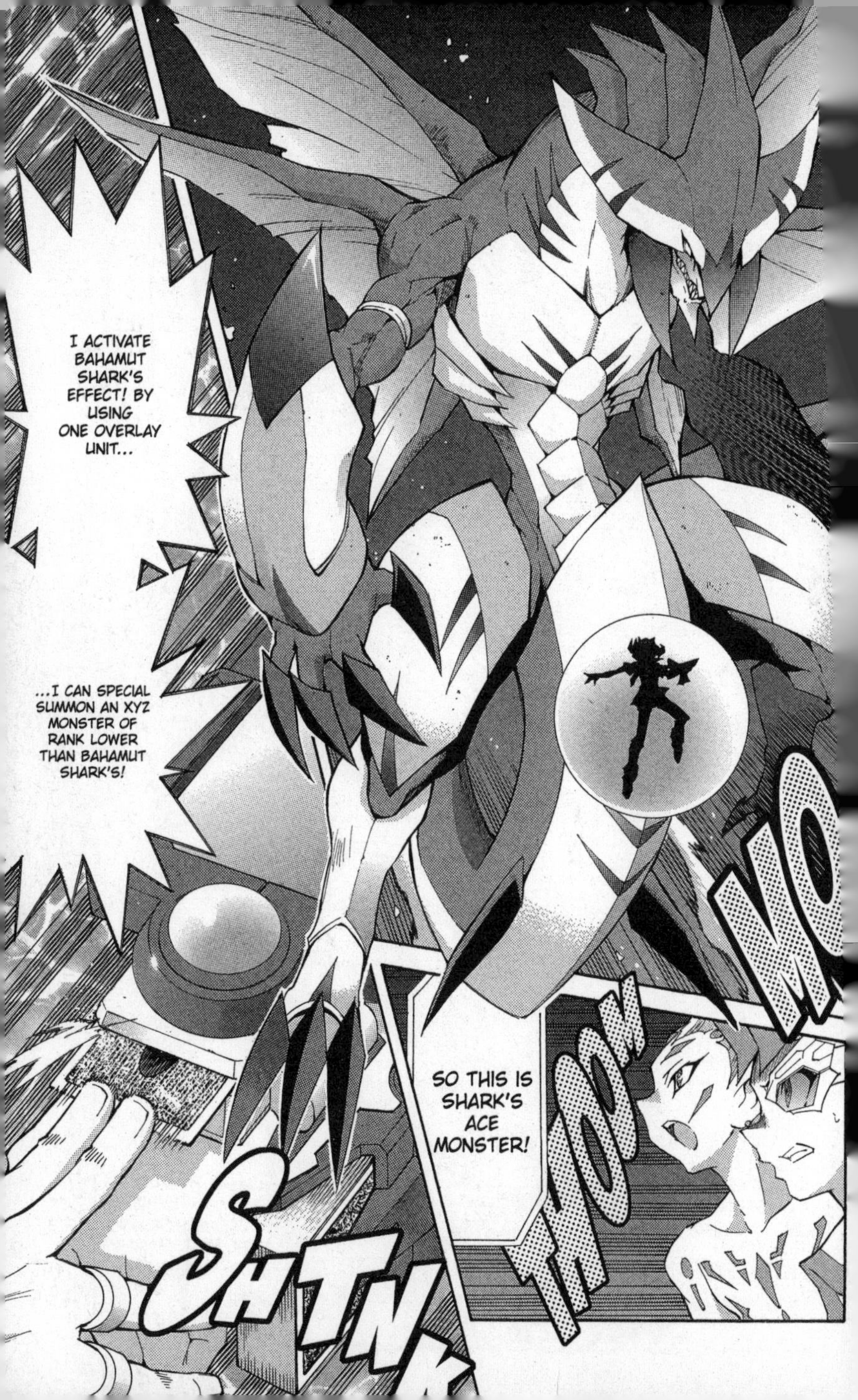
I ACTIVATE BAHAMUT SHARK'S EFFECT! BY USING ONE OVERLAY UNIT...
...I CAN SPECIAL SUMMON AN XYZ MONSTER OF RANK LOWER THAN BAHAMUT SHARK'S!
THOOM
SO THIS IS SHARK'S ACE MONSTER!
SHTNK

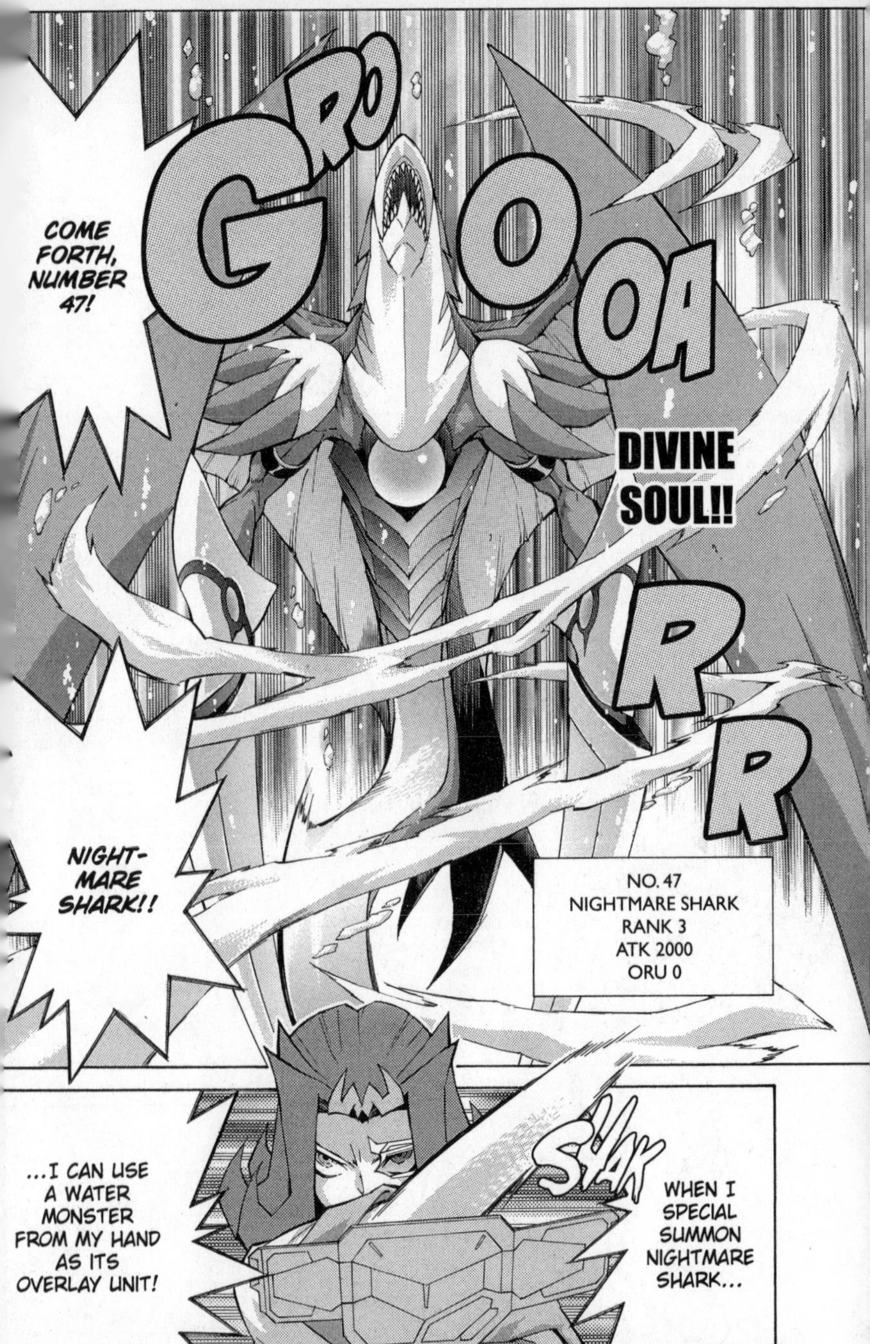
GROOOARR
DIVINE SOUL!!
COME FORTH, NUMBER 47!
NO. 47
NIGHTMARE SHARK
RANK 3
ATK 2000
ORU 0
NIGHT-MARE SHARK!!
WHEN I SPECIAL SUMMON NIGHTMARE SHARK...
SHAK
...I CAN USE A WATER MONSTER FROM MY HAND AS ITS OVERLAY UNIT!

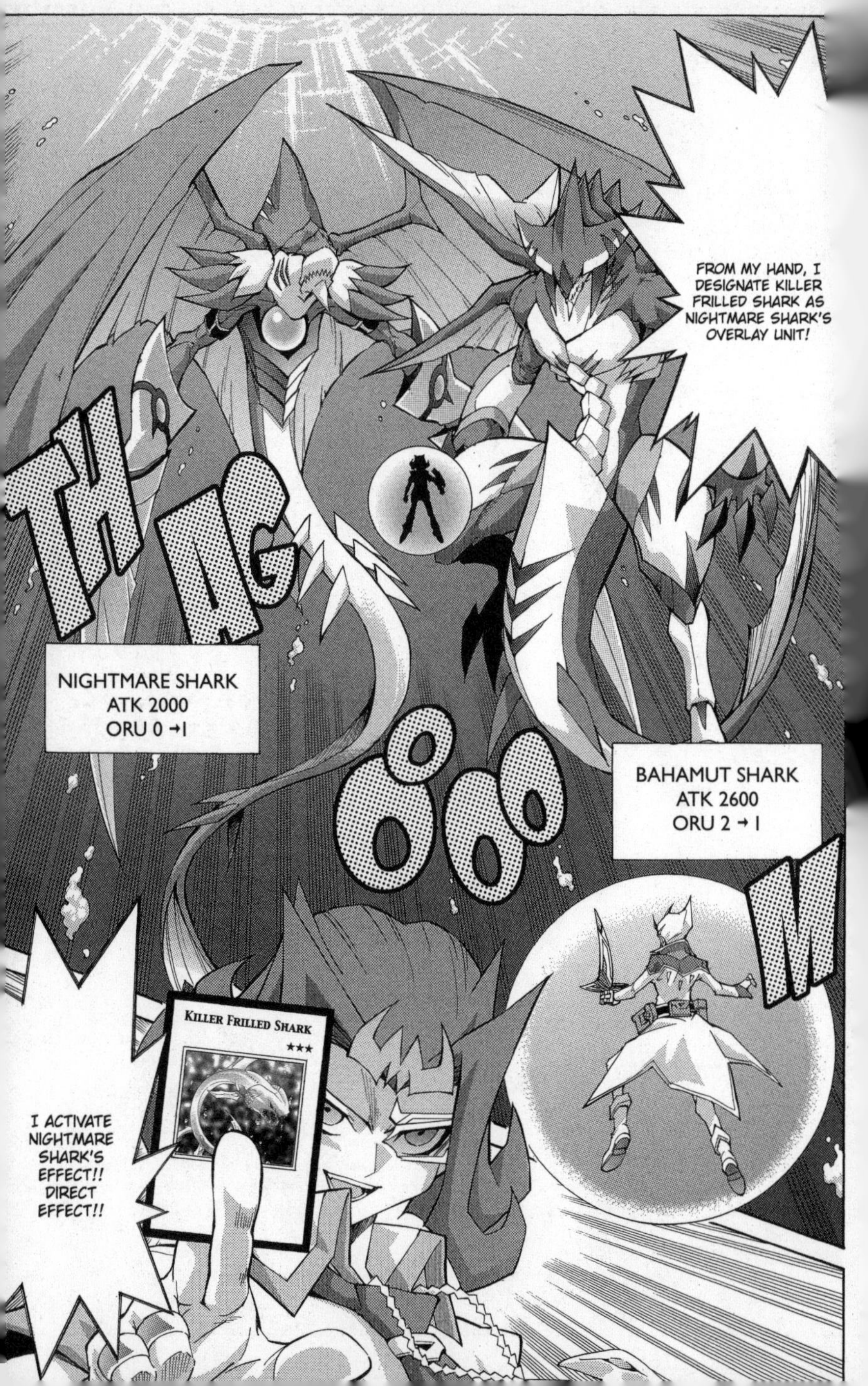
FROM MY HAND, I DESIGNATE KILLER FRILLED SHARK AS NIGHTMARE SHARK'S OVERLAY UNIT!
TH AG
NIGHTMARE SHARK
ATK 2000
ORU 0 → 1
BAHAMUT SHARK
ATK 2600
ORU 2 → 1
OOOO
M
KILLER FRILLED SHARK
I ACTIVATE NIGHTMARE SHARK'S EFFECT!! DIRECT EFFECT!!

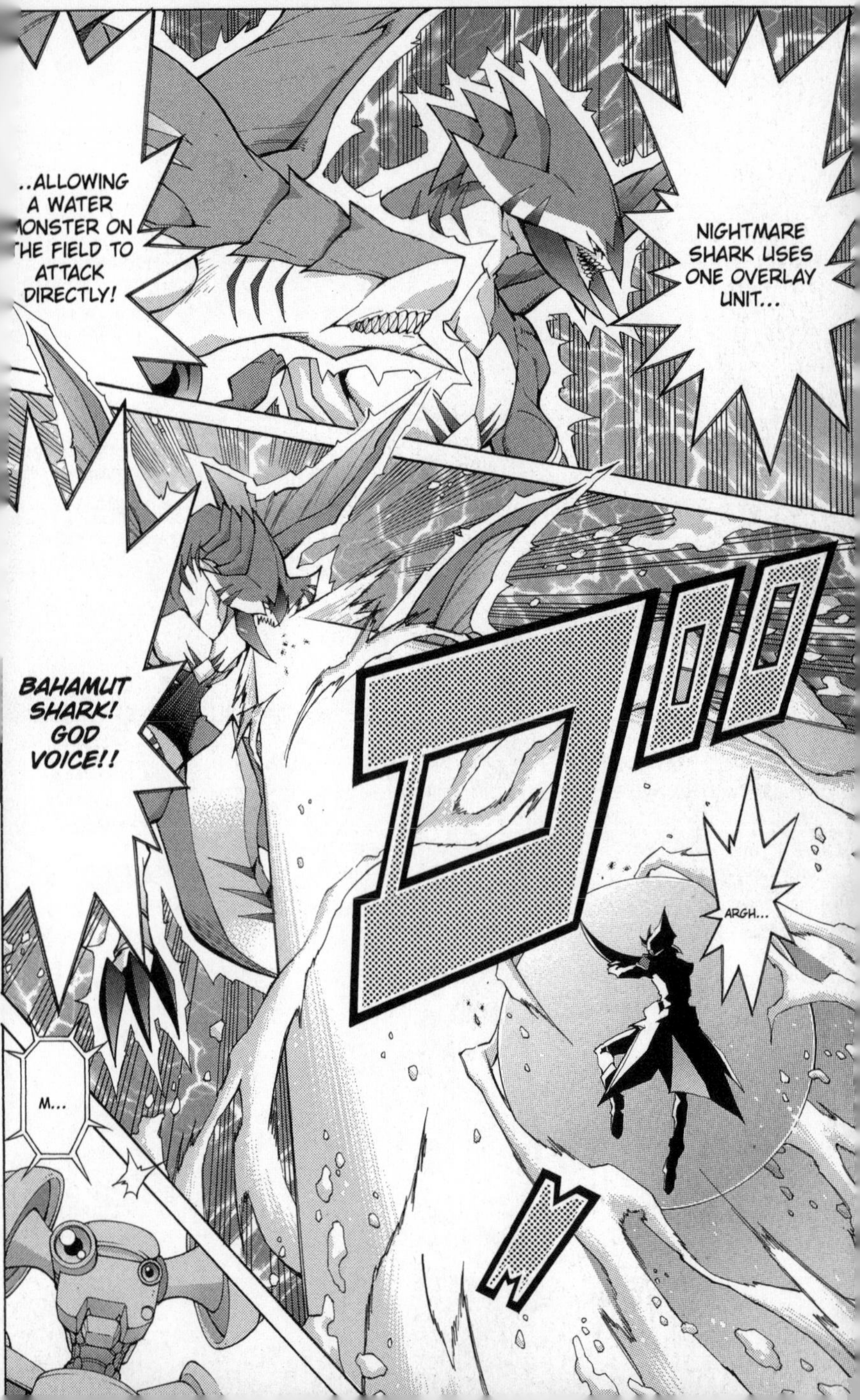
NIGHTMARE SHARK USES ONE OVERLAY UNIT...
..ALLOWING A WATER MONSTER ON THE FIELD TO ATTACK DIRECTLY!
BAHAMUT SHARK! GOD VOICE!!
ARGH...
M...

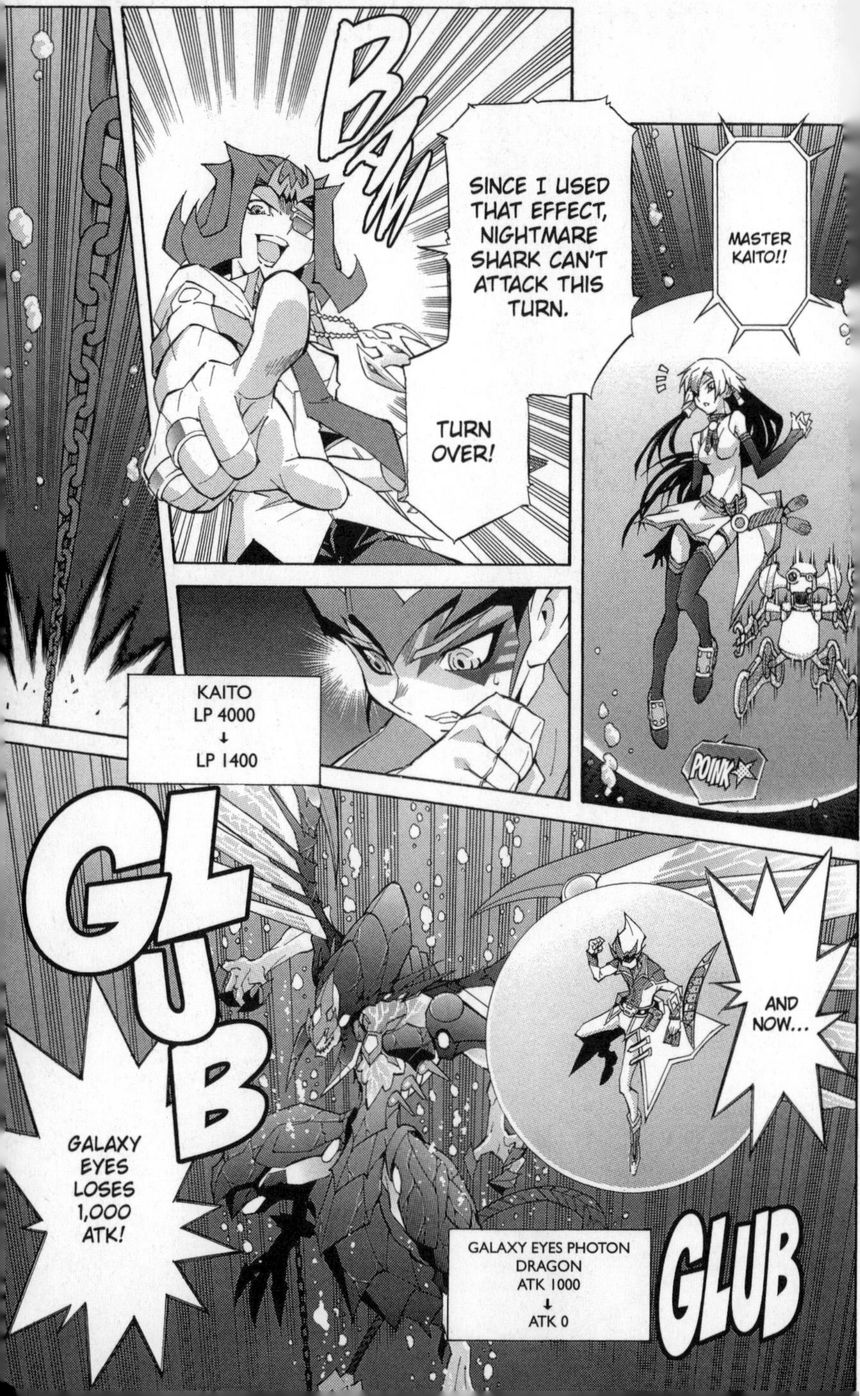
MASTER KAITO!!
POINK
BAM
SINCE I USED THAT EFFECT, NIGHTMARE SHARK CAN'T ATTACK THIS TURN.
TURN OVER!
KAITO
LP 4000
↓
LP 1400
AND NOW...
GLUB
GALAXY EYES PHOTON DRAGON
ATK 1000
↓
ATK 0
GLUB
GALAXY EYES LOSES 1,000 ATK!

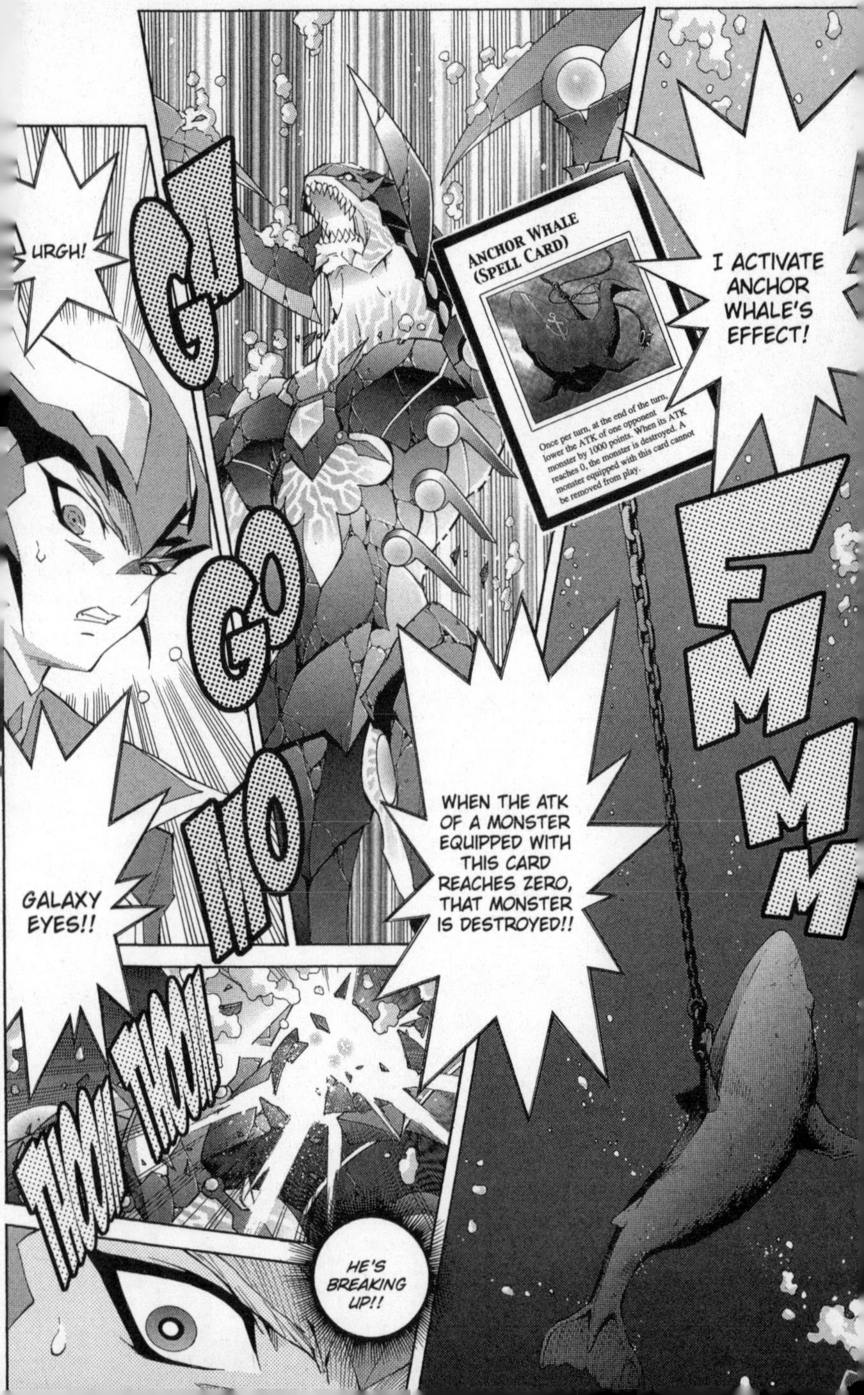
I ACTIVATE ANCHOR WHALE'S EFFECT!
ANCHOR WHALE (SPELL CARD)
Once per turn, at the end of the turn, lower the ATK of one opponent monster by 1000 points. When its ATK reaches 0, the monster is destroyed. A monster equipped with this card cannot be removed from play.
FMMM
URGH!
GO GO GO
WHEN THE ATK OF A MONSTER EQUIPPED WITH THIS CARD REACHES ZERO, THAT MONSTER IS DESTROYED!!
GALAXY EYES!!
THOOM THOOM
HE'S BREAKING UP!!

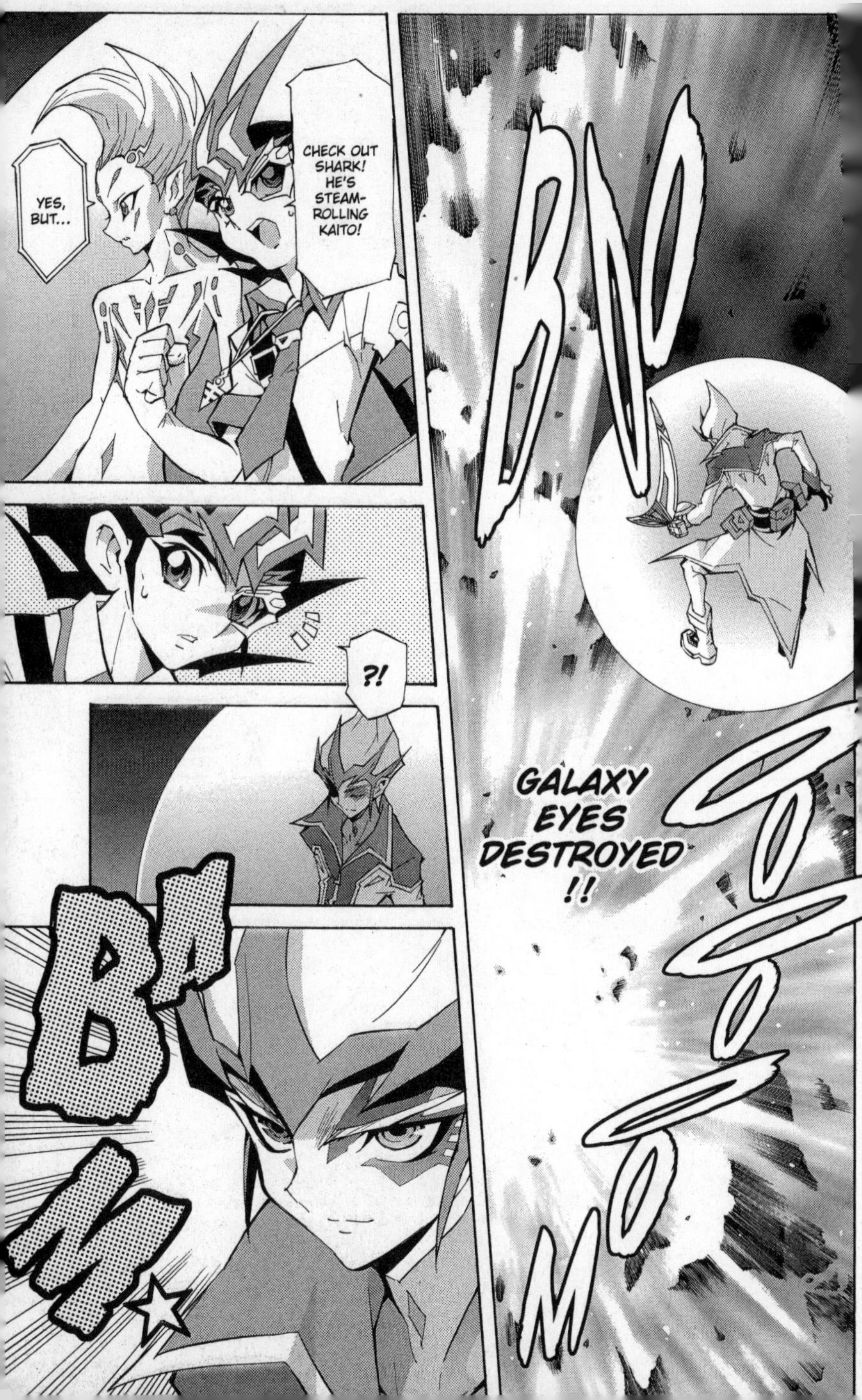
GALAXY EYES DESTROYED!!
CHECK OUT SHARK! HE'S STEAM-ROLLING KAITO!
YES, BUT...
?!
BAM☆

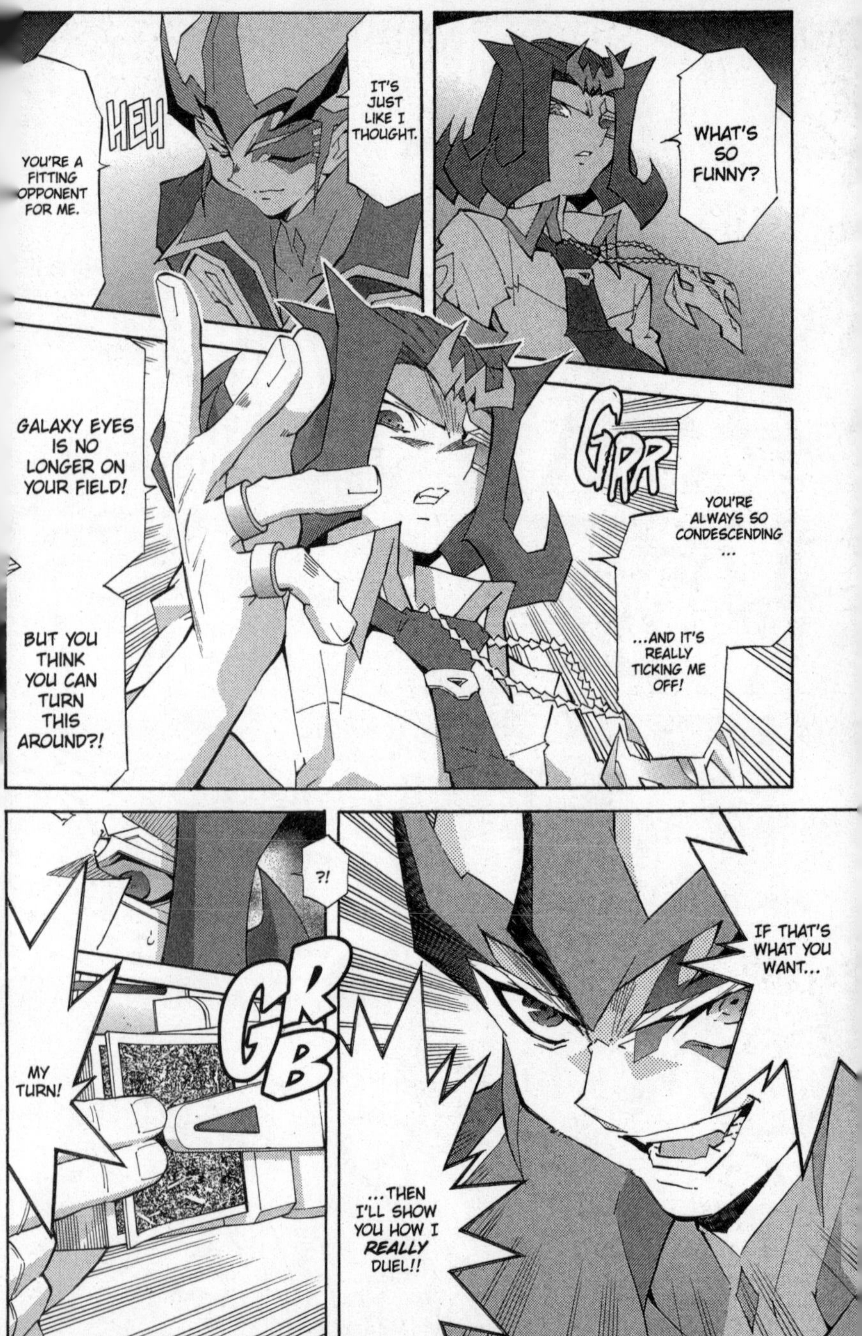
WHAT'S SO FUNNY?
IT'S JUST LIKE I THOUGHT.
HEH
YOU'RE A FITTING OPPONENT FOR ME.
GRR
YOU'RE ALWAYS SO CONDESCENDING...
...AND IT'S REALLY TICKING ME OFF!
GALAXY EYES IS NO LONGER ON YOUR FIELD!
BUT YOU THINK YOU CAN TURN THIS AROUND?!
IF THAT'S WHAT YOU WANT...
...THEN I'LL SHOW YOU HOW I REALLY DUEL!!
?!
GRB
MY TURN!

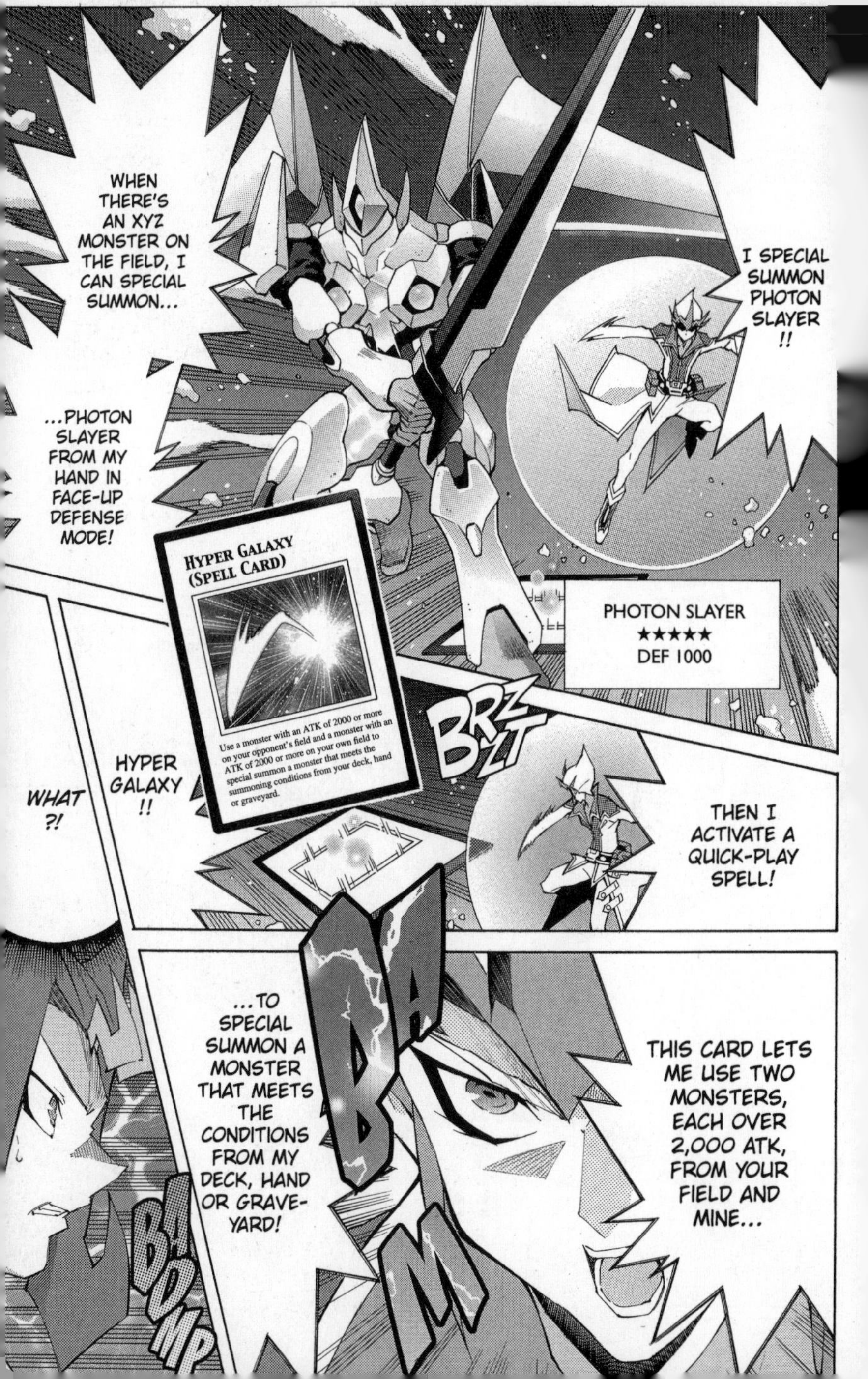
I SPECIAL SUMMON PHOTON SLAYER!!
WHEN THERE'S AN XYZ MONSTER ON THE FIELD, I CAN SPECIAL SUMMON...
...PHOTON SLAYER FROM MY HAND IN FACE-UP DEFENSE MODE!
PHOTON SLAYER
★★★★★
DEF 1000
THEN I ACTIVATE A QUICK-PLAY SPELL!
BRZZT
HYPER GALAXY (SPELL CARD)
Use a monster with an ATK of 2000 or more on your opponent's field and a monster with an ATK of 2000 or more on your own field to special summon a monster that meets the summoning conditions from your deck, hand or graveyard.
HYPER GALAXY!!
WHAT?!
THIS CARD LETS ME USE TWO MONSTERS, EACH OVER 2,000 ATK, FROM YOUR FIELD AND MINE...
...TO SPECIAL SUMMON A MONSTER THAT MEETS THE CONDITIONS FROM MY DECK, HAND OR GRAVE-YARD!
BAM
BA-DUMP

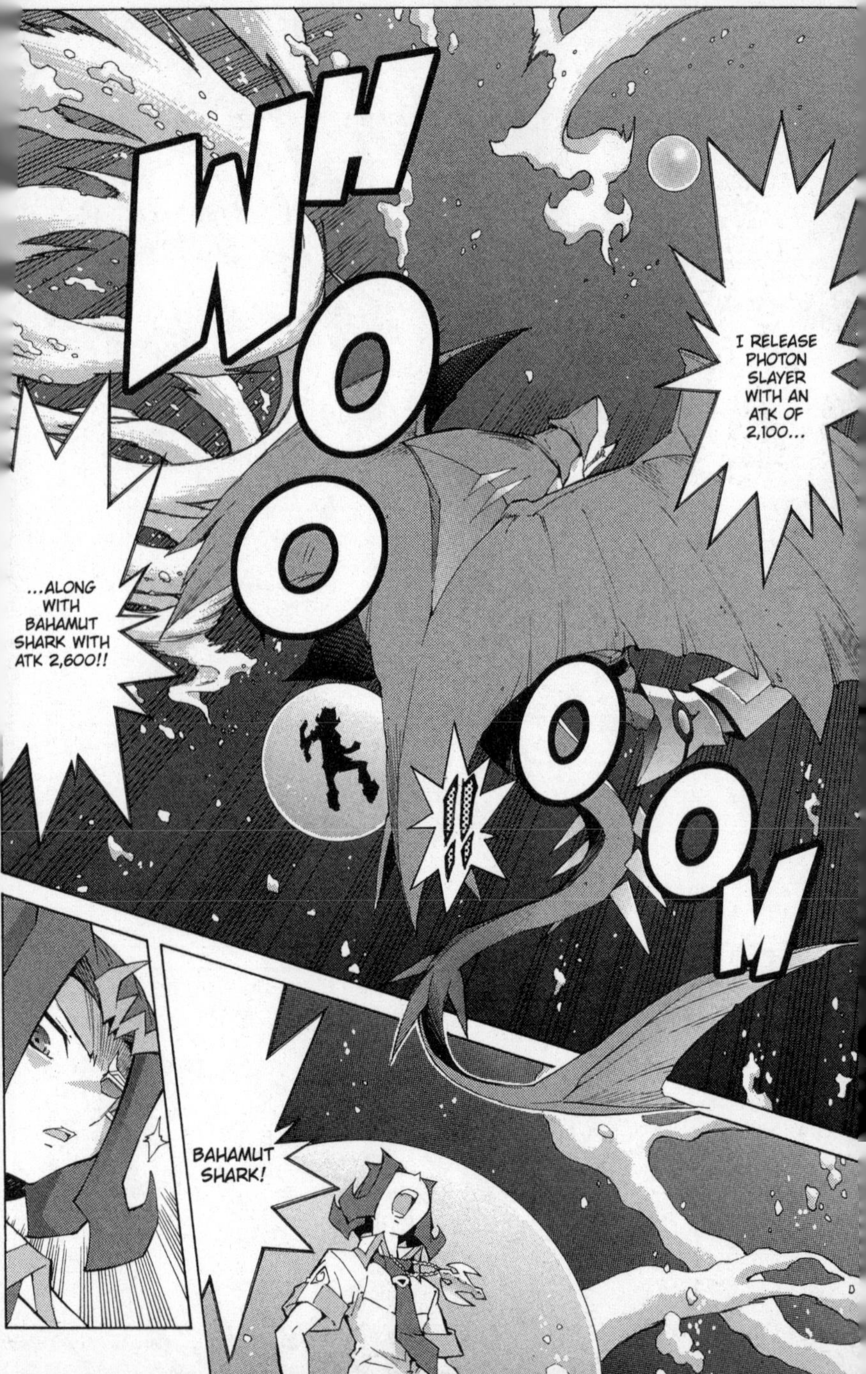
I RELEASE PHOTON SLAYER WITH AN ATK OF 2,100...
WHOOOOM
...ALONG WITH BAHAMUT SHARK WITH ATK 2,600!!
!!
BAHAMUT SHARK!

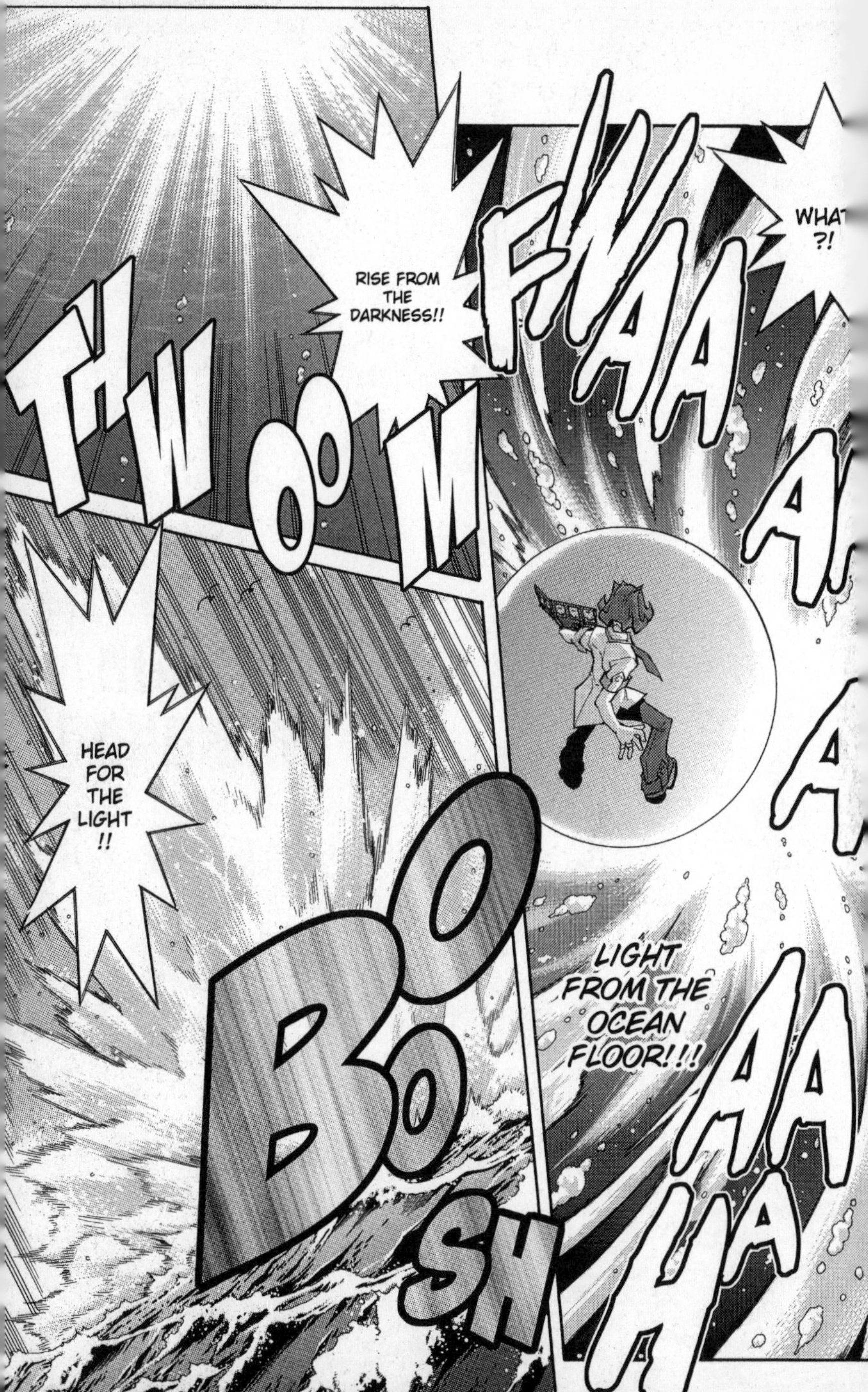
WHAT?!
FWAA
RISE FROM THE DARKNESS!!
THWOOM
LIGHT FROM THE OCEAN FLOOR!!!
BOOSH
HEAD FOR THE LIGHT!!

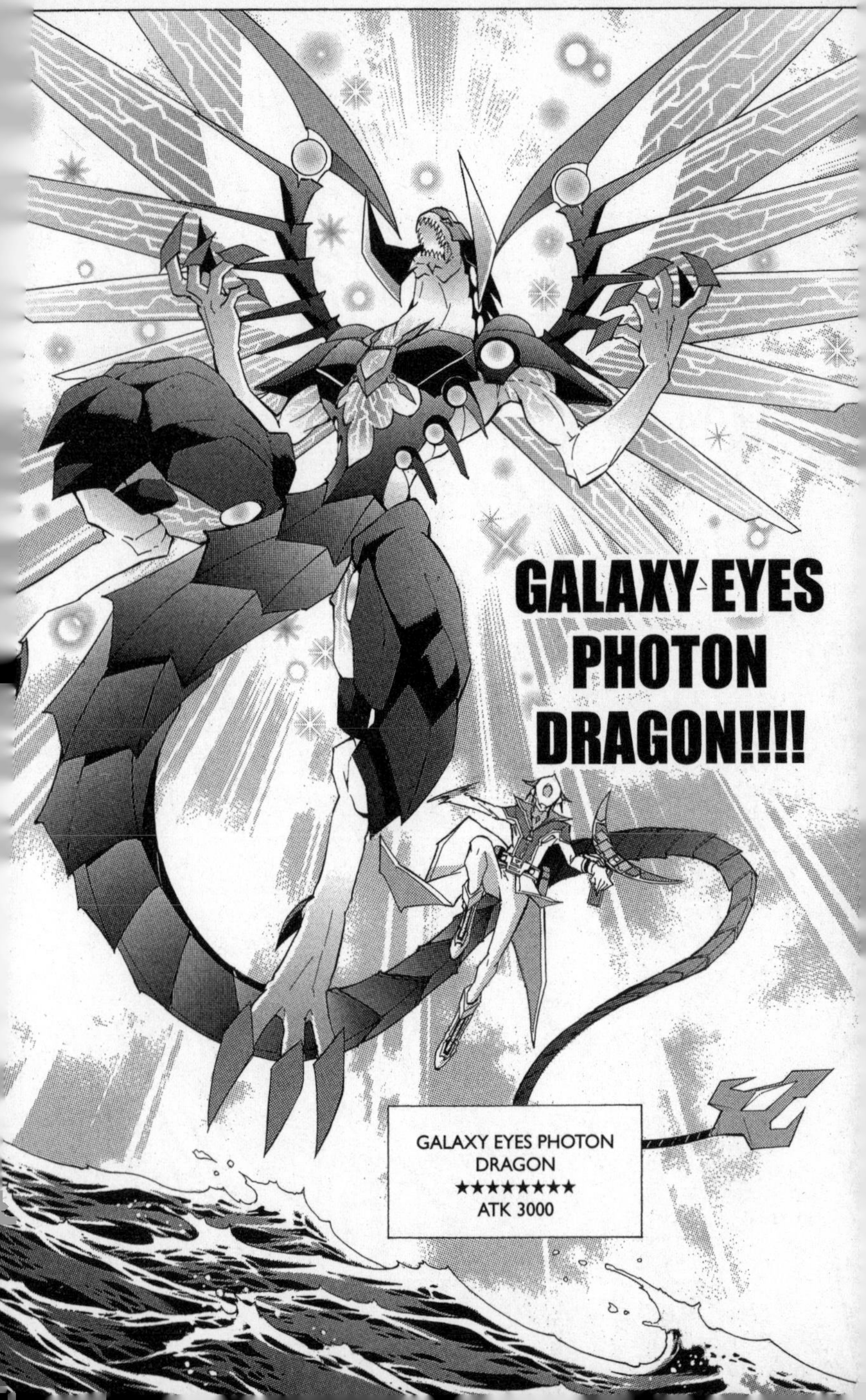
GALAXY EYES PHOTON DRAGON!!!!
GALAXY EYES PHOTON DRAGON ★★★★★★★★ ATK 3000

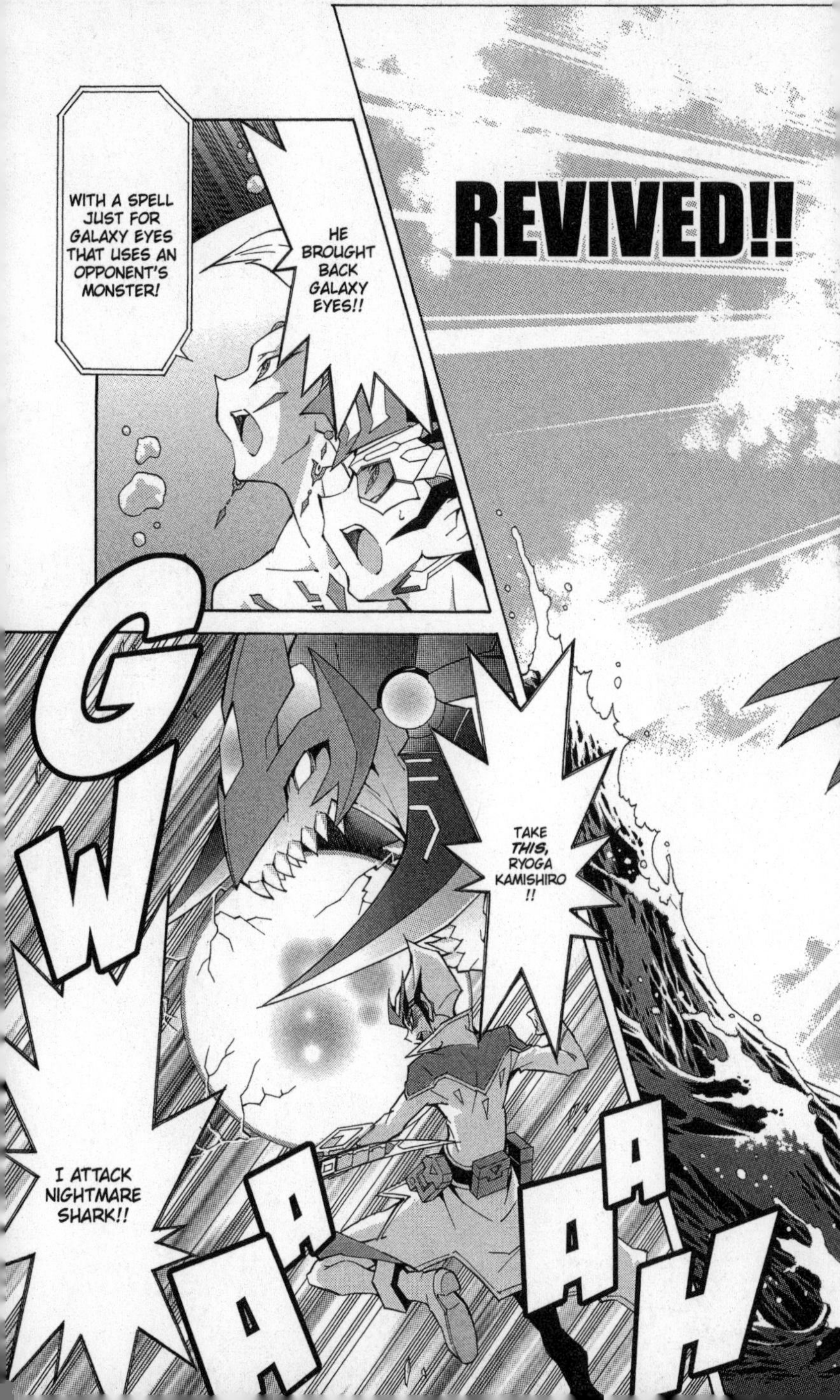
REVIVED!!
HE BROUGHT BACK GALAXY EYES!!
WITH A SPELL JUST FOR GALAXY EYES THAT USES AN OPPONENT'S MONSTER!
TAKE *THIS*, RYOGA KAMISHIRO!!
I ATTACK NIGHTMARE SHARK!!
GWAAAAH!

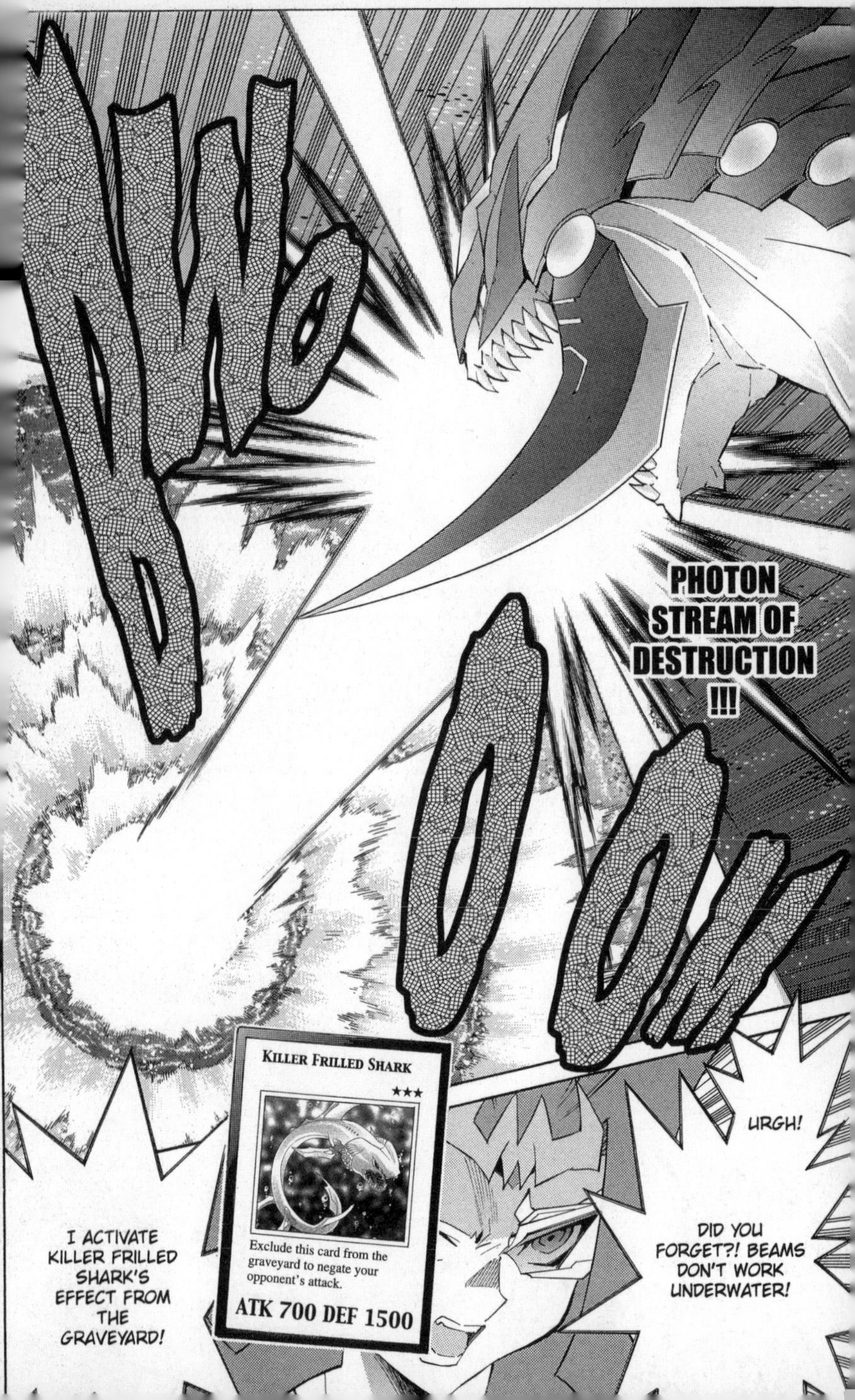
PHOTON STREAM OF DESTRUCTION !!!
URGH!
DID YOU FORGET?! BEAMS DON'T WORK UNDERWATER!
KILLER FRILLED SHARK
★★★
Exclude this card from the graveyard to negate your opponent's attack.
ATK 700 DEF 1500
I ACTIVATE KILLER FRILLED SHARK'S EFFECT FROM THE GRAVEYARD!

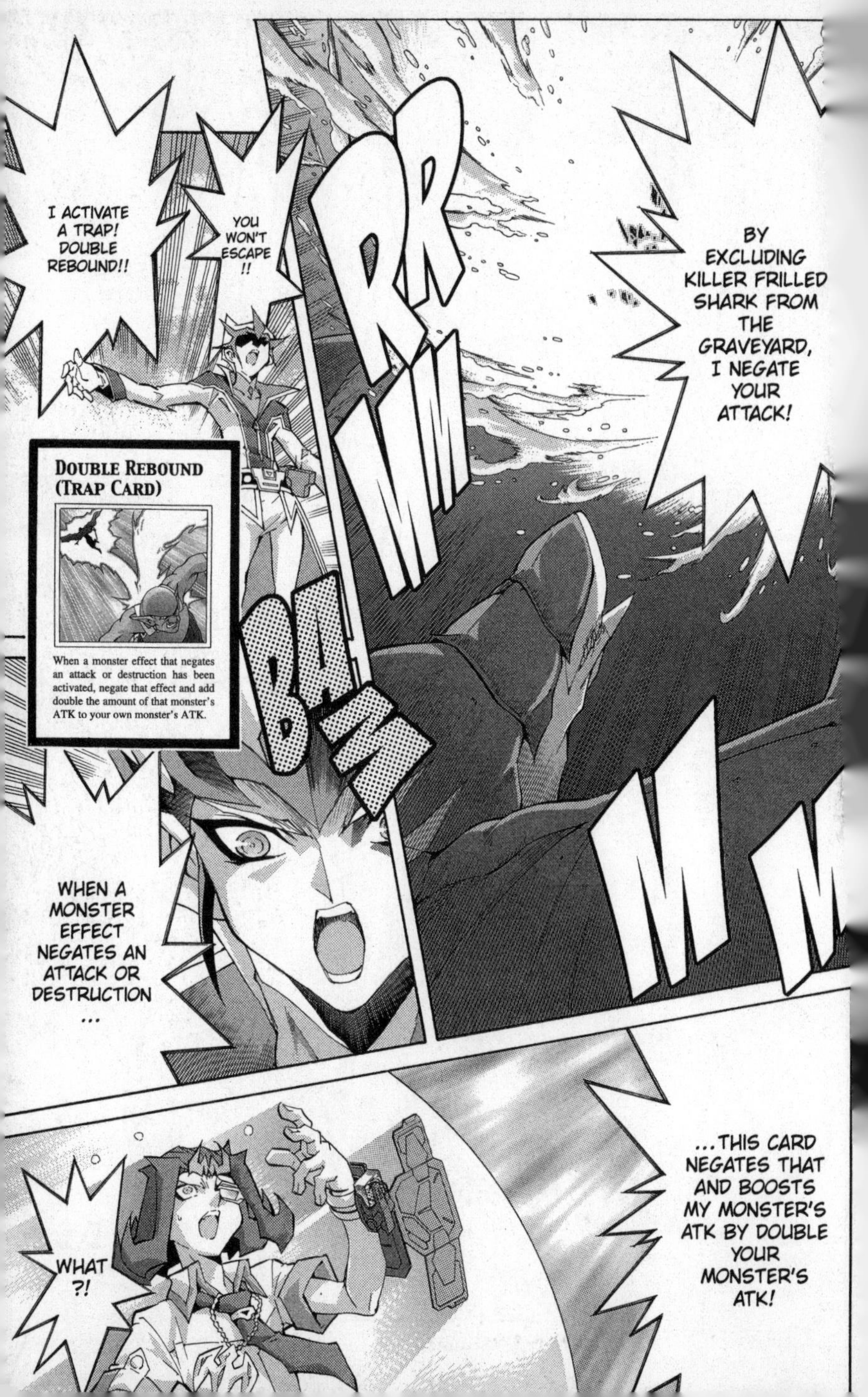
BY EXCLUDING KILLER FRILLED SHARK FROM THE GRAVEYARD, I NEGATE YOUR ATTACK!
YOU WON'T ESCAPE!!
I ACTIVATE A TRAP! DOUBLE REBOUND!!
DOUBLE REBOUND (TRAP CARD)
When a monster effect that negates an attack or destruction has been activated, negate that effect and add double the amount of that monster's ATK to your own monster's ATK.
BAM
WHEN A MONSTER EFFECT NEGATES AN ATTACK OR DESTRUCTION...
...THIS CARD NEGATES THAT AND BOOSTS MY MONSTER'S ATK BY DOUBLE YOUR MONSTER'S ATK!
WHAT?!

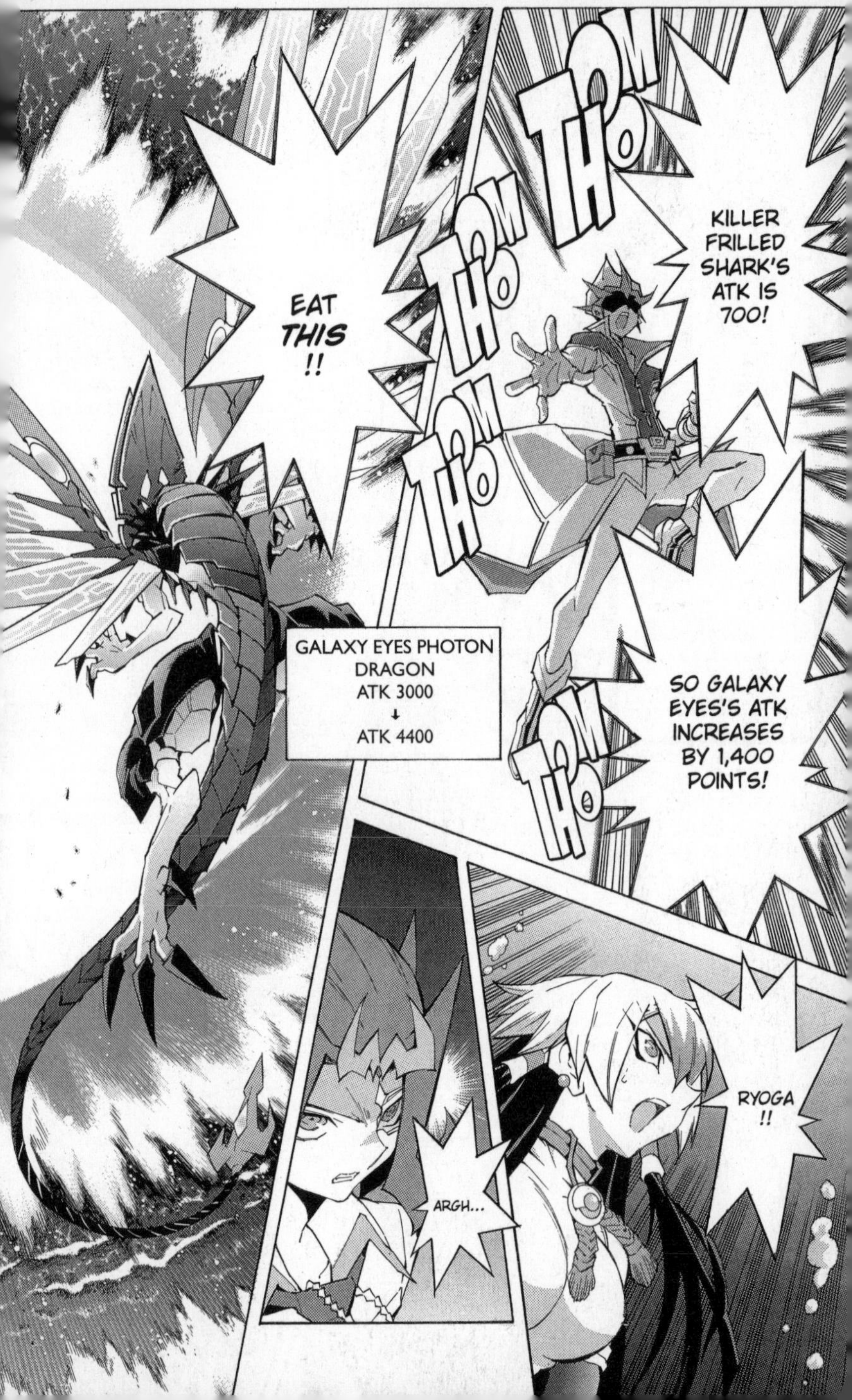
THOM
THOM
THOM
KILLER FRILLED SHARK'S ATK IS 700!
THOM
SO GALAXY EYES'S ATK INCREASES BY 1,400 POINTS!
RYOGA!!
ARGH...
EAT THIS!!
GALAXY EYES PHOTON DRAGON ATK 3000 ↓ ATK 4400

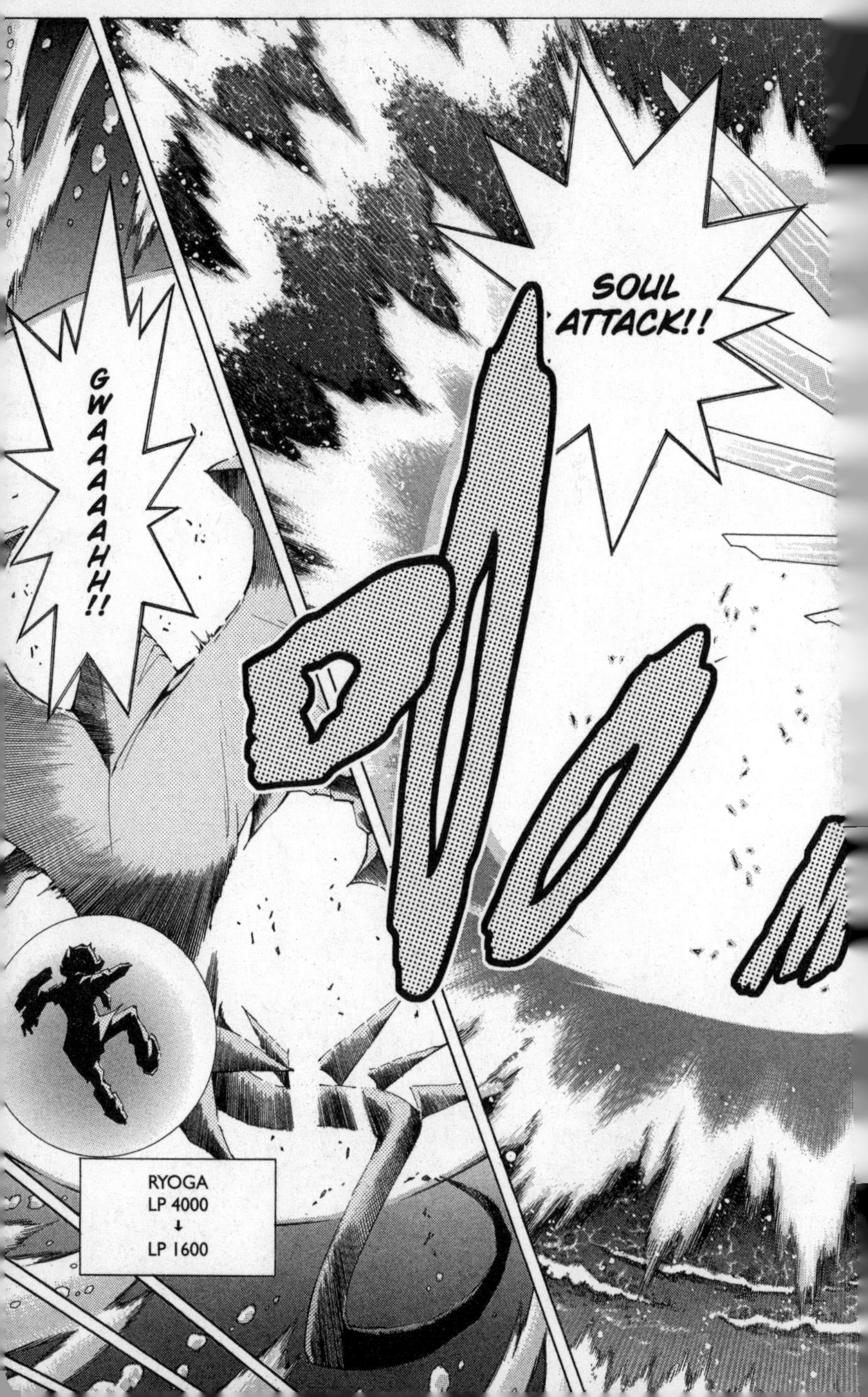
SOUL ATTACK!!
GWAAAAAHH!!
RYOGA
LP 4000
↓
LP 1600

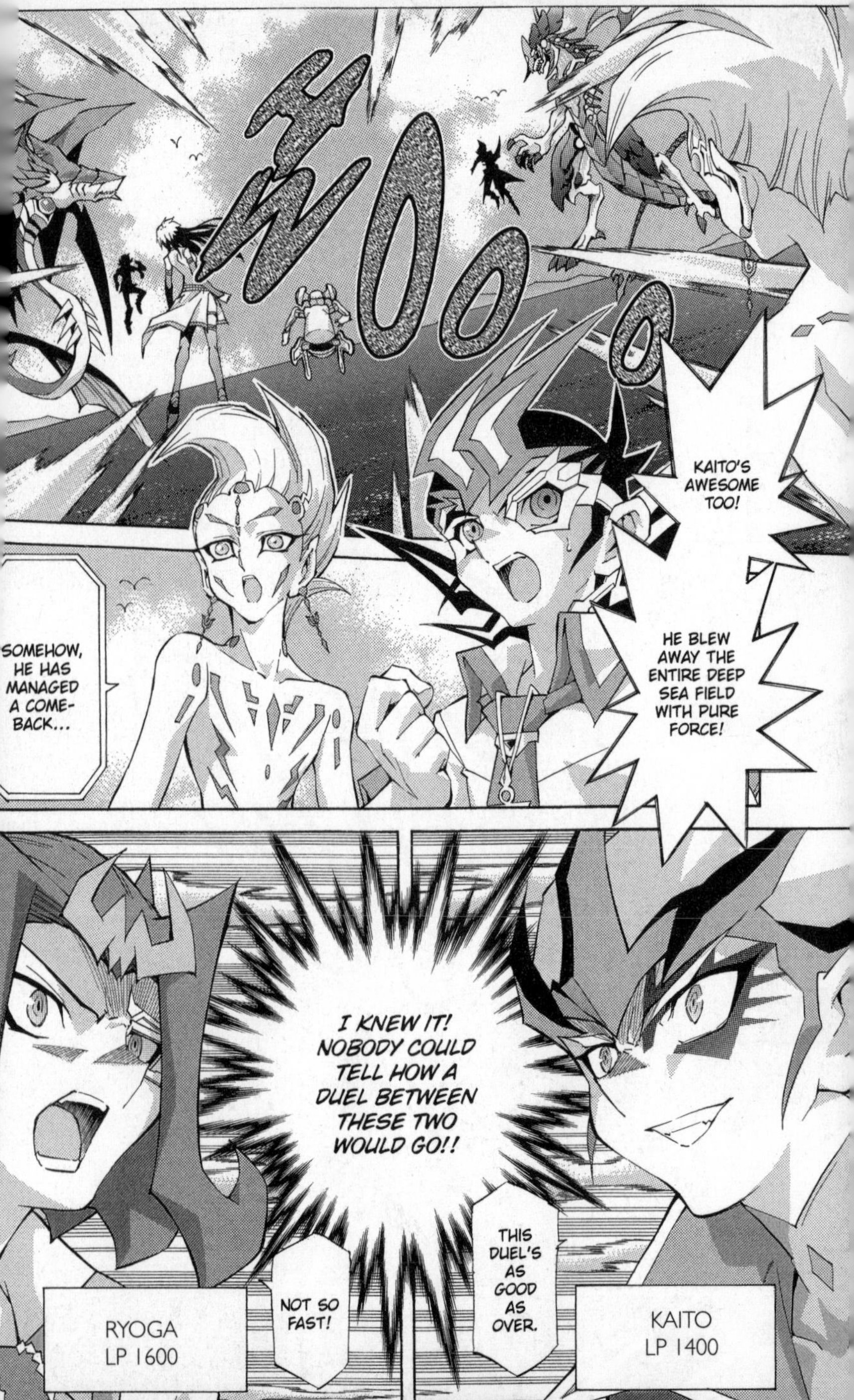

SHWOOOO
KAITO'S AWESOME TOO!
HE BLEW AWAY THE ENTIRE DEEP SEA FIELD WITH PURE FORCE!
SOMEHOW, HE HAS MANAGED A COME-BACK...
I KNEW IT! NOBODY COULD TELL HOW A DUEL BETWEEN THESE TWO WOULD GO!!
THIS DUEL'S AS GOOD AS OVER.
KAITO LP 1400
NOT SO FAST!
RYOGA LP 1600

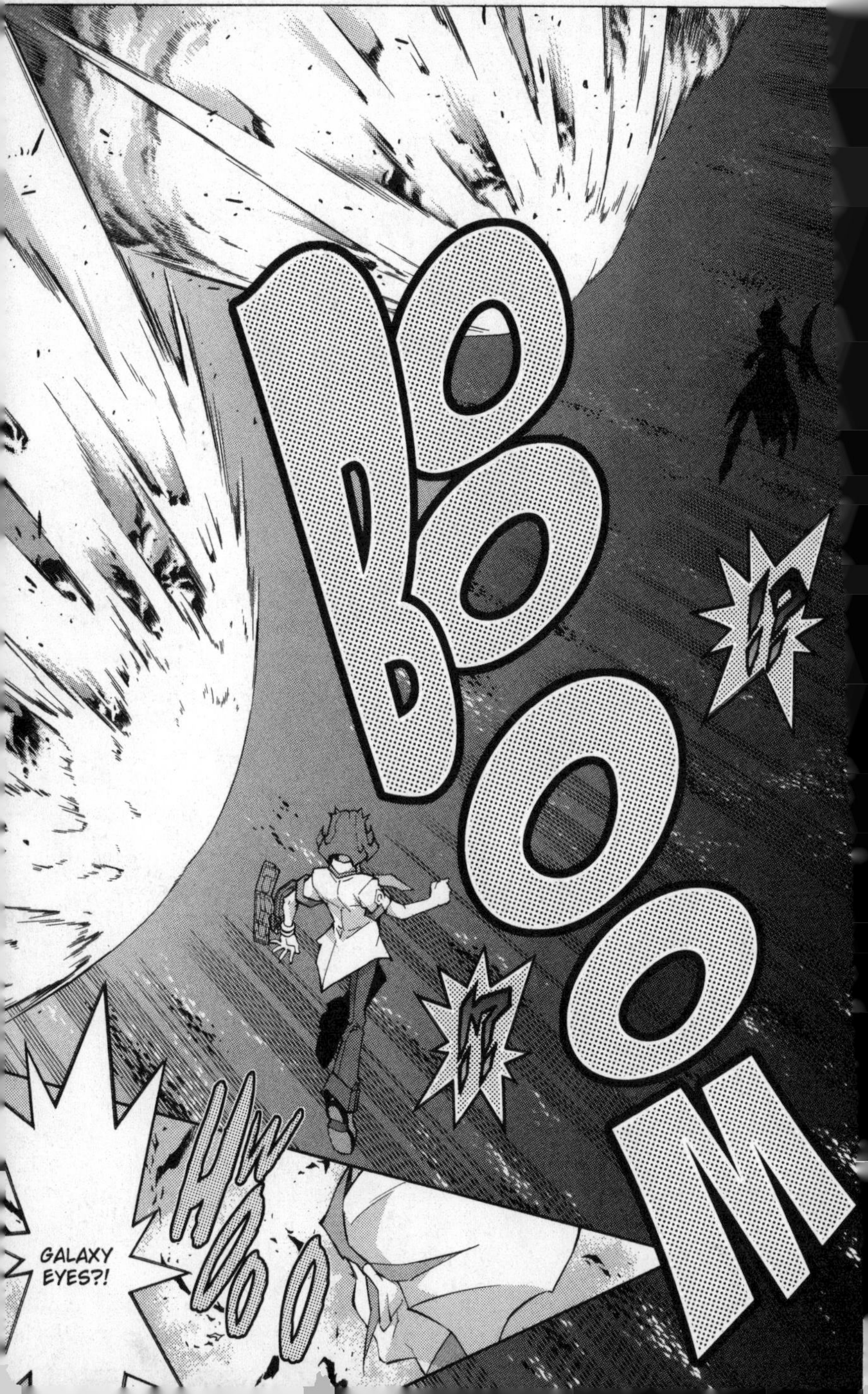
BOOOOM
HWOOO
GALAXY EYES?!

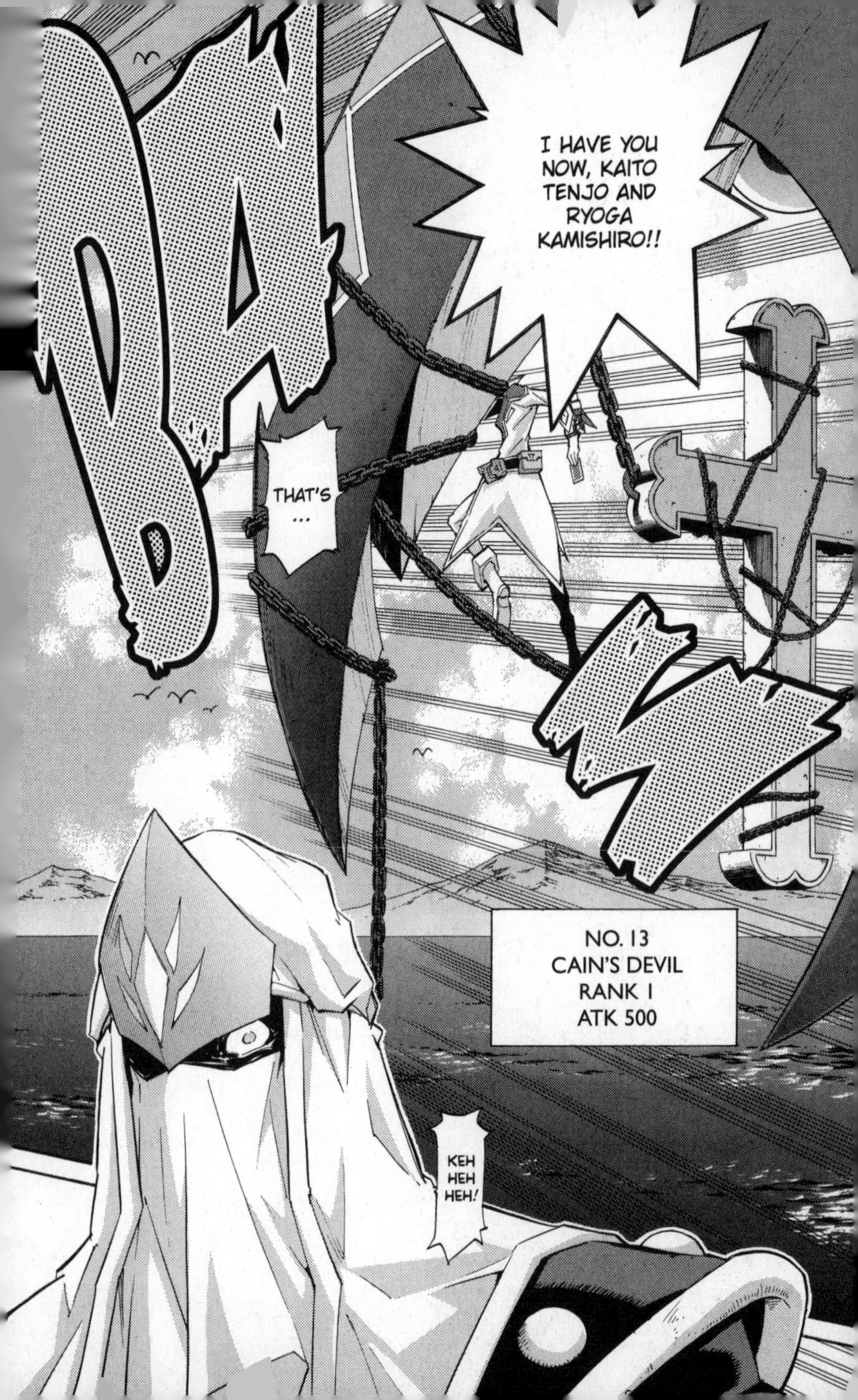
I HAVE YOU NOW, KAITO TENJO AND RYOGA KAMISHIRO!!
THAT'S ...
NO. 13 CAIN'S DEVIL RANK 1 ATK 500
KEH HEH HEH!

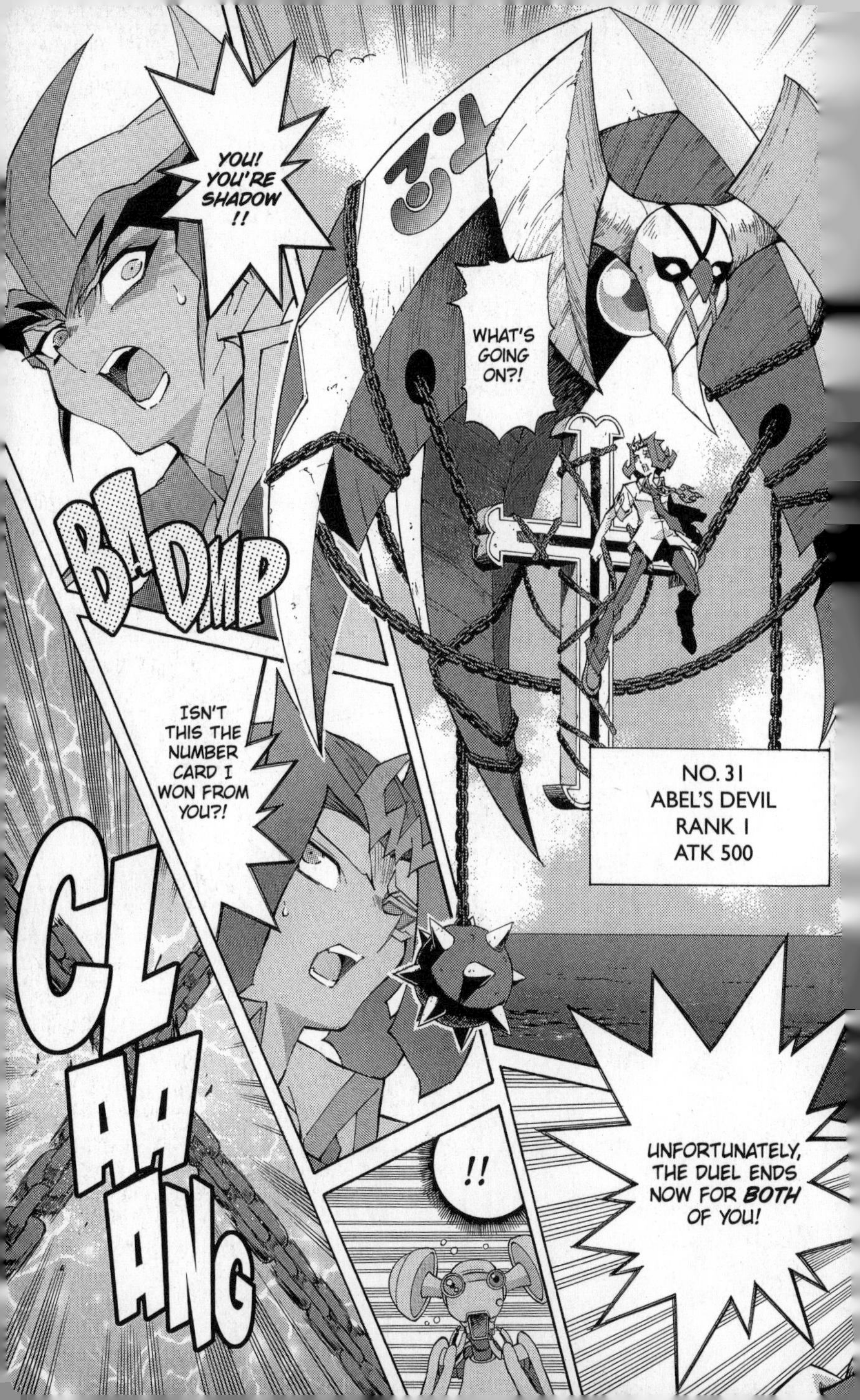
WHAT'S GOING ON?!
NO. 31 ABEL'S DEVIL RANK 1 ATK 500
YOU! YOU'RE SHADOW !!
BADUMP
ISN'T THIS THE NUMBER CARD I WON FROM YOU?!
CLAAANG
UNFORTUNATELY, THE DUEL ENDS NOW FOR *BOTH* OF YOU!
!!

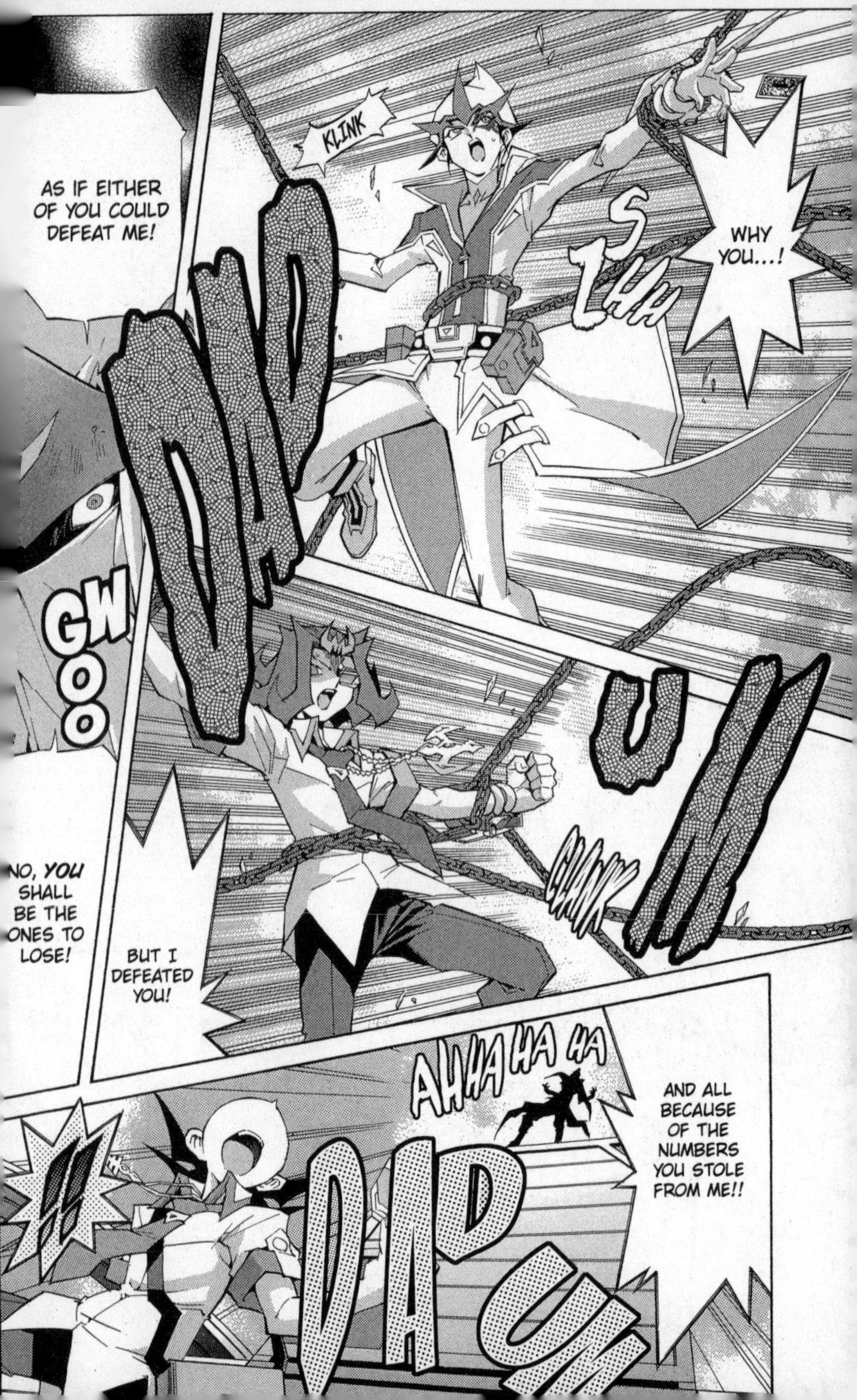
KLINK
WHY YOU...!
SZHA
DAD
UM
CLANK
GWOO
BUT I DEFEATED YOU!
AS IF EITHER OF YOU COULD DEFEAT ME!
NO, YOU SHALL BE THE ONES TO LOSE!
AHHA HA HA
AND ALL BECAUSE OF THE NUMBERS YOU STOLE FROM ME!!
DADUM
!!

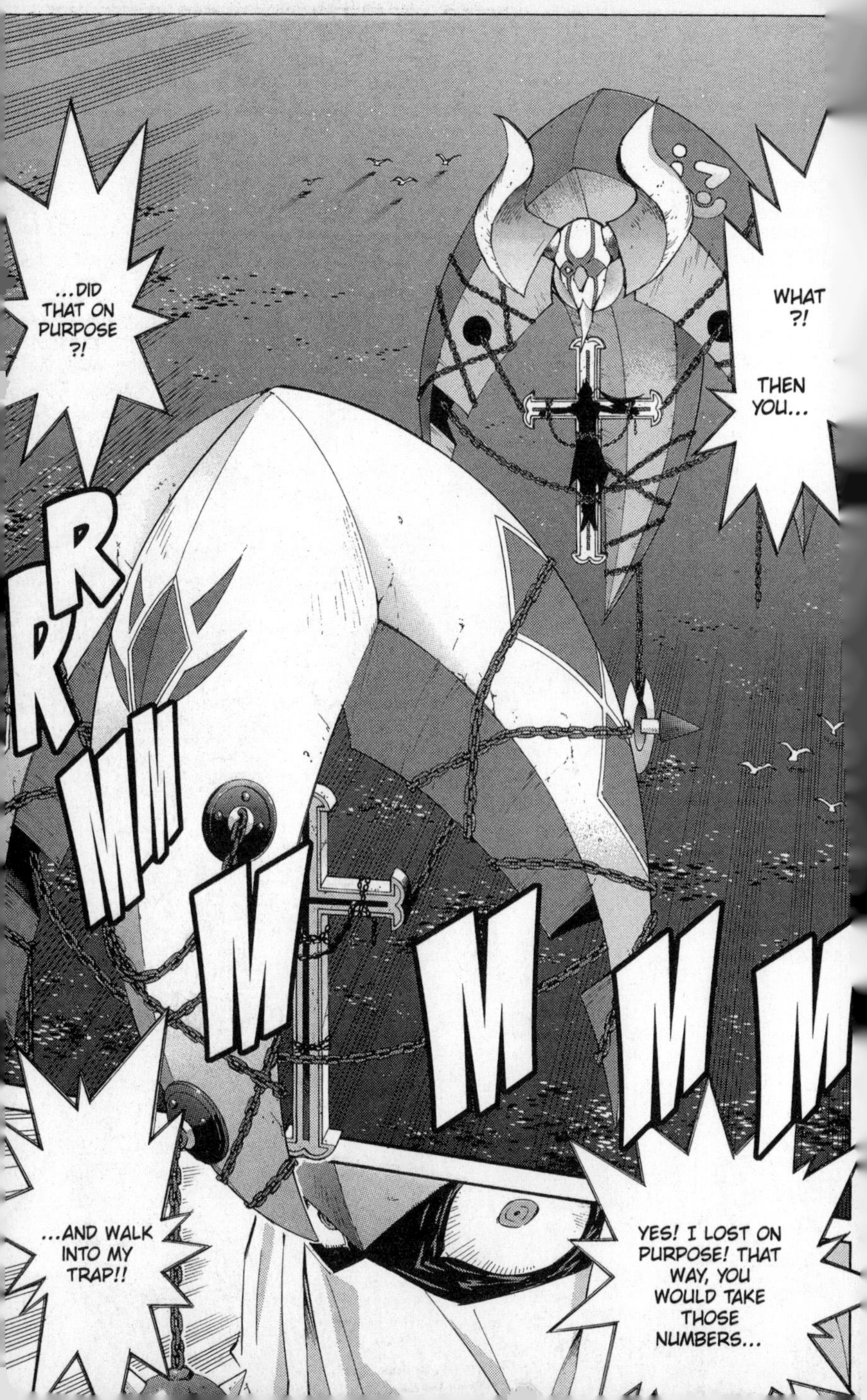
WHAT ?!
THEN YOU...
...DID THAT ON PURPOSE ?!
RRMMMMMMM
YES! I LOST ON PURPOSE! THAT WAY, YOU WOULD TAKE THOSE NUMBERS...
...AND WALK INTO MY TRAP!!

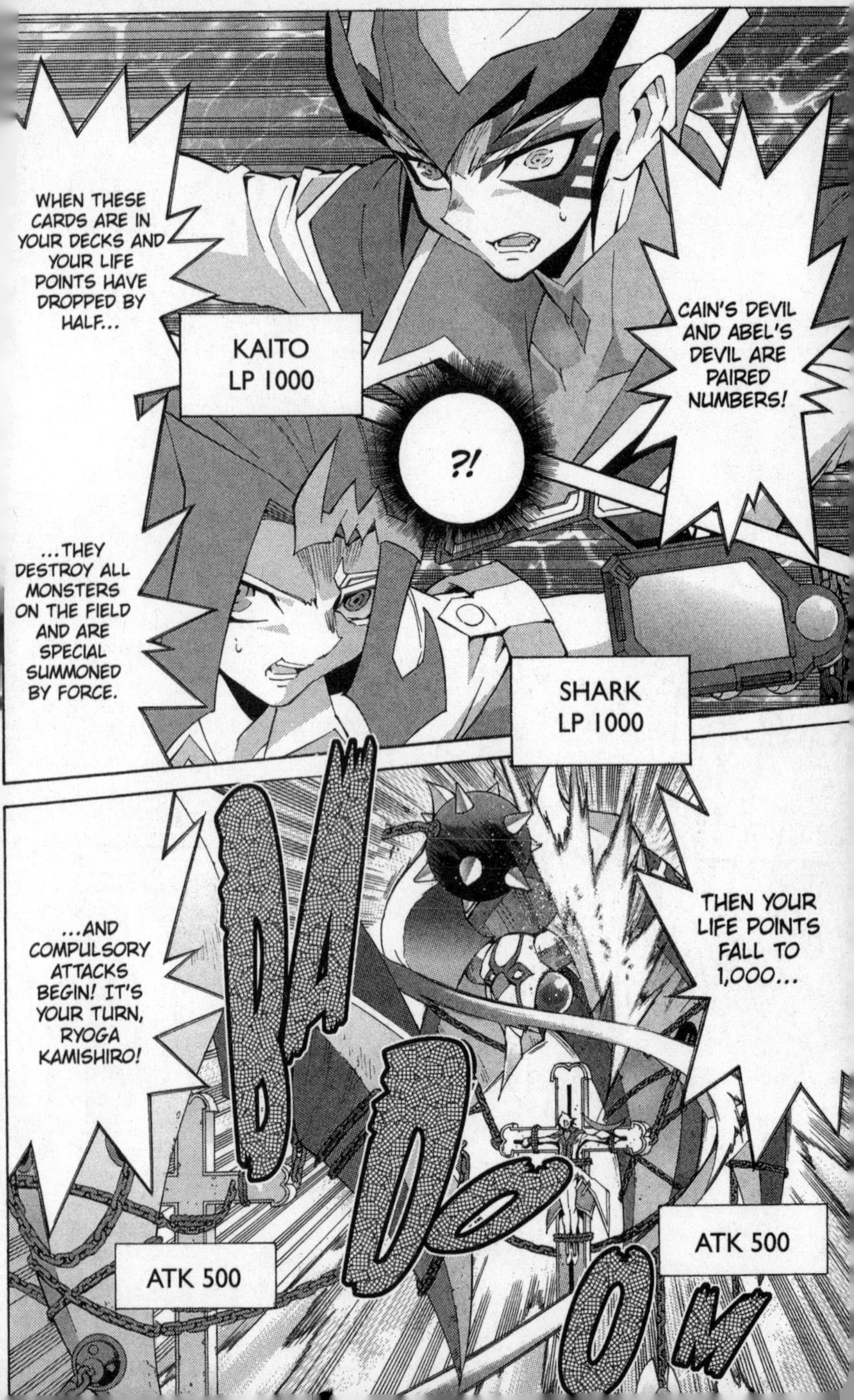
CAIN'S DEVIL AND ABEL'S DEVIL ARE PAIRED NUMBERS!
WHEN THESE CARDS ARE IN YOUR DECKS AND YOUR LIFE POINTS HAVE DROPPED BY HALF...
KAITO LP 1000
?!
...THEY DESTROY ALL MONSTERS ON THE FIELD AND ARE SPECIAL SUMMONED BY FORCE.
SHARK LP 1000
THEN YOUR LIFE POINTS FALL TO 1,000...
...AND COMPULSORY ATTACKS BEGIN! IT'S YOUR TURN, RYOGA KAMISHIRO!
BADOOM
ATK 500
ATK 500

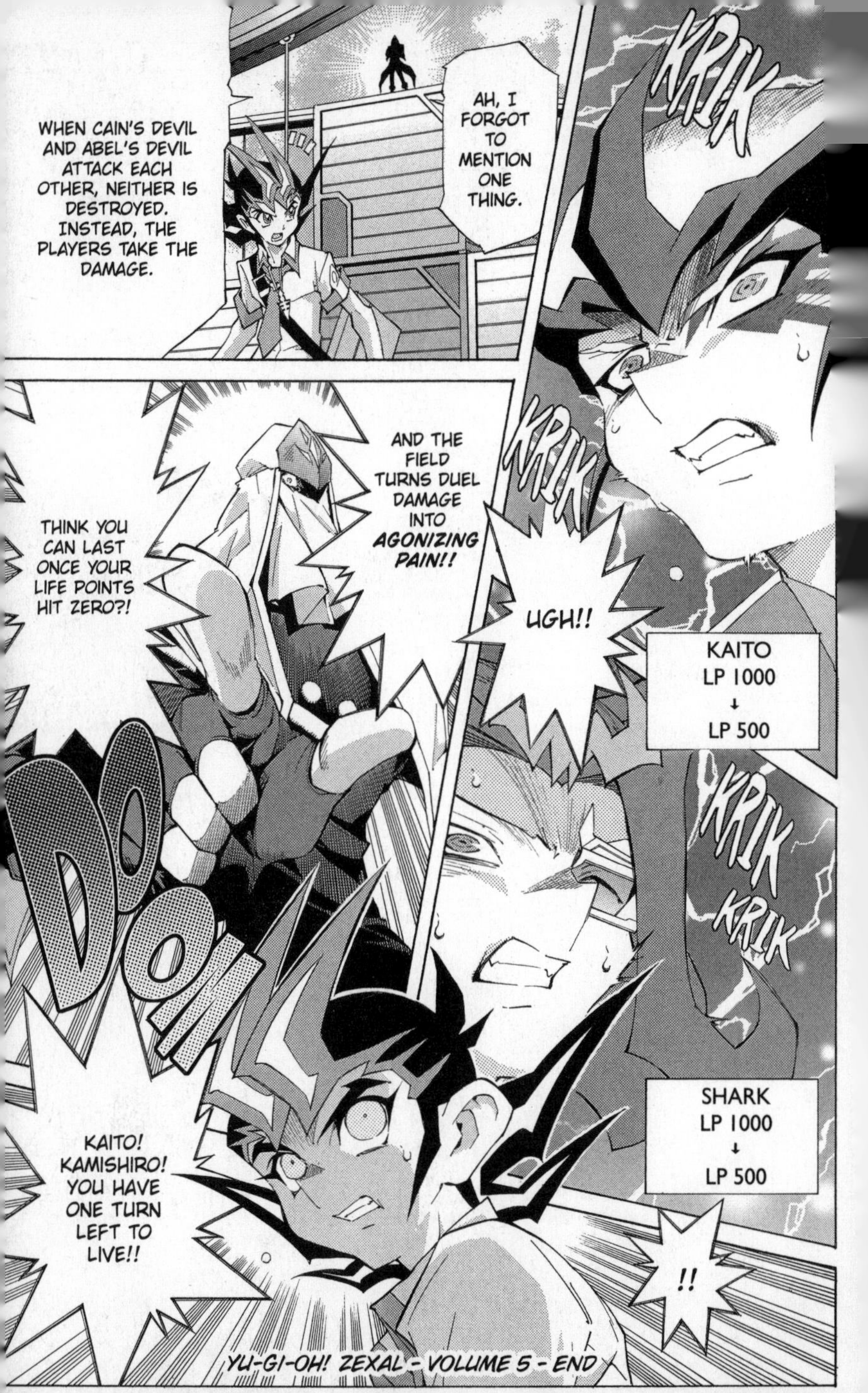
KRIK
KRIK
UGH!!
KAITO
LP 1000
↓
LP 500
AH, I FORGOT TO MENTION ONE THING.
WHEN CAIN'S DEVIL AND ABEL'S DEVIL ATTACK EACH OTHER, NEITHER IS DESTROYED. INSTEAD, THE PLAYERS TAKE THE DAMAGE.
AND THE FIELD TURNS DUEL DAMAGE INTO *AGONIZING PAIN!!*
THINK YOU CAN LAST ONCE YOUR LIFE POINTS HIT ZERO?!
DOOOM
KRIK
KRIK
SHARK
LP 1000
↓
LP 500
!!
KAITO! KAMISHIRO! YOU HAVE ONE TURN LEFT TO LIVE!!

YU-GI-OH! ZEXAL - VOLUME 5 - END

STAFF
Junya Uchino
Kazuo Ochiai
Toshiaki Kat
Masahiro Miura
Fumitaka Murayama

Coloring
Toru Shimizu [cover]
Studio Tac - Takumi Yokooka

EDITOR
Daisuke Terashi
Takahiko Aikawa

SUPPORT
Gallop

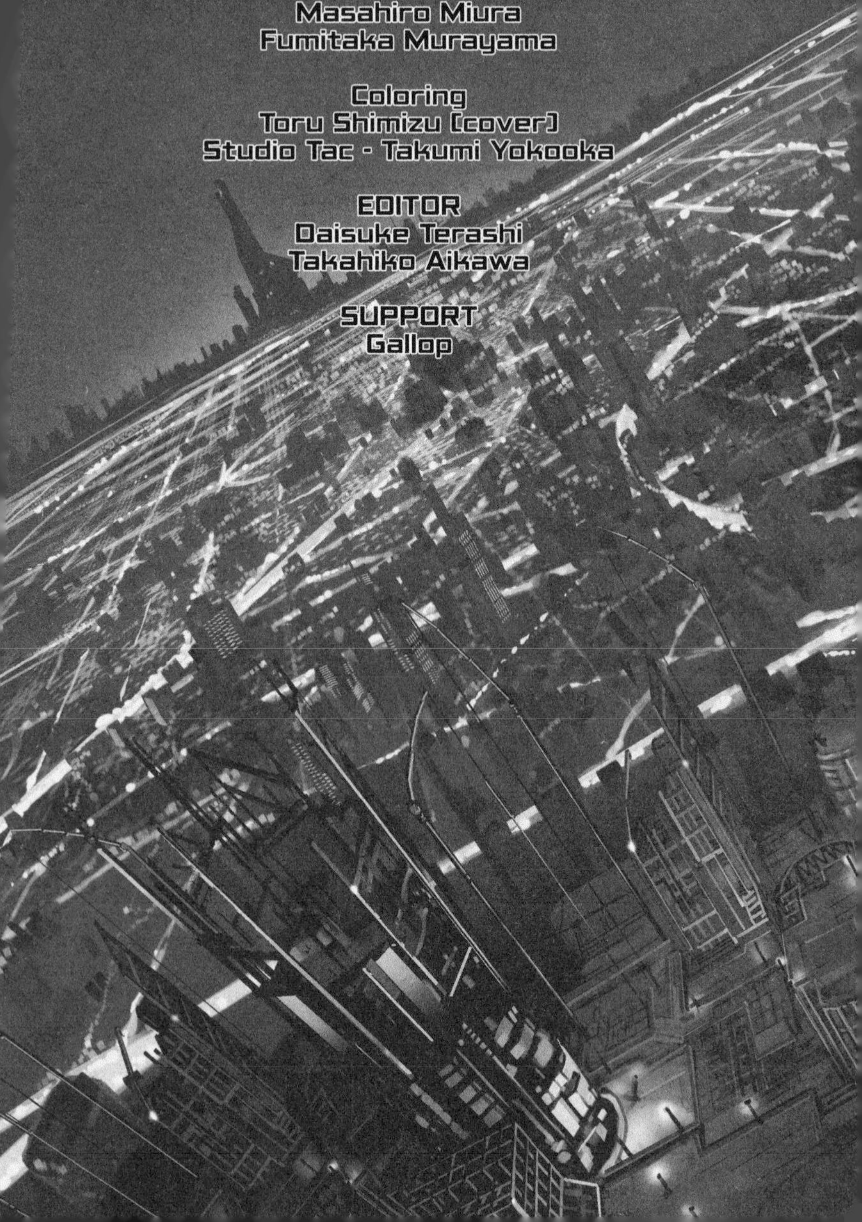

YOU ARE READING IN THE WRONG DIRECTION!!

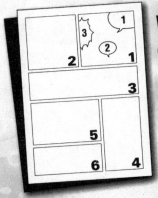

Whoops! Guess what? You're starting at the wrong end of the comic!

...It's true! In keeping with the original Japanese format, *Yu-Gi-Oh! ZEXAL* is meant to be read from right to left, starting in the upper-right corner.

Unlike English, which is read from left to right, Japanese is read from right to left, meaning that action, sound effects and word-balloon order are completely reversed... something which can make readers unfamiliar with Japanese feel pretty backwards themselves. For this reason, manga or Japanese comics published in the U.S. in English have sometimes been published "flopped"—that is, printed in exact reverse order, as though seen from the other side of a mirror.

By flopping pages, U.S. publishers can avoid confusing readers, but the compromise is not without its downside. For one thing, a character in a flopped manga series who once wore in the original Japanese version a T-shirt emblazoned with "M A Y" (as in "the merry month of") now wears one which reads "Y A M"! Additionally, many manga creators in Japan are themselves unhappy with the process, as some feel the mirror-imaging of their art alters their original intentions.

We are proud to bring you Shin Yoshida and Naohito Miyoshi's *Yu-Gi-Oh! ZEXAL* in the original unflopped format. For now, though, turn to the other side of the book and let the duel begin...!

—Editor